THE S. MARK TAPER FOUNDATION

IMPRINT IN JEWISH STUDIES

BY THIS ENDOWMENT

THE S. MARK TAPER FOUNDATION SUPPORTS

THE APPRECIATION AND UNDERSTANDING

OF THE RICHNESS AND DIVERSITY OF

JEWISH LIFE AND CULTURE

The publisher gratefully acknowledges the contribution to this book provided by the following organizations and individuals:

Wake Forest University, honoring the memory of Camillo and Bianca Artom, supporters of scholarship in Italian culture

Deborah Low Doppelt

Thomas J. Fleish

The David B. Gold Foundation

Florence and Leo Helzel

The Lucius N. Littauer Foundation

Joseph Low

The Skirball Foundation

The S. Mark Taper Foundation

Evan and Terri Wein

The Jews of Europe after the Black Death

The Jews of Europe
after the Black Death

Anna Foa

Translated from the Italian by Andrea Grover

UNIVERSITY OF CALIFORNIA PRESS
Berkeley · *Los Angeles* · *London*

University of California Press
Berkeley and Los Angeles, California

University of California Press, Ltd.
London, England

© 2000 by the Regents of the University of California

Originally published as *Ebrei in Europa: Dalla Peste
nera all'emancipazione, XIV–XVIII secolo* in 1992
by Editori Laterza. © 1992 Gius. Laterza & Figli.

Please see illustration credits at back of book.

Library of Congress Cataloging-in-Publication Data

Foa, Anna.
  [Ebrei in Europa. English]
    The Jews of Europe after the black death /
  by Anna Foa ; translated from the Italian
  by Andrea Grover.
      p.   cm.
    Includes bibliographical references and index.
  ISBN 0-520-08765-8 (cloth : alk. paper)
    1. Jews—History—70–1789. 2. Jews—
Europe—History. 3. Europe—Ethnic relations.
I. Title.
DS124.F6213   2000
909'.04924—dc21   00-022315
                             CIP

Manufactured in the United States of America
09 08 07 06 05 04 03 02 01 00
10 9 8 7 6 5 4 3 2 1

To my father

Contents

.

Preface   ix

Acknowledgments   xi

Introduction   1
1. Beyond the Catastrophe   7
2. The Church and the Jews   23
3. The Boundaries of Identity   49
4. The Jews of Spain   74
5. The Jews of Italy   108
6. The Age of the Ghettos   138
7. The Modern Era   154
8. Beyond the Ghetto   192
Afterword   215

Bibliography   221
Illustration Credits   261
Index   263

Preface

Creating a synthesis encapsulating a period as long and varied as the one discussed in this book poses significant methodological problems. In particular, one has to come to grips with the particularity of the material. To tell the story of the Jewish presence in Europe means to bring together into one whole both Christian and Jewish perspectives. The Jewish perspective, in turn, must be seen both in its own self-representation—the way Jews saw their own culture and how they created a sense of identity—and in the way in which that self-perception was judged from without. My basic principle has been constantly to interweave the internal history of the Jews with that of their relations and relationships with the non-Jewish world, a problem that defies easy solutions. The borders between the two worlds must constantly be crossed, and this also means dealing with historical opinion that sees these two worlds in permanent opposition, with sharp lines distinguishing opening from closure, identity from assimilation, and halcyon from lachrymose times. In reality, such clear lines have never existed, and it is only recently, thanks in large part to what has been learned from the social sciences—anthropology, in particular—that scholars have begun to abandon their quest for clear-cut borders and, in their place, to search for points of cultural contact, as well as the existence of a Jewish sub- or microculture, and to do so, for that matter, without resort to apologetics.

These problems recur with respect to periodization. Jewish history has its own time brackets—which are not always congruent with those of general history. Neither the expulsion from Spain nor emancipation, for example, both of which created sharp breaks in Jewish history, has a parallel in the non-Jewish world. Christian and Jewish chronicles and other parallel sources emphasize diverse issues, which, in turn, determine how periods of time are bracketed. At the same time, Jewish history and Jewish time have not existed in a vacuum. Rather, they have a rapport with general history that is much like that which general social history has with political or diplomatic history: namely, however individual or individually discussed these types of history and the historiographical methods used to study them are, one cannot properly tell the story of one without being conscious of the existence and importance of the other.

But then the story of the Jews does not have the sole function of re-creating the world of the Jews that has passed and of recounting the tale of a minority alone. It would be virtually pointless to limit oneself to sectarian and sectorial history that reflects only on itself. The history of the Jews is an indispensable chapter in what is sometimes called general history, and it illuminates, or should be made to illuminate, that history, that past, no less than it illuminates the past of the Jews themselves. History is history, period. And only by viewing all history as integral will the presence of the Jews and their history cease to be viewed only in terms of influences on outside cultures or of Jewish figures of distinction. At a certain deeper level, one might say that Christian society can be properly understood only in the context of the Jewish presence it has harbored, which over the centuries has affected that society profoundly, forcing it to come to grips with difference and pressing it to elaborate mechanisms for confronting the Other, albeit this confrontation was long framed in terms of spontaneous or codified intolerance, repugnance, or violence. The same may be said of the Jews, obligated to avoid complete separation even at times of maximum segregation, pricked by myriad external stimuli even when they were most spurned. The history of the Jews in Europe has thus been a complex chain of distance and proximity, of segregation and contiguity. Our problem now is to unveil the back-and-forth movement between Jewish and Christian worlds, in which the borders between the two are forever blurred and never clearly seen. My narrative is cut from fabric such as this.

Acknowledgments

The writing of this book and now its translation into English have taken many years, and many friends and colleagues have come to my aid with suggestions, ideas, and willingness to read parts of the manuscript or even the manuscript as a whole. I particularly thank Vittorio Vidotto for his generous counsel and encouragement, and Lucetta Scaraffia, who has been at my side from the inception of this project, always ready to share with me her critical intelligence and firm friendship. I have equally benefited from the help and careful readings of Luciano Allegra, Manuela Consonni, Denise Despres, Riccardo di Segni, Judith Goldstein, Elisabetta Mondello, Marla Stone, and Katja Tenenbaum. Work on the volume was also facilitated by the privilege of being invited to engage in periods of study and research in the United States, for which I am indebted to the members of the departments of history at the University of Michigan and the University of Washington and to the entire faculty of Smith College in Northampton, Massachusetts.

I would like to thank Franco Zerlenga, who had the idea to have this book translated. He found the translator and was instrumental in finding both a publisher and funds to pay for the translation. It was his strong determination and his belief in the project that kept it going, even in the most trying moments. Andrea Grover translated the entire book with intelligence and perspicacity. Her passionate devotion to this task has been limitless. Our work together blossomed quickly into close friendship. I am also indebted to Alan Mandelbaum for bringing the book to the attention of the University of California Press, and to the Littauer Foundation for providing funds for the translation. To Stanley Holwitz of the University of California Press, I owe an unpayable debt for standing by me and sustaining this project during its lengthy period of gestation.

My father, Vittorio Foa, has been a constant source of illumination, even when our opinions on history and Judaism have diverged. Over the course of time, I have come to realize that his opinions were sometimes more courageous and less conventional than mine. Kenneth Stow has been close to me throughout all these years, supporting me through his wide knowledge in the field of Jewish history, his intelligence and creativity, and especially his constant companionship and deep affection. No words can thank him enough.

Needless to say, the responsibility for the final product is all mine.

Finally, I wish to thank my son, Andrea, and my granddaughters, Nicole, Viviana, and Morgana. They have had little part in the writing of the book, but they have played a great role indeed in keeping me in a good mood.

Introduction

In 164 B.C.E., Roman emissaries offered their services as mediators in the dispute between the Jews of Palestine and the Seleucid Greek rulers of Syria, an intervention that culminated three years later in a formal treaty between the Jews and Rome. Roman hegemony inevitably followed, leading eventually to the Great Revolt of 66–70 C.E., after which thousands of Jews were brought to Rome as slaves. Jews had also voluntarily come to live along the European Mediterranean littoral before 70 C.E., from Sicily and Apulia to Spain.

The long history of Jewish settlement and life in Europe was thus initiated under conditions of both force and free will, and the interplay between the two would remain a constant over the centuries. The role of external force in determining Jewish life was regularly balanced by creativity and self-determination. It was in the western Mediterranean countries that had once been part of the Roman Empire that the Jews produced the structures that would underlie Jewish activity, thought, and formal organization over the ensuing centuries, structures they took with them when they migrated from the Mediterranean world to northern Europe.

Yet these Mediterranean centers, especially the Italian ones, had already served, especially in the early Middle Ages, as crossroads for the Jewish culture that had sprung from the Babylonian (Iraqi) Talmudic academies of the Geonim. In Italy, that culture was assimilated and melded into an Italian Jewish product, whose roots can be traced to the academies of late ancient Israel. The result was a profound transformation of both the form and direction of Jewish culture as a whole, whose origins are enshrined in quasi-mythical legends of cultural origins: of mythical learned persons who dramatically arrive and mysteriously disappear once their learning has been absorbed, legends that took shape in the towns of Apulia during the tenth and eleventh centuries. Similar legends arose in Provence and Muslim Spain, although there the mythical scholars were made to disappear through marriage into existing local rabbinic lineages.

So armed, Jews from these centers moved northward, driven by economic and demographic impulses to cross the Alps or go up the Rhône river and settle in the north of France or in the valleys of the Moselle and the Rhine, laying the foundations of what would eventually be known as the world of Ashkenaz and Ashkenazi Jewry. And thus were achieved the basic elements of Jewish European culture, whose broad outlines would remain stable—in terms of communal organization, family structure, the socialization of knowledge, and practical traditions (with certain noticeable shifts of emphasis), but also of relations with the non-Jewish world—practically up to the time of Jewish emancipation during and after the French Revolution. For its part, that non-Jewish world, too, remained fixed in its basic attitudes, predicated on an equilibrium between superiors, the Christians, and obedient inferiors, the Jews, albeit this equilibrium was severely rocked in the sixteenth century following the Protestant and Catholic Reformations.

As for the kingdoms and states, they were moved by growing pressures for religious homogeneity and alternating concerns about whether to protect the Jews or to bow to those other elements in society that firmly believed the Jews to pose an irresistible threat. From the time of the Crusades, these pressures were often popular in nature, fueled at times by extreme interpretations of Christian teachings of Jewish negativity and—especially in the regions of Germany—they ended in attacks and large-scale massacres, or acts of Jewish mass suicide, especially in the year 1096, the time of the First Crusade. A less violent variation on this theme was expulsions resulting from struggles between kings, barons, and sometimes high clergy, in which the Jews were caught in the middle.

Our particular story begins in the fourteenth century, when the Black Death devastated Europe. In its wake, radical changes occurred in demographic and economic structures, as well as in mentalities and in the ways in which men and women perceived the world. Great changes occurred, too, in the ideology of the Church. Jews were the special victims of these events and processes, devastated during popular violence that accompanied the passage of the plague. The Jewish communities of Germany suffered a massive decline, adding to the blows they had already received at the end of the thirteenth century. These pogroms (the term really belongs to a much later, modern age) symbolically mark a divide between what I see as two distinct historical periods. This divide was predicated on more than destruction alone. In central and northern Italy, this was a time of the growth of dozens of small settlements and communities, composed sometimes of immigrants fleeing the German massacres, but also of Jews, from Rome in particular, seeking new commercial opportunity, primarily as operators of small institutions of lending. In addition, this was the time of a last burst of glory in the communities of Spain, just prior to the massacres and the mass conversion and conversionary pressures of the epoch 1391–1418, whose denouement would be the expulsion of 1492 and the mass forced conversion in Portugal in 1497. Small communities in France were reestablished (following the major expulsion of 1306), only to be eliminated anew, first in 1322 and finally in 1394, except for communities in Provence, from which Jews were expelled definitively in 1498; we must not forget that the Jews had been expelled from England in 1290.

In each of these regions, communal life also meant cultural and economic endeavor—which is a way of saying that this book is not a history of anti-Semitism. Anti-Semitism in its various expressions, religious and even racial, is but one facet of a much larger story. I am primarily interested in the creative aspects of Jewish life: culture, both high and low, daily and personal life, and the structures of the community and the family, as well as of the various modes of organization, such as confraternities and social networks, that form the backbone of continuing existence. Indeed, far more important than the violence and hatred that Jews endured are the ways in which the Jews perceived these phenomena and gave them added meaning.

Nonetheless, the periods subsequent to the fourteenth century, those of the Italian Renaissance and after—on which my narrative dwells—were difficult ones for the Jews of western Europe. For these were the times of the expulsion from Spain and of an expanding Jewish Diaspora that penetrated every corner of the vast Mediterranean region. These were also the times of forced conversion on a massive scale, unprecedented in the brief and limited episodes of forced conversion in the past, and which resulted in placing these unwilling converts under continuous surveillance to defend against the crypto-Judaizing and Marranism that these conversions in fact spawned. As for the remaining Jews, they were ghettoized; the institution of the ghetto spread throughout Italy, wherever Jews were allowed to live. This was, it goes without saying, an epoch of contraction in European Jewish settlement—in the West, that is, but not in the East, where a great explosion of Jewish population was about to begin. In the West, these trends did not begin to reverse themselves until near the end of the seventeenth century, most notably in the "communities of return," composed of Spanish and Portuguese Marranos who returned openly to Judaism, first and especially in Amsterdam, but also in Hamburg, Bordeaux, London, and Leghorn. This return was marked by a gradual acceptance of the legality of these Jews openly practicing Judaism, the flourishing of Dutch communities, and even a rebirth of Jewish life in Germany. Only in Italy, and especially in the papal states, did Jewish life grow ever more closed, and impoverished.

The eighteenth century witnessed dramatic changes in Jewish life and in the relations of the Jews with the non-Jewish world, both stimulated by fundamental changes congruent with a growing laicization and secularization in Christian society, as well as by notable changes among the Jews themselves, the result of internal crisis and a growing desire for transformation. These changes determined the often tortuous paths of emancipation and the attempted entrance of the Jews into wider European society. They initiated a radical break in Jewish history: the end of social segregation, on the one hand, and of semi-autonomous communal privilege, on the other.

Our story concludes at the end of the nineteenth century, when Jewish emancipation and social integration—in those countries where these were achieved at all (in Russia, for example, they were not)—had reached their apogee. The twentieth century would usher in a new brand of anti-Semitism accompanying a radical revision in European society itself, propelled forward by the bloody war of 1914–18. The effects of this revision—the birth of Zionism and, eventually, the state of Israel, major upheavals in Jewish identity, and, to be sure, the cataclysm of the Shoah—are outside the scope of the present work.

The purview of this study is long and vast, which has forced me to select and privilege certain events, certain spheres, certain issues more than others. The heaviest concentration is on themes that most affected the Jewish experience in the West, the most important of them being perhaps the relationship between the Church and the Jews. Accordingly, an entire chapter has been devoted to the principal aspects of this relationship, treated by subject rather than chronologically; the conclusions of this chapter, in turn, are balanced by a long discussion of Jewish identity, which forms a separate chapter. In fact, the relationship between the Church and the Jews is a theme that reappears like a scarlet thread throughout the book, sometimes becoming a prime criterion of interpretation, for instance, in showing how religious and ideological motivations outstripped those of segregation and separation with respect to the ghetto and its establishment.

Another principal theme is that of conversion. The drive to convert Jews in large numbers was marginal until at least the thirteenth and fourteenth centuries, and it was not embraced by Rome until the sixteenth century. The ability of such a drive to destroy longtime equilibria between Jews and Christians has yet to be properly evaluated and appreciated. This drive was directed principally at the Jews of Spain and Italy, and, for this reason, the story of events in these two regions is carefully discussed. Nevertheless, there is no intent to diminish the importance of Jewish life in France, England, and Germany, whose discussion is linked, in turn, to the rise of national monarchies and to the growth in these monarchies of lay powers much different from those in Italy. The treatment of the Jews of Poland and other areas of eastern Europe is less intense. There, Jewish life reached its peak toward the end of our period, in the eighteenth century and afterward, especially in such expressions as the Hasidic movement. This movement is still significant in contemporary Jewish life, but its origins were late, and, hence, the movement was not central to the development of Jewish life in the long period between the time of the Black Death and emancipation.

The same minor treatment has been accorded Jewish life in the Muslim world. This is not to deny its significance, which was actually great during much of our central period, especially in the sixteenth and seventeenth centuries, when so large a proportion of all Jews lived in Islamic countries. (Jews had lived there for centuries, and their numbers were strengthened by refugees fleeing Spain after 1492.) In 1666, these Jews also experienced at first hand the failed messianic movement of Shabbetai Tzevi, a pretender who ended his career by converting to Islam. To give these important issues their due would, however, take us too far afield.

CHAPTER ONE

Beyond the Catastrophe

A s the Plague raged throughout Europe in the middle of the fourteenth century, a wave of violence broke out against the Jews living in Christendom. Mobs attacked Jewish quarters, massacring
their inhabitants or forcing them into exile. Elsewhere, Jews accused by
Christians of poisoning wells and streams and of spreading the Plague
were tried and burned at the stake. Centuries-old communities were
thereby decimated or destroyed, significantly altering the geography of
the Jewish presence in Europe. The events connected to the Plague profoundly marked the history of western European Jewry, but the Black
Death of 1348 was a watershed not only for the Jews. Perhaps as much
as one-third of the entire European population died, and the demographic expansion of the thirteenth century came to a halt (Bowsky
1971). The haunting presence of death left an indelible imprint on the

medieval mentality. It affected material life, literary and artistic expression, worldviews, and, most of all, men's basic sense of trust.

In this anguished universe, the centuries-old attempt to define the role of the Jewish presence in Christian society came to a head. The consequences of the Black Death alone did not determine the fate of European Jewry. By 1348, both England and France had already expelled their Jews. In Spain, meanwhile, campaigns of violence, initiated chiefly by the Dominicans, aimed—and not without some success—at bringing the Jews to the baptismal font. The Rindfleisch massacres in 1298, followed by those of Armleder in 1336, had decimated the German Jewish population. Legally, the Jews were excluded from the civil judiciary system and thus fully dependent on their sovereigns. But, more crucially, from 1348 until at least the close of the sixteenth century, no Jewish community—not even those in southern France that survived until the end of the fifteenth century—experienced real growth or expansion, with the sole exception of those of northern and central Italy. Moreover, the image of the Jews fostered by the Christian world was by now deeply permeated with myths powerful enough to fuel the vilest accusations against them. These myths penetrated even the peaceful communities of Italy, arousing a desire for a world without Jews there as well.

PRESENCE, MOVEMENT, EXPULSION

It is difficult to determine the precise composition of fourteenth-century European Jewry. One hypothesis tends to overestimate the total number of Jews but accurately lists the communities in order of respective size. According to this hypothesis, the total Jewish population in Europe was around 450,000 at the opening of the fourteenth century, 1 percent of a total estimated population of 44 million. England had already expelled the Jews by this date. In France there had been 100,000 Jews before the 1306 expulsion. Southern France, from which they had not yet been driven out, counted 20,000 Jews by 1490. In the Holy Roman Empire, there were about 100,000, down to 80,000 by 1490. Italy, in contrast, witnessed an increase from 50,000 to 120,00 at the beginning of the fourteenth century. The Jews of Spain numbered around 150,000, and notwithstanding the seesawing events of the fifteenth century, this hypothesis posits an increase to 250,000 on the eve of the expulsion in 1492 (although this figure seems truly excessive). The number of Jews in Portugal increased from 40,000 at the opening of the fourteenth century to 80,000 by 1490. The communities of eastern Europe were just beginning to form: there were 5,000 Jews in Poland and an equal number in Hungary. In his article on population in the *Encyclopaedia Judaica,* Salo Wittmayer Baron noted that by 1490, these communities had grown to 30,000 and 20,000 respectively.

The Jewish presence in Europe was unstable and constantly in flux, however, and these figures are therefore only estimates. Displacement and exile characteristically marked the moments of crisis, such as 1348, but they were part and parcel of Jewish history even in less dramatic circumstances. Jews traveled more than Christians. They moved around and passed from one region to another. Their history was one of migration and the creation of new settlements. In the ninth century, for example, the northward migration of Jews originally from southern Italy gave rise to the Ashkenazic communities of Germany (from the Hebrew *Ashkenaz,* meaning approximately Germany). The formation of communities in Piedmont and Savoy—destined for a long history in Italy—resulted from the dispersion of Jews driven out of Languedoc during these centuries. Displacement and migration thus represented the norms of a life marked by a precariousness imposed on the Jews by a world that created laws and extraordinary justifications to explain the presence of a foreign body within the medieval social fabric.

Between the end of the thirteenth century and the beginning of the sixteenth, Jews were expelled from a large part of Europe in two successive waves. The definitive expulsion from England took place in 1290. A provisional expulsion from France (or, rather, from the royal French dominions) occurred in 1306, followed by another in 1322. Even the last few Jews readmitted to France were compelled to leave in 1394. Between the middle of the fifteenth and the first years of the sixteenth century, they were driven from most of Germany, Spain and the Spanish possessions of Sicily and Sardinia (1492), Provence (between 1498 and 1501), and the kingdom of Naples (1511). The ways in which these expulsions were carried out depended upon the interpretations of juridical doctrines that allowed for the Jewish presence in Christian society. In what ways, during these centuries, did conditions change so as to permit expulsion?

Medieval Christendom had accepted and tolerated a Jewish presence, in specific situations and for varying lengths of time, an acceptance officially denied all other religions. Pagans had no place in the victorious Christian society; they had no choice but to convert. In contrast, the acceptance of the Jewish presence resulted from a complex process—essentially juridical and theological in nature—of defining the Jew and his place in the Christian world. During the course of the Middle Ages,

Italy and some other countries maintained the tradition of Roman law, which despite the strict limitations of the Theodosian (fourth- and fifth-century) and Justinian (sixth-century) codes considered Jews to be citizens of the Empire. Thus the Jews' juridical status derived from an amalgam of the legal tradition with the theological tradition of the Church. It was probably in this way that, between the eleventh and the thirteenth centuries, canon law fully elaborated a complex theory that firmly guaranteed a Jewish presence in the midst of Christian society.

But in the Holy Roman Empire—and later in the new kingdoms of England and France—Roman law was no longer in place. With the creation of new juridical forms between the ninth and tenth centuries, the Jewish presence required a different justification. Eventually, it came to be based on special privileges, similar to those of the charters of *tuitio* of the Carolingian period, first granted by Emperor Henry IV in 1090. A direct and particular relationship with the emperor formed the basis for these privileges and justified the protection they guaranteed. The Jews, a charter of Frederick Barbarossa declared in 1157, were protected because *ad cameram nostram attineant,* that is, because they were dependent on imperial power. In 1234, Frederick II defined the Jews as *servi nostrae camerae.* Their juridical status was thus characterized by a direct dependence on the state.

How was this condition of servitude to be interpreted? What were the characteristics of such a direct and privileged relationship between the Jews and the monarchy? Much has been said on the subject. Some scholars have considered this "servitude" a mere juridical artifice. Others have stressed the Jews' loss of freedom and concrete legal status. This condition of servitude can be interpreted either as a means of protecting and guaranteeing the Jewish presence or, conversely, as a strategy for a more pronounced financial exploitation of the Jews (Kisch 1949; Baron [1937] 1967, vol. 11; Langmuir 1990b).

With the emergence of national monarchies and their growing secularization, the arbitrary and unreliable nature of this relationship led, in large part, to a widening rift between the state power and the Jews. This rift seriously compromised the security of the Jews' very existence. As this relationship of servitude with the monarchy and the most important feudal lords became more defined, in fact, it radically curtailed Jewish freedom of movement and increased financial pressure on the Jews to the point of expropriation. In several instances, kings and lords held Jews hostage until the latter paid a ransom to the royal treasury.

In Europe, this process was characterized by parallelisms: there is a similar time frame and an underlying sense of unity. England presents a particularly meaningful case. Here the turning point that signaled the first years of the deterioration of the Jews' legal situation took place around the beginning of the thirteenth century. Until then, a series of royal privileges had guaranteed Jewish freedom. But little by little this status changed. About 1200, the juridical status of free men came to derive from the right to choose their own court of law and to avoid the arbitrary imposition of taxes on the part of the king and feudal lords. Jews received no benefit from this development. Rather, being directly dependent on the king, they ended up consigned to the category of serfs and indentured peasants. As such, they were unable to avail themselves of other than royal courts and were subjected to arbitrary fiscal impositions. The creation of a "status singular," the growing civil and religious isolation of Jews, and the unpredictable nature of the king's actions together opened the way to expulsion in 1290 (Stacey 1992b).

From the thirteenth century on, this process affected both northern and part of southern Europe. The two great monarchies, the English and the French, eventually rid themselves of Jews. The Spanish sovereigns followed their example at the end of the fifteenth century. The only exception appears to have been Italy, or at least those Italian states not subject to Spanish rule. The fact that the expulsions were a general phenomenon encourages a search for consistency and homogeneity among them, whereas the analysis of specific cases leads to an emphasis on the different forms the process assumed in various European countries. Is it possible to move beyond the differences in order to stress common elements? Can political, social, or even psychological climates favorable to the growth of the project of expulsion be singled out?

Beyond the specificities of each monarchy, one element that England and France had in common was that both had governments on the road to centralization. Intent on creating the tools of their countries' growth, English and French monarchs made use of consensus and mobilization. This mobilization involved integrating a role for the people into the policy decisions of the sovereign (Kriegel 1978a). To activate this strategy, age-old interpretive schemes were used. These reassuring and well-established models represented an effective way of creating consensus. As such, they were adopted once again to a newly emerging process of amalgamation. Hostility to the Jews was one of the most powerful and efficacious of the traditional schemes reactivated.

The first expulsion of the Jews was from England, where they formed a community of modest size with a history of only two centuries on English soil. These Jews had originally settled in England only after the Norman Conquest, on concessions from—or, perhaps more precisely, at the request of—William the Conqueror. It appears that they came principally from Rouen, other cities in northern France, and the German Rhineland. They were merchants until the twelfth century, when they became primarily moneylenders. Initially, they lived only in London, but their numbers grew, giving rise to numerous communities. The English Jews were, however, a very small minority. Out of a total population of two million, they never exceeded 5,000, or .25 percent of the population.

In the years between 1240 and 1260, when the juridical status of the Jews had already severely deteriorated, extremely heavy fiscal impositions levied by Henry III ruined the communities. Severe restrictions on moneylending in 1275 further aggravated the crisis. In order to satisfy the demands of the tax collector, Jews sold or ceded directly to the crown the lands forfeited to them as unredeemed pledges by insolvent debtors. This practice, which turned expropriated noble lands over to the monarchy and involved members of the royal family, could not help but create strong hostility toward Jews on the part of the barons and squires. It is therefore not surprising that the decision to expel the Jews finally resulted from a bargain struck among the king, the barons, and the squires. In exchange for the imposition of an extraordinarily heavy special tax that would resolve his financial exigencies, the king agreed to expel the Jews. It follows from this interpretation that their expulsion from England was not the necessary and well-planned outcome of the monarchy's centralizing politics, but the result of unforseeable contingencies (Stacey 1990, 1992b).

The practice of moneylending generated similar anxieties and fears in France, where, however, concern about illicit profits was usually expressed by the kings. Although it is not possible to trace the stages leading to the expulsion of the Jews from France with the same precision as for England, the facts suggest that they were not qualitatively different. However, unlike the English sovereigns, the French kings began to believe their own propaganda, inventing concepts such as that of the *corpus reipublicae mysticum* to create a consensus. In this Christian and sanctified—albeit political—*corpus*, Jews had no place.

In Germany, in contrast, there were no expulsions during this period. Anxiety about Jews led directly to mob attacks aimed at "paying hom-

age to the city," as Rindfleisch, the head of the butchers, asserted in
1298 when he invited the middle class of Regensburg to the massacre
(Lotter 1988: 413). But violence was not limited to Germany. The Jews
of southern France also experienced great suffering in 1320 during the
so-called Crusade of the Little Shepherds. This was the context in which
the Plague made its appearance in 1348.

THE BLACK DEATH

The Plague was not unknown in Europe and the Mediterranean, where
in the Late Middle Ages it had raged for more than two centuries. But
memory of it had faded when it reappeared in Sicily between September
1347 and January 1348, brought by the Genoese galleys arriving from
the East (Biraben 1975–76). From Sicily, it spread throughout the Mediterranean, striking Marseilles, Pisa, and Venice before moving northward. In the spring, it exploded in Provence, Catalonia, and, eventually,
Savoy. Only at the end of 1348 did it make its appearance in Switzerland, northern France, and Germany.

From the spring of 1348 on, the epidemic was accompanied by pogroms against the Jews (Ginzburg 1991). The first massacres took place
in April 1348 in Toulon, where the Jewish quarter was sacked and forty
Jews were murdered in their homes. Shortly afterward, violence broke
out in Barcelona and in other Catalan cities. In similar episodes, which
can only be described as outbursts of mass hysteria, spontaneous and
uncontrollable mob violence erupted in the Jewish quarters. It is not by
chance that the first massacre took place on Palm Sunday, the beginning
of Holy Week, which, in the Christian world, is a period traditionally
marked by the ritualized and codified manifestation of hostility against
the Jews. The spontaneous violence was unleashed by new fears but
found old and well-known paths in which to channel itself. In both
Provence and Catalonia, the authorities condemned the pogroms deci-
sively (Shatzmiller 1974). We know that those responsible for the massacre of Toulon were imprisoned, because we have evidence that the
authorities granted an amnesty in 1351 in response to a labor crisis
that followed in the wake of the Plague. The crisis in the Provençal Jewish communities that resulted from the massacres and sackings owing
directly to the epidemic forced the monarch to reduce by half the tax
levied against them.

Even the Church defended the Jews. Clement VI expressed the official
Church position in a bull issued in Avignon in July 1348. The Plague,

the pope stated, was not caused by the action of men. It could only derive from natural causes—particularly the alignment of the stars—or from divine will. By the time of the epidemic's first appearance in Narbonne, Carcassonne, and Avignon, however, the theory that the Plague was the result of a conspiracy had already found credence among the authorities, resulting in trials and burnings at the stake. In the early phase, beggars and people on the margins of society were held responsible, not the Jews. In the Dauphiné, Jews were accused for the first time in July 1348 of poisoning wells and fountains in order to spread the Plague among Christians. From there, the accusation spread rapidly to Savoy, where the count of Aosta, Amedeo VI, ordered an inquest into the persistent rumors of poisoning. Twelve Jews were arrested and tortured; many confessed. Similarly, in Châtel on Lake Geneva, a Jewish silk merchant named Agimet admitted that while traveling on business, he had spread poison powder in the wells and cisterns of Venice, Calabria, Puglia, and Toulouse on the orders of a rabbi from Chambéry (J. R. Marcus 1979: 44). Others accused in this case gave similar confessions, painting the picture of an authentic Jewish plot against Christianity. A collective responsibility was hinted at; all Jews, including children from the age of seven up, were said to have taken part in the conspiracy (Ginzburg 1991). A summary of the trial with the statements of the confessors was sent to the authorities in Strasbourg and other German and Swiss cities. Thus, the image of Jewish poisoners spread along with the Plague, resulting in trials, executions, and massacres. Even the confessions given under torture by the Jews of Freiburg very clearly expressed the theme of a Jewish plot and vendetta: "You Christians killed so many Jews . . . and we too want to rule, you have done it long enough" (Breuer 1988: 141).

In October of 1348, Clement VI issued a second bull, strongly reaffirming the Jews' innocence. He held that they could not have spread the disease, because their mortality rate equaled that of the Christians. The erudite Konrad of Megenberg supported this argument in *Das Buch der Natur,* written in 1349–51, in which he confronted in naturalistic terms the problem of the Plague's origin. He recalled, among other things, that the death rate among the Jews of Vienna was so high that they had had to enlarge their cemetery (Guerchberch 1948).

Following the trail of the Plague, massacres of Jews spread to the Swiss and German cities at the close of 1348. In many cases, violence against the Jews preceded the appearance of the epidemic. This does not mean, however, that we are dealing with independent and unconnected phenomena (Wickersheimer 1927). The Plague was, in fact, a widely announced catastrophe; it had been well forecast. The news of its advance, its anticipation, and the resulting panic are sufficient to explain the violence. Additionally, the course of the epidemic was preceded by bands of flagellants, particularly in Germany and Switzerland (Ziegler 1969). The origin of this movement and its complex rituals of pilgrimage and self-flagellation lay in the idea that through repentance, hard work, and individual mortification, one could avoid the collective punishment unleashed by the Lord with the epidemic. Soon the movement took on a subversive bent, characterized by violence against municipal authorities, the ecclesiastical hierarchy, and the rich. But its main target was the Jews. All over Germany, massacres of Jews accompanied the arrival of flagellants. In many German cities, the Jewish communities were wiped out. In Frankfurt, Mainz, and Cologne, as well as in Brussels and the Low Countries, the flagellants, together with the common people, attacked and exterminated the Jewish communities. The idea of a plot coalesced with the theory that the Plague was the result of divine punishment. However, the raison d'être of the bands' anti-Jewish propaganda lay primarily in the desire to take a direct hand in the job of purifying Christianity, placating divine rage by "pleasing God in this way" (Cohn 1961: 180). This was more important than the conviction that the Jews were spreading the Plague out of hatred of Christians.

The Church condemned the movement, rejecting the subversive character of the flagellants. The latter, in turn, envisioned their movement increasingly in messianic terms, clashing with the Church hierarchy and adopting heretical positions. Several cities tried to close their doors to the processions of flagellants, but the popular consensus in their favor and the anti-Jewish bias of the lower classes made this a difficult choice. In February 1349, the Strasbourg city council, accused of favoring the Jews, was replaced by one that decreed the stake for the entire Jewish community, two thousand in all. A hundred or so accepted baptism and were saved. "Thus were the Jews of Strasbourg and all the cities of the Rhineland—free cities, imperial cities, or feudatories—burned at the stake in that same year," reported a Jewish chronicle of the period. "In some cities Jews were burned after a trial, in others, before. In some cities, the Jews themselves set fire to their own houses and perished in the flames" (J. R. Marcus 1979: 47).

The events depicted were nothing out of the ordinary in medieval German Jewish life. These venerable Ashkenazic communities dated back to the tenth and eleventh centuries, when Jews arriving from Italy settled in the Rhineland at Worms, Cologne, Metz, Speyer, and Mainz. Once

before, in 1096, the German communities had been attacked and decimated along the route of the First Crusade, much as they were in these
pogroms. (Like the violence associated with the Plague, these earlier attacks were characterized by lower-class hostility, a preponderance of
marginal people in mob violence, and the relations of the mobs' orga-
nizers with the local and feudal powers.) Other cases of widespread
slaughter took place, as has been noted, between the end of the thirteenth century and the first decades of the fourteenth. But the consequences of the events of 1348 added to those of the preceding decades
were even more profound and led to the wide-scale destruction of the
Jewish communities. Even where Jewish communities were reestablished, they merely survived. The vigorous rabbinic culture of the past
had been destroyed, despite attempts to resuscitate it. The wave of expulsions that eradicated the Jewish presence in a large part of the imperial lands did not take place until the second half of the fifteenth century.
But for the medieval Ashkenazic world, the material, cultural, and psychological consequences of the dramatic events of 1348 were truly a
point of no return.

THE CONSTRUCTION
OF THE ANTI-SEMITIC STEREOTYPE

The fourteenth century represented a significant threshold, not only for
the Jewish presence, but also for the construction and consolidation
of the anti-Semitic stereotype as well (Langmuir 1990b). In this period,
in fact, all the Christian fantasies concerning Jewish ritual murder of
Christian children, profanation of the host (Christ's body), and the poisoning of wells and streams reached maturation. What united these accusations—linking the image of the Jew as poisoner to that of ritual
murderer of children—was the new definition of the Jew in terms of his
physical nature, not his religious beliefs. (This did not stop his detrac-
tors from giving this too an essentially religious interpretation in later
centuries.)

The parallel between the German pogroms of 1348 and those of
1096 may illustrate the transformation of the stereotype. In the eleventh
century, Jews had been attacked as murderers of God and massacred
as killers of Christ. These attacks were also linked to the ideology that
viewed the Crusade as a recovery of the Holy Sepulcher (Langmuir
1980a). Often, Jews were given the choice between conversion and
death, but for the most part they chose martyrdom (what they called

Kiddush ha-shem, "sanctification of the Name"). In the fourteenth century, however, Jews were rarely offered this choice. Even circumstances such as those present at Strasbourg—or in Toulon, where the pogrom broke out during Holy Week—appear mechanical repetitions of earlier events. The true religious and ideological motivation in 1348 was a desire to restore a universal order whose violation the disease had unleashed, not to punish the Jews' refusal to convert. The new view held that the evil they represented could not be canceled, not even by baptism. This indicated a transformation of the stereotype and an accentuation of its negativity. Most important, it now insisted that a kind of natural Jewish evil was the source of the disturbance in the natural order and the contamination of the Christian world.

The age-old concept of contamination lies at the very origin of anti-Jewish polemics. Formulated within the ecclesiastical tradition, it is discernible in some of St. Paul's texts, including the Letter to the Galatians (Stow 1992a). But this concept of contamination undoubtedly made an imperceptible but fundamental semantic shift away from its first formulation by Paul, to the point where the contamination was seen to result from the nature of the one who erred, rather than from the error. In recent times, the idea that the Jews are different or inferior by nature, and therefore capable of contaminating whoever comes in contact with them, has been denoted by the term "anti-Semitism." Anti-Semitism and anti-Judaism (the theological hatred of the Jews by the Christian world) therefore have a common and interwoven history.

The anti-Semitic stereotype grew stronger and more vigorous in the centuries following the eleventh, nourished, above all, by accusations of host profanation and ritual murder of Christian children. Despite their obvious differences, these two charges had the same form and delivered the same message: that the Jews ritually repeated the killing of Christ. We can observe evidence of the first accusation in the splendid images of a famous polyptych by Paolo Uccello on view in the ducal palace of Urbino. In the first panel, we find the shop of a Jewish moneylender, to which a Christian woman has consigned a sacred host stolen during communion, in exchange for the restitution of a cape she had pawned. In the next panels, we see the Jew in the act of profaning the host with the help of his family. The blood flowing from the tortured body of Christ reveals the misdeed to Christians. Thus the Jews—children included—end up at the stake, while the Christian woman dies repentant and eternally saved. The episode described in these panels purportedly took place in Paris at the end of the thirteenth century (Francastel 1952; Grayzel

1989). This fifteenth-century work in Urbino certainly illustrates the propagandistic exigencies of the Church—intent on stressing the divine presence in the Eucharist—as well as polemics against Jewish money-lending by minor orders of the Italian cities. But the clarity of the images strongly reinforces the rigidity of the stereotype: a stereotype evolving through history, but now solidly crystallized.

There are many cases documenting charges of host profanation, especially in Germany, where only the advent of the Reformation and its polemics against Holy Communion put an end to such episodes (Hsia 1988). The most sensational case occurred in 1478 in Passau, a city on the Danube, where the entire Jewish community was brought to trial for having profaned a host bought from a Christian woman. Although a few converted, many were burned at the stake, and the rest were expelled. A church was built on the site of the synagogue where the sacrilege was alleged to have occurred, a place of subsequent miracles.

The charge of ritual murder—in which Jews were accused of killing a child out of contempt for Christianity and in order to use the child's blood for ritual, medical, or magical purposes—had an even more complex form. These accusations usually coincided with Holy Week, making more plausible their connection to the ritual repetition of the killing of Christ. The frequent overlap of Easter and Passover gave credence to the widespread belief that Jews used Christian blood in the preparation of matzoh, the unleavened bread eaten during Passover. The accusation assumed two distinct forms in the course of its history. In the first, documented from the middle of the twelfth century on, the alleged killing took the form of a crucifixion. In the second, whose first appearance dates to the thirteenth century, and which has been called "ritual cannibalism," Jews killed a Christian child and drained its blood to use for magical and medicinal purposes (Langmuir 1990b). Both accusations very much stressed ritualism and represented the murder of the child, not as an episode of sporadic violence, but as a collective Jewish ritual regularly repeated and codified by Jewish law. The oldest example of this type of accusation is from Norwich in England, where, in 1144, the disappearance of a child and the subsequent discovery of its body gave birth to the first definition of the ritual crucifixion myth. The author was a monk, Thomas of Monmouth, who, as has been shown, fabricated the accusation, taking advantage of the opportunity to create a new saint, William of Norwich (Langmuir 1984). Composed several years after the events, his account of the murder had no juridical consequences for the Jews of Norwich, a small and recently formed community. But the stereotype had been created, albeit from bizarre personal fantasies. From then on the stereotype pervaded the collective imagination of educated and common people alike. The idea that Jews gathered every year at Passover to crucify a Christian child in order to redeem—by means of this repeated sacrifice of Christ—their destiny as slaves became familiar in vast areas of Europe. Such fantasies found fertile soil in which to take root. England and northern France were, in the century following the episode in Norwich, the scenes of other blood libels. There were accusations against the Jews in Gloucester in 1168, in Pontoise in 1163, and in Blois in 1171. Similar events took place in many other cities, until in 1255 the English king, Henry III, intervened directly in the judicial action against the Jews, in Lincoln, backing the accusation with the authority of the sovereign for the first time.

The first documented accusation of ritual cannibalism took place in Fulda, Germany. Thirty-four Jews were burned at the stake in 1235, accused of having killed Christian children to use their blood for rituals. The sources report two different versions of the event. In one, the Jews are said to have been massacred by crusaders, in the other by the citizens of Fulda. This was a case of indiscriminate murder without trial; a pogrom based on a rumor of ritual murder. The blood libel in Fulda was important not only in itself but also because it provided the opportunity for the first public stand on this problem taken by a state authority. Emperor Frederick II, in fact, interested the other European sovereigns in this issue, and gathered together a throng of converted Jews in Germany to answer the charges on the basis of their knowledge of the Hebrew texts. The converts responded that not only did neither the Bible nor the Talmud prescribe this ritual, but also both reflected a horror of blood, which they considered impure. Frederick II officially declared the accusation false. There was another blood libel in 1247, in Valreas, where Jews were imprisoned and killed. Several of them appealed to Pope Innocent IV, who condemned the accusation in no uncertain terms. But it returned repeatedly, notwithstanding papal bulls and the statements of sovereigns and central authorities.

There is plentiful documentation of these accusations, but it is limited to episodes that left a trace in either procedural documents (having resulted therefore in actual judicial proceedings) or in the clarifying intervention of some religious or lay authority. These charges must have been much more numerous. We wonder how many there were when we run into other kinds of evidence regarding cases that did not arrive at a conclusion. Such is the case of the so-called failed plot, reported in

Barcelona on the eve of the fourteenth century, when the body of a child was discovered in the Jewish quarter, near the meat market (Lourie 1986). The evidence obtained from the Jews during a hearing that found them innocent throws light on both their keen understanding that the whole community might be accused of homicide and their precise knowledge of the blood libel syntax. The case challenges the belief that there were no ritual murder accusations in southern Europe, at least until much later (Langmuir 1977). It also draws our attention to a common knowledge of the language of the stereotype and the accusation, understood by victims and accusers alike.

The success of this myth calls for a consideration of its genesis. Even though we can determine that Thomas of Monmouth wrote the script, we cannot but wonder where he obtained all the elements of his invention, and why it enjoyed such success and wide circulation. Can one hypothesize that classical pagan culture and anti-Jewish myths that were widespread in the Alexandrian world influenced the formation of the charge of ritual murder and, even more generally, the origin of the Jewish physical stereotype? It does not appear that Thomas of Monmouth had the opportunity to read the only text through which this anti-Jewish tradition could have reached the medieval world: Flavius Josephus's *Contra Apionem,* written in the first century of the common era (Langmuir 1984). But even if its direct influence on the monk from Norwich cannot be documented, the hypothesis that the classical anti-Jewish tradition was not extraneous to the myth of ritual murder remains worthy of attention.

This accusation had enormous political impact. It frequently appears, in fact, among the charges leading to expulsion as one of the most serious violations of the pact that bound Jews to Christians and that determined their submissive presence in society. Even the expulsion of the Jews from Spain in 1492 was immediately preceded by a sensational, although anomalous, trial for ritual murder. Thus, whereas in theory the Church rejected the charge, the secular authorities, and even the marginal ecclesiastics involved, quickly appropriated the myth and assimilated it into their system of beliefs and images. At the least, they did not hesitate to take advantage of its practical applications. Paradoxically, the accusation used religious terminology, elicited emotions connected to the passion of Christ, and expressed clear-cut Christian imagery. What's more, its supporters were friars and ecclesiastics. From Thomas of Monmouth to Bernardino of Feltre—whose preaching preceded and laid the groundwork for the charge against the Jews of Trent in 1475 of having murdered a Christian child named Simon, who was later beatified—the accusers often purposely adopted Church language, even though papal bulls continually refuted the accusations unequivocally, save in exceptional cases such as that of little Simon.

Thus, the image of the Jew intent on ritual murder supported the idea of the Jew poised to take revenge on Christians, poisoning them en masse during the Black Death. Both of those charges gave special consideration to the development of the myth that the Jew was an enemy of Christian society, and that it was therefore necessary to eliminate him, or at least reprimand him harshly, in order to protect the physical and spiritual health of Christian society and the Christian state. One should not be surprised to discover that the myth of the Jews as poisoners of wells also had its precedents before the Black Death—in Vaud in 1306, in the region of Eulenburg in 1316, in Franconia in 1319 (Trachtenberg 1943), and above all in France in 1321. This last was a sensational episode in which lepers and Jews were accused, as King Philip V asserted, of having "put lethal poisons in the wells and fountains . . . to kill the people and the subjects of our kingdom" (Ginzburg 1991: 22). The confessions of lepers and Jews, and the inquisitorial documents, as later on in 1348, gave shape to the idea of a plot, organized in this case by lepers together with Jews and Muslims to wreak revenge on Christians and take over the government. Massacres, trials, and burnings followed, in which the monarchy, the state, local authorities, and inquisitors participated. Anonymous mobs slaughtered Jews and lepers without benefit of trial. The lepers who escaped the massacres and flames were shut up in leper colonies, while the Jews were expelled from the kingdom several months later. But the association of Jew with leper continued for a long time. At the close of the fifteenth century, Europe would look for a reason for the appearance of a new and unknown disease: syphilis. As in the case of the Plague, the discussion would stray far afield from scientific neutrality. Anxiety provoked the need to provide external causes for the disease, and it was attributed to the Jews driven out of Spain, among others. This time there would be no hypotheses about poisoning. The accusation, limited to the findings of doctors and naturalists, would be supported by obscure correlations—explicable only in symbolic terms—to leprosy and prostitution (Foa 1990).

Thus Christian anxieties about contamination fueled the construction of a physical stereotype of the Jews that drew the flesh and blood of its myth from disease and epidemics. The history of its formation is obviously very obscure, as are all histories of fears, anxiety, and irrational thinking. The weapons of knowledge and reason appear blunted when confronted with these images that single out the body of the other in order to emphasize the contaminating, evil power of what is alien. The evolution of this stereotype is a history of base passions and uncontrollable fears. And even if its success boils down to an irrationality that one finds in every record of the past, it is found more often in Jewish memory than elsewhere, perhaps because the symbolic weight Jewish history has borne has so often obfuscated reason's neutrality.

This symbolism, this significance conferred on the Jew, has been a creation of the Christian religion, at least until the modern era (Langmuir 1990a). Thus the Church, which had been capable of developing a theory that guaranteed a Jewish presence and gave it stability, also furnished the cultural and symbolic tools to transform this presence into a dark menace, against which it was necessary to take up arms.

CHAPTER TWO

The Church and the Jews

THE INVERTED MIRROR

In June 1493, Jews driven out of Spain, who had been decimated by epidemics, were encamped on the Appian Way at the gates of Rome. The Spanish ambassador protested to the papal court that whereas "his king had expelled the Marranos [the Jews] from his kingdom as enemies of the Christian faith, the pontiff, the head of the faith, had welcomed them to Rome" (Infessura 1890: 288). This was not the first time that the Jews had turned to the head of Christianity for aid and protection, and it would not be the last. Over the course of centuries, they had come to see the pope as their protector, not only against arbitrary and violent acts, but also against attempts to worsen their legal status.

At first glance, the Jews' perception that the pope was their protector is inexplicable. From its origins, Christianity had built a great deal of its theology on the negative concept of the Jew, and this construct had left a very strong imprint on Jewish life through the centuries. The history of the Jewish presence within the Christian world is also the history of how this negative interpretation—in essence, the fruit of a religious conflict—has shaped mentalities, cultures, sociopolitical behavior, and symbolic constructs. At heart, this is a history of how the enduring anti-Jewish stereotype—a product of the same original building blocks as Christian identity—evolved and, because of its basic ambiguities, came to regulate the relations between Christians and Jews and to mark the boundaries between them.

This relationship originated in the period when nascent Christianity differentiated itself from Judaism, at the very inception of the complex relations between the religion of the law and that of Christ. Christianity based its truths on the same books as Judaism. But the newborn religion constructed its image on a foundation of anti-Jewish polemics, particularly concerning the obstinate fidelity of the Jews to their ancient law. In his Letter to the Romans, St. Paul expressed for the first time the idea that Jews had a fundamental role in the economy of salvation. Although it reviled them for their stubborn refusal to accept Christ as the messiah, the new society nonetheless demanded that the Jews remain within it, as the inverted mirror image of the emerging Christian identity.

The Jews thus served as witnesses to the truth of Christianity, according to St. Paul and later St. Augustine (who would more fully elaborate Paul's theory). According to the evolving doctrine, the people of God had been stripped of their primogeniture and had ceded their place to the true Israel, Christianity (Blumenkranz 1960; Simon 1986). In an image that would enjoy great success in medieval Christian thought, Jacob's descendants became Esau's children (G. Cohen 1967). Although the older brethren had lost their primogeniture, they were not to disappear; they would have a place within Christian society, a subordinate position that would be fully defined only in the course of the subsequent centuries. Their role would become central at the time of the final judgment, when only the conversion of all infidels—first and foremost the Jews—would allow for the establishment of the Kingdom of God. For centuries this doctrine would furnish the theological foundation necessary for the acceptance and maintenance of an element of diversity within the homogeneous universe of medieval Christianity.

But Paul had also formulated a more antagonistic attitude toward the Jews, one more concerned with the contamination they might bring to the Christian world. "A little bit of leavening leavens all the dough," he had written in his Letter to the Galatians (5.9), referring to Jewish ritual. And with the very same words in the First Letter to the Corinthians (5.7), he had recalled idolatrous rites. Moreover, he averred (1 Cor. 10.21), "You cannot drink the cup of the Lord and the cup of demons" (*New English Bible*). Much early Christian thought centered around the interpretation of these passages. Eventually, Christian thinkers constructed an image of the Jew featuring, not only his stubborn reluctance to recognize the truth, but also his sensuality and immorality (Bori 1983), and, ultimately, the diabolical and idolatrous nature of his religion. This line of thought finds its most radical expression in St. John Chrysostom's invective, according to which the Jew is the very symbol of evil, and the synagogue is Satan's abode. Despite imperial protection, the iconoclastic wrath of the monks and the faithful had toppled both synagogues and pagan temples in the East during the fourth and fifth centuries. Nevertheless, coexistence was a distinct possibility in the West. Although not out of the question, it would have been more difficult to destroy the synagogues in western Europe or make them into churches. If an equilibrium was reached, it was owing to Augustine's revival of the Pauline tradition of the Letter to the Romans, with its pivotal theory of the theological need to safeguard a Jewish presence within the Christian world. This theory represented an unswerving point in the western Christian tradition, which resisted attempts to erode it through the centuries by the anti-Jewish formulations of the intransigent wing of the Church.

Whatever position it took regarding the Jews, the Church never seriously put Jewish presence in doubt, at least not until the sixteenth century. To justify this presence, however, it was necessary to make it functional in Christian society, not only in the eschatological future outlined by Augustine, but in the earthly life of Christians. Consequently, the Church constructed a complex theory in which a Jewish presence became conditional on the maintenance of its inferiority and subordination to Christianity. As long as the correct scale of values was maintained—that is, as long as the inferiority of the Jews was assured—the Church would repulse all violations of religious freedom and guarantee a Jewish presence. Not hatred of the Jews, but love of the Church, as demonstrated by a preoccupation with the destiny of Christian people, inspired ecclesiastical policy (Stow 1988b). This theme would be reformulated and elaborated upon innumerable times in the long history of the relations between the Church and the Jews. Ultimately, Pope Paul IV opened his 1555 bull instituting the Roman ghetto, *Cum nimis absurdum*, with the words, "Since it is absurd and improper that Jews—whose own guilt has consigned them to perpetual servitude—under the pretext that Christian piety receives them and tolerates their presence should be ingrates to Christians, so that they attempt to exchange the servitude they owe to Christians for dominion over them" (Stow 1977: 294; Milano 1963: 247), thus providing the required, traditional theological support for the creation of the ghetto.

THE JEWS IN CANON LAW

In order to define this process of theoretical construction, it is necessary to define the juridical state of the Jews during the first centuries of the common era. The concession of citizenship to all inhabitants of the Empire in the third century also guaranteed the right of the Jews to be Roman citizens. Jews thus gained civil rights equal to those of others. Restrictions were introduced, however, immediately after the victory of Christianity. Under Constantine, Jewish proselytizing was prohibited, and conversion to Judaism became a crime. At the same time, the first limitations on Jewish ownership of Christian slaves were established. Subsequently, in 388, marriage between Christians and Jews was prohibited. This legislation was joined with the Theodosian Code and systematized around the middle of the fifth century. It was made still more restrictive in the sixth century by the Justinian Code, which, however, was only introduced in the West many centuries later. The explicit affirmation that the Jewish faith could not be denied by any law was fundamental to the Theodosian Code. This formulation disappeared, by contrast, in the Justinian Code. But in late medieval western Europe, the Theodosian Code remained in place even after the so-called barbarian invasions, and this fundamental principle continued to guarantee a Jewish presence by preventing Judaism—or the "Jewish sect," as it was legally defined by then—from being interpreted as a heresy. With the limitations stated above, the Jew therefore remained a citizen in the countries in which Roman Law was enforced, never becoming a foreigner without a specific juridical status. The Church played a fundamental role in this process. Its ecclesiastical formulations were joined with the Roman juridical tradition to create a solid theoretical body of law to define and justify the Jewish presence in the midst of the Christian world (Parkes 1934).

A fundamental stage in the elaboration of this policy took place at the close of the sixth century, under the pontificate of Gregory the Great (Boesch 1979). One debate centered on forced conversions. The Church also debated whether synagogues should be confiscated and transformed into churches, which was occurring in the West on the initiative of the local clergy, and whether the laws demanding the release of Christian slaves owned by Jews should be fully enforced, in contrast to what was happening in France and under the Visigothic kings in Iberia. When Jewish merchants complained that the bishop of Marseilles had tried to convert Jews by force, Pope Gregory condemned the use of force and reaffirmed the belief that conversion should be spontaneous. (Several decades later, contrary to Roman sanction, the Visigothic kings opted for forced conversion.) Moreover, the Theodosian Code protected synagogues from attacks and destruction, although it also prohibited the construction of new synagogues or conspicuous restoration of existing ones. When the synagogues of Palermo and Cagliari were forcibly transformed into churches, Gregory condemned this as a denial of religious freedom and requested the bishop of Cagliari to give back the synagogue there, which was as yet unconsecrated as a church. He asserted, however, that the synagogues in Palermo, which had already been consecrated, could not be returned. Instead, the bishop had to compensate the Jews for their losses and restore to them their books and synagogue ornaments. But when asked about Christian slaves, Gregory responded that acquiescence in Jewish possession of Christian slaves was a violation of the principle of Jewish subordination, equivalent to allowing "Christ's enemies to step on his limbs" (Migne, *PL,* 77: 1038). In these cases, as well as in others, the pope thus relied firmly and consistently on Roman law. He thereby provided Rome with a clear-cut basis for a continued Jewish presence and for the toleration of Judaism, provided, however, that Jewish inferiority was constantly reaffirmed.

In subsequent centuries, canon law united the disparate formulations of pontiffs, theologians, and councils and sanctioned a Jewish condition based on the complementary aspects of servitude and protection. The bull *Sicut Iudaeis* was a fundamental step along the path to a legitimate settlement of the contract between the Jews and Christian society. Its original text dated back to the pontificate of Callistus II (1121), but it was often republished and revived in canon law. Of equal importance was the bull *Etsi Iudaeos,* issued by Innocent III in 1205, which defined Jews as being in a state of "perpetual servitude," a term understood as meaning a position of inferiority sanctioned and formalized by clauses limiting freedom. Only their "perpetual servitude," it was stated, permitted the Jewish presence in the Christian world. Likened by many historians to the concept of *servi camerae* elaborated in these centuries by the English and French monarchies (Baron [1937] 1967, vol. 11), this concept was, in reality, quite different. The former was designed to sanction the boundaries of an essentially stable juridical status. The latter, however, was aimed at reducing the freedom of Jews in the nascent monarchies pending their ultimate expulsion.

This theoretical systematization thus sought to strike a balance between the Jews' inferiority and their necessary presence in the economy of salvation. Even as the theory's basic meaning remained unchanged through the centuries, however, many areas were left open for reinterpretation. The possibility of change implied the possibility of a deterioration of Jewish legal status, which was thrown into doubt by every shift of political and ecclesiastical power. But until the sixteenth century, no one in the ecclesiastical world went so far as to maintain that the Jews' behavior violated the basic pact that joined them to Christian society, much less that they should be expelled from Christian society because of it (Stow 1988a).

THE POPE, THE FRIARS, AND JEWISH LAW

The security of the law gave papal policy toward the Jews an element of stability. The Jews were clearly aware of this when changes under way in Europe at the end of the medieval period resulted in the formation of secular states with arbitrary Jewish policies. They appealed to Calixtus II's bull *Sicut Iudaeis* when these states seemed ready to question Jewish rights and privileges.

As a contract that guaranteed protection in exchange for submission, the terms of *Sicut Iudaeis* in fact closely resembled those of the *tuitio* charters of the Carolingian period. At times, submission might reach the point of making the pontiff the absolute arbiter, not only of their safety, but of their religious beliefs as well. In a text from a French-speaking area, traditionally dated to the beginning of the eleventh century, but recently placed in a historical context that cannot have preceded the middle of the thirteenth, Jews appealed to the pope in the matter of persecutions by the secular powers, while at the same time acknowledging his total control over their faith:

> I have found none, save God, who stands above you in the lands of the Nations, because you are the Head of the Nations and the ruler over them. So, I came to cry out about my ills from the Jews who live under your jurisdiction. For evil men have arisen without your sanction and they have attacked the Jews [using force to make them convert to Christianity, which is wrong. . . . For

they] do not have the governance over the Jews to make them leave their Torah. . . . that belongs only to the Pope of Rome. (Stow 1984: 35–36)

Direct papal jurisdiction over Jews was never explicitly claimed before 1245 in Innocent IV's *Apparatus* to the *Decretals* of Gregory IX. Pope Innocent asserted jurisdiction over Jewish orthodoxy, that is, over Jews' obedience to the principles of their own religion, not the power to force them to convert. Although the Jewish writer was keenly aware of the risks involved, he at least accepted the idea that the head of the Church of Rome enjoyed such authority, for recourse to a Church guided by principles of equilibrium was preferable to dependency on arbitrary secular leaders who offered no guarantees. In the sixteenth century and in a completely different context—the inverse of the thirteenth century, in which attacks against Jews were provoked by zealous converts and led directly by the popes—Solomon Modena wrote, with obvious exaggeration, "from the Pope comes the Torah"; that is, the papacy should maintain its traditional role of safeguarding, not destroying, both Judaism and the Jews (Ruderman 1979; Stow 1984).

But what happened when, not only the head of the Church, but also religious orders, ecclesiastical courts, and writers of treatises aspired to become the guarantors of Jewish orthodoxy and sought to establish what Jews must believe and to determine which doctrines were correct and which would introduce pernicious innovations into Judaism? This compromise of their freedom opened the door to limited inquisitorial jurisdiction over the Jews, and hence to censorship and book burning. Created to combat heresy, and formalized as a juridical institution around 1231 (when Gregory IX entrusted it to the Dominican order), the Inquisition did not, of course, have direct jurisdiction over Jews. Judaism was a religion tolerated within Christian society, a deviation from the correct faith, not a heresy. Nevertheless, the connection between Judaism and heresy became more complicated as the concept of heresy broadened and focused on the struggle for religious conformity. The Dominicans sought to broaden the authority of the Inquisition to include Jews. So, especially, did the Franciscans, who immediately took a role in the activities of the Inquisition and were bound to a less rigorous legal and traditionalist interpretation. They accomplished this by inventing a new kind of heretic, Judaizers, a category that included forced converts attempting to revert to Judaism by practicing their true faith in secrecy. In a 1267 bull, *Turbato corde,* reissued twice by later pontiffs in the course of the thirteenth century, Clement IV gave the Inquisition jurisdiction over Judaizers:

> With a troubled heart we relate what we have heard: A number of bad Christians have abandoned the true Christian faith and wickedly transferred themselves to the rites of the Jews. . . . We order that . . . you make diligent and thorough inquiry into the above, through Christians as well as through Jews. Against Christians whom you find guilty of the above you shall proceed as against heretics. Upon Jews whom you may find guilty of having induced Christians of either sex to join their execrable rites . . . you shall impose fitting punishment. (Grayzel 1989: 15)

The term "Judaizer" thus also came to include not only converts who "Judaized" but any Jew who urged or merely facilitated their return to Judaism. Although it maintained a distinction between Jews and converts, the bull extended inquisitional power over the Jews. The new jurisdiction covered heresies within Christianity, but Jews were subject to the Inquisition if they were found to be accomplices of heretical Christians. The fact that these Christians were, for the most part, forcibly converted Jews did not change the nature of the Inquisition's intervention (Yerushalmi 1970; Kriegel 1978b).

The Inquisition exerted a completely different kind of control over the nature of the Jewish religion and the orthodoxy of Hebrew texts. The first step in this direction was the condemnation of Maimonides' writings in Languedoc about 1232, at about the time of the Inquisition's founding. This episode pitted the traditionalists of the Jewish world against its rationalists. According to extant sources, all from the philosophical wing, opponents of Maimonides' ideas requested that the Inquisition of Montpellier denounce them as heretical. As reported by two eminent representatives of the Barcelona community, Judah and Abraham ibn Hasdai, the opponents said to the friars and the priests: "Why do you concern yourselves with heretics and go to the ends of the earth to persecute them, hoping to be rid of the evil in your midst? We too have heretical works . . . guilty of terrible crimes. It is your duty to preserve us from error in the very same way you preserve yourselves" (J. Cohen 1982: 55). For the first time, Christian theologians intervened in matters of Jewish orthodoxy, delivering Maimonides' works to the flames. Although the episode remains extremely vague, at least regarding the authors of the denunciation and the actual scope of the bonfire (perhaps limited to some parts of Maimonides' works), it is nonetheless significant, because it opened the door to inquisitional meddling in internal

Jewish affairs (J. Cohen 1982). With the burning of Maimonides' writings, the way was open for intervention against the Talmud.

THE ATTACK ON THE TALMUD

In 1236, the convert Nicholas Donin sent Pope Gregory IX a petition containing thirty-five accusations against the Talmud, the basic text of rabbinic Judaism. Donin charged not only that the Talmud contained attacks and blasphemies against the Christian religion but also that it introduced a new oral law that took the place of the written Torah. "So," wrote Gregory IX, taking up this last point, "they are not content with the ancient written law given to Moses by God, but ignore it and declare that God has given them another Law called 'Talmud', the 'teaching precepts' given orally to Moses" (Grayzel 1966: 240–41). The charge brought to the fore the previously marginal idea that the Talmud represented a heretical line within Judaism, in contradistinction to the authentic biblical tradition shared with Christianity and expressed in the Pentateuch. Three years later, in 1239, the pope ordered the confiscation of Hebrew books and their examination by the mendicant orders. The order to confiscate Hebrew books was sent to all the European kings, but only Louis IX of France complied. In a public disputation, one of the most representative figures of French Jewry, Rabbi Jehiel ben Josef, defended the Talmud against Donin's charges. After a trial at the University of Paris before the king, the Talmud was condemned and burned in the place de Grève. Ten or twelve thousand volumes were destroyed.

This episode has been interpreted as a radical change in the Church's policy toward Jews: an orchestrated attack by the mendicant orders and the papacy on the Talmud, the normative and exegetical text of the Jews, and their constant point of reference for daily life and thought (J. Cohen 1982). But this poorly documented episode can also be interpreted in light of a preexisting struggle between the secular clergy and the mendicant orders for control of the University of Paris. Moreover, one can see it as a disguised attack on papal interpretative authority. For if this could happen to the Talmud, why not to canon law, which derived its authority mainly from the pope and could therefore be viewed as a superimposition lacking legitimate scriptural authority (Stow 1972)?

Many elements seemed to indicate a noteworthy ambivalence in Rome's policy toward the Talmud. For one thing, the traditional respect for Jewish law and freedom stood in opposition to the indiscriminate confiscations of Hebrew books. In 1247, Pope Innocent IV acceded to Jewish requests and formally reopened the inquest on the Talmud following several attempts by the French to confiscate Hebrew books. "Since the Jewish masters of your kingdom," he wrote to Louis IX, "have explained to us ... that without the book that in Hebrew is called the Talmud, they are unable to understand the Bible and other ordinances of their Law according to their faith, we, who in accordance with a Divine Mandate are obliged to permit them to observe their law, consider it our duty to respond that ... we do not want to unjustly deprive them of their books" (Grayzel 1966: 275–81). Moreover, except for the special case of John XXII in 1321, no pontiff confiscated and burned rabbinic books until the sixteenth century. The Church wanted to censor the Talmud, eliminating the portions considered blasphemous to the Christian religion, but not to suppress it.

The interpretation developed by the followers of Raymond de Peñafort among the Aragonese Dominicans during the mid thirteenth century was similarly motivated. They argued that the Talmud itself might be useful in convincing the Jews of the truth of Christianity, and that the concept of Christ as the messiah (Christology), together with the doctrine of the Trinity and other precepts of the Christian religion, was foreshadowed or actually found in the Talmud. These doctrines were at the center of the public disputation initiated by the Dominicans and held at Barcelona in 1263 in the presence of King James I of Aragon and Raymond de Peñafort. It pitted the convert Pablo Christiani against one of the greatest authorities of the Jewish world, Moses ben Nahman, known as Nahmanides. In his attack, Pablo Christiani emphasized the distinction between the old and new rabbinic literature. He saw the former as potentially useful but argued that the latter was heretical and had to be rigorously prohibited. Either to defend the Talmud from the charge of blasphemy, or to refute its Christian interpreters, Nahmanides felt compelled to maintain that only the normative, or *halachic,* part of the Talmud should be accepted. He viewed the narrative, or *haggadic,* part as having lesser authority.

The disputation resulted in a theological victory for the Christians. In the context of the debate with the Christian world, the position Nahmanides took was laden with consequences, and although it might be the expression of the rationalistic wing of the Spanish Jewish world, it was certainly not that of a mystic and kabbalist like Nahmanides himself. "Know that we have three types of books," the rabbi had stated.

The first category comprises the twenty-four books you call the "Bible," in which all of us have complete faith. The second group is called the "Talmud," and consists of the interpretations and precepts (*mitzvot*) of the Torah, because there are six hundred thirteen precepts in the Torah, which are all explained in the Talmud. And we have faith in this explanation. We have at our disposal a third kind of book that we call "Midrash," sermons. It is almost as if a bishop delivered a sermon and one of his listeners wrote it down word for word. If one believes in this book, all the better. If not, there are no consequences. (Moses ben Nahman 1982)

Another de Peñafort disciple, Raimon Martini, the author of *Pugio fidei* (1278), one of the most important thirteenth-century treatises on the *veritas fidei*, also took issue with the narrative parts of the Talmud. He made the *midrashim*, the books in which God's activities are described in an anthropomorphic manner, the object of a particularly harsh attack. The stories that depicted the Lord spending his days studying, instructing schoolchildren, and playing ball with the Leviathan for relaxation seemed to the Spanish Dominican to constitute a dangerous heresy expressing a concept of divinity completely different from the biblical one. "Neither God nor any other living creature, but only a fiction produced by their imagination; which does not exist, has never existed and will never exist" (J. Cohen 1982: 150). It would appear that cultural misunderstandings also created a gulf between Talmudic literature and its Christian censors, despite the Hebrew schools founded by de Peñafort to study Talmudic texts. Even the *Pugio fidei*, however, despite the harshness of its attack on the Talmud, called for its censorship only and for a retention of those sections most suited to conversionist purposes, not for its total elimination.

Even when the Church took the initiative in the sixteenth century and directly attacked the Talmud, it would not completely abandon its previous course. Rome's policy would continue to waver between the need to destroy the Talmud and the impulse to amend it; between the need to safeguard the law, which tolerated Jewish observance, and the need to suppress the source of Jewish incredulity. Julius III would go so far as to ban the Talmud and burn it in 1553. In 1557, the Inquisition would prohibit Jews from possessing books in Hebrew other than the Bible. Additionally, the Talmud would be included in the Index of Prohibited Books in 1559. These prohibitions would not be vigorously enforced, however, and various pontiffs would either ease or renew them from time to time. The debate on the ambiguous value of rabbinic literature that raged deep in the bosom of the Catholic world would not die (Stow 1972).

In addition to the creation of the mendicant orders and the attack on the Talmud, the thirteenth century saw yet another caesura in the relations between the Church and the Jews. The Fourth Lateran Council (1215) opened the century, or so it seemed, with a series of segregationist and discriminatory measures against the Jews. The obligation of the Jews to wear a special identifying badge was perhaps the most significant and well known of these measures. It is also the one most fervently and continuously opposed by the Jews, who tried every imaginable way to circumvent it or render it ineffectual. Of possible Muslim derivation, the badge was imposed on the Christian world in 1215, but not adopted everywhere. It was created expressly to distinguish Jews from Christians and to curb illicit sexual contacts between the two groups. It only subsequently became associated with discrimination. The shape of the badge varied according to circumstances and locale. It could take the form of a highly visible yellow or red cloth circle sewn on clothing, a yellow hat, a special cloak, or even a pair of earrings, an ornament that in Italy had fallen into disuse from the fourteenth to the sixteenth centuries and was only worn by Jewish women and sometimes by prostitutes to set them apart from honest Christian women. In fifteenth-century Ferrara, laws decreed that every Jewish male over the age of twelve had to wear a yellow badge and every Jewish woman over the age of ten clearly visible hanging earrings, "Because," explained the Franciscan preacher Giacomo Della Marca, "earrings are jewelry that Jewish women wear in place of circumcision so as to be distinguishable from other women" (Hughes 1986: 24). Whatever the original meaning of the badge, Jews as well as Christians quickly came to perceive it as signifying inferiority and shame. In the thirteenth century, however, the badge was generally ignored in many parts of Europe, despite the decree of the Lateran Council. It appears to have been enforced primarily in France and England. In Italy, Franciscan preaching in the course of the fourteenth and fifteenth centuries was responsible for its formal imposition in the communes and cities, where the *condotte,* charters that bound Jewish moneylenders to their localities, provided that they would not in fact be obliged to wear it.

Other dispositions of the Lateran Council regarding the Jews proved just as difficult to enforce, from the proscription against having Christian servants and wet nurses, to the acceptance of Christian testimony against Jews, to the bans against Jews holding public office and appearing in public during Holy Week. But even had these measures been enforced, they would hardly have been innovative. Rather, they merely renewed old and oft-repeated prohibitions. Despite its guidance in legal areas, the Fourth Lateran Council does not represent a watershed in Jewish history. The council did introduce significant innovations in the areas of interest and moneylending, which owing to the previous lack of urgency were without precedent. But rather than reinforcing the bans that prohibited lending money at interest, the council's decisions, in fact, cleared the way for the development of Jewish loan banks in the late medieval Italian cities and communes.

THE CHURCH AND USURY

Ecclesiastical doctrine viewed any interest gained from lending money as usury. In 806, the first medieval definition of the word "usury" was "to demand in return more than what has been given" (Gilchrist 1969: 63). Canon law condemned usury in the twelfth century, calling it "all that is added to capital." Similar definitions and condemnations appeared to leave little room for moneylending, at exactly the moment when burgeoning commercial and economic development made it necessary as a way to furnish capital. Did the Church, thus, obstruct socioeconomic development with a rigid theological and moral barrier? In reality, the ecclesiastical position was more complex, and there was room for substantial consensus on the development of moneylending. In fact, what the Fourth Lateran Council did in 1215 was to prohibit excessive and immoderate usury (*graves immoderatasqve usuras*) on the part of Jews. This does not imply that moderate usury was permitted; the canon simply limited itself to forbidding immoderate usury. However, the distinction between moderate and immoderate usury served to undermine the rigid conceptual opposition of the canonists to lending and opened the way to a limited and possibilist interpretation of the prohibition. All this, however, concerned only Jewish moneylending. Lending money at interest undoubtedly remained a sin and was rigorously denied Christians, although the ban was commonly circumvented. Opposition to moneylending derived from the view that interest was a profit on time, because money was, in Aristotelian terms, sterile. Such profit was illicit: time belonged to God, not man. "Since usurers sell nothing but the hope of money, that is time," wrote the Dominican Stefano di Bourbon in the thirteenth century; "they sell the day and the night. But the day is the time of light, and the night the time of rest; therefore, they sell light and rest. It would not be right, therefore, for them to enjoy eternal light and rest" (Le Goff 1977: 4).

The formulation of the 1215 decree on immoderate usury, with its openings for moneylending, was the result of an internal clash between the most rigid canonists, who were intent on forbidding lending, and more moderate elements, at that point substantially tied to papal politics. From a theoretical point of view, even the most radical position presented many problems. It was, in fact, theoretically possible to forbid the practice of usury to Christians. But denying it to Jews violated the canons that permitted them to continue the free practice of their customs, provided they were not contrary to Christianity and did not indicate superiority of Jews over Christians. Jewish moneylending had until then been practiced without prohibitions. In order to forbid the practice, it was therefore necessary either to condemn usury absolutely as a sin in any form or to assert that Jews in their capacity as moneylenders exerted an improper supremacy over their Christian debtors. Both rationales motivated the attack on moneylending launched from the thirteenth century onward by the most virulent canonists and the preaching orders, particularly the Franciscans.

The Church made a different choice, at least until the seventeenth century. During the fifteenth century, most canonists eventually supported the permissibility of moneylending based on a series of exceptions, including the *lucrum cessans* (the sum that a debtor paid to a moneylender to compensate him for the inability to make a profit on the use of his money during that period). When it came to Jewish moneylending, the canonists permitted its practice, but were careful not to allow any erosion of traditional Church theory. Instead, they devised dispensations and suspensions of penalties. Italian communal authorities often required that Jewish loan bankers wanting to settle and carry on their business in their towns possess such a dispensation, which only the pontiff could confer. In the middle of the sixteenth century, the legislator Marquardus de Susannis undertook a new discussion of the entire question of usury. In his *De Iudaeis et aliis infidelibus,* he maintained that usury was forbidden by divine law and that therefore not even the pontiff, much less the secular authorities, could permit it. The pope could resort to a legal fiction, however, and establish that Jews not be punished for this crime (Stow 1977).

Despite the very concrete economic motives that propelled it, this policy indicated not only a pragmatic compromise but also one of principle. The compromise on moneylending reflected the Church's overall Jewish policy and the desire to maintain the delicate balance between restriction and facilitation that allowed for the Jewish presence within Christian society. Like the monarchies, which after having granted Jews the right to lend money ended up sharing the qualms of the most radical canonists and expelling them, the Church had concerned itself with the financial role of the Jews, and this concern became closely linked to the political and religious problem of the Jews' role in Christian society. All things considered, the policy of compromise supported by the Church permitted a very realistic approach to the question of usury. Those opposed to moneylending, on the other hand, increasingly attributed mythical and irrational values to usury, thus making it the main source of friction between Jews and Christian society.

USURY: REALITY AND MYTH

In the thirteenth century, St. Bernard of Clairvaux wrote that Christian usurers were like "baptized Jews." The 1213 Council of Paris denounced Christian moneylenders for the *synagogas* they had erected. (Poliakov 1977: 27). "Jew" and "moneylender" were by then synonymous terms. Jews had not, however, always been moneylenders. It was only beginning in the tenth and eleventh centuries that this activity became increasingly significant within the Jewish world. Important and far-reaching development in the outside world constantly increased the need for the capital that Jews had at their disposal. Church condemnation of Christian usury, coupled with the need to employ Jewish capital obtained from trade, made moneylending the prevalent activity among Jews, although in different ways according to specific local conditions. At the same time, growing competition from Christian commerce and limitations imposed by the guilds increasingly interfered with Jewish artisan and commercial activities.

What was the Jewish position regarding usury? In Deuteronomy, it is written: "You may lend money at interest to the stranger, but not to your brother" (23.20). The teachers of the Talmud generally interpreted this passage as sanctioning interest charged to non-Jews. The Talmud was ambiguous on this point, however, and objected to moneylending in principle on both moral and religious grounds. This objection was based on Talmudic reasoning that forbade commerce with idolaters near the time of their holidays, so as to avoid contact with their cult. Since Christians were considered idolaters and there was at least one feast day each week, not only moneylending but any type of business would have to be forbidden. This reasoning implied very serious consequences for Jewish life in the Diaspora and was only resolved by eleventh-century

Ashkenazic and French scholars (J. Katz 1961). In the twelfth century, Rabbenu Tam, one of the highest authorities of the French rabbinate, affirmed: "Today we are in the practice of loaning money at interest to non Jews . . . because we have to pay taxes to the king and to the lords, and all these things are necessary for our survival. We live in the midst of non Jews and we cannot earn a living if we do not have commerce with them. Therefore, it is no longer forbidden to charge interest" (Poliakov 1977: 30). An Ashkenazic text from the end of the fifteenth century was less defensive, valuing moneylending because, in addition to being well remunerated, it provided free time for study: "If the Torah and its interpretation are better developed in Germany than elsewhere, it is because Jews here are sustained thanks to the money trade with Christians and therefore they do not have to work. Consequently, they have time available for the study of Torah. And those who do not study, can provide with their earnings for the needs of those who do" (Poliakov 1977: 35).

Nonetheless, Jewish criticism of lending already existed in the 1100s, and it persisted through the centuries (Soloveitchick 1972). When Jewish loan banks were in the midst of a serious crisis in the seventeenth century, and attacks were coming from all sides, Jewish criticism of lending reached its height. In this context, Leon Modena, in his *History of Jewish Rites* (1616), apologetically constructed a connection between moneylending and external restrictions. "It is all too true," he wrote, "that the straitened circumstances to which they have been reduced by their long confinement, being prohibited almost completely from owning land and from plying most other trades . . . have dampened their spirit and weakened their loyalty to Israel. Thus for the same reason, they have become traffickers in usury" (Modena 1979: 44).

Separation from the land and restrictions on trade were thus at the root of the choice of loan banking. The alienation of the Jews from the land was imposed, however, only at the close of the Middle Ages. In Italy, a widespread ban on owning land and real estate only came into effect in the sixteenth century. In reality, Jews had already been separated from the land for a thousand years, expressing a preference for an urban and commercial life over an agrarian one. Since the fourth century, laws preventing Jews from owning Christian slaves, and thereby large estates, had determined this state of affairs, not those prohibiting Jewish ownership of property. The ban on Christian slaves had the effect of keeping Jews from cultivating large areas. But they did own small plots of land, on which they produced wine, which was essentially permitted during the entire medieval period. Motivated also by rituals,

Jewish vineyards were widespread throughout Europe, from Sicily to Provence and Navarre. Apart from this limited phenomenon, however, even when lands pawned by insolvent debtors came into their possession, as happened in England, Jews sold them. Their juridical status deprived Jews of the opportunity of converting their assets into land, a choice the bourgeois bureaucrats of sixteenth- and seventeenth-century states were free to make.

As moneylending became the primary Jewish profession between the twelfth and sixteenth centuries, the identification of the Jew as moneylender underwent a mythic elaboration. The stereotype of the Jewish usurer created in these centuries assumed a religious connotation that relied only marginally on the actual history of moneylending. Usury was interpreted as an act of war by Jews against Christianity, a means of destroying Christians by metaphorically sucking their blood, just as the charge of ritual murder accused them of sucking the blood of Christian children. Formulated in this way by the preaching orders, especially in fourteenth- and fifteenth-century Italy, and echoed by the commonfolk, the anti-Jewish imagination of these centuries conceived of a war against Christians conducted by Jews with the weapon of money (moneylending). This was the connection between the image of the Jewish usurer and the accusation of host desecration, another form of ritual murder, depicted in Paolo Uccello's altarpiece in Urbino (see p. 17 above). In Shakespeare's *The Merchant of Venice,* as well, Shylock the Jew is motivated by hatred of Christians and a desire for revenge, not by the wish to accumulate money: "Hath not a Jew eyes? . . . [Is he not] fed with the same food? Hurt with the same weapons? . . . If you prick us, do we not bleed? . . . And if you wrong us, shall we not take revenge?" The emphasis of the polemics and the target of the stereotype are not cupidity and avarice but hate and religious war, the preferred weapons of which are the funds used in moneylending.

In truth, the collective perception of the Jewish moneylender was not always so negative. More positive images emerge when we abandon Franciscan polemics for other sources documenting everyday life. In the fourteenth century, a Provençal Jew charged with having demanded undue restitution from a Christian creditor sustained his credibility and honesty by bringing a series of Jewish and Christian witnesses to testify on his behalf. The testimony paints him as a highly regarded person, secure within the economic context and, one historian believes, well liked by the citizenry. This image enables us to reconsider Shylock, at least in the chief commercial areas of Mediterranean Europe (Shatzmiller

1990). These glimpses of reality force a modification of the image of a Europe uniformly in the grip of the preaching orders. Nevertheless, from the twelfth century on, the question of usury weighed heavily on the relations between Christians and Jews and offered wide scope for the strengthening of a negative Jewish image.

CONTINUITY AND BREAK: THE SIXTEENTH CENTURY

Despite the Fourth Lateran Council, the thirteenth century does not appear to mark a significant turning point in the relations between the Church and the Jews, at least not in terms of ecclesiastical doctrine. Nor did it witness an alteration in the recently consolidated equilibrium upon which the Jewish presence depended. From the thirteenth to the fifteenth centuries, however, despite the continuity in relations between Jews and the Church, the Church's policies began to change. The most dramatic moment of this deterioration dates to the fourteenth century, but it was only documented—very dubiously—by Jewish chroniclers in the sixteenth century. These sources report that Pope John XXII, then residing in Avignon, decreed the expulsion of the Roman and Avignonese Jews and the burning of the Talmud. The episode was said to have taken place in 1322, contemporaneous with the slaughter of French lepers and Jews accused of poisoning wells. According to the chronicles, the edict of expulsion, later rescinded by the pope, caused an outbreak of anti-Jewish violence in Rome, culminating in the public burning of the Talmud. The Roman Jews, backed by Robert of Anjou, king of Naples and "senator of Rome," traveled to Avignon and resolved the crisis by paying enormous sums of money to both the pontiff and the king (Milano 1963).

Surely the most telling sign of the new papal ambiguity, or rather of the seeming inability of the Church to guarantee the Jews safety and stability, was the attitude of the fifteenth-century popes toward Franciscan preaching, whose virulence had become a source of serious tensions, above all in the time of St. John of Capistrano (1386–1456), one of the order's main representatives. Capistrano was active against heretics and Jews in Italy, Germany, and Poland in the first half of the century, baptizing himself "scourge of the Jews." Faced with such preaching, popes from Martin V to Nicholas V adopted a policy that alternated between toleration of the violence and attempts to limit the preaching. Such vacillation did little to oppose the Franciscan hard line.

The episode of Simon of Trent in 1475 represented another disquieting change in the Church's Jewish policy, because Rome seemed to retreat from its traditional repudiation of ritual murder charges. After a highly illegal, viciously one-sided trial that ended in death sentences for several Jews accused of having killed little Simon, the Vatican sent to Trent an apostolic commissioner, the Dominican Battista de' Giudici, bishop of Ventimiglia. He returned to Rome, professing the innocence of the Jews and the illegal procedures of the trial. But in the Curia he found himself facing authoritative supporters of the charge, among them the humanist Bartolomeo Platina, and got the worst of the dispute that followed. The Church's solution was to avoid expressing an opinion on the validity of the charge, only affirming the regularity of the judicial proceedings (Quaglioni 1987). In truth, the affair was unique and never to be repeated. Still, one cannot help but see it as a sign of noticeable cracks in the wall of Church-Jewish relations.

Nevertheless, from a theological point of view, neither the fourteenth century nor the fifteenth witnessed the introduction of radical changes in the Church's position. The break came only with the establishment of ghettos in the sixteenth century, the age of the Counter-Reformation. At that time an unprecedented debate arose within the Church, undermining the traditional stance and calling into question the meaning and viability of the Jewish presence in the Christian world. The debate involved only the Catholic world, however, since the reform branch of Christianity did not share the prevailing opinion. The theoretical Lutheran position, in particular, was strongly anti-Jewish and picked up the thread of the radical ecclesiastical tradition introduced by St. Paul in the Letter to the Galatians (Stow 1977). The Catholic Church, for its part, profoundly modified its traditional policies. It embarked upon a conversionist project of enormous scope, creating new instruments—the first of which was the ghetto—of intervention in Jewish daily life and religious practices and systematically causing the deterioration of the Jews' condition and of the basic modus operandi of their presence in Christian society (Stow 1977). This process was full of ambiguity; in fact, the Jewish presence ended up being confirmed despite changes in tone. By the end of the century, a new equilibrium would once again ensure the continuation of the traditional position. In the second half of the sixteenth century, the Church had appeared to undertake the urgent elimination of infidels from a Christian society approaching an eschatological denouement. By the close of the century, however, it felt compelled to reorganize the scope and sense of its conversionist project, weakening it and rendering it so ambiguous that it became, in fact, unfeasible.

The reasons for the change, or rather attempts at change, in the Church's perennial position toward the Jews were complex and can be identified with more general changes during the Church's sixteenth-century crisis and transformation. The first to push for change were the supporters of the project of internal reform who, from the first decades of the sixteenth century onward, undertook a thorough renovation of ecclesiastical politics and its relationship to temporal power (Prosperi 1989). From their perspective, in fact, tolerance of Jews seemed geared more to the earthly concerns of power and wealth than to eternal salvation. Like the massacres during the Crusades, or the intemperance of Franciscan preaching, which could easily have unleashed a pogrom, the currents of change and reform in the Church encouraged the usually contained hostility typical of ecclesiastical anti-Judaism to overstep the bounds of the law.

There was a contemporaneous movement toward a clear-cut break with the Jews, even in environments more connected to the Counter-Reformation and its entreaties of restoration. It developed out of the tensions tied to the rupture of Christian unity and from the perceived need to be vigilant against every form of heresy and to reject any diversity. Additionally, one should not underestimate the Catholic Church's awareness of the innumerable links of fifteenth-century humanist culture to that of the Jews—namely, the humanist fascination with Jewish exegesis and with Cabala. Generated by cultural influences more than by authentic fears that Judaism might have a direct influence on the Christian world, these anxieties were nevertheless behind the complex rapport—characterized simultaneously by interest and rejection—that Christian exegetes established with Jewish tradition (Morisi 1988). These anxieties were not unrelated to the Counter-Reformation's distancing of itself from biblical texts, which from then on, barring their study by Catholic ecclesiastical scholars, became a virtual patrimony of the Protestant.

Thus, various prevailing trends within the Church of Rome converged to force a change in the rules that regulated the pact between Christians and Jews. Eventually, they united in a common cause: to convert the Jews. This desire also sprang from the eschatological fervor of both the most enthusiastic exponents of the Counter-Reformation and the most radical reformers. Indeed, in the first half of the sixteenth century, history appeared to be hastening toward the end of the world and the advent of the Kingdom of God. Heresies and wars were interpreted as the final convulsions of a world in ruin, and the hastening of the coming of the Kingdom seemed the urgent and necessary duty of every Christian. At the beginning of the sixteenth century, Christians viewed with renewed interest the tradition of Paul and Augustine, previously revived in the twelfth century by Gioacchino da Fiore, which saw the conversion of all infidels as a necessary and preliminary condition for the end of the world. First and foremost among the nonbelievers, burdened by the weightiest symbolism and expectations, were the obstinate Jews. This was the eschatological climate in which Paul IV became pope. In his youth, he had been a gifted member of the Oratory of Divine Love, which in the third decade of the sixteenth century united religious rigor and internal reform and formed the breeding ground of both the most typical representatives of the Counter-Reformation and illustrious reforming cardinals like Reginald Pole, Gasparo Contarini, and Giovanni Morone. Connected to the world of reform were two Camaldolite monks, Pietro Querini and Paolo Giustiniani, who in 1513 wrote *Libellus ad Leonem Decem,* a work that reverberated far and wide and went on to help reform the Church from within. They proposed a politics of conversion, later adopted along broad lines by Paul IV, that provided for the expulsion of the Jews from Christian society when conversion could not be effected. But the document that most thoroughly expressed the new politics of reform, without insisting on the Jews' expulsion from Christian society, was Marquardus de Susannis's *De Iudaeis et aliis infidelibus,* which notably included the principal plans for conversion in a global discussion of all preceding canon legislation on the Jews. Written in Udine in 1558, only three years after the creation of the ghetto, this work enjoyed great fame (Stow 1977).

A prudent mixture of innovation and tradition seems finally to have guided Paul IV's shift vis-à-vis the Jews. In fact, a case of ritual murder, the very charge that had so often initiated radical discussions of the Jewish presence and expulsions, occurred right at the center of Christianity on the eve of his accession to the papal throne in 1554. The only such episode in Roman Jewish history, it remains obscure, and Jewish sources document it in purely stereotypical terms. The story is similar to many others of its genre. The crucified corpse of a child was discovered in the cemetery of Rome during Holy Week in 1554, and a convert, Hananel of Foligno, incited the mob against the Jews. The resolution, however, was not the usual one. Although Pope Marcellus II was sympathetic to the mob's cries for the massacre or expulsion of the Jews, Cardinal Alessandro Farnese discovered the real culprits: two Jew-hating Spaniards who had committed the crime for money. The newly elected Paul IV sentenced the Spaniards to death and thus assured the status quo, a status quo, however, inside the rapidly enclosing walls of the ghetto (Foa 1988).

THE POLITICS OF CONVERSION

The Church's Jewish policy continued to fluctuate between guarantees and threats. The principal element of change was the new emphasis on conversion, which somewhat ambivalently involved two separate aims: the first was concrete and realistic, the conversion of the Jews by means of a series of incentives and pressures; the second was mythical and eschatological, the hastening of the arrival of the Kingdom of God. The resulting broad policy used both persuasive methods, such as conversionary sermons, and coercive ones, including fiscal pressure, arbitrary incarceration, and the creation of homes and schools for converts. The house for converts founded under the guidance of St. Ignatius of Loyola in Rome in 1543 housed Jews and other infidels, particularly Muslims, who wanted to become Christians. A house for female converts was founded in 1562, and in 1577 a school to instruct novices in the Christian religion. Incentives for entering such a place ranged from the right to keep one's possessions, or to receive charity if poor, to the ability to obtain an education. Personalities destined for brilliant careers as preachers, Hebraists, and librarians graduated from these schools. Any Jew who displayed the slightest interest in converting spent several weeks exposed to intense propaganda, which worked especially effectively on children. Typically, parents or grandparents, themselves new converts, would offer their children for conversion. Sometimes, children were handed over by only one parent. In controversial cases, the community fought to recover children they considered to have been kidnapped. Although there were cases of forced conversion (or close to it), they were few in number and did not go unnoticed. On the contrary, they elicited outcries and appeals to the pontiff, who, despite the undisputed arbitrariness of the whole procedure, eventually resolved them according to the law. In practice, this meant that in cases where there was even a slight legal pretext, the house of converts returned its victims only after they were baptized, and thus lost to the Jewish world. When the Jews clearly had the law on their side, however, the novices were generally released. Except in a few dramatic cases, it seems that the authorities aimed to provoke and frighten the Jews, and to foster in them a feeling of legal insecurity, but not to stretch the limits of the law. For example, while the house of converts maintained the legitimacy of controversial conversions of children offered by tutors, or relatives other than parents or grandparents, the Holy Office regularly ruled to return them to the Jewish community (Milano 1964). During the second half of the sixteenth and the entire seventeenth century, a string of convert houses based on the Roman model spread to Venice, Bologna, Ferrara, Modena, and Reggio. More than in Rome, the other locales housed substantial groups of marginal and poor people, who found in conversion a solution to their marginality and in the institutes' assistance an answer to their economic problems (Prosperi 1989). This was the situation in the Turin house of converts, founded in 1653, which, unlike its counterpart in Rome, seemed more like a poorhouse than a place of captivity and coercion. (The registers for the Turin house dating from 1720 have been preserved [Allegra 1990].)

The compulsory sermon represented the most dramatic undertaking in the years of conversionary zeal. A long-established tradition in preceding centuries, particularly in Spain, where the Aragonese Dominicans made it the mainstay of their proselytistic activity, it was institutionalized by the Church in 1584. Every Saturday, all the adult members of the Roman Jewish community, men and women alike, were required to listen to a sermon that was, in effect, a Christian interpretation of the weekly portion of the Pentateuch read that morning in synagogue. Some of the preachers were among the most celebrated converts of the sixteenth century, sound in their knowledge of the world from which they had departed and in their newfound religious zeal. "There are excellent preachers," observed Michel de Montaigne, "like that renegade rabbi who preaches to the Jews Saturday afternoon in the oratory of the Trinità. There are always sixty Jews forced to attend. He was one of their wisest scholars, and now he combats their faith with their own arguments, the words of their rabbis, and the text of the Bible" (Montaigne 1906: 254). This eloquent preacher was Andrea de Monte, whom Montaigne went to hear on his trip to Rome in 1581 as if he were attending a performance. De Monte preached to the Jews from 1576 to 1582, and he was effective enough to elicit protests from the community, which may have even obtained his removal (Parente 1983). As the seventeenth century progressed, there was no longer a prevalence of converts among the preachers, probably indicating that knowledge of Hebrew and of the Jewish world had spread beyond the restricted number of neophytes (Satta 1987).

Jews evidently experienced attendance at conversionary sermons as an unmitigated humiliation, and there were many attempts, individual and collective alike, to escape them. Failing this, they tried everything to avoid hearing the preachers, from putting wax in their ears to talking among themselves. All the while, Christians watched the performance from the balconies. If conversionary policy was effective at all, it was certainly not because of these methods. What then was the value of such activities? In truth, they can be interpreted as theater as well as described as such. This humiliation of Jews was staged for, first and foremost, non-Jews and represented an escape valve, conscious or unconscious, for the violence that might at any time erupt between Christians and Jews. Rome had long been acquainted with these kinds of mechanisms. Until they secured their release with the payment of a tax at the beginning of the fourteenth century, Jews were forced to endure the mockery and violence of the masses at the carnival games at Agone and Testaccio. The participation of naked Jews in the Palio also became continually more humiliating during the sixteenth and seventeenth centuries, until the community paid a tax, a kind of ransom, of three hundred scudi in 1668. Analogous manifestations employed theatricality to unleash a controlled, symbolic violence that ended up reinforcing order after exhausting itself through ritual. Other examples of this genre include such sacred medieval performances and phenomena as the Holy Shower of Stones (Sassaiola Santa) in fifteenth-century Umbria, a regulated ritual in which a controlled mob stoned Jews during Holy Week (A. Toaff 1989c). In sixteenth-century Rome, ruled by a temporal sovereign who was also the highest authority in the Christian world, religious exigencies did not seem to clash with social ones. The Church's need to maintain the Jewish presence despite everything coalesced with the demands of the social order. The violence of the lower classes had to be contained and ritualized. The sermon-as-theater was one of the means adopted to control it, reiterating nevertheless the humiliation and inferiority of the Jews.

But how many Jews converted? What was the success rate of the Church's policy? It cannot be said that it failed and that no Jews converted. Conversions were a mainstay of Italian Jewish history, and recent studies show how widespread the phenomenon was. In fifteenth-century Umbria, for example, a constant trickle of conversions accompanied economic and political situations unfavorable to Jews, leading to the complete disappearance of many small communities. (This came at a time when conversionary pressure was in the hands of the Franciscans and not yet undertaken by the Church [A. Toaff 1988].) In Rome, according to the archives of the house of converts from the years 1614 to 1679, the average number of conversions was ten a year. The rate increased slightly in the following century. Although close to one-third of these conversions were Jews from other cities or countries who traveled to Rome to be baptized, this is a higher percentage of conversions than previously estimated (Milano 1964), amounting to between 3 and 5 percent. It would not in itself erode group identity, but it was sufficient to make conversions a daily occurrence in Jewish life. The presence of neophytes was a fact that nearly all families in Rome had ultimately to acknowledge (Rudt de Collenberg 1986–88.)

Nevertheless, we can safely state that the Church's conversionary policy was not successful in eroding the solidarity of Jewish identity in the ghetto. The campaign involved an enormous organizational effort by the Church, the expenditure of considerable energy, and the assembly of a complex machinery. It should have been able to worm its way violently, by means of threats and incentives, or subtly, with promises, into the chinks that from time immemorial had existed in the armor of a threatened and oppressed identity, and to exploit the fears that made up those points of weakness. Despite all this, conversions were an individual phenomenon, never assuming a group dynamic. Indeed, the policy was a failure, especially given the extent of its radical aims: the termination of the Jewish presence within Christian society and the end of relations between Christians and the Jewish "other." Moreover, these objectives were to be reached without force, without an expulsion, with only propaganda and ideological pressure. For had they opted for expulsion, Christians would have had no choice but to expel the Jews from the entire Christian world, and that would have meant abandoning the Augustinian precept that for centuries had allowed for a Jewish presence, which would have constituted a radical theological shift. There were frequent attempts to circumvent this obstacle, concealed by accusing the Jews of having violated the pact that bound them to Christian society. But this path was difficult and beset by contradictions. For that matter, the same difficulties burdened the alternative of conversion, even as it was developing into a global and generalized campaign that sought to put an end to the Jewish presence. Such inherent contradictions were at the root of the conversion policy's ambiguity. They accounted for the hesitancy with which it was conceived and for the evident fact that its methods were inadequate to the task, thereby allowing Jewish identity to remain unscathed.

In the middle of the sixteenth century, therefore, the Roman world seemed for the first time to have been influenced by pressures to alter its traditional policy of equilibrium in regard to the Jews and by agitation for the Jews' elimination from Christian society. It boiled down to a change in continuity, or, rather, a partially failed attempt to change traditional policy. The product of this change was the ghetto, which enclosed the Jews behind walls and gates, in an effort to tame their perennial stubbornness. This did not, however, have the desired effect, which from its inception was, above all, conversion. The ghetto was the last hurrah of a policy that found it necessary to aggravate and worsen the conditions of Jews in order to obtain their conversion. Of all the instruments created to lead the recalcitrant flock to conversion, the ghetto was the only concrete attempt to alter the social reality of the community and its cultural, religious, and family bonds. All the others, from conversionary sermons to houses of converts, proved to be little more than public performances, a theater of conversions.

CHAPTER THREE

The Boundaries
of Identity

A STRONG IDENTITY

As the difficult job of reflecting on the Holocaust began in Europe, Jean-Paul Sartre wrote that the Jew is someone whom others consider Jewish (Sartre 1946), thus maintaining that the Jew was a creation of an anti-Semitism existing primarily in the mind of the anti-Semite. The question that elicited Sartre's egalitarian response denying difference was one of identity: Who was the Jew, and what were the elements that constituted his identity? This had been an easy question to answer when the criteria had been religious—religious affiliation and the observance of the law—but it had became far more complex as a result of the secularization of both the Jewish and non-Jewish worlds after the nineteenth century.

It was not, however, a new question. Theologians and the collective Christian sensibility had repeatedly posed it ever since Christianity, demanding the role of the new Israel, had been compelled to give meaning to the presence of a minority in its midst that was obstinately opposed to the new faith. What meaning was one to attribute to Jewish identity, and thereby to the possibility of the existence of Jewish history in a Christian world? The Christian response—elaborated in particular through a polemical reading of prophetic passages dealing with Israel's sins—turned the Jewish idea of election into a sort of negative election characterized by an obstinate persistence of error. From a theological point of view, this negative election allowed for the possibility of a Jewish history. But it was a history of a people without a kingdom, without a nation, without power, and destined, like the legendary Jew Ahasuerus, to wander in expiation of the guilt of having denied comfort to Christ as he climbed Golgotha. Like Ahasuerus, the Jews made their way through history, indestructible.

Eventually, historiography confronted this interpretation and its providentialism. How was one to interpret the history of the Jews in a more rationalistic vein? How could one avoid a false distinction between sacred and profane history? Posed in a different way by such thinkers as Spinoza, Bayle, and Vico, this problem was inextricably tied to the birth of modern historiography in the seventeenth century. Only by undermining the separation between sacred and profane history, in fact, could historiography emerge as an autonomous discipline. Nor was it easy for Jewish historiography (launched as a scholarly field only at the beginning of the nineteenth century) to find criteria that allowed for its integration into the larger sphere of universal history (Yerushalmi 1982b). Thus, in the middle of the nineteenth century, Heinrich Graetz attributed the survival of Jewish identity through the ages—and hence the possibility of Jewish history—to a sort of eternal spirit of Judaism (Graetz 1946). And, more recently, Yizhak Baer wrote that "Jewish history, from its origins to our times, constitutes an organic whole. Each subsequent stage in its development reveals more fully the nature of the unique force that guides it" (Baer 1961: 1). Conversely, Jewish history could be seen to exist only because of persecution, the passive response to a constant and eternal anti-Semitism.

The best way, in fact, to avoid the sterile arbitrariness of myth has been to look at the history of the Jews as a process of construction and elaboration, a continual refinement of the internal mechanisms and modalities of Jewish society, its perceptions of the outside world, and its social and cultural creativity. Thus, Jewish history becomes a history of the development of concrete and subtle strategies of survival, around which the Jewish nation's identity takes shape, as it alternates creatively between immutability and transformation. The concrete social, organizational, and cultural forms industriously built by the Jewish people through the centuries have formed the strongest bulwark against every attack on its identity. Jewish identity is not a spirit that travels through history; nor has some mysterious divine election enabled the world to witness the miracle of the Jews' inexplicable survival. Jewish identity is not the product of a succession of uninterrupted pogroms, in which the battle against persecution has become the driving force of Jewish life; nor does it arise from a "lachrymose conception" of Jewish history, a term coined by the illustrious historian Salo Baron.

Indeed, the elements of this strong identity are concrete and well documented: community and family organization, the sacred texts and their study, separateness, and a complex relationship with the outside world. The law and its rabbinic interpretation, the Halakhah (literally, "way of proceeding"), are the most important elements of all. The Halakhah is the body of oral law, expressed in the fundamental legal texts of the Mishnah and the Talmud and regulating even the most ordinary aspect of Jewish life. It constitutes a true "hedge around the Torah" (*Pirqe Avot*), which, after the destruction of the Temple in the first century C.E., permitted the defense and maintenance of the Jewish religion and, consequently, of Jewish identity.

THE PERCEPTION OF SELF: SEPARATENESS

With a few periods of exception, the internal pull for separateness and distinction in Jewish history has often accompanied the external push toward segregation. Jews originally saw even the ghetto, the very symbol of discrimination, as a means of defense and protection from the aggression of the outside world. Jewish identity has been perpetuated and maintained throughout history primarily through a sense of difference from the surrounding world. This difference has manifested itself in the organization of communal structures, the family, and social institutions. But basic differences have also arisen from a fundamentally different mentality regarding the perception of time, as well as from the distinction between the sacred and the profane, and from the dietary laws.

Jews perceive time in a decidedly different way than do Christians. In preindustrial Europe, the Christian world, like the Jewish world, was characterized by a fluidity in the day's rhythm. The real difference between the two worlds is not just that the Jewish day begins at sunset, nor that the year commences in autumn. More significant is the difference regarding the day of rest, the division of the week between work and the Lord. Jews, of course, observe the Sabbath on Saturday (Shabbat), while early on Christianity moved the holy day to Sunday, thus seriously modifying the Pentateuch's definition of the Sabbath. On Shabbat, all work is prohibited, as are lighting a fire, using means of transportation, writing, and traveling far on foot. In this tight net of prohibitions, the observance of the Sabbath on Saturday constructs a barrier between the Jewish and Christian worlds and thus rigorously perpetuates a sense of difference. Certainly there are moments at which the surrounding society, regulating its relations with the Jewish world, recognizes the other's time. Medieval privileges like the clauses of *condotte* in Renaissance Italy guaranteed that Jews would not have to appear in court as witnesses or conduct any other transactions connected to their work as moneylenders or merchants on Saturday. But recognition of the Jewish Sabbath does not imply the acceptance of a plurality of times. The very same regulations required Jews to respect Sunday, the Christian Sabbath, and abstain from work on that day as well.

The separateness created by the different divisions of time found expression in many other aspects of everyday life. Among them was the fundamental difference in diet founded on the biblical distinction between permitted and prohibited animals. Jewish law permits the consumption of only those quadrupeds that chew their cud and have a cloven hoof, and those fish that have fins and scales. Of the various prohibitions, the best known is the one concerning pork. This prohibition ultimately assumed special symbolic meaning for Christians as well as Jews. Adopted by Islam, this distinction had no theoretical basis, because the dietary laws do not provide a hierarchical scale of impurity. Nevertheless, the fact that Jews did not eat pork had already struck the imagination of pagan writers (Foa 1990). When, after some hesitation, pork became a basic ingredient of the medieval rural diet, Christians were responding openly and knowingly to the need to differentiate themselves from Jews and Jewish laws. And the Inquisition, in its efforts to uncover continued observance of Jewish law among *conversos* in fifteenth-century Spain, considered abstention from eating pork proof of guilt. In addition to distinguishing between permitted and prohibited animals, Jewish dietary laws mandate that even acceptable animals be eaten only if they have been slaughtered in the ritually prescribed manner (*shehitah*) and have had the sciatic nerve and all blood and fat removed. Moreover, it is forbidden to mix milk and meat. Based on the biblical commandment "Thou shall not cook the kid in its mother's milk," rabbinic law eventually extended this regulation to any combination of meat and milk products. Drinking wine made or poured by non-Jews was also proscribed, because of the connection wine might have with pagan cults or the Christian Mass, that is, with acts considered idolatrous.

The severity of the dietary laws, which extended to cooking and serving vessels as well, made it impossible for Jews to eat in Christian homes. The opposite—a Christian sitting down at a Jew's table—was less complicated, but the Church severely condemned such practices because of the possibility of contamination. Nevertheless, it must have been quite a common occurrence judging from the very frequent canonical bans against it. Both Jewish dietary restrictions and Christian prohibitions against eating at the home of Jews concerned the problem of contamination. But a basic difference underlay the apparent similarity in the two approaches. Christians feared contamination from the Jews' hands, from their persons. This was a fear of contagion from something simultaneously impure and evil. For Jews, contamination—perhaps even more worrisome—did not come from the Christian himself but rather, as with wine, from the connection with a rite considered idolatrous. The conceptual system of reference was therefore different, even though the practical consequences were identical: to erect a rigid barrier between the two universes and limit the relations between Christians and Jews as much as possible. Such a strategy of isolation naturally also firmly guaranteed the maintenance of a religious and cultural identity and was not just an accidental consequence of it. In fact, Jewish tradition explicitly regards the barrier that Jewish dietary laws erect around Jews as the true function of these laws (J. Katz 1961).

Still other barriers divide the Jewish world from Christianity based on fundamental differences in their criteria for interpreting the sacred and the profane, and their different relationships with the written word and with the study and concept of religion. The Jewish religion expresses itself not so much in a credo as in concrete practice that continually reminds the Jew of his relationship with God through rituals that embrace even the simplest gestures of everyday life. The word "religion," one of the basic terms in the Christian world's lexicon, hardly exists in biblical texts. Only in the Middle Ages did the corresponding Hebrew term (*dat*) take on the meaning of "religion."

The Jewish relationship with the sacred is much different than that of

Christianity. First of all, a profound difference marks the respective conceptions of sacred space. For Jews, sacredness never issues from a quality immanent in the space itself, but from the function that the space performs (Smith 1987). Biblical description of the trials undergone by the Jews in the desert placed sacredness in the holy ark, which functioned as the mobile seat of communication with the divinity. With the establishment of the Jewish people in Eretz Israel and the construction of the Sanctuary in Jerusalem, sacredness was placed in a fixed location (the innermost part of the Sanctuary, the "Holy of Holies"). Still this place retained an essentially symbolic function, as the words with which Solomon consecrated his Temple demonstrate: "But is it therefore true that God resides on the earth? Behold, the heavens and the heavens of heavens cannot contain You; how much less this house that I have built for You!" (1 Kings 8.27). After the destruction of the Temple, sacredness came increasingly to reside in the symbolic and immaterial space of the community, called, in fact, kehilla kedoshah (sacred community). Sacredness defines the boundaries of this community, separating it from the surrounding non-Jewish world. (The Hebrew word kadosh, sacred, first and foremost means separated.) Thus, the heir of the Temple in the Diaspora is the sacred and immaterial space of the community much more than the space of the synagogue. The latter is sacred only for the function it fulfills during the service, being in reality a house of study and prayer (Stow 1992e).

Even more striking is the absence of any differentiation between priests and laymen in the Jewish world. The rabbi is not a priest, but a teacher and judge. His main duties are to instruct in Torah and Talmud and to formulate judgments and opinions on problems of everyday life, family matters, and religious behavior. In the early Middle Ages, "rabbi" was an honorific title, generally reserved for important personages and wise men, and did not differentiate its holder from the lay leaders of the community. Although it has links with an institution already present in the Palestinian era, authentic rabbinic ordination—the semikhah—originated only in the fourteenth-century Ashkenazic world. It grew out of the need for internal reorganization and reinforcement of rabbinic authority in the German communities after the crisis of 1348. It spread throughout Italy, in analogous forms, between the middle of the fifteenth century and the end of the sixteenth (Bonfil 1990). But ordination did not convey any holiness to the figure of the rabbi. Rather, it served solely to enhance his professionalism and to redefine his social role.

The figure of the rabbi embodies several closely linked aspects of Judaism: piety, juridical normativism, study, and the transmission of cultural identity. Study, in Jewish tradition, is directed for the most part toward the sacred texts: the Torah, the other books of the Bible, and the complete exegetical tradition, including the Talmud and medieval commentaries. The scroll of the Torah exudes an aura of authentic sacredness and assumes, it could be said, that status of sacred place that the synagogue lacks. Richly and sumptuously adorned, the scrolls of the Torah are the centerpiece of the religious service and in some communities become objects of adoration. The Torah, the Pentateuch (accompanied by an appropriate selection of the prophetic corpus), is read in weekly portions in the synagogue, and Jews are called in turn to read it aloud in public. To write as a scribe, copying the holy books in a sacred manner, is truly a religious obligation. Moreover, it is the duty of every Jewish male to read and study every day of his life, from the day he becomes a man in the eyes of the synagogue until he dies. "Everyone should fix an hour during the day devoted to study," decreed the medieval communal synods. "Anyone who cannot study the Talmud all the time should, if possible, study half a page of the Talmud each day, or the Midrash or part of the weekly portion of the Torah" (Finkelstein 1924).

But what were the channels of transmission of Jewish culture and tradition? In this, the family played a fundamental role, seconded by the synagogue. It was there that children learned the rudiments of Hebrew and began to acquaint themselves with the Hebrew texts of the prayers and their accompanying chants. Primary instruction began at a very early age, between three and five. Wealthy families entrusted their children to private tutors, and the poorest children attended the community-organized school. Instruction concentrated first on the study in Hebrew of the Torah and subsequently on the other books of the Bible, the vernacular translation of these books, and the version of the Torah in Aramaic (Targum, the language spoken in antiquity by the Jews of Israel, in which several books of the Bible and the text of the Talmud are written). There was no fixed age for graduation to the next level; it generally took place at around twelve or thirteen, but sometimes much earlier. In the Mediterranean area, the next level of instruction included nonreligious subjects such as Latin and arithmetic, and, in Renaissance Italy, even music and dance (Bonfil 1994), in addition to traditional Hebrew studies. True higher education, the yeshivah, concentrated on the study of the Talmud and the entire exegetical tradition. Students who completed

their studies in a yeshivah generally came from far away and lived for
years in a close communal relationship with the teacher and the other
students. This was particularly true in the post-sixteenth-century Ashkenazic world (J. Katz 1961), but as described by Elijah Capsali in his
Venetian Chronicle, the situation was not very different at the famous
academy of Padua directed by the Ashkenazic rabbi Judah Mintz at the
beginning of the sixteenth century. Formal discussion—in which pupils,
teachers and auditors of all ages participated—formed a central part of
yeshivah life and aimed to investigate method, more than content:

> There were desks and benches, and everyone sat down, the rabbis and the
> other (private) tutors with their pupils. At this point the Master would ask a
> series of questions and everyone answered according to his ability. Then they
> began a discussion, asking each other questions: this is what they call an aca-
> demic disputation (*pilpul ha-Yeshivah*). Everyone discussed with his neigh-
> bor, grown-ups with grown-ups and youngsters with youngsters. The discus-
> sion was held without consulting the text, since everyone knew it perfectly.
> The only book in the room was the Master's in which he would indicate the
> passage for the day's study. (Quoted in Bonfil 1994: 119–20)

Jewish tradition reserved Talmudic studies for men. It was not that
women were absolutely denied access to education, and examples to the
contrary are not lacking, but these were exceptional cases. A traveler
from Germany, Rabbi Pethahiah of Regensburg, wrote in the twelfth century that the only daughter of the Gaon of Sura (the leader of the Babylonian academy of Sura) "was so knowledgeable in the Scriptures and
the Talmud that she was permitted to teach her students through a win-
dow. She stayed inside while her students, who were not permitted to see
her, remained outside" (Adler 1987: 71). This topos is also clearly present in other stories, including Christian versions about women of exceptional learning (Baskin 1991b). The level of instruction received by
women in the Jewish world varied according to time and place. In some
cultural environments, men preferred to emphasize the *halachic* (that is,
legal) exemption of women from the male duty of learning the Torah
and transmitting it to their children. In others, however, much more
attention was paid to the education of women, especially in rabbinical
families. Dulcia, the wife of Rabbi Eleazar ben Judah of Worms, who
was killed along with her two daughters by crusaders in 1197 and
mourned by her husband in a commemorative poem, not only wrote
and did arithmetic, like many other women of her standing, but taught
the law and the rules of observance to other women in the community

(Stow 1987). "Even the poorest Jew, even if he has ten children, sends them to school . . . and not only the boys, but the girls as well," wrote a twelfth-century disciple of Abelard (Grabois 1975: 633). This was a very widespread custom, if not the rule. It has been generally reported that the education of Jewish girls in the Middle Ages did not differ greatly from the one received by Christian girls living in urban areas: reading, some writing, and a basic knowledge of religion. But for Jews, this implied the need to read Hebrew and a more demanding knowledge of religious laws than that required in the Christian world. Furthermore, whereas the conduit of instruction for Christian girls was primarily the convent, for Jewish girls it was the family (Baskin 1991b).

Although illiteracy was not completely unknown, the Jewish world had an extremely high rate of literacy with regard to writing as well as reading. In the Jewish world, the relationship with the written word was a privileged one, much more so than it was in the Christian world. The comparison with Christian society must not, however, be made with the illiterate rural population of preindustrial Europe, but rather with the bourgeois or protobourgeois classes. This considerably reduces a discrepancy that would otherwise seem abysmal.

THE COLLECTIVE PERCEPTION OF SELF

In the web of Christian society, life for Jews in the Diaspora involved a complex collective perception of reality. Jews necessarily linked their interpretation of the gentile world to their interpretation of themselves and their role in the surrounding world. First of all, what was the Gentile (the non-Jew) for the Jew? What value did Jews ascribe to Christianity, a monotheistic religion different from theirs? And what kind of relationship between the two worlds did Judaism permit? In Talmudic formulations and in the subsequent tradition, Christianity was considered idolatrous, *avodah zarah*, as paganism had been. The consequences of this theory might have led to the erection of very inflexible barriers against Christian society. But the situation in the Diaspora—unlike that in ancient Palestine—made relations with Gentiles essential for survival. Hence there began a process of reinterpretation of halachic texts aimed at permitting this relationship without undermining religious principles. Without contravening the basic principle that Christianity was an idolatrous religion, therefore, Rabbenu Tam (1100–1170), one of the most outstanding figures of twelfth-century France, was able to reinterpret the Talmudic stricture that established that "one must not do business

with the idolaters for the three days preceding their feast days"—a law
that, if enforced, would have prevented virtually any commercial interaction with Christians (J. Katz 1961). Wine traffic with Christians was
subject to specific analogous proscriptions, because theoretically wine
could be used in the Mass. But although it was renewed for the entire
duration of the Middle Ages, even this regulation was often disregarded.
Moreover, it was subsequently reinterpreted and subjected to numerous
limitations (J. Katz 1961; A. Toaff 1989c).

If this was the religious perception that Jews had of non-Jews, what
was the political perception Jews had of the outside world? And how did
it differ, if at all, from their religious perception? Jews lived for centuries
in exile, called in Hebrew *galut*. As we have seen, Christian theology saw
the Jewish exile as nothing more than divine punishment for the crime
of deicide. But what did Jews think of their history in exile? What connection did they see between life in the Christian world and life in the
land of Israel? Where were they to rebuild the Temple, and where did
they hope to return to in a historic or messianic future?

In reality, the Jewish relationship with Eretz Israel, the land of Israel,
is an ongoing although distant one. "My heart is in the East and I in the
furthest West," sang the poet Jehudah Halevi on the threshold of the
twelfth century. Halevi, who lived in the refined Córdoba of Muslim
Spain and died while he was on his way to settle in the land of Israel,
was the author of the important theoretical work *Al Kuzari*. The relationship with Eretz Israel goes beyond the ritualistic phrase from the
Haggadah pronounced during the Passover service, which recounts the
story of the liberation of the Jews from slavery in Egypt: "This year in
exile, next year in Jerusalem." The messianic expectation of Passover is
a mixture of spiritual and earthly expectation that is very much of this
life. Although it exists completely within the religious sphere, the relationship with Israel assumes concrete, everyday aspects. On the one
hand, the *mitzvot* (religious obligations) are more efficacious in Eretz Israel, where they reach their apogee; moreover, some religious obligations
pertain only to those residing there, particularly those who live in relationship with the land and its products. On the other hand, from the
sixteenth century on, Jews migrated to Palestine not in their messianic
dreams but in reality. In fact, Jews had never completely left Palestine,
where several thousand continued to reside, especially in Jerusalem,
Galilee, and Hebron. This steady movement prompted the aged to go
to the Holy Land to be buried, but also the young to study and train
in the academies of Jerusalem and Safed. Contracts between the families

of these students and institutions in Palestine, mentioned in Roman fifteenth- and sixteenth-century matrimonial agreements, document this phenomenon well.

The existence of a reference point, the land of Israel, did not imply per se the need to formulate a strategy of return. That remained entrusted to messianic dreams. But it did lend a sense of precariousness to the perception Jews had of their presence in the Christian world. To a much greater extent, however, this sense of precariousness came from their juridical status. Jews were increasingly compelled to bargain for a presence that, at the end of the Middle Ages, no law granted them uncontestedly. Their special status profoundly influenced Jewish political thought. The relationship with power was the first political problem Jews faced in the course of their history. A group that based its existence on the strict observance of a law found itself facing the problem of establishing a rapport between its law and the dominant and alien law, the latter powerful enough to dictate the rules and enforce them. The principle that was developed in the twelfth-century Ashkenazic world was a reworking of the Talmudic precept *Dina de-malkhuta dina* (the law of the kingdom is law), which based the law of the community on its submission to external law. But what courts should have jurisdiction over Jews? The rabbinical tribunal, or the tribunal of arbiters—not necessarily rabbis—was a fundamental institution in the Jewish world, regulating tensions and settling complicated halachic issues. What relationship did state law mandate between the secular and Jewish courts? If these were the principles by which the relationship with the outside world was articulated, what were the rules governing the internal life of the community? And first and foremost, what was the source of the communal organization? The community (in Hebrew *kehillah* or *kahal*) had its origins in medieval European Jewry; there are no actual precedents in the sociopolitical organization of the Jews in antiquity. It originated as a collective organization of Jewish life within Christian society, hence in the Diaspora.

COMMUNAL ORGANIZATION

The question of the origin of the community is subject to much debate (Baron 1942; Baer 1989). The Jewish communal structure already in existence in southern Italy in the tenth to eleventh centuries probably served as a model for other communities to emulate. As Italian Jews moved into the Rhineland, they played a role in the organization of the Ashkenazic communities in Rhineland Germany and Provence in the eleventh century. This communal structure thereby became the norm for medieval Europe. But it is much more difficult to establish whether this model derived from within, evolving out of early medieval Jewish settlements influenced by relations with the eastern Jewish world, or if instead it followed the pattern set by the outside Christian world, that is, by the organization of the Italian communes.

In order to analyze the modalities and structures of the community, I shall cite several particularly significant or well-documented examples belonging to diverse geographic areas and different periods. Our points of reference will be the Ashkenazic communities of the twelfth century, the fifteenth-century Italian communities, those in Poland in the seventeenth century, the thirteenth- and fourteenth-century Spanish communities, and the Marrano communities of the seventeenth century. Organizing the discussion of life in the European communities by themes instead of chronology allows for a comparative discourse, but it implies a decision to forgo a thorough investigation of the differences among various communal models and various historic periods. But Jewish communal structures in different times and places retained enough similarities to make possible a generalized theoretical discussion that points toward a specific communal model (J. Katz 1971). Even the organization adopted by the new settlements of the seventeenth century—reconstituted after an interruption of centuries in England and France, or springing up in such places as Holland, where there had not previously been a Jewish presence—did not really involve a break with tradition and the past (Baron 1942, vol. 2). Until the dissolution of the communities in the age of emancipation, the foundations on which the communal organization rested remained substantially the same.

Throughout the long period from the second to the eighteenth century, Jewish society may be defined as a "traditional" one (J. Katz 1971). In reality, a wise mixture of old and new lay at the root of communal organization. The juridical foundation on which the life of the community rested, and on which its entire theoretical justification and the judgments of its courts were based, was the law expressed in the exegetical texts, that is, the interpretative apparatus of the Torah handed down by rabbis. It was through that fundamental instrument of conservation and relationship with tradition that the Jewish world expressed itself and regulated its existence. At the same time, it was never truly static; by means of *taqqanot* (decrees and ordinances), it assimilated historic contingencies, adapted the juridical process to the times, and changed in order to preserve tradition.

The community, or, as it was called in Italy, the Communitas Hebreorum or Universitas Hebreorum, was, however, an entity recognized by the external Christian authorities, who saw it as a responsible interlocutor. Thus in Perugia, where a Jewish presence is documented from 1262, the community appeared under the name "Universitas Hebreorum" only in 1394; the term *judeis* was used in documents of the preceding period, but implying an individual and not a group (A. Toaff 1975). Similarly, in Mantua, where a Jewish presence is first documented in 1145, the term "Universitas Hebreorum" appears only in 1511. The Jews of Assisi, numbering around one hundred in the second half of the fourteenth century, never developed a communal organization but referred to Perugia if necessary (A. Toaff 1979). In addition to the formation of an organ to direct community life, communal organization implied the presence of a sufficient number of Jews to require a synagogue, a ritual bath (for monthly purification of women), an oven, and a ritual slaughterhouse. Organized around the civic authorities' concession of a *condotta,* the settlements of moneylenders in fourteenth-century Italy were initially so meager as to not require a communal organization, even though by law they allowed for the presence of at least ten adult men, the *minyan* (the number necessary for collective prayer).

The governing body directing the communal organization varied according to time and place. Its members were generally chosen directly from the general assemblies, whose representativeness also varied. In general, voting rights in the assembly were reserved for those who paid community taxes. There were various Hebrew names for the members of the council: *parnassim, memunnim,* or *Shivah tove-ha-ir* (the seven *boni homines* [good men] of the city), a Talmudic phrase that did not imply a specific number. In sixteenth-century Rome, we find a congregation of seventy members, governed by a smaller council of twenty members drawn from its body, and other officials, among whom were three administrators possessing executive powers. Owing to a high degree of social diversification in communities in which prominent individuals predominated, the administrative organisms in Spain were much more restrictive. In Poland, significantly, the councils exercised very similar functions to those of the Christian municipal councils, administering the Jewish city. Despite the existence of a strong overarching communal organism, these communities enjoyed very broad powers and considerable administrative and juridical autonomy.

The members of the community organizations were mainly laymen. Rabbis formed an additional element that can be defined as both religious and legal. After the thirteenth century, the rabbinic tendency to concentrate halachic decisions in their own hands created considerable conflicts within the community. At times, civil authorities or sovereigns tried to strengthen the role of the rabbi. Such was the case, for example, during the crisis of the Black Death in Germany in the second half of the fourteenth century, when the institution of the communal rabbi made its appearance in the Ashkenazic communities. The history of the inconsistent relationship between the rabbinate and the lay leadership is complex. As in the German communities, the rabbi was inserted into the organizational structure of the sixteenth-century Italian communities and became a salaried official. His functions were the traditional ones: to teach, to express opinions in ritual matters, to be a judge in matrimonial and other matters over which the rabbinic courts had jurisdiction, and to proclaim the *herem* (excommunication), which represented the community's sole means of enforcing its ordinances (not the least of which were the fiscal ones). This last function, in particular, made the rabbi indispensable to the community (Bonfil 1994).

Only small, homogeneously Ashkenazic communities such as those of Verona, Padua, and Casale created the post of communal rabbi, however. The process was more complex in larger communities, such as those of Mantua or Venice, where excommunication was subject to the agreement of the most important rabbis. In sixteenth- and seventeenth-century Rome, on the other hand, there were several communal rabbis, each evidently possessing limited authority. The absence of charismatic scholars facilitated this. Between the fifteenth and sixteenth centuries, only the Provençal rabbi Bonet de Lattes, the pontiff's personal physician, received the title "rabbi of the community." He exercised authority bestowed on him not only by the community but by the pope, who permitted him to "rule and issue edicts" (Bonfil 1990: 180). But this was a case of an individual possessing great prestige. During the fifteenth and sixteenth centuries, the most prestigious heads of yeshivot in the communities of northern Italy often expressed opinions and issued decrees and ordinances such as those drafted by Judah Mintz of Padua in 1506. These were accepted by all the Italian communities, even when their authors lacked community positions.

INTERCOMMUNAL ORGANIZATION

In the medieval Jewish world, local communities were autonomous; there were no centralized, overarching community organizations, and rabbinic courts did not have any jurisdiction over the decisions of other communities. Community boundaries were rigid and well defined. The Catalan rabbi Solomon Ibn Adret, one of the foremost halachic authorities of the period, formulated a theory of reciprocal independence in 1305 in a text intended for the communities of Languedoc: "We have issued a ban that prohibits the study of philosophy under a certain age in our territory. What can you find wrong with this? We have not imposed this ban in your territory. God put a boundary between us; our children are not your children, you may do whatever you wish" (Saperstein 1986: 28). The controversy referred to in the text can serve to illustrate both the mechanisms of this independence and the contradictory drive to widen the sphere of influence of rabbinic ordinances. It is a well-known case; the ban issued in Barcelona by Ibn Adret assailed the study of philosophy and forbade it to those under twenty-five, thus severely subordinating it to Talmudic studies. Whereas the ban was applied without incident in the Catalan communities, in the culturally similar Provençal communities, it unleashed a spirited polemic on the pros and cons of adopting the measure. The debate clearly demonstrates that an out-and-out jurisdictional conflict was developing, one that went beyond the merits of the question. The French authorities were absolutely opposed to the influence of non-French rabbis, whose involvement they construed as external meddling in the internal affairs of the kingdom. We find the same attitude in England regarding the possibility of Jewish recourse to Continental courts. There the monarch formally forbade both Jews and non-Jews to appeal to foreign courts.

There was, however, a great need for rabbinical ordinances that transcended the narrow confines of the community, and this was fulfilled by the frequent convocation of extracommunal synods in Italy, France, Spain, and Germany between the twelfth and sixteenth centuries. These assemblies took their cue from the development of communal forms in Christian Europe—principally in Italy—from which they acquired models and administrative functions. Synodal decrees had wide jurisdiction and covered every sort of issue, from ritual and behavior to the imposition of regional taxes and the issuance of sumptuary laws (Finkelstein 1924).

At times, such efforts represented a response to external pressures rather than to the need for internal regulation. Intent on reestablishing the Castilian communities after their demise in the years between 1391 and 1420, Abraham Benveniste, *rab de la corte* (rabbi of the Castilian court), realized in 1432 a level of centralized power previously unknown by the Jewish communities. His taqqanot, known as the statutes of Valladolid, intervened in the areas of internal communal taxes, teaching, and choice of judges and other community functionaries. Beyond the value of the ordinances in the reorganization of the Castilian communities, one must stress the central role played by the *rab de la corte,* who had recognized authority over the autonomous communities. (The office of *rab* was conferred from outside the community, and the title did not indicate a rabbi in the usual sense of the word.) In the event of disagreements within the community, he represented the highest decision-making authority on such fundamental matters as the distribution of taxes, rulings of communal courts, and the choice of community representatives (Baer 1961).

The main incentive for this thorough imposition of centralized power was, however, the reorganization and defense of the communities. Additionally, the need to share the expense of extraordinary or even ordinary taxes levied by an external power (to whom the communities were collectively responsible) was often at the root of attempts to organize and coordinate the autonomous communities. The most protracted and perfected example of intercommunal centralization took place in Poland, where the Council of the Four Lands governed Jewish life for close to two centuries (from the sixteenth century to 1764). A central representative body made up of the heads of the communities and a tribunal of the chief rabbis, it had fiscal, administrative, and legal jurisdiction.

In this kind of society, highly important figures often assumed the role of mediator between the internal and external worlds and ended up managing the community's relationship with the state, as they had in Spain. They personally guaranteed the community's payment of levies to the king, while acting on behalf of the community and defending it against threats. Precedents for these figures existed at the very origins of Jewish communal organization. Sovereigns often appointed an authority to supervise Jewish affairs: in the ninth-century Holy Roman Empire, for example, the *magister judaeorum,* a non-Jew, supervised Jewish affairs. The *archisynagogus,* the *episcopus judaeorum,* and the *presbyter judaeorum* were all titles of Jews appointed to communal leadership positions by the state in post-eleventh-century England and the Empire. They were similar to such figures of the early modern era as the chief rabbi of France, the *Landesrabbiner* of the Empire, the *rab de la corte* of Castille, and the *dayan kelali* of Sicily. They also resemble such figures in the Islamic East as the *rosh golah* (exilarch) and the *nagid* (chief) of Egypt, although these derived their authority from within the community. In Europe, on the other hand, such appointments originated outside the community, although, to be effective, they needed, in reality, to be the community's choice, thereby reflecting its needs. Frequent conflicts arose between community organizations and these intermediaries. In 1447, after much tension, the Sicilian communities succeeded in abolishing the office of *dayan kelali,* the supreme arbiter installed by the monarchy in 1396 (Ashtor 1983). It was rare indeed to find Jewish authorities at the close of the Middle Ages possessing the power exercised by Rabbenu Tam, who ruled over the Jewish communities of Champagne and France in the twelfth century.

INTERNAL SOCIETY

The degree of social and ethnic homogeneity is one of the first issues encountered when dealing with the internal organization of the communities. Did they contain significant social stratification? If so, did it generate conflicts and tensions, or were these the result of the communities' diverse ethnic components? We know that a high degree of geographic mobility characterized the Jewish world, and that this was augmented by migrations forced by external persecutions. Thus, Jews of diverse ethnic backgrounds lived together, especially in Renaissance Italy and in the modern era. What tensions did this situation consequently produce, and, conversely, how strong was the push for assimilation among the various ethnic groups?

Partly because of its limited size, Jewish communal society was generally characterized by a high degree of social homogeneity. Sealed off as it was by often hostile forces, potentially threatening to its existence, the very situation of the community necessitated cohesion and reduced tension, even in places with a higher degree of differentiation and conflict. Confraternities, which became ubiquitous in the Jewish world at the beginning of the seventeenth century, contributed effectively to the reduction of tension. This is not to say that there were no areas of significant social diversity in the Jewish world. On the contrary, such diversity appears to have existed in Spain. The Spanish communities were characterized by a high degree of internal conflict provoked, to be sure, by the enormous differences in wealth and lifestyle, but above all by intrafamily struggles. Strictly speaking, therefore, this was a political rather than a social clash (Kriegel 1979). Social homogeneity was evidently linked to the range of activities within a community. Many fewer conflicts, therefore, arose in small communities organized around moneylending and populated mainly by bankers and their families. The Italian communities of Venice and Rome, on the other hand, were extremely heterogeneous. The high degree of internal conflict in Rome is apparent both in the frequency of such crimes as brawling, acts of violence, and theft, as documented in the state judicial records, and in the numerous civil lawsuits dealing with rent, inheritance, and business transactions that have left a trace in notarial documents (Stow 1989; Feci 1991).

In general, however, internal cohesion overcame the forces of disintegration. Such forces were, in fact, considered especially dangerous, because when exacerbated by particularly intense external pressure, they might cause individuals to flee the Jewish community, and hence to pass into Christian society. Thus, the containment of social tensions came to be identified with the maintenance and defense of cultural and religious identity. Confraternities played a fundamental role in this area. Probably founded on the model of analogous contemporary Christian confraternities, these institutions played an important part in organizing religious life, and ultimately performed an important series of vital social functions as well, from burying the dead and assisting the poor to underwriting the dowries of poor young women. Sumptuary laws also substantially furthered the process of social homogenization. The communities of Germany, Spain, and Renaissance Italy repeatedly issued such laws, which they modeled on those promulgated in Christian society. Principally an attempt at self-censorship, they aimed to prevent adverse Christian reaction to excessive displays of opulence on the part of Jews. Nevertheless, they ultimately exerted a leveling influence, as well, at least on lifestyle and customs (Adelman 1991).

Ethnic as well as social diversity could provoke tensions within the communities. Ethnic differences obviously entailed cultural, religious, and behavioral conflicts. It is difficult to establish where ethnic conflicts left off and political or social conflicts began. In Rome, for example, the influx of refugees in the wake of 1492 profoundly altered the community's organization, doubling the population and broadly dividing Roman Jews into Italians and *ultramontani* (as the Ashkenazim, French, and Spanish were called). According to a famous account by the historian and chronicler Ibn Verga, the Roman Jews petitioned Pope Alexander VI in 1492 to bar Spanish refugees from entering Rome. Ibn Verga's story lacks confirmation by other sources and is probably highly exaggerated. To the extent that it can be believed, however, relations between the Italian Jews and the Spanish refugees left much to be desired. Although ethnicity has been identified as the source of these tensions, did they really boil down to conflicts between different "nations" of Jews, as many sources maintain even today (A. Toaff 1979 and 1988; Esposito 1990)? Let us consider the reform of the Roman Jewish community instituted in 1524 by Daniele da Pisa's *Capitoli,* which, among other things, modified the distribution of communal jobs by dividing them among Italian Jews and *ultramontani.* This is usually interpreted as a confirmation of the obvious ethnic character of the clashes in the Roman community (Milano 1964). The *Capitoli* did not, however, simply divide power within the community. Rather, they promoted real unity between Sephardim and Italians, pointing the way to a progressive amalgamation of the community's different ethnic groups. After the middle of the sixteenth century, mixed marriages—already widespread among the upper classes since the beginning of the century—became commonplace at all levels of Roman Jewish society. Jews joined together in business ventures with Jews of different ethnic backgrounds and served as their best men or tutors. Synagogue membership was not as strictly regulated as one might have assumed from the toponymic identification of the congregations. Rather, affiliation with the Scola Tempio (Italian), Scola Siciliana, Catalana, Aragonese, and so on was sufficiently flexible to make one believe that it was a matter of choice and not obligation, a sure indication that the process of unification was solidly under way (Stow 1988c and 1992d). Moreover, the tensions apparent in the *Capitoli* of 1524 seem more revealing of a political conflict among bankers than of actual ethnic tensions.

The examination of communities such as Venice, Amsterdam, or London, which were formed in the seventeenth century, underscores the difficulty of defining ethnic conflict as such, that is, of isolating the ethnic features of a conflict from those that are cultural and ideological. All of these cases concern the birth of separate and autonomous communal organizations of Sephardim (for the most part Marranos [Spanish or Portuguese converts who had reverted to Judaism]) and Ashkenazim. A comparison between the community of Venice and that of Amsterdam can shed light on the dynamics of this separation. In Venice, the division that proved successful was the one that grouped together Ashkenazim (Germans, mostly moneylenders) and native Italians, on the one hand, and Sephardim, Levantines, and Ponentines (some Spanish, but principally Portuguese, who were mostly merchants), on the other. The division was perpetuated in the 1530s by the institution of two ghettos, the Ghetto nuovo for the Ashkenazim and Italians, and the Ghetto vecchio for the Sephardim, but the division was not rigid: the wall they shared was sufficiently porous to encourage cultural fusion, rather than inhibit it.

This laboriously slow process would have taken longer had it not been for the fact that the Portuguese had no choice but to join one of the other communities until it became possible to organize the Ponentine community in 1589. Usually, they affiliated with the Levantine community (Bodian 1987). The first Jews to settle in Amsterdam were Portuguese, but from the Thirty Years' War onward, a large number of Ashkenazim settled there as well. The two communities, Portuguese and Ashkenazic, remained, however, strictly divided. This separation resulted from the high degree of internal cohesion in the Portuguese community, which maintained extremely close ties with other Portuguese throughout the Diaspora. The society created in Amsterdam in 1615 for the purpose of providing dowries to destitute young girls of the "Portuguese nation" excluded Ashkenazi girls from its philanthropic activities. It did, however, include those of the "Portuguese nation" who were formally Christian and lived in France or in other countries that did not tolerate Jews. Interest in proselytizing among Marranos still not openly practicing Judaism may have motivated the Dutch confraternity (Israel 1989), but its activity was nonetheless based on ethnicity (Kaplan 1989c; Bodian 1987).

There is no doubt, moreover, that Portuguese Jewish cultural life characteristically accentuated the importance of blood and lineage during these years. In this regard, it first of all evoked memories of age-old Spanish Jewish myths of supremacy and nobility. Second, it reflected the Jews' long involvement with Spanish culture and their assimilation of the values that inspired the anti-Jewish defense of purity of blood on the Iberian peninsula. Those Portuguese who reverted to Judaism appeared now to revive these myths, altering their symbols and values (Kaplan 1988). And yet, even more than in other cases, ethnic categories here ultimately concealed what in truth were other cultural realities. The accentuation of ethnic criteria was, in fact, a particular legacy of the Marranos, those who had shared the experience of conversion to and practice of Christianity. In addition to being the product of Christian cultural influences, this emphasis on ethnicity therefore also arose as a kind of camouflage—or rather a kind of collective repression—of the realization that what really united the Portuguese of Amsterdam and Bordeaux was not so much that they belonged to the same "nation" as that they had shared the experience of traversing the Christian world through conversion. If this factor, which was religious, not ethnic, was canceled, there remained only one basis for their common identity: blood. The resultant ideology thus emerged to blot out the Christian experience and console individuals as they interpreted their own voyages to include uninterrupted membership in a "nation" bowed but not broken by conversion.

FAMILY STRUCTURE

Transmission and preservation of Jewish identity were entrusted to both the political organization of the community and its social structures. The family assumed a fundamental role in this area, representing the nucleus around which not only daily life but also ritual, social relations, and knowledge revolved. While Christians often compare the family ideal unfavorably to that of chastity and sublimation of sexuality, Jews regard chastity with suspicion, seeing marriage as the fulfillment of personal and religious life. Marriage and transmission of tradition to the next generation constitute a religious duty, a *mitzvah.* The laws and prohibitions limiting sexuality do not spring from a conception favoring abstinence, but rather from obligations connected to the laws of ritual impurity that restrict a woman during her menstrual cycle. This concept is based on the rejection of blood, a system globally different from that of Christianity, which instead largely focuses on the denial of sexuality. The Jewish husband's fulfillment of his conjugal duty, the *onah,* is a strict obligation of married life and if disregarded can constitute grounds for the dissolution of a marriage.

The Jewish family is patriarchal. Although permitted by the Bible, polygamy had all but disappeared when Rabbenu Gershom, one of the most important figures in the German Jewish world, issued an ordinance in the eleventh century formally abolishing it. This *taqqanah,* universally adopted in Germany and France, was extended only much later to Spain, where for a long time a second marriage was considered valid provided that the first produced no offspring after ten years. Even as the social and family life of Spanish Jewry underwent drastic reform in the thirteenth century, the rabbi of Barcelona, Ibn Adret, referred in a responsum precisely to such cases of sterility and affirmed that "there are many men in our community, and among them scholars and leaders of the communities, who marry a second time without divorcing their first wife, and no one has questioned the appropriateness of their behavior" (Baer 1961, 1: 254).

Jewish marriage, unlike that of Christians, was not indissoluble, but allowed for divorce (*get,* from the term that designates the document of divorce). Originally reserved for men as an act of repudiation of one's wife, divorce became contingent on the consent of the woman in the eleventh century in a taqqanah issued by Rabbenu Gershom contemporaneously with the one on polygamy. Under the legal designation "the rebellious wife," a detailed set of rules regulated broken marriages and even based the economic dispositions of the divorce on the couple's behavior. Despite its patriarchal character, the series of laws regulating married life guaranteed women economic and emotional security and protected them from the potentially difficult situation of being abandoned. Abused women existed, but they enjoyed the protection of rabbinic courts and the surrounding Jewish world. Although rabbis handed down differing opinions concerning the punishment of abusive husbands (Ashkenazim were the harshest), the Jewish world, unlike its Christian counterpart, condemned wife abuse in no uncertain terms (Grossman 1991). In France, Rabbenu Tam issued a significant ordinance in the area of family relations, limiting the duration of absences by husbands for reasons of business or education and making them conditional on the wife's consent. Limitations already present in the Talmud were thus restated and transformed into law (Finkelstein 1924).

Women play a fundamental role in Jewish life, and it would be a gross simplification to define it in terms of mere subordination, even though that term might contain strong elements of truth. The transmission of Jewish identity is entrusted to the mother. Despite the fact that the juridical structure is patriarchal, the system, is, in fact, bilinear, and each parent is recognized as such. The role of the father is, for the most part, "juridical," whereas the role of the mother is seen as "natural" and takes precedence in abnormal situations, including mixed descent. Symbolically, the maternal link represents the indissolubility of divine election, which is transmitted through the mother (Di Segni 1989). Unions between Jews and Christians were exceptional in the centuries under discussion, but in such cases the children of Jewish mothers and non-Jewish fathers were Jewish, whereas the children of Jewish fathers and non-Jewish mothers were Gentile. Legitimate marriages between Jews and Christians were naturally impossible, since both the Church and the Jewish world (where marriage was a strictly religious act) viewed them as illegal.

The family is as much, if not more, at the heart of Jewish religious life as the synagogue. Home ritual finds space and privileged expression within family life. Women play a fundamental religious role inside this space, although Halakhah limits their public religious role. To this day, the placement of women's galleries emphasizes their exclusion by preventing them from participating in the synagogue service and Torah reading (for which the men gather in the temple's real space). At home, however, many religious duties are in women's domain. Their role in the transmission of ritual practices and religious lore is fundamental. In fifteenth-century Spain, women were the ones who transmitted the hidden tradition of Jewish teachings in Marrano families. Yet its function and structure, its clear boundaries with the outside world, and its differentiation from the Christian family all make the institution of the Jewish family as a whole one of the principal links in the chain of transmission of Jewish identity through the centuries.

This does not mean that we are dealing with an absolutely immutable institution. As a closed system, rigidly organized along basic principles derived from Halakhah, even small changes and adjustments were likely to transform the family fundamentally. We have exceptional documentation on Jewish family life in Rhenish Germany during the eleventh and twelfth centuries, a product of the dramatic massacres that accompanied the First Crusade. The lists of martyrs are divided according to nuclear family and are accompanied by poems composed to preserve the memory of the victims. Together they shed light on Jewish demographics and family history (Stow 1987). The Jewish family in Germany during these years appears to have been a nuclear family comprising only two generations: parents and their children. Its size was limited, with an average of fewer than two children per family. Among family values, emotional life received ample attention. In short, Jewish families of this time bear comparison to protobourgeois Christian families of Renaissance Italy. Both possessed similar family ethics, internal structures, and socioeconomic functions.

The memoirs of Glückel of Hameln, a late-seventeenth-century German Jewess from a well-to-do family of Hamburg merchants, present us with a very different family model. She wrote her memoirs—an exceptional and extremely significant document—in two separate phases of her life to find consolation after the deaths of each of her husbands (Glückel of Hameln 1984). Glückel was twelve when she first became engaged and fourteen when she married. It was of course an arranged marriage, following a custom that had been a constant factor in Jewish family life for centuries. (Jews shared the tradition of arranged marriage and other distinctive matrimonial strategies with similar Christian

families.) The importance of the family structure as the foundation of
Jewish society in that era led to frequent ordinances against clandestine
marriages lacking family consent. Falling in love did not necessarily lead
to marriage, nor were feeling and affect always necessary components
(J. Katz 1971). In Glückel's case, however, her memoirs display a strong,
albeit contained, affection for her husbands and children. Glückel's family was a nuclear one. She and each of her husbands spent the first years
of their married life in his parents' house—as was the custom—but this
period was only temporary and was regulated by a contract. Her family
was large: she gave birth to fourteen children, eight of whom survived.
The Ashkenazic family of 500 years earlier was much smaller, as has been
noted, with an average of fewer than two children (slightly fewer than
the medieval Christian family). Families in the Roman ghetto had an average of three children, although some well-to-do families, especially
those in banking, had as many as six.

Glückel's memoirs bring us to the threshold between the seventeenth and eighteenth centuries. With its accentuation of patriarchal
power, the family structure at this time became increasingly rigid and
narrow-minded in its values and behavior (J. Katz 1971; Stow 1987). Indicative of a clear-cut discontinuity with the preceding period, this
narrow-mindedness arose from various factors, including the undoubtedly important fact that the Polish Jewish communities were then only in
a very limited sense urban. Moreover, one must not underestimate the influence that mystical and cabalistic thinking had in turning Jewish life in
a much more severe direction than had the rabbinic tradition. A comparison with the narrow-mindedness that was typical of European family
models during the first phase of the nuclear family from the sixteenth
century onward is also important (Stone 1975). In the eastern European
Jewish world of this period, the role of women was decidedly subordinate to that of men. Women customarily worked, at least in rabbis' families, and earned money so that men could dedicate all their time to
study of the law. This general marriage strategy accentuated tendencies
already present in the Jewish world and thus served to greatly limit social mobility.

At least until assimilation took hold, the very distinctive life of Jews
within the Christian world proceeded within these various spheres created by the family and other social and cultural structures. Save for the
formal breach represented by conversion—a step that was taken only by
a minority and never deeply eroded Jewish identity or blocked its transmission through the generations—the deeply rooted structures of Jewish

life and organization never altered, even at the moments when they most resembled those of the Christian world. Through the centuries, daily Jewish life has been inspired by constant Jewish models, and Jews have developed finely tuned instruments with which to modify them. The exegesis of sacred texts and the tradition of Talmudic study have been the building blocks of Jewish organization, ideology, and mentality over the centuries. Despite transformations and inevitable changes over the course of time, this cultural and ideological structure has left a deep imprint on the development of Jewish history. It is at the core of all forms of Jewish society. It is at the origin of collective Jewish identity and creates the framework of its history.

CHAPTER FOUR

The Jews of Spain

A DIFFERENT HISTORY

Jews have been in Spain since antiquity, and their historical legacy there has been filtered through myths and legends. Thus, Spain, the land furthest west, became identified with the biblical land of Sepharad—probably ancient Sardis in Asia Minor—and the reference to the "exiles from Jerusalem in Sepharad" in Obadiah 20 became the first record of a remote exile. Hence Sepharad came to be the Hebrew name for Spain, and the term "Sephardim" came to designate Jews of Spanish origin. Originating in the tenth-century cultural milieu of the Talmudic academy of Córdoba, these legends recounted a very different story than did those about other Jews, and conveyed the image of a sort of preeminence of Spanish Jews vis-à-vis the other communities in the Diaspora. Thus, Abraham Ibn Daud, a twelfth-century Toledan philosopher and historian, recounted how several of the most noble Jews in Jerusalem—all of royal blood—were sent to Spain after Titus's victory. Under the veil of the myth of four wise prisoners, he also described the emergence in Spain of rabbinical academies to replace those in Babylonia (G. Cohen 1960–61; Shatzmiller 1985). Other versions of the legend dated the origin of the Spanish Jews to an even earlier period, particularly to a mythical voyage to the West by the Babylonian Nebuchadnezzar. Jews were thus said to have settled on Spanish soil long before the fall of the second Temple (and well before the killing of Christ). Such myths clearly reveal the Jews' intent to defend themselves against the charge of deicide, and they take on greater significance in the tormented century preceding expulsion (Martínez Marina 1799).

In reality, the first evidence of Jews in Spain dates from the last centuries of the Roman Empire. It consists of inscriptions in three languages (Greek, Latin, and Hebrew), conciliar canons such as that of Elvira from the fourth century, and a letter of uncertain date and authenticity by Severus, bishop of Majorca, recounting the forced conversion of the Jews of Minorca in 418. Evidence from the Muslim period portrays a substantial, strong, and firmly established presence. A responsum by one of the greatest Babylonian rabbinic authorities of the eleventh century describes Lucena as a "city of many Jews, where no gentile lives," while Córdoba, the capital of the Caliphate, is said to be a place where few Jews live and Muslims are in the majority. Arab geographers of the tenth and twelfth centuries refer to Granada and Tarragona as "cities populated by Jews" (Baer 1961).

In general, it is difficult to arrive at valid estimates of the European population during the late Middle Ages (Cipolla 1976), and we therefore know very little of the composition of the Jewish population in Spain beyond these images. It is only from the thirteenth century on that fiscal registers of the Spanish Jews, albeit partial and sporadic, allow for less approximate estimates. When compared with other types of sources these data confirm that Castile had no more than 3,600 Jewish families at the end of the thirteenth century, in all 20,000 people, or .4 percent of the entire population. The Jewish population of Aragon was probably the same, but constituted a higher percentage of the total population (2 percent). According to these sources, even such larger communities as Toledo and Zaragoza each had only 200 to 400 families (Baer 1961). These are indeed scanty figures; still, they are higher than those for any other contemporary European Jewish community.

In Spain, as in the rest of Europe, Jews thus seem to have been a small minority. These figures force a radical reappraisal of demographic estimates made by both contemporary and nineteenth-century historians. Indeed, they contrast starkly with other sources that paint an image of a Spain densely populated by Jews. One must take into account, however, that until the fifteenth century, when the population dispersed throughout Castile, the Spanish Jewish world was predominantly urban, although not exclusively so, given its ongoing relationship with the land. Indeed, throughout Europe the Jewish population was mainly urban. An analysis of the percentage of Jews in the major cities with Jewish communities allows us to evaluate the real weight of the Jewish presence, as well as its visibility to the outside world. In most of the cities that had Jewish communities in the fourteenth century, Jews must have constituted more than 10 percent of the population. In some places, such as Avila and Tudela, Jews made up as much as 30 percent of the population, which, however, did not exceed 5,000 in total. The percentage of Jews in the Muslim kingdom of Granada was very low, less than 1 percent (Kriegel 1979).

The common historiographic interpretation of Spanish history during these centuries suggests a stereotypical image of growing intolerance linked to the centuries-long Reconquista of Spain from the Muslims by the Christian kings. The spirit of the Crusades had dissolved the values of tolerance and cultural and religious syncretism characteristic of both Muslim Spain and the first centuries of Christian Spain, thereby opening the way to the Inquisition, persecution, and expulsion. The reality was perhaps less clear-cut, more nuanced, and rife with contradictions.

The best-known and most sensational episode of Jewish history in pre-Muslim Spain was undoubtedly the attempt by the Visigoth kings, recently converted from Arianism to Catholicism, to convert the Jews forcibly. Sisebuto issued an edict sanctioning the forced conversion in 613. It was, however, only partially implemented, thanks in part to the opposition of the aristocracy, which protected the Jews. The converts must have remained in some way faithful to Judaism, since Visigothic legislation strictly regulated their orthodoxy over the course of the century. After fruitless attempts to bring the project of religious uniformity to a close in 694, a council convened at Toledo in the presence of the kings resolved that Jews be placed in slavery, that their property be confiscated, and that their children be raised by Catholic families. By this time, legislation lumped Jews and converts together under the designation "Jews." This period's history remains quite obscure because of lack of documentation. It can nevertheless be deduced that several basic trends of Spanish history were already present in the years preceding Muslim domination: forced conversions, crypto-Judaism, and, most significantly, the belief that baptism could not change a Jew into a Christian.

In 711, Arabs invaded and settled the Iberian peninsula. Contemporary chronicles relate that Jews betrayed the Visigoth kings and opened their doors to the invaders. This legend dates from the twelfth century, and probably only echoes the anxieties and suspicions that the world of the Christian Reconquista felt concerning the Jews. But the Arab conquest did indeed represent the end of religious persecution for the Spanish Jews. As elsewhere in the Muslim world, Jews in Muslim Spain were considered infidels, on a par with Mozarabs (Spanish Christians). They lived in a juridical situation of inferiority, and their presence was conditional on the payment of an annual tax, which took the place of military service and guaranteed protection. The pact of Omar introduced these laws to regulate the relations of Muslims with the "peoples of the Book," that is, with Christians and Jews. Although these laws originally discriminated against all non-Muslims, the Christian world would later revive them in part in order to underscore the inferiority of the Jews. Among the most significant of these laws were the requirement that non-Muslims wear an identifying badge, the ban on riding a horse and carrying arms, and the limit on the height of churches and synagogues. But within these clearly defined limits, Jews enjoyed religious freedom under Muslim rule. There were no legal restrictions on movement, professions, or property; they were farmers and landowners, merchants and artisans. And Jews, rather than Mozarabs, always constituted the entire administrative class, despite the fact that, in theory, infidels were forbidden to hold government offices.

It was in this period that the Talmud was introduced into the western Jewish world through contact with the Jewish culture of the East, particularly with the Babylonian academies. The push for wide acceptance throughout the Diaspora of the Talmud (the oral law developed in Palestine and Babylonia) was a very important turning point. Hebrew became established during this period as the official language of the Jewish community, replacing Aramaic, Greek, and Latin, and equaling Arabic in its importance. A bilingual culture was formed in Hebrew and Arabic that would long remain a characteristic of Spanish Jewry. This period remained in the historic memory of the Spanish Jews as one of great creativity. Jewish poets have handed down to us an image of a cultured and refined civilization replete with seductive and fascinating attractions. When the poet Moshe Ibn Ezra fled to the north, following the dispersion of the important Jewish community of Granada during the civil wars of the second decade of the eleventh century, he sensed the great contrast of the Christian kingdoms: "Destiny has brought me to a land / where my daunted spirit rebels / Barbarians speaking a coarse language / just the sight of them fills me with despair"(Avisar 1980: 427).

In this period, Jews increasingly moved to the Christian world, a trend that became more marked in the twelfth century, when the conquest of Andalusia by the Almohades gave rise to a policy of outright persecution that left Jews and Mozarabs alike with the choice of conversion or death. Many of those waiting for more propitious times or the chance to emigrate probably converted. This was the end of the Hebrew-Arabic civilization of Andalusia. The exiles left for more favorable lands, such as the other shore of the Mediterranean, southern France, or the Christian kingdoms in northern Spain that were engaged in the Reconquista. In fact, during the twelfth century, increasing numbers of Jews settled in Aragon, Catalonia, and Castile, where the Christian kings protected them. The rise of the new communities was contemporaneous with the birth of the urban civilization of Christian Spain, and the Jews made a paramount contribution to this transformation. Even cultural life had a resurgence in "barbarian" Christian Spain. The Castilian city of Toledo, the seat of the largest Jewish community in the Christian territory, was a major cultural center in the twelfth century, where Toledan Christians and Jews translated the works of ancient Greek philosophers and scientists from Arabic into Latin.

JEWISH SOCIETY IN CHRISTIAN SPAIN

The presence there of three different religions has traditionally led to the view that medieval Spain was a tripartite society founded on the principle of limited tolerance and coexistence. This is an image that suffers from a certain simplification. Another point of view interprets the very specificity of Spanish history, its "anomaly," as the consequence of this coexistence of three religions, considered in turn as three castes with different functions and roles (Castro 1966). In reality, the Spanish Christian world of these centuries regarded both Jews and Muslims as "microsocieties" within the larger Christian society. The direct relationship that bound the Jews to the monarchy, to the juridical person of the king himself, characterized and legitimized them (Suárez Fernández 1983). At the root of this bond of dependence to the crown was the fact that the Jews were legally the property of the king. They made up part of the "royal treasure" and were defined in official terminology as "the crown's coffer," the equivalent of the German emperor's *servi camerae*.

The juridical terminology reveals that the Jews were a docile source of income for Spanish monarchs. Their taxes, already higher than those levied on Christians, were often increased by all sorts of extraordinary levies. Protection was naturally the quid pro quo for their financial contributions: the kings protected their Jews and guaranteed the conditions of their existence. All in all, it was a situation of extreme vulnerability and marginality. Even at times of greatest prosperity and social advancement, the Jews' situation remained extremely precarious. The great fortunes of Jewish financiers at the courts of the thirteenth-century Castilian kings were often subject to sudden reversals, and the crown frequently confiscated their patrimony. Dependent as they were on the goodwill of the monarchy, Jews were highly exposed to political shifts or dynastic crises. The frequent periods of civil war, regency, or weakness in the central power generally plunged the entire Jewish world into very serious crises.

Marked social differentiation characterized Spanish Jewish society during the last centuries of the medieval period. The "court Jews" stood at the highest level of the hierarchy appointed first by the Muslims and then by the Christian kings as the main administrative officers, tax collectors, functionaries, and court treasurers. Jews thereby contributed directly to the construction of the administrative and financial structures of the Spanish state, playing a role unparalleled in other modern states (Kriegel 1979). Even in Languedoc, where they initially performed analogous functions, although to a much lesser degree, they had already been excluded from the central administration and the most important positions by the thirteenth century. On the other hand, in Spain, especially in Castile, Jewish involvement in the organization of the state reached its peak in the fourteenth century, only to decline in the fifteenth. Even then, moreover, court Jews continued to perform an important role until the expulsion. Particularly in the last decades of the fifteenth century, Ferdinand and Isabella, the Reyes católicos ("Catholic kings"), resumed the use of Jewish services in the transformation and centralization of the state. On the eve of the conquest of Granada and the expulsion, Jews were still among the most important administrators, from Isaac Abrabanel, the tax collector and renowned financier, who was later exiled to Naples and Venice, to Abraham Seneor, tax collector general and, from 1477, "chief rabbi" by royal decree, who converted at the age of eighty when the decree of expulsion was promulgated (Gutwirth 1989a).

Descending the social scale, we find numerous and diversified professions within the *aljamas* (a word of Arabic derivation used to designate Jewish communities). Jews were landowners and farmers and, in particular, vineyard owners and wine producers, as they were in Languedoc. In the course of the thirteenth century, documents increasingly show a clear prevalence of land sales over acquisitions, marking the Jewish propensity for liquidity that accompanied the growth of commercial and artisan activities in the cities, related to the first bans on owning land and real estate. These restrictions had been disregarded when they first appeared in late-thirteenth-century legislation, but they became more effective in the first decades of the fourteenth century.

Commerce and moneylending became the privileged terrain of Jewish activity in the thirteenth century. In Castile, Jews engaged in a vast range of artisan work, perhaps because of the absence of a Christian artisan class (Kriegel 1979). In Aragon, Jews engaged in more specialized activities, or, at the other extreme, more humble ones: the coral trade, silk manufacturing, the jewelry business, and expensive bookbinding, on the one hand, and the sale of rags, on the other. Jews were active in international trade with Muslim countries in both the Maghreb and the Orient. In the fourteenth and fifteenth centuries, Spanish kings granted commercial opportunities in the Balearic Islands to North African Jews, resulting in the growth of the Jewish community of Majorca. Another important Jewish function in the Mediterranean was the ransoming of Christian prisoners in the East and of Muslim prisoners in Christian countries. But the Spanish Jews did not limit themselves to large commercial trade in the Mediterranean. They were brokers and small businessmen as well. They traveled with merchandise hanging around their necks and were involved in the retail sale of goods of every kind, including livestock. In the fourteenth century, municipal laws obstructed or forbade all of these intermediary activities.

Moneylending, however, remained a fundamental Jewish activity. It caused the greatest friction with the surrounding world, and the crown constantly tried to regulate it, at least by reducing the interest rate. It appears that lending reached both rural and urban areas at every level of the social hierarchy. Polemics against usury assumed wide proportions in the fourteenth century, consistently denouncing it as the main source of impoverishment and decay in the rural world, particularly in times of famine and epidemics. However, the data available stress the productive role of agricultural lending and its connection to both the seasonal exigencies of agriculture and the development of a rural economy. On the other hand, indebtedness might have a very negative effect in the case of a natural disaster. Lending seems to have catalyzed or accelerated inherent processes of both development and pauperization (Kriegel 1979). In the fourteenth century, Jewish banking entered a period of crisis. The tendency, already present in the preceding period, to make Jews intermediaries and front men for Christian financiers became more marked. The growing limitations imposed by legislation, the reduction of interest rates, and competition from new Christian forms of moneylending all took the currency monopoly away from the Jews and assigned Jewish banking an increasingly marginal role in the Spanish economy.

THE *ALJAMAS:* INTERNAL
CONFLICTS AND JUDICIAL AUTONOMY

Several important elements distinguished the organization of the Spanish Jewish communities from those in the rest of Europe, despite substantial political, social, cultural, and religious similarities. One basic difference was that Spanish Jewry exhibited a high degree of internal conflict, more than any other part of the Jewish world. This resulted not only from tensions caused by the existence of privileged classes but also from Spanish Jewry's peculiar structure of families or clans and other kinship groups, differentiated socially and continually agitated by power struggles. Another fundamental difference was the judicial autonomy enjoyed by the Castilian and Aragonese Jewish communities, giving them the right to exercise full judicial powers in civil as well as criminal matters. This legacy of the Muslim era had been reinforced in the thirteenth century, although the Church had resisted it as an abuse of sovereignty. Despite its temporary abolition in 1380 in Castile, and notwithstanding subsequent attempts to limit its scope, this judicial autonomy was abolished only in 1480, as a consequence of Ferdinand and Isabella's policy of centralization.

Jurisdiction in criminal matters gave Jewish tribunals the opportunity of meting out corporal and capital punishment, the execution of which was delegated to the civil authorities. This was certainly a case, as has been stressed, of a derogation—in favor of the adoption of "barbaric medieval procedures"—of Talmudic provisions that surround the death sentence with an almost insurmountable barrier of cautions and guarantees (Kriegel 1979: 116). On the other hand, it also constituted a basic means of controlling the Jewish communities and—when not made into a vehicle of internal conflict—of safeguarding their cohesion (Suárez Fernández 1983).

The fourteenth-century extension of local Jewish jurisdiction to cover the *malsinos* was also an important development. A Hebrew word that later found its way into Castilian, *malsinos* means *slanderers* or *informers*. Slandering rivals, or informing on them to the outside world, in order to settle power struggles within the community had, in fact, become a very serious problem during the fourteenth century. Between 1380 and 1390, the campaign against malsinos in some communities became a mere pretext for bitter conflicts between groups and clans accusing each other of treachery (*malsineria*). In these years, the legal procedure against malsinos, previously an abbreviated and "exceptional" procedure, became more clearly based on the judicial model of the Inquisition, which itself had recently been codified by the Catalan inquisitor Nicolas Eymerich in his *Directorium Inquisitorum* (1376). Side by side with the fight against the malsinos, the communities increased their control over religious and communal obedience and submitted it to exceptional procedures as well. By the end of the fourteenth century, Solomon Ibn Adret, the highest rabbinic authority in Aragon, was able to write: "He who works for the reform of the social order of the communities must not adjudicate in conformance with the laws stipulated in the Torah, but according to the requirements of the situation." This was tantamount to opening the door to innovations and derogations of the fundamental principles of Jewish law (Kriegel 1979: 140).

Judicial autonomy not only represented an element of great importance to the internal life of the communities but also considerably conditioned relations with the outside. Unique among the communities of the Diaspora, the *aljamas* could execute ordinances, issue judicial sanctions against violations of community regulations, and control the customs and religious observance of their members. The role this power played in the maintenance of internal cohesion is subject to a variety of interpretations. Nevertheless, there is no doubt that the reestablishment of judicial autonomy by the law against resorting to Christian courts and the renewed campaign against malsinos were among the cornerstones of the reconstruction of the Castilian communities in 1432 by the Valladolid synod. Internal conflict, which weakened the bonds of communal solidarity, may also have helped the breakup of the Spanish Jewish world between the end of the fourteenth century and 1492. But some scholars believe that the polarization and conflicts served to integrate Spanish Jewish society rather than dissolve it. They point, for example, to the obvious internal consensus on which court Jews based their power. The court Jews' role as mediators between court and community was essential in such a context of political uncertainty and dependence on the will of the crown. Their activities justified not only that consensus but also the great privileges they enjoyed, the most important of which was exemption from the taxes imposed on the community by the kings (Kriegel 1979).

The political shift that drastically changed the situation of the Jews in Castile and Aragon took shape in the middle of the fourteenth century during the period of civil wars and dynastic changes known as the Trastámara Revolution (Suárez Fernández 1983). By the thirteenth century, however, legislative pressure on the Jews had already increased, progressively circumscribing their place in Spanish society. The ban on landowning and the limitations on moneylending were the most significant and far-reaching aspects of this turnabout. But restrictions on Jewish activity reached well beyond the socioeconomic sphere. Beginning in the second half of the thirteenth century, the kings seemed disposed to enact a whole series of civil regulations banning Jews from employing Christians; from eating, drinking, or bathing with them; and from providing them with medical treatment. These prohibitions had been part of canon law for some time. But their reconfirmation by the ecclesiastical synod of Zamora at the onset of the fourteenth century is an indication of a new focus on the issue of contamination in both the religious and secular spheres. All these regulations were taken up again by Alphonso X of Castile, whose famous codex *Las siete partidas* was issued in 1265 but only applied in the fourteenth century, and even then very partially. James I of Aragon (1208–76) also raised these issues but at the same time confirmed and extended the privileges of the communities in his kingdom. Concerns about contamination led municipal authorities in nearby Languedoc to issue ordinances in the late thirteenth century aimed at keeping Jews from contaminating food on sale in the markets. Likening Jews to lepers and prostitutes, a 1293 Provençal edict, one of many issued in the region during these centuries, ordered "that no Jew, courtesan or leper dare touch bread, fish, meat or fruit without buying it" (Kriegel 1979: 40). A "mysterious, strange passion for purity" characterized the western Mediterranean in the last centuries of the Middle Ages and, according to several scholars, nearly transformed the Jews into a caste of untouchables in their relations with the predominant society (Kriegel 1976 and 1979).

The Jews' situation became particularly critical in the kingdom of Aragon, which was concerned about a constant migration of Jews expelled from France at the beginning of the fourteenth century. In 1320, the Crusade of the Little Shepherds, after having devastated the south of France, slaughtering and forcibly converting Jews, turned toward Aragon and Navarre and massacred the Jews of Monclus. While the persecution of Jews and lepers raged in France, some Jews were tried and condemned in Teruel in 1321, accused of having poisoned Christian wells. In 1328 a pogrom of enormous scope once again devastated the communities of Navarre. During the pestilence of 1348, Catalonia and Valencia were at the center of violence and killings. The Inquisition accompanied the crescendo of violence, investigating the lives of Jews and hunting down converts among the survivors of persecution in Germany and France who had reverted to Judaism. Thus Jews began to migrate in the search for a safe haven toward Castile, a land free from the jurisdiction of the Inquisition. But the spark that brought about the almost total destruction of the Spanish Jewish world was struck at Seville, in Andalusia, then ruled by Castile.

THE YEAR OF DESTRUCTION

The pogrom that destroyed the greater part of the Castilian and Andalusian Jewish communities in 1391 originated in Seville, where the immensely popular Ferran Martinez, archdeacon of Ecije and archbishop's vicar, preached for more than a decade to a large following, inciting mobs to destroy synagogues and segregate or drive out the Jews. Martinez had continued to foster tensions and hostility against the Jews despite repeated orders by the crown to cease preaching and the accusation of heresy made against him by the archbishop. Finally, the unexpected death of John I of Castile in 1390, followed by that of the archbishop, gave him free rein. The pogrom broke out on June 6, 1391, following the usual course: attacks on the Jewish quarters, destruction of the synagogue, massacres, and baptisms.

The movement quickly enough spread throughout the kingdom of Castile and then to Catalonia. Just the news of the events in Seville was enough to unleash violence in Valencia. During the attack on the Jewish quarter, word spread that the archdeacon was coming with a cross to baptize all the Jews (Kriegel 1979). Between the dead and the converts, the Jewish community of Valencia was completely wiped out. Not only sailors, vagabonds, and people of the lower classes, but also bourgeois and perhaps even aristocrats participated in the slaughter. News of the events in Valencia, delivered with great speed thanks to the arrival of numerous agitators, helped detonate violence in Barcelona too. Despite the attempt by dignitaries and the municipality to form a militia to protect the *aljama,* it was assaulted and sacked on the night of August 5. About a hundred Jews were killed. Those who survived the massacre found refuge in the castle. In the next two days, during which calm seemed to have been restored, the authorities imprisoned some of those responsible for the violence and sentenced them to hang. To cries of "Long live the king and the people!" the townspeople rose up again, freeing the prisoners and threatening to attack the houses of the patricians. At that point, apparently, a nobleman named Pons de la Sala diverted the attackers to the castle in which the Jews had taken refuge. The siege was lifted by a procession of monks coming from the cathedral and advancing toward the castle, brandishing the cross. Many Jews were carried directly to the baptismal font. Others, including many women, refused to convert and were killed. Another two months would pass before order could be restored in the city (Wolff 1971). Similar events took place in Majorca, Gerona, Lérida, and many smaller cities.

For the most part, municipal authorities did not condone the violence. But they often behaved ambiguously and in any case were too weak either to prevent the attacks or to quickly reestablish order. The pogroms were allowed to continue and to spread, with particularly devastating effects for the community. The participation of dignitaries and members of the nobility, as in the case of Valencia, encouraged the sense of ambiguity. Although, with a few exceptions, the highest levels of the ecclesiastical hierarchy tried to stop the violence, the clergy led the way everywhere. So widespread was the participation of monks and priests that, in December 1391, the archbishop of Barcelona had to ask the king for a kind of amnesty for the ecclesiastics involved in the riots. The Castilian crown consistently maintained a position of stern condemnation. But, weakened by a very unstable regency, it was not able to protect the Jews and their belongings. In Aragon, where, on the other hand, the monarch's much firmer attitude limited the disaster, the Jewish communities survived the destruction. The great *aljama* of Zaragoza, seat of the court, was not touched by the pogroms.

The events of 1391 have been interpreted as the religious expression of an essentially socioeconomic crisis, a struggle between the upper and lower classes in which the Jews represented only a secondary target. In short, the crisis of 1391 can be seen as one of the numerous revolutionary crises—from the Ciompi uprising in Florence to the Lollard riots in England—that shook all of Europe during the second half of the fourteenth century (Wolff 1971; MacKay 1972). In fact, the dynamic of the

1391 events confirms the image of the pogrom as an act of religious violence and not, at least in this instance, a social phenomenon. In all cases, the Jews were in fact the primary object of the pogrom (Kriegel 1979). And the religious motive, the desire to convert the Jews, was always at the center of the mob's activity. This was true even in Barcelona, where the social dynamic seems more explicit, with a clear-cut distinction between the lower classes, whipped into a frenzy against the rich and the Jews, and the dignitaries, saddled with their defense. Central to each pogrom was the mob's unflinching, direct participation in the act of religious purification, which was justified by acquiescence, compromise, and the absence of central power. The pogrom was, of course, an example of social behavior. But it represented a collective appropriation by one or more social groups of the whole society's pressing need for religious purity. As in the wars between Protestants and Catholics in sixteenth-century France, the rites of violence expressed in pogroms were of an essentially religious nature (Davis 1975b).

By the end of the wave of violence, nearly all of the large and small Jewish communities in Andalusia had been destroyed, while those in Catalonia and Castile had been significantly diminished and impoverished. During the crisis, the Christian world had revealed a burning hostility toward the Jews. Only the monarchy and some of the nobility had respected the law and the traditional policy: the Jews belonged to the crown; they were the king's "coffer" and should be protected. But the ambiguities of this policy made continuation of the status quo increasingly untenable. Only after the second decade of the fifteenth century were the Jewish communities able to set off on the road to a partial reestablishment. Even then, as the kings facilitated the effort to rebuild the communities in a situation of reconstituted legality, a new element made the previous equilibrium even more precarious: the crown's own conversionist policy.

THE DRIVE FOR CONVERSION

Before the project to convert the Jews became the domain of the kings of Aragon and Castile, however, it had been the centerpiece of the Dominican order's missionary effort accompanying the Reconquista since the thirteenth century. It was thus that the Aragonese Dominicans, led by Raymond of Peñafort, conceived new methods for obtaining the conversion of Jews and Muslims, methods later directed in particular toward the Jews. The most important of these methods was the forced sermon, introduced in 1242, when the king authorized preachers to enter synagogues and deliver conversionist sermons. The Church approved this practice, although indirectly, without making the sermons compulsory, in a 1278 bull, *Vineam sorec*. In thirteenth- and fourteenth-century Aragon, forced sermons in synagogues or cathedrals were usually authorized by the sovereigns, despite the resistance of the Jewish world, which saw in them a violation of the laws that guaranteed Jews the right to live according to their own religious principles. Most of the preachers were converts able to read Hebrew and discuss Hebrew texts. But in the second half of the thirteenth century, the Dominicans attempted, without much success, to develop Hebrew and Arabic schools capable of providing preachers of non-Jewish origin with adequate linguistic knowledge. In that way, they hoped to become less dependent on the original culture of the conversos. Forced sermons and the teaching of Hebrew, as we have seen, would be revived and perfected by the sixteenth-century Church of the Counter-Reformation. On the other hand, disputations between Christians and Jews, in which rabbis were obliged to respond to Christian attacks and polemics, took place only in Spain. Converts played a fundamental role in these cases as well.

The missionary effort of the Dominicans met opposition from a medieval Spanish society that basically did not favor conversion. Although theory dictated support for the passage of Jews into the ranks of the Church, customs and laws severely limited the conversions in practice. First of all, it was the practice of the crown to confiscate the convert's assets in compensation for the financial loss incurred with the passage of the Jew from the status of "servant of the crown" to that of Christian subject. The Dominicans saw to it that these laws were abrogated in Aragon between 1242 and 1311. But the new ordinances were probably adopted without much conviction, since the use of confiscation is still documented at the end of the fourteenth century. Nonetheless, the introduction of the principle of creating material and spiritual incentives for conversion was an obvious sign of a radical change in the general climate. Conversion, seen as a time of passage and imbalance in the subject's system of beliefs and rituals, began to be represented as a gratifying and exemplary goal, laden with incentives and rewards.

Until 1391, however, conversions did not assume the scope of mass defections. They remained, rather, a constant trickle, fostered by the outside world's erosion of the Jewish communities' power by growing limitations on the social mobility and activities of Jews. But with the consolidation of the monarchies, the end of the Reconquista, and the precarious peace within Spain after the civil wars of the fourteenth century, the drive to convert the Jews became an integral part of the political dynamic of the country. The basic contradiction between the maintenance of the status quo and the pressing need for religious uniformity would mark the politics of the Aragonese and Castilian crowns during the fifteenth century.

The crisis of 1391 did not come to a close with the end of open acts of violence. Attacks on Jewish quarters and destruction of synagogues continued to occur, particularly between 1415 and 1417. But preaching played a more important role in the new offensive than did the pogroms. The leading player in this drama was St. Vincent Ferrer, who, from 1411 onward, was able to rouse the Castilian people to a frenzy of religious fervor and to drive—as if by miracle—entire groups of Jews to the baptismal font. Municipal councils supported his efforts by passing severely discriminatory laws segregating Jews and strictly prohibiting them from dealing with Christians. Ferrer's preaching is traditionally compared to that of Ferran Martinez. The former—eventually made a saint by the Church—appears to have rejected violence and coercion, and to have been careful not to overstep the bounds of the law, whereas the latter seems to have been a coarse organizer of bands of assassins. In fact, it is only in comparison with the massacres of 1391 that the actions of Vincent Ferrer appear moderate and legal. During a forced sermon delivered to the Jews of Toledo in 1411, for example, he rushed into the main synagogue and, brandishing a cross, consecrated it as a church dedicated to the Virgin, with the name of Santa Maria La Blanca.

Probably inspired by Ferrer, the Castilian crown issued very stringent legislation at Valladolid in 1412 that obliged Jews to live in secluded quarters, to wear an identifying badge, and to dress differently from Christians. It forbade them to cut their hair or beards or to loan money, and excluded them from government service and almost all professions. Jewish doctors could not treat Christians, nor Jewish artisans sell them products. Meanwhile, Aragon was racked by a serious problem of succession and had forged an alliance with Pedro de Luna (the anti-pope Benedict XIII) who would be deposed by the Council of Constance in 1414. While Vincent Ferrer traversed Aragon delivering sermons, Benedict XIII, with the aid of the convert Jerónimo di Santa Fe, organized a great public disputation in Tortosa with the rabbis of the kingdom of Aragon. The last disputation before this one had occurred in Barcelona in 1263 between Nahmanides and Pablo Christiani. Unlike Barcelona's disputation, where the debate had unfolded in a climate that guaranteed

Nahmanides the right of free speech, the Tortosa disputation constituted nothing less than a trial of the Talmud involving all forms of intimidation. Thousands of Jews were forced to attend the sessions of the disputation between 1413 and 1414. A great number of conversions appear to have taken place, particularly among the upper classes, rabbis, and court Jews. The debate was described as "the defeat of Jewish theology," a term that seems to record aptly the scope of the event, which was perhaps more destructive for the Spanish communities than the 1391 pogroms (Kriegel 1979). Between 1412 and 1419, the preaching of Vincent Ferrer alone seems to have led to 15,000 to 20,000 conversions at the very least. In 1415, Benedict XIII issued a bull that revived the dispositions of the Valladolid ordinances. In addition, the pope now called for the confiscation of the Talmud and all rabbinic literature, and required that Jews attend three sermons a year. Ferdinand I of Aragon confirmed the validity of the bull in his kingdom. The situation of the Jews in both Castile and Aragon had reached a nadir. Although fluctuating between segregation and elimination, the attack on the Jewish world had by now seriously called Jewish existence into question.

AVERROISM AND APOSTASY

In the first years of the fifteenth century, the Jews of Spain thus seemed to have entered a crisis with no way out. Unlike that in fourteenth-century Germany, however, this crisis was provoked not only by massacres and the destruction of the communities, but by renunciation, abandonment, and conversion on a vast scale. How can one not wonder why such a substantial segment of Spanish Jewry defected, when neither the violence visited repeatedly upon the Ashkenazic Jewish world nor the Church's proselytizing in the age of the ghettos was able to undermine the religious identity of Jews in other Diaspora communities? Undoubtedly, these conversions were to a large extent forced. But by preferring conversion to death, and circumventing forced conversion by maintaining a secret fidelity to Judaism, the Jews of Spain made conscious theoretical choices. Not that cases of martyrdom were lacking; in fact, evidence documents such cases during the 1391 pogroms. But in Germany, where massacres had marked the life of the communities from the time of the Crusades, the Jews had responded by choosing martyrdom (*Qiddush ha-Shem,* the sanctification of God's name), either by Christian hand or ritualized suicide, in which Jewish men killed their wives and children and then themselves (J. Katz 1961; G. Cohen 1967b). In

Spain, *Quiddush ha-Shem* remained a very limited phenomenon; given the choice between conversion and death, the majority of Spanish Jews chose the former.

The reasons for this choice have been variously interpreted. Some have attributed it to the high degree of contact between Spanish Jews and the Christian milieu. The diffusion of philosophical/rationalistic and skeptical theories might have undermined religious identity and facilitated passage to the dominant religion. The centuries-old rapport with other cultures, and the study of the classics of antiquity and of the knowledge of other nations, could thus have been at the root of a crisis leading to conversion, the ultimate capitulation of a conscience under siege (Baer 1961). "Perhaps philosophical meditations have driven you to turn basic concepts upside down and to consider observant men vain and frivolous, and it is for this reason that you aspire to that which brings greater bodily pleasure and spiritual tranquillity, in order to be free of worries, fears and anguish," wrote Josue ha-Lorki to his friend Solomon Halevi, a convert who had forged a brilliant career—capped by his ordination as bishop of Burgos—under the name Pablo de Santa Maria. Soon afterward, Josue ha-Lorki also chose Christianity and, as Jerónimo de Santa Fe, became one of the authors of the Tortosa disputation (Kriegel 1979: 204–5).

In the medieval Jewish world, on the other hand, this cultural climate existed outside Spain as well. Analogous experiences characterized the history of the Provençal-speaking Jews of Languedoc. In fact, during the persecutions of the Almohades, the intellectual Jews of Andalusia took refuge in the Provençal city of Lunel, where they founded a school of translators (from Arabic). Their translations of the works of medieval Jewish philosophers and the Aristotelian/Averroistic tradition helped give a decidedly rationalistic character to the Provençal culture of those centuries. While a reaction against philosophy—also induced by the arrival of Ashkenazic masters—spread through the world of Spanish Jewry in the early fourteenth century, and the most unorthodox philosophical currents were banned, the interest in philosophy was at its height in the Provençal Jewish world. A spirited debate ensued between Spanish and Provençal traditionalists regarding Maimonidean thought and the relationship of Judaism with non-Jewish science in general. Nonetheless, when violence and expulsions struck the communities of southern France about 1320, mass conversions on a par with those at the end of the century in Spain did not occur. But the passage from Averroism to apostasy was not taken for granted even in Spain, as is demonstrated by apologetic writings composed after 1391, which continually defend the Jewish religion against Christianity by marshaling traditional rationalistic and philosophical arguments (Ben-Sasson 1989). On the other hand, the argument that an inclination toward philosophy might contribute in various ways to the impoverishment of tradition, although a recurring theme in Jewish polemics since antiquity, was not merely rhetorical. In the rationalistic environment of the Spanish and Provençal cultures of the late Middle Ages, in fact, allegorical interpretations of sacred texts represented a crisis of traditional religion. They introduced the concept that biblical texts could be read on two levels: one literal, intended for the masses; the other allegorical, earmarked for the select few capable of grasping the philosophical truths hidden behind the veil of allegorical narration, and basically devaluing observance.

But the mystical and cabalistic thinking widespread in fourteenth-century Spain may have had similar consequences, since it opted to value a symbolical reading of the texts and to interpret the observance of the law as a way of comprehending the divinity. Unlike the philosophers, the mystics marked the boundaries with the outside world quite rigorously and eliminated all contact with gentile culture (Kriegel 1979). Nevertheless, a mystical interpretation of the texts would have undermined the foundations of normative rabbinic Judaism just as fully as a rationalistic interpretation would have done. It is therefore no contradiction to argue that the trend toward renunciation of the ancestral faith that characterized the Spanish Jewish world in these centuries was linked to mysticism itself, and in particular to messianic expressions. Continual messianic speculations, born often in the mystical milieu of medieval Spain, in fact raised expectations of and projections toward the future and led to disappointment and forms of "extreme religious inertia." The tranquil acceptance of divine will that constituted the "classic faith" of the Ashkenazim, by contrast, resulted not in messianic enthusiasm but in the sacrificial ritual of *Qiddush ha-Shem,* a sort of voluntary expiation of mankind's sins (G. Cohen 1967b). Thus, mysticism, despite its apparent alliance with traditional Judaism, contained the same seeds of dissolution of Jewish life as did philosophy and skepticism (Kriegel 1979).

Cultural factors can explain several admittedly unique cases. But can they account for the thousands upon thousands of conversions that took place during the violence of pogroms and in the period of distress following the Tortosa disputation? What kind of general cultural climate provided the proper conditions for the diffusion, from the twelfth century on, of a doctrine that justified, although always within the limits of the law, conversion under the threat of death? The man responsible for giving theoretical force and firm halachic foundation to a choice that at first sight might seem essentially pragmatic was the greatest thinker and exegetist of medieval Judaism, Moses ben Maimon, better known as Maimonides (1135–1204).

It was in his *Treatise on the Sanctification of the Name,* written in 1162–63 in Fez, that Maimonides took issue with those who maintained that it was necessary to accept martyrdom rather than profess Islam and defended those who "forced by persecution, practice the commandments in secret." At the heart of Maimonides' treatise was the distinction between spontaneous and forced violation of the commandments, "because, how can one judge equally a man who has responded to force and one who has acted voluntarily?" As a consequence, it was necessary to safeguard the principle of secret observance when confronted by those who, denying the importance of such observance in the name of martyrdom, ended up accepting that the children of Israel "should assimilate among the nations." From this followed Maimonides' fundamental recommendation: "To whomever inquires of us whether one must choose martyrdom or recognize Mohammed we respond: recognize Mohammed and spare your life." Maimonides argued that God considered the secret and limited observance of the *anussim,* the forced converts, worthy, because "he who applies a commandment without fear does not receive the same reward as he who acts with the knowledge that, if his actions become known, he will lose his life and all that he possesses." But this view did not lead Maimonides to acquiesce in conversion, or to accept duplicity calmly. In order not to become voluntary transgressors of the commandments, argued Maimonides, Jews accepting forced conversion should abandon the place of persecution: "You must go, leaving all your belongings and travel day and night until you find a place where you can practice your religion. And it is a great and vast world" (Maimonides 1983; my translations).

Maimonides consistently formulated his conclusions in relation to Islam, since, in the period in which he was writing, Muslims were converting Christians and Jews by force. But, apart from exegetical references to the sacred texts and the Talmud, Maimonides referred to other persecutions frequently enough to validate his point even in different situations. He did not, however, deny the basic principle that Islam and Christianity were idolatrous. The first to question the identification between Christianity and idolatry on a theoretical level, not just in a limited and pragmatic way, was R. Menahem ha-Meiri, a defender of

Maimonidean thought in the dispute with the traditionalists, who lived in Provence in the thirteenth and fourteenth centuries. He made his point of departure a distinction between the idolatrous nations of Talmudic times and the Gentiles of his day, maintaining that the Gentile nations were capable of developing religions that, although they might be inferior to Judaism, were not to be confused with idolatry (J. Katz 1961). Conclusions such as this, fraught with consequences for the Jewish world, naturally helped to reduce conflict with the Christian world (Shatzmiller 1973b). But they did not necessarily lead directly to conversion.

The diffusion of these doctrines and their penetration of the Jewish mentality present a different set of issues. We do not know to what extent philosophical skepticism, mystical speculation, and the Maimonidean debate on the lawfulness of forced conversion became commonly known beyond restricted intellectual and rabbinic circles. We can only hypothesize that this diffusion of ideas took place, and that in the long run it affected mentalities, changing them and reconfiguring boundaries. We know, for example, that Jacob Anatoli, one of the most noted Provençal philosophers at the turn of the fourteenth century, read his homilies, laden with allegorical interpretations, in the synagogue before the entire community every Saturday (Kriegel 1979). We may also suppose that physicians facilitated contact and cultural exchanges as they moved between the Jewish and Gentile worlds.

But these seeds fell on very distinctive ground, marked for more than two centuries by a conversionist offensive completely without precedent. Involving all of Spanish society, this offensive could not but change Jewish perceptions in the long run. The Jews may have been driven to consider baptism a possibility, but they still feared it. Rabbis very frequently chose to facilitate the return of converts to Judaism, basing their actions on the halachic principle that a baptized Jew remains a Jew. And this, in conjunction with the Maimonidean tradition on conversion, may ultimately have given birth to the idea that conversion was not a significant threshold and that return to Judaism was always possible. But external pressure, which became unbearable after the 1391 pogroms and the theological defeat at Tortosa, lay at the root of the conversion of so much of Spanish Jewry. Other factors may have helped to create a climate favorable to conversion, to blur the boundaries between Christianity and Judaism in the name of a higher philosophical truth, or to reduce baptism to a mere pretense. But the Jews of Spain accepted baptism only when it became too difficult—even impossible—to remain Jewish.

BETWEEN CONVERSION AND RECONSTRUCTION

After the election of Pope Martin V in 1417, the Aragonese and Castilian communities, which had been heading toward a catastrophe, gradually reestablished themselves. In 1419, the new king of Aragon, Alfonso V, revoked his kingdom's pragmatic royal sanction of the bull of the anti-pope Benedict XIII. This immediately allowed Jews once again to possess and read both the Talmud and rabbinic literature, to exercise the professions from which the bull had excluded them, and to have their own tribunals. In short, they could return to the situation that had preceded 1391. The Valladolid ordinances had already been abrogated in Castile in 1418. Twenty years of restrictive legislation, pogroms, and mass conversions had, however, left their mark on the life of Spanish Jewry. While the conversions were a mass phenomenon, they had their greatest repercussions on the most privileged social groups. Court Jews, rabbis, doctors, and notables had accepted Christianity, changing the social composition of Spanish Jewry. Physicians were now at its pinnacle, for the most part, while small artisans, moneylenders and impoverished merchants constituted the vast majority of the population. Even the geography of the Jewish communities had changed. Most of the communities in the kingdom of Aragon, especially those in Catalonia, had been destroyed or greatly reduced in size. In all, there were probably no more than 600 Jewish families in Aragon in 1492. Most Spanish Jews now lived in Castile, free from the Inquisition, and scattered in a great many small communities, small cities, or even rural areas. The great *aljamas* of Seville and Toledo had lost their age-old splendor, and very few communities contained more than 50 or 100 families. Nevertheless, if, as some have maintained, there were 30,000 families living in Castile at the time of the expulsion, then the fifteenth century witnessed new demographic growth and the reestablishment of substantial communities (Baer 1961).

The process of reconstitution was facilitated by the crowns, in particular that of Castile, preoccupied by the overall impoverishment of Spanish Jewry and its reduced capacity to contribute financially. Immediately after the massacres of 1392, the crown of Aragon had attempted without success to reconstitute the Jewish communities of Barcelona and Valencia, but had soon abandoned the project. Hasdai Crescas, the influential rabbi of Zaragoza, who had close connections to the court, stood at the center of efforts to reconstruct the Aragonese communities. In 1396, he launched a campaign to restructure the community of

Zaragoza so that its elite would be in power, which the crown extended to all the Aragonese *aljamas*. The revival of the Castilian Jewish communities after 1419 was the work of Abraham Benveniste, a "court Jew," at a time when Jews were out of favor in the highest positions at court and converts were preferred. Named "chief rabbi" in 1429 by the king of Castile, Benveniste initiated the synod of the Castilian communities that met in 1432 at Valladolid and gave life to a successful attempt at communal reorganization. The synod provided for close coordination among the Castilian *aljamas*, allotted communal taxes in such a way as to finance instruction and, hence, to consolidate a religious identity threatened by conversion, reinstated communal administrative and juridical structures, issued sumptuary laws, and attempted to reinstate the anti-*malsino* laws abolished in 1380.

In addition to economic and organizational problems, however, the crisis of the preceding decades confronted the Jewish world with the problem of establishing a policy vis-à-vis those who had chosen, more or less under duress, to convert and who now attempted to return to the community. It was hardly a new problem, but its very dimensions were now charged with serious political and religious implications. In theory, a converted Jew remained a Jew: according to the Talmud, "even if Israel has sinned, it remains Israel." From the eleventh century on, this Talmudic formulation was transformed into a juridical principle, expressed for the first time in a *responsum* by one of the greatest authorities of the Ashkenazic world, Rabbenu Gershom, and later by Rashi of Troyes (1040–1105), the greatest exegetist of the Middle Ages. The determination that a Jew remained a Jew after being baptized raised concrete juridical problems concerning marital bonds, inheritance, and commercial enterprises. Their solution was linked to the definition of the legal status reserved for converts by the community. Could a woman married to a convert remarry, or did she first have to obtain a divorce from her now Christian husband? The law forbade collecting interest from another Jew, but was it permissible to loan money at interest to a convert? The Ashkenazic masters had continuously based their responses to these questions on the presumption that a sinful Jew remained a Jew, with all the legal consequences attached to his condition. The Jewish world generally perceived converts to be Christians, a perception justified by the zealous Catholicism and support for the persecution of Jews voiced by many of them. Jews found themselves confronting particularly complex problems when they continued to consider Jewish those who according to Christian law were Christians in every sense of the word.

How was one to behave, thus, in fifteenth-century Spain in situations in which support for conversos planning to reenter the community might expose Jews to the jurisdiction of the Inquisition? Beginning in the fourteenth century, when this problem had begun to recur insistently, Jewish authorities had chosen to support conversos intent on returning to Judaism. The struggle against malsinos had been one of the weapons of this strategy. Another may have been the adoption of readmission ceremonies. These rituals were not contemplated by Jewish law, since they had not been necessary, but they are documented in these centuries by inquisitorial and Jewish sources alike. The Judaizer Baruch described a ceremony of this kind before the inquisitor Jacques Fournier in Pamiers in 1320: "The apostate who returns to Judaism does so in this way . . . : He must cut his fingernails and toenails, shave his head, and wash his entire body in running water in the same manner that a foreign woman marrying a Jew purifies herself according to the law, because it is believed that baptism contaminates whomever receives it." Bernard Gui's inquisitorial manual, *Practica Inquisitionis,* recounts a similar ceremony in the same years, as does a document of the Inquisition in southern Italy from 1292, which refers to a case in Salerno. On the other hand, rabbinic sources also describe readmission rites for apostates between the fourteenth and seventeenth centuries. These ceremonies must have been widespread in Spain as well: such a ritual is, in fact, recounted during a trial of the Huesca Inquisition, in reference to a collective return to Judaism by conversos and descendants of conversos that took place in 1465 (Yerushalmi 1970). There must have been a strong need to mark the reentry into Judaism with the crossing of a threshold—a counter-baptism, as it were—in a society like that of medieval Spain, characterized by such a high number of conversions and by a considerable reintegration of conversos into the Jewish community (Kriegel 1979).

THE SPANISH INQUISITION

In the course of the fifteenth century, attacks on the Jewish world shifted their main focus from the open Jew, who had rejected conversion, to the converso. Until the first decades of the fifteenth century, converts had assimilated very thoroughly into Spanish society. This integration was cemented by extensive matrimonial alliances between the old aristocratic Christian families and the upper strata of the new Christians, and was marked by a high degree of social interaction and cultural acceptance.

In the first half of the fifteenth century, however, the process of integration came to a halt and the policies aimed at converting the Jews appeared to fail. Paradoxically, this failure was caused not by the scarcity of conversions but by both their abundance and doubts about their sincerity. Such doubts had always been a topos, but they had become increasingly alarming in the course of the century. The Dominican order in particular fostered these suspicions, especially in Seville. In this context, Ferdinand and Isabella decided to introduce into Castile what had been present in Aragon since the thirteenth century: the Inquisition. Thus the Spanish Inquisition was born. Pope Sixtus IV approved it in a bull on November 1, 1478. The power to nominate and depose inquisitors was entrusted completely to the sovereigns. For its part, the monarchy instituted the Council of the Inquisition in 1480, at which the Inquisitor General also sat. From 1483 until the year of his death in 1498, the Dominican Tomàs de Torquemada, Isabel's confessor, served as Inquisitor General, thus tightening the indissoluble bonds between the inquisitorial apparatus and the politics of the monarchical state.

By 1480, trials of Judaizers had begun. The first burnings took place following a rebellion by some conversos. From then on the macabre spectacle of the auto-da-fé (act of faith) appeared frequently in Spanish cities. The Inquisition would pronounce sentences in public with elaborate formality. Because the Inquisition was not allowed to spill blood directly, the condemned were burned at the stake by the secular authorities at the conclusion of the ceremony. Opposition to the creation of the Inquisition came not only from conversos but also from supporters of municipal and civic self-government, and even from local clergy. In his *Shevet Iehudah*—a historic work written at the beginning of the sixteenth century and packed with literary topoi—Solomon Ibn Verga describes how the inquisitors could have responded to these objections: One Saturday, the inquisitor of Seville had the governor of the city accompany him to the top of a high tower and, showing him the city at his feet, said: "Lift your eyes and look at all those houses inhabited by conversos. No matter how cold it is, you will never see smoke rising from their chimneys on Saturday, because on that day the *conversos* will not light a fire" (Poliakov 1974b, 2: 191).

Old and new Christians alike thus initially opposed the new tribunal. In 1482, their opposition led to a bull by Sixtus IV, in which he condemned inquisitorial methods and returned control of inquisitional courts to the diocese. But the anti-inquisitional front was broken in 1485, after conversos assassinated the inquisitor Pedro de Arbues in the

Zaragoza cathedral. Trials, held first in Zaragoza and later in Valencia and Majorca, dealt a blow to nobles, intellectuals, physicians, and bourgeois. Entire upper-class families ended up at the stake, ensuring, at least for one generation, the decline of new Christian political and social influence in Aragon (Brault-Noble and Marc 1980). Although the Inquisition's jurisdiction was not limited to Judaizers, but covered all crimes against the Catholic faith, almost all of the condemned during the entire fifteenth and first quarter of the sixteenth centuries were conversos accused of Judaizing (Dedieu 1980).

The creation of the Inquisitional tribunal reinforced rather than diminished concern about the success of conversionist policies. The trials continually demonstrated, with greater or lesser truthfulness, that the new Christians remained faithful in their hearts to the religion of their fathers. They also exposed the complicity between Jews and conversos: not only did the open Jews not convert, but they also abetted conversos' reentry into the bosom of Judaism. Old networks, friendship, and kinship survived conversion. Jews and new Christians continued to share customs, memories, and even the use of Hebrew (Gutwirth 1985). Beginning in 1484, Aragonese Jews were called to testify against Judaizers in inquisitorial proceedings, a practice that overturned judicial precedents, inasmuch as it allowed Jews to testify against Christians (Edwards 1984b). The circle was closing, and more than on the Jews, it seemed to be closing in on the new Christians.

THE "SANTO NIÑO DE LA GUARDIA" CASE

In the Spain of the Reyes católicos, Ferdinand and Isabella, bent on centralization, there was no lack of traditional ritual murder accusations. The santo niño de La Guardia case of 1490 was not the first in Spain of this type. In 1435, a similar accusation had caused the forced conversion of the large Jewish community of Majorca. In 1454, there had been a similar case in Valladolid, but the accused Jew had been acquitted, despite the incendiary preaching of a Franciscan, Alonzo de Espina, who continued to maintain the Jew's guilt. In his work *Fortalitium fidei*, de Espina subsequently reaffirmed the nexus between the blood libel accusation and the political response of expulsion. Both England and France, de Espina recalled, had expelled the Jews because by committing ritual murder the latter had violated the pact of subordination with Christian society.

The offensive launched by Alonzo de Espina and his followers had come to a standstill in the 1460s. But by 1490, things were different. The La Guardia accusation originated in that year after the casual arrest of a converso in possession of a consecrated host. Interrogated under torture, the accused confessed to having killed a child in order to use its body magically to cause the deaths of Christians and inquisitors and bring about the triumph of Judaism. In doing so, he implicated other Jews and new Christians. The child—who never existed and therefore had no name—passed into history as the "santo niño de La Guardia" and became the object of a popular cult, although it never ascended to sainthood. The trial, which concluded with a solemn auto-da-fé, echoed far and wide throughout Spain (Lea 1967).

This case was anomalous among accusations of ritual murder in that it implicated both Jews and conversos. Traditionally—as has been noted—converts had assumed a different role in such cases: that of instigators of the charge and guarantors of its truthfulness. But it was not by chance that in the La Guardia trial, conversos were accused along with open Jews. Indeed, the accusers meant to create an image of a plot by Jews and new Christians against Christianity. Thus, the trial expressed, through the mythical image of the blood libel, the anxieties provoked by the existence of conversos and the fear of their subterranean and persistent bond with Judaism. The burnings in La Guardia demonstrate once again that the problem of the conversos had by then become widespread, and that the obsessive fear of an agreement between Jews and conversos spurred the decision to expel the Jews. By demonstrating that Jews and conversos together violated the pact that bound them to Christian society, an accusation of this type could only serve to facilitate the choice of radical means. In this sense, the theories expressed by de Espina in the *Fortalitium fidei* opened the debate on the expulsion of the Jews from Spain.

THE EXPULSION

Many historians have interpreted the measures taken against the Jews in the years preceding their expulsion as successive stages of an ineluctable and consciously prepared process that had expulsion as its goal. In reality, another interpretation is possible, one that sees expulsion as the unforeseeable and unnecessary outcome of the vacillation of the Reyes católicos, Ferdinand and Isabella, between the conservation of traditional laws and a destabilizing drive toward religious and political homogeneity. Thus, the decrees of segregation of 1480, although they doubtless represented a considerable worsening of the Jews' condition and sanctioned rather severe conditions for their continued presence, actually indicated a policy opposite from that of expulsion. Although it is usually seen as being closely connected to the general expulsion of 1492 (Beinart 1985), even the 1483 decree expelling the Jews from Andalusia, which gave them one month to liquidate their holdings and leave, and resulted from an initiative directed by the Inquisition of Seville, can be interpreted from the perspective of the Jewish policies of the Reyes católicos. These policies were marked until the eve of the expulsion by the staunchest conservatism. They strictly adhered to the tradition of protection and guarantees, together with the desire to stop Jews from in any way overstepping the limits imposed on them by their necessary condition of inferiority and servitude (Kriegel 1978a).

The expulsion in 1492 resulted from the insertion of a different element; neither popular pressure, middle-class pressure, nor even a supposed anti-Jewish hostility on the part of the aristocracy (Kamen 1988), but rather the knowledge that conversionist policies had failed together with a last-ditch attempt to save whatever had been achieved until then by definitively cutting the umbilical cord that still bound public Jews and conversos. The solution of expulsion did not arise from gradually mounting hostility and restriction. Rather, it was the result of a fragmented policy that ranged from a traditional concern for stability to an essentially contradictory destabilizing conversionary policy. Moreover, a religious motive—the necessity of isolating new Christians from Jews—was the basis of Ferdinand and Isabella's edict. As its preamble clearly states:

> The Jews try by all possible means to draw faithful Christians away from our Holy Catholic Religion, to detach them, to deviate them and attract them to their cursed faith and opinions. They instruct them in the rites and observances of their law, organize meetings where they teach them what they must believe and practice according to their law, circumcise them and their sons, give them prayer books, inform them of the fasts to respect, gather with them to read and teach them the history of their law, let them know when Passover is coming and advise them of what they must do to observe this holiday, giving them, bringing it from home, matzah and kosher for Passover meat, warn them of the foods from which they must abstain and which they must eat in obedience to the law, and persuade them to observe and practice the law of Moses to the extent that they are able, having them believe that there exist no other law or truth besides these. (Suárez Fernández 1964: 392)

How many Jews left Spain in search of a land where they could maintain their identity? And how many accepted, with greater or lesser reluctance, the conversion imposed by the edict of the Reyes católicos? Contemporary Jewish and Catholic chroniclers who have handed down a record of the expulsion and who, from one perspective or another, emphasize the trauma, report very high figures, which reach into the hundreds of thousands of exiles. The figures of 35,000 families for Castile and 6,000 for Aragon (in all, about 170,000 individuals) are related by André Bernaldez, the curate of Los Palacios and a witness to the events, and have been considered reliable by some historians because they are also found in a letter by the chief rabbi of Spain, Abraham Seneor (Baer 1961). Much lower recent estimates place the Jewish population of Spain in 1492 at between 70,000 and 100,000, that is, about 1.5 percent of the total population (Ladero Quesada 1975; Suárez Fernández 1983; Kamen 1988). The number of converts is also very much a subject of debate and has been estimated by some to be much higher than that of exiles. It is particularly important to keep in mind that exile was not always definitive, especially for the many who found refuge in Portugal and Navarre without having to face a long and dangerous ocean voyage (Cantera Montenegro 1979; Kamen 1988). At least until 1499, the crown facilitated the reentry of exiles, restoring possessions that were sold or confiscated in Spain to all those who had converted before crossing the border. Thus, in a case that is documented by petitions to the crown for the restitution of possessions, a converso who returned to Aragon with his family claimed that he had emigrated to Navarre for the sole purpose of buying time to convince his wife—who wanted to go abroad with the children—to convert (Meyerson 1992). The choice between conversion and exile divided families, tearing them apart. Often the women chose to leave for distant shores, while the men opted for baptism.

In 1492, some of the exiles took refuge in Navarre. The vicissitudes of this kingdom—the smallest state in medieval western Europe and ruled by a French dynasty—are in some sense typical (Gampel 1989). The seat of flourishing communities since the twelfth century, Navarre had offered refuge to Andalusian Jews driven out by the Almohades, to French Jews in 1294 and in 1306, and even to Castilian Jews after the pogroms of 1391. Not that the Jews of Navarre had never faced any crises of their own; in the first decades of the fourteenth century, they were attacked during the Crusade of the Little Shepherds and again in 1328, with serious losses and vain attempts at armed resistance. But

apart from these isolated incidents, Navarrese Jews led a life characterized by a remarkable socioeconomic integration. They could live among
Christians as well as in quarters set aside for them, and they enjoyed
full rights of ownership of their lands and houses. Another indication of
their integration was the fact that they could live not only in the main
cities of Tudela and Pamplona but also in villages and hamlets. The
Jews of Navarre were engaged in a wide range of professions: in addition to commerce and moneylending, they had an important role in the
production of wine (Leroy 1985). This situation—analogous to that in
Spain in preceding centuries—had not deteriorated in the course of the
fifteenth century.

   In 1485, a jurisdictional dispute pitted the Aragonese crown against
the city of Tudela, where some of the conversos accused of having assassinated the inquisitor of Zaragoza, Pedro de Arbues, had taken refuge. Ultimately, this conflict weakened the kingdom's political autonomy and introduced the Inquisition to Navarre in 1488. Nevertheless,
despite some difficulties, the Jews who took refuge in Navarre in 1492
managed to find acceptance and to create separate communities, which
became part of the economic life of the kingdom. The growing Spanish
influence—which would lead to Navarre's annexation by Spain several
years later—caused the Navarrese kings to expel the Jews in 1498. We
do not have the text of the edict of expulsion of March 1498, but we do
know that it gave Jews a choice between conversion and exile. It was,
however, a purely theoretical choice. Those choosing exile could not
legally travel across the surrounding territories, because these were controlled by the Reyes católicos, and hence were not able to leave Navarre.
"The way was barred and they were not able to emigrate, and so they
abandoned the God of Israel," wrote the chronicler Joseph Hacohen in
his chronicle *Emech Habacha* (Hacohen 1971: 67). Most Navarrese
Jews chose conversion. Many of the 1492 exiles returned to Spain, taking advantage of the provisions of the Reyes católicos allowing reentry
and joining the conversos (Meyerson 1992).

THE JEWS OF PORTUGAL

As has been noted, many of the Spanish Jewish exiles found refuge in
nearby Portugal, encouraged by the protection of King Manuel. Viewing the influx of refugees as an opportunity to reap the benefits of Jewish
wealth and economic acumen, the Portuguese monarch offered all Jews
residency rights at the time of the expulsion from Spain. These rights

were limited to a period of eight months and subject to the payment of a per capita tax. Special dispensations, however, were granted to the richest and most influential families, which were able to pay a higher entrance tax. But in 1496, following his marriage to the infanta Isabella, the king yielded to Spanish pressures and agreed in substance to the forced conversion of all Jews living in Portugal. At first, a ban of expulsion was issued that gave the Jews ten months in which to convert or leave the kingdom. In March 1497, however, this was followed by a decree that imposed conversion on all children between the ages of four and fourteen. After having been dragged to the baptismal font, the children were assigned to Christian families to be raised according to the Christian religion. Imprisoned and subjected to violence of every kind, the adults too were converted in the following months (Roth 1947).

An initiative of the crown, the edict encountered determined opposition from the Portuguese Church, which declared it contrary to ecclesiastical canons. It was unprecedented in Iberian history since the time of the Visigoths and constituted a true example of forced conversion, since exile was not an option. The motives of the crown were financial and economic, not religious. In the first place, the crown needed to safeguard the Jewish community as a source of income and as a spur for the country's economic and commercial development. When this need clashed with the Spanish request to "purify the kingdom of the Jewish presence," the king turned his back completely on tradition, making an objective decision to keep the Jews in his kingdom, but to subject them to baptism (Yerushalmi 1972).

It was indeed a traumatic event, one that remained impressed on the memories of both contemporary and subsequent generations of Portuguese Judaizers. The words that a Portuguese Marrano, on trial by the Inquisition in Venice in 1555, used to describe it still have a strong emotional charge after all these years: "As the Jews of Portugal were baptized by force, they took the children from their parents and put them among Christians and baptized them voluntarily or by force.... My father told me that I was taken from my mother's breast and baptized" (Ioly Zorattini 1980–94, 1:252–53). Very painful and distressing, as well, are the words of the Portuguese bishop Fernand de Coutinho. Describing the episode many years later, he recalled seeing many people dragged by force to the baptismal font. Fathers carrying their children to be baptized kept their heads covered as a sign of mourning, protesting that they preferred to die with their children in the faith of Abraham (Roth 1941).

In no time at all, Portugal became a kingdom without Jews. No one had illusions about the sincerity of such conversions. In the meantime, the crown had closed the borders, forbidding new Christians to emigrate and, at the same time, promising not to introduce controls on their religious beliefs for twenty years, in the hope that they would gradually accept the Christian faith. The edict had very severe consequences: the community structure was destroyed and links among the crypto-Judaizers now depended on the will of individuals. Moreover, the obligation to maintain a pretense of Christian religiosity confronted the new Christians with a considerable element of change and constituted a crisis in their religious identity and perception of self. But even the crown realized that it had badly miscalculated, because the conversion of the Jews gave them equal rights with Christian-born subjects, depriving the monarchy of its traditional avenues of control and financial expropriation. The rulers therefore introduced laws intended to differentiate old from new Christians and attempted to devise new ways to tax and control new Christian merchant groups. The introduction of the Inquisition after 1536 would serve these ends (Yerushalmi 1972).

In 1506, as plague devastated Lisbon, a pogrom of alarming proportions broke out against conversos in the city, claiming more than 1,000 victims. The violence developed along the usual lines, and it was very much like other pogroms, except that it was directed at new Christians instead of Jews. Beginning with the lynching of a new Christian who had seemed skeptical about the miraculous virtues of a crucifix, it spread rapidly, striking at all the conversos. The mob was led by two Dominicans (executed after order was restored) who incited their followers to massacre that "abominable people." The pogrom revealed that both citizens and the Dominicans who led them continued to perceive the conversos as Jews. There seemed to be a powerful need to restore religious order, which had been upset by the king's tolerance of converso fidelity to Judaism, and to assuage the divine punishment raging over the city in the form of the plague. In addition to this fundamental dynamic, other factors lay at the root of the Lisboners' uneasiness. One such factor was the resentment provoked by the king's policy of progressive elimination of citizens' privileges, accomplished with the active participation of conversos. This resentment found an outlet in the slaughter of a new Christian tax collector (Yerushalmi 1976).

After order was restored, the conversos asked the king to reopen the borders and allow them to leave the country. The decree that liberalized emigration was, in fact, issued in 1507, permitting many to leave for the more hospitable lands of the Ottoman Empire. Most stayed, however, calmed by the decree's promise to abolish all discrimination between old and new Christians. An attempt was made to assimilate the remaining conversos (presumably those least attached to their former religion) into Christian society. This policy allowed them to live under the protection of the crown until 1515, when the king unexpectedly changed his stance and asked the pontiff to introduce the Spanish Inquisition into Portugal. Besides the realization that the politics of assimilation had substantially failed, the roots of this drastic change of policy probably lay in the need to identify new channels of control over converso assets. The first attempt failed. John III, King Manuel's successor, tried again in 1522. Even then, however, negotiations with the papacy dragged on for a very long time, either because of Rome's reluctance to grant to the small kingdom of Portugal a weapon it already regretted having accorded to powerful Spain or because of the spirited fight put up by the conversos. They bargained with the pontiff and offered to pay exorbitant sums in order to prevent this turning point, which would mean ruin for their world (Yerushalmi 1972). Only in 1536 did Portugal get its way, and the Inquisition made its appearance among the Portuguese conversos. When the negotiations with the Curia began in 1522, the borders were closed again, and emigration from Portugal began once more, this time clandestinely and under extremely dangerous conditions. From 1536 on, leaving countries that were under the control of the Inquisition became a prerequisite for survival for the Portuguese conversos.

LIMPIEZA DE SANGRE

Not even exile succeeded in completely breaking the ties between Jews and Iberia. Sefarad remained a myth in their collective memory, the country that had represented, in the course of centuries, much more than a land of refuge and exile. But the Spaniards, too, kept alive the record of the Jews that they had exiled or destroyed, continually redepicting the ghost. This record assumed the form of a genuine obsession, a fear that profoundly influenced life and culture, behavior and thought, and left its imprint on the entire course of Spanish history (Castro 1966). In a world permeated by the Christian concept of the equality of men, and in which baptism canceled all faults, the fifteenth century gave rise to a totally new idea, that of pure blood (*limpieza de sangre*), which profoundly altered the ideological framework of relations between Christians and Jews. In fact, there was a deep and irremediable contradiction between the idea of conversion and a concept that stressed blood, regardless of avowed religious belief. Discrimination arose from suspicion of crypto-Judaizers, but in the end, it rapidly assumed a decidedly racist tone. Despite conversion, those who had Jewish blood coursing through their veins remained Jews.

Discriminatory measures directed at new Christians converted after 1391 first appeared in the middle of the fifteenth century and prevented them from entering government service, religious orders, and guilds. Such measures subsequently multiplied, until they assumed the force of law by the middle of the sixteenth century. The guilds were the first to adopt them, followed at the end of the century by the orders of knighthood. University faculties, the *colegios mayores,* also excluded new Christians at that time. The Spanish Church introduced these discriminations as well, and the Franciscans embraced them in 1525. St. Ignatius of Loyola, founder of the Jesuit order, opposed the statutes, and one of its generals, Lainez, was a descendant of conversos, but the Jesuits eventually approved them in 1592. From then on, to be admitted into a religious order or a faculty of the university, or to obtain a government position or practice a profession regulated by a guild, one had to prove, with genealogical documents, the absence of Jewish ancestors. Although the system was corrupt, obtaining a family tree without blemishes became a veritable obsession and profoundly affected sixteenth-and seventeenth-century mentalities. In 1536, Charles V bestowed imperial sanction on the statutes of pure blood, and the Church was soon forced to give up its long-standing opposition to the idea and follow suit, although, of course, just for Spain.

In early modern Spain, the laws of pure blood did not strike only Jewish conversos. They were also applied, although much less rigorously, to descendants of Muslim converts, the Moriscos, who would be expelled from Spain in 1609. But the relationship between old Christians and new Christians of Jewish origin remained Spain's real concern. In trying to explain this concern, scholars have turned to the imperial messianic ideology dominating sixteenth-century Spain, which viewed the Spanish as the new chosen people, destined to supplant the Jews in a pact with the Lord. The Jews, not the Muslims, stood at this center of the ideology of election. It was their role that had to be passed on to the Spanish nation (Y. Kaplan 1988). This helps explain the obsessive attention fixed on those suspected of a secret connection to Judaism, but the genesis of the racial concept introduced by the laws regulating purity of blood was even more complex. It was, in any event, a violation of the fundamental tenet of Christianity that baptism and not blood determined religion. As a result of these laws, the very possibility of the conversion of the Jews was now called into question.

The Jews of Italy

While for the Jews in the rest of Europe the fourteenth century brought violence, expulsion, and exile, in Italy it signaled the beginning of a period of great expansion. New communities formed, and Italian states and cities became places of refuge for the exiles of Germany, France, and, lastly, Spain. The Jews in Italy thus appear to have taken a different road from the one traveled by the Jews in the rest of the continent. Italy truly became that island of divine dew, the *I-tal-ya*, described in the fanciful etymology known by Jews since antiquity. Numerous dense clouds gathered over this happy "island," however, and its ambivalent history is often interpreted as an anomaly.

A marked mobility characterized the Italian Jewish world in the first decades of the fourteenth century. When Italian Jews migrated, they left behind settlements that had been established for centuries. In some cases, including that of the kingdom of Naples, they were expelled by force; in others, they were driven out by commercial and financial needs. The transfer of the papal seat to Avignon (1305–77) created a void in Rome and turned the capital of Christianity into a marginal and isolated city, outside the mainstream of commercial traffic and cultural life. This development prompted many Roman Jews to look for more propitious places to live in the communes and lordships of northern and central Italy. Moreover, from the end of the thirteenth century on, a large number of Ashkenazic Jews came to Italy, driven out of Germany by massacres and repeated local expulsions, and out of France by the general expulsions of the fourteenth century. This influx became even greater after the Black Death. The twofold migratory flow—from Rome northward and from the transalpine territories southward—gave life to the communities of loan bankers that studded the cities and communes of northern and central Italy from the end of the thirteenth through the entire fourteenth century. Additionally, a policy of forced conversion drove many Jews in the kingdom of Naples to accept baptism or exile in 1290, resulting in the temporary disappearance of heavily populated, age-old communities, and further transforming the Italian Jewish world in these decades.

Southern Italy recovering with difficulty from a crisis, Rome marginalized, and northern and central Italy just becoming populated: this was the map of the Jewish presence in Italy at the beginning of the fourteenth century. The key factor in fourteenth-century Italian Jewish history—something that remained virtually unchanged until the end of the fifteenth century—was the rise of small and medium-sized Jewish communities founded on loan banking in the burgeoning communes and *signorie* (lordships) of Italy.

LOAN BANKS

We do not know whether the Jews who left Rome because of the city's economic stagnation had formerly been bankers and moneylenders. But this was certainly true of the Ashkenazim who began to make their way to the more hospitable Italian territories around the same time. Settling in Italian cities, Roman and German Jews alike gave birth to communities centered around the activity of one or more lenders. Only subsequently did a milieu composed of artisans and merchants form around the bankers in the larger communities.

In need of cash for civic necessities or eager to create small loan banks to mitigate the scourge of poverty, municipal authorities usually invited

Jewish moneylenders to settle in their localities. In other cases, the initiative came from the lenders themselves. They offered services to the authorities, generally soliciting invitations with substantial loans to the cities, which they promised to forgive. Before Jews could settle in a city or commune and open a bank, however, the authorities first had to determine the Jews' legal status and the terms of their settlement. Hence, cities generally entered into agreements granting citizenship to the bankers and their retinues for a certain number of years and established conditions for opening and managing their banks. These documents, the *condotte,* have been preserved in great numbers, allowing us to trace the origins of these settlements and understand their main characteristics. The contracts of the condotte all share very similar clauses and formulae. They were as a rule temporary, fixing the number of years for which the commune—and reciprocally the lender—was bound to keep the bank going. Additionally, they stipulated the amount of capital that the banker was committed to invest in the bank and limited the amount of interest that could be charged.

The average interest on pawnbroking was 20 percent, but it was often less or much more, depending on the type of loan and the scarcity of capital—that is, on the laws of supply and demand and the risks run by the lender. An interest rate of 20 percent corresponded to the limit set by the Church to distinguish moderate interest from usury. A rate that was too low might prove unproductive for the lender, who could then choose to look for a more favorable place to open a bank. The clauses of the *condotta,* moreover, specified certain items that could not be pawned—religious objects, for example—and guaranteed security and religious freedom for the moneylender. Specific laws, in fact, dealt with the synagogue, the cemetery, the ritual slaughterer, and the observance of Jewish holidays, as well as with the prohibition against conducting business on Christian holidays.

From the end of the thirteenth century on, Jewish bankers, originally from Rome, thus created a far-reaching and extensive network by opening loan banks in a great many centers of Umbria, the Marches, Tuscany, Emilia, and the Veneto. Many Ashkenazic Jews left Germany for the Italian cities at the same time, opening banks in the Veneto, Istria, Trentino, and Lombardy. Milan was a special case; in 1320, a decree excluded Jews from the city, a prelude to a policy that substantially blocked any kind of stable Jewish settlement there. Milan's policy was similar to the one maintained by Genoa until the seventeenth century. In the cities of the Po Valley—Padua, Mantua, Vicenza, Verona, and Ferrara—lenders originally from Germany and, to a lesser extent, France, mingled with those from Rome to create composite communities. By contrast, the Jews who settled in Piedmont and Monferrato were chiefly French, although there were some Germans as well. From the first years of the fourteenth century on, Jews arriving from France gave rise to a network of communities destined to have a long history (R. Segre 1986).

Not all Italian cities accepted or solicited settlement by Jews. Cities in which Christian bankers were numerous and organized in guilds were generally hostile to Jews, in whom the former saw dangerous competition. Jewish bankers were admitted to Florence, for example, only in 1427, and competition from Florentine banking prevented Jewish lending from fully developing there. In other cases, a city's security concerns or its distance from centers of commercial trade and finance prevented Jews from taking up residence. Notwithstanding these limitations, the spread of Jewish banking was vast and far-reaching. Several thousand people gave rise to hundreds of communities scattered throughout northern and central Italy. In actuality, this meant that in some places there was only one Jewish family, and that the average was not much greater than those four families living in Trent when the accusation of ritual murder destroyed the entire community in 1475. Bologna—one of the largest cities in Europe, with 50,000 inhabitants and a renowned university—had more than twenty Jewish banking families, a rare situation indeed. In fact, although the largest cities provided the opportunity to join an organized Jewish community, they also already had established networks of Jewish lenders and therefore did not provide ample room for expansion.

Life in such small and scattered communities posed significant problems of organization. One of the most important clauses of the condotta—along with those regarding the possession of a synagogue and a cemetery—was the concession of a ritual slaughterer to provide kosher meat. But this concession alone was not sufficient. Because dietary laws forbade the use of the hind parts of the animal, the price of kosher meat would have been prohibitive had Jews not been able to sell these parts to Christians. This practice, however, roused the Church's hostility. Franciscan preachers, in fact, immediately made the scandalous sale to Christians of meat butchered according to Jewish law the primary target of their sermons. As part of its traditional policy of safeguarding Jewish subordination, the Church requested a halt to the paradoxical situation that allowed Jews to sell their scraps to Christians while refusing to touch meat butchered by them. Moreover, this issue was just a smoke screen for the traditional anxiety about the dark specter of contamination. The right to slaughter meat and sell it to Christians thereby became emblematic of the establishment or deterioration of friendly coexistence with the civil authorities and the surrounding Christian world in general (A. Toaff 1989c). In everyday situations, both civil authorities and ecclesiastics were very flexible. This does not mean that the Franciscans had no success in stirring up emotions by their preaching and wrenching prohibitions from the civil authorities. On the contrary, they prevailed in Perugia in 1439, in Spoleto in 1451, and in Norcia, Terni, and many other communities as well. But the Jews were usually able to neutralize such pressures and have the bans invalidated. They even threatened to abandon the condotta, because, as the Jews of Todi stated in 1438, "being prohibited from buying meat, we cannot live in good health" (A. Toaff 1989c: 86).

Ritual slaughter demanded the presence of a skilled *shohet,* a Jew specially trained in both the observance of religious laws and technical expertise. The rules governing ritual slaughter were part of the curriculum of Jewish children's studies in Renaissance Italy, and many children performed this function. Judah Mintz, the rabbi of Padua, issued an ordinance at the beginning of the sixteenth century prohibiting boys under the age of eighteen from performing ritual slaughter, but it appears that this ruling was not observed (Bonfil 1994). We also find a great many cases at this time of women—more or less instructed in the law—executing this function in Italy. These cases did not violate any regulation, but they did form an exception to the established custom that permitted only men to perform *shehitah.* This phenomenon, however, did not indicate a particularly high degree of emancipation of Jewish women in Renaissance Italy. Rather, it was a consequence of the dispersion of so many isolated communities, where, especially during the long absences of men, it became necessary to assign to women and children the job of supplying meat (Bonfil 1984).

Around the middle of the fifteenth century, Jewish communities in Italy began to band together and decrease in number, reversing the earlier trend toward dispersion. This shift was primarily the result of new external pressures generated by Franciscan anti-Jewish propaganda, of the Franciscan order's creation of the *monte di pietà,* and of the civil authorities' consequent adoption of new policies. Preaching against usury was not, in fact, enough to eliminate Jewish moneylending. Rather, it was necessary to find a replacement for it. The monte di pietà, created by the Franciscans in the second half of the fifteenth century, filled this role precisely. The foundation of the monte di pietà significantly blurred the boundaries between socioeconomic and religious motivations. In fact, an intensive campaign of preaching intended to create a consensus among the masses and arouse their eagerness to participate in the purification of Christian society from Jewish usury preceded its creation. Moreover, the Franciscans hoped that their campaign would stir up the civil authorities' never completely placated religious scruples and eventually drive many of them to cancel the contracts with Jewish moneylenders and to expel the Jews from the city. The monte di pietà's first goal was to supplant Jewish usury and demonstrate that the Christian world was capable of resolving from within, using Christian principles of charity and love for the poor, the problems that Jews had resolved until then. Thus the Franciscan attack on Jewish lending had essentially religious and ideological characteristics, although many purely economic factors also contributed to its success. In its initial phase, the monte di pietà steered a middle course between banking and charity. It confined its assistance to very small loans to the poor, which it rigorously regulated to prevent their transformation from aid to the needy into profitable and unnecessary lending. The monte di pietà set its interest rate at between 5 and 10 percent, the amount needed to cover operating expenses. This did not stop the Dominicans and Augustinians from attacking the Franciscans for charging interest. Nevertheless, by the sixteenth century, the monte di pietà was on its way to becoming a legitimate credit institution with investments and legalized interest rates. The Christian bank had thus usurped the Jewish one.

Although the foundation of the monte di pietà failed to put an end to Jewish lending in some cities, most communes were quick to cancel their condotte with the Jews. The primary function of the monte di pietà, however, was to take care of the needs of the poor, not to provide for more extensive lending or meet the communes' and cities' need for liquidity. This does not necessarily imply that Jewish banking, which the monte di pietà hoped to replace, served primarily to ameliorate social tensions provoked by growing poverty, as some have maintained (Bonfil 1994) in contrast with those who have emphasized its role in the development of the urban economy (A. Toaff 1989c). In this situation, poverty became, in effect, an essential matter for propaganda. Just as the cities had justified the concession of a condotta on the grounds that the poor were needy, so now they used the institution of the monte di pietà to justify the end of their long relationship with Jewish capital. In reality, the need for cash had diminished, and the Christian bank was growing. At the same time, ideological and religious concerns about Jewish lending were assuming greater significance. Whatever the economic role of Jewish banking had been—whether it had participated widely in the city's development or been kept out of the real economic sphere and limited to stabilizing social needs—the monte di pietà catalyzed the crisis and transformed it into a victory of religion over evil. The Franciscan struggles against poverty and Jewish usury were inextricably intertwined, and did not—as some have argued—represent a war on poverty in which the attack against the Jews was only an inevitable secondary consequence (Meneghin 1974).

It is impossible to analyze here in detail the development and modalities of Jewish banking in Italy in the fourteenth and fifteenth centuries, but we are able to look at several cases more specifically, selecting them from among the most significant or best documented. Venice is a very special case. Lending had been prohibited to both Jews and Christians there since 1254. Christian loan banks existed in both Mestre and Treviso, however, and Venetians did business with them, despite prohibitions. During the fourteenth century, there were several failed attempts to introduce moneylending to Venice as well. In 1356, for example, during a very unfavorable economic situation after the Black Death and the extremely costly war of 1350–55 against Genoa, the city proposed an interest rate of 10 percent on pawnbroking and 12 percent on unsecured loans. In 1366, the Great Council authorized the Venetian *podestà* (chief magistrate) in Mestre to negotiate with "other persons" inclined to be satisfied with an annual interest of 20 percent rather than with the bankers of Mestre, who charged 25 percent. This may be the first reference to Jewish lenders, although there is no proof that the reference was to Jews and not Christians (Mueller 1975).

It was only after the war of Chioggia (1378–81) caused a severe money shortage in Venice that the city on the lagoon altered its traditional policy against lending and gave permission to Venetians and foreigners alike to lend money for five years at a maximum rate of 10 percent interest on pawnbroking and 12 percent on unsecured loans. Although the invitation was not explicitly directed at Jews, only one Christian, who was in partnership with several Jews, accepted the offer. The concession was renewed in 1385 for another ten years, this time with explicit reference to Jewish moneylenders. They could choose between paying 4,000 ducats a year to the Venetian treasury and maintaining the previous interest rate or reducing the rate by 2 percent. The Jews chose to reduce the interest rate, indicating that 4,000 ducats was more than they would have earned from a higher rate. Additionally, the Jews were promised a place where they could live together *pro commodo eorum*. In 1386, they received a plot of land to use as a cemetery. But this period proved to be only an interlude. In 1394, the Venetian Senate decided not to renew the condotta when it expired in 1396, but instead to expel all Jews from the city at that time. The motives given were that the Jews preferred to make contractual loans to the rich, at 10 percent, rather than to the poor against a pledge, at 8 percent, and that "all the convertible assets of the Venetians risked ending up in their hands" (Mueller 1975: 1291). Venice had by then undoubtedly weathered the unfavorable economic conditions that had forced it to abandon its traditional opposition to moneylending: the presence of the Jews had thus become superfluous.

They had been forbidden by then to reside in Venice for periods of longer than fifteen days, a limitation subsequently narrowed even further to fifteen days a year. But not all Jews had been banished. Also in 1394, a Senate decree exempted Jewish physicians from the restrictions as long as they did not engage in lending. Moreover, in 1408, Jewish merchants were authorized to conduct business and reside temporarily in Venice provided they abided by the same conditions. This policy was subsequently confirmed, but with a significant restriction: both merchants and doctors legally residing in Venice had to wear a distinguishing badge, a yellow circle (Ravid 1987b).

It appears, therefore, that even after this first episode of Jewish banking had ended, Jews continued to live in Venice, albeit without engaging in moneylending and in conditions of extreme precariousness. Considerable limitations were also placed on the practice of Judaism. In 1443, the law requiring Jews to wear a distinguishing badge was confirmed, in a continued attempt to prevent sexual contacts between Jews and Christian women. At the behest of Jews "who live in or frequent Venice," and in compliance with Pope Pius II's excommunication of anyone who prevented Jews from practicing their religion, the limits on religious practices were attenuated in 1464. The first mention of a Jewish community, or *università* (the Italian word used to designate Jewish communities), in Venice and other cities of the Venetian *terraferma* dates from 1492, and it is mentioned again by legislation in the early sixteenth century. In 1503, the operators of three loan banks in Mestre obtained permission to live with their families in houses they rented in Venice. This ordinance was a prelude to the transfer of the banks from Mestre to Venice. It allowed Jews to lodge in Venice, conduct services there, and keep pawned items in their houses, but not to reside permanently in the city or maintain synagogues. In the event of war, however, the law permitted them to transfer to Venice. This, in fact, took place after Venice's defeat at Agnadello in 1509 in the war against the League of Cambrai. After an attempt to return the lenders to Mestre in 1513, Venice finally agreed to allow loan banks in the city. A few years later, the creation of the Ghetto nuovo segregated Jews in an area on the outskirts of the city near Cannaregio, definitively sanctioning their presence in Venice (Ravid 1987a).

The Jewish community of Venice thus began life as a community of bankers similar to those in northern and central Italy in the thirteenth and fourteenth centuries. It was a different type of settlement, however, and its relations with the authorities differed significantly. Financial, religious, and social concerns overlapped considerably in Venice: the first drove the Republic to accept the settlement of the Jews initially in the fourteenth century and definitively in 1513; the second led to the obsessive insistence on the badge; and the last gave loans to the poor top priority, keeping interest rates very low. Subsequently, banks were transformed into "banks for the poor," making Venice, as one sixteenth-century observer put it, the only city where "the *Monte di Pietà* is run by the Jews" (Bonfil 1994: 46). Venice also provides us with a clear instance in which lending passed from Christian to Jewish hands. This transfer was motivated by the disadvantages of Christian banking: interest rates that were difficult for the authorities to control and profits that were less easily subjected to fiscal impositions. Moreover, one must not forget that, although its origins were linked to lending, the Venetian community did not remain one of bankers for long. Beginning in the 1530s, an influx of Jewish merchants, and their strong commercial ties with the city, changed the Venetian Jewish community into one whose importance to the economic life of Venice went far beyond banking.

Bologna is an important case. There, Christian bankers—Bolognese and later Tuscan—organized a guild of *campsores* (moneychangers and lenders) and succeeded in excluding Jewish lenders until the second half of the fourteenth century. During a period of brisk economic and demographic development, the city opened its gates to Jewish banking, initially allowing free immigration, without condotte. A 1387 census, taken for the purposes of regulating the tax on salt, allows us to know, albeit only fragmentarily, how many heads of families resided permanently in the city. In that year, according to the census, there were at least thirty-five Jewish families in Bologna, about two hundred individuals. Other sources document the existence of seventeen loan banks in the city and the surrounding countryside in 1388, of which eleven were Jewish. In 1392, there were thirteen moneylenders, nine Jews among them. Eight banks opened between the close of the fourteenth and the first years of the fifteenth century, not in the city but in the countryside. The creation of a monte di pietà in 1473 led to the expulsion of the Jews, but only the establishment of the papal dominion in Bologna and the expulsion decree in the 1593 bull *Caeca et obdurata* put an end to the community. Jews left Bologna for good, in fact, in November 1593. They set out for Ferrara and Mantua, carrying the bones of their dead to bury in Estense soil (Pini 1983).

The case of Siena is exemplary of the development of small communities of bankers in northern and central Italy. The commune invited Jewish lenders to settle in the city in 1309. The Jews completely replaced their Christian counterparts and, in addition to making loans to the poor, appear to have performed the more important role of financing the communal treasury. About 1420, the commune refused to renew the condotta and attempted to manage the banks directly, replacing the Jews with Christian bankers. But only a few years later, in 1437, it was again necessary to call upon the Jews to fill the hard-pressed public coffers, this time to pay the mercenary armies. New statutes in 1457 confirmed the presence of Jewish bankers in the city. The public function of Jewish lending in Siena explains why the creation of the monte di pietà in 1472 threatened the Jewish banks only temporarily and never seriously. In fact, the statutes of 1477 document the sharp resurgence experienced by Jewish banks. Despite St. Bernardino da Siena's preaching against usury, particularly in the first two decades of the fifteenth century, the Sienese commune appears to have enforced restrictions against Jewish banks only temporarily. Most of the time, they used the liquidity made available by Jewish banking to reinforce civic structures and eliminate poverty and social tensions (Boesch 1983).

The experience of Siena is not, however, to be seen as paradigmatic. Let us consider Umbria, an area with one of the longest traditions of banking, in the last decades of the thirteenth century. Aided by lower interest rates, Jews seem to have completely replaced Christian bankers—particularly the Aretine—at the beginning of the fourteenth century. There were about fifty Jewish settlements in Umbria, with a total Jewish population of no more than five hundred persons. It was a dispersion of great breadth. Only Perugia counted more than one hundred Jews, while most of the communities had fewer than fifty, and sometimes even fewer than twenty. Many Jewish communities, therefore, consisted of one or, at most, two families, including their retinues of bank employees and servants (A. Toaff 1989c). Jewish merchants and artisans arrived after the bankers, without undermining the latter's economic supremacy. Franciscan activity increased in the fifteenth century, multiplying the number of *monti di pietà* and stirring up the civil authorities' religious scruples against "Jewish usurers." As a result, Jewish banks experienced a crisis. At this time we find Jews engaged in numerous and varied mercantile and artisanal activities: they worked as carriage makers, saffron merchants, leather merchants, rag sellers, and peddlers, and three Perugian Jews were even members of the painters' guild in the early sixteenth century. The change to mercantile and artisanal activities was not, however, sufficient to avoid a crisis. In many Umbrian cities preaching by such Franciscans as Bernardino da Feltre, together with the creation of monti di pietà, led to the Jewish communities' demise through expulsion and conversion. This was the case in Gubbio, Assisi, Spello, and even Perugia, where, about 1485, a third of the Jews chose conversion and many others, although not formally expelled, opted for exile (A. Toaff 1989c).

By and large, Italian communes chose to allow the establishment and growth of Jewish banking between the fourteenth and fifteenth centuries. It was a realistic choice, not only because it took into account the local economies' need for liquidity, which Jews could provide more advantageously, but also because it recognized the real Jewish presence, its everyday relationships and way of life. Within these boundaries, the Jew was in a certain sense somewhat relieved of his heavy symbolic burden. The radical wing of the Church continued to oppose lending, both absolutely and from a utopian point of view, however, and to see the Jew as a stereotyped interloper—or, rather, enemy. The stereotypical Jew evoked by Franciscan preaching and the mentality of the friars had no basis in reality. This does not mean that Christians and Jews lived together in a kind of serene symbiosis during these centuries, broken only by Franciscan preaching and later by the Counter-Reformation's ecclesiastical policy. On the contrary, the two worlds were separated by predetermined, guaranteed boundaries, and Jewish inferiority was taken for granted. But even if the legend of a carefree Jewish golden age in Italy during these centuries must be reconsidered, nevertheless, rarely in the long history of the Jewish presence in the Western world have Judeo-Christian relations afforded Christians the opportunity both to relate to Jews as real people—not mythic creations—and to understand the true dimensions of lending as they did at that moment. This alone, and not a special benevolence on the part of contemporary Christian society toward Jews, is perhaps what allowed Christians and Jews to coexist more easily in Italy during these centuries.

THE JEWS IN SOUTHERN ITALY AND SICILY

As has been noted, the fourteenth century began disastrously for the Jews of southern Italy, with the forced conversion imposed by the Angevin kings in 1292. The Dominican Giordano da Rivalto memorialized this event in terms more mythic than historic in a 1304 sermon. It originated in Apulia, where the king took immediate advantage of an accusation of ritual homicide to expel the Jews, giving them the choice of conversion or death. In reality, the mass conversion of the Jews in the Angevin kingdom took place between 1290 and 1294, less suddenly than it would appear from da Rivalto's narration. Moreover, the conversions left many problems unresolved (Starr 1946; J. Cohen 1982). The Inquisition appears to have played a major role in these events. This role at first appears anomalous in light of the fact that the kings, not the clergy, initiated expulsions from France and England at approximately the same time. There are many indications, however, that the Angevin monarchy played a role in the conversionist policy. The first was the heavy fiscal burden to which it subjected the Jews in the preceding decades, severely impoverishing their communities and leaving them vulnerable to external pressures. The crown's decision to exempt converts from the payment of taxes was also important. It is precisely these requests for exemption that provide the documentation with which we are able plausibly to reconstruct the scope of this unmitigated catastrophe, in which nearly half of the Jews in southern Italy—7,000 out of 15,000—chose conversion. Jews who did not accept conversion joined the migratory flow northward, where their presence is documented in Mantua, or southward, probably to Sicily (Starr 1946).

In the years immediately following the conversions, however, the destroyed communities began to reconstitute themselves. In the fourteenth century, the Jews enjoyed renewed protection from the Angevin rulers of Naples, especially Robert, Joan I, and Ladislas. They also, however, faced such renewed acts of violence on the part of the clergy and the populace as took place in Trani in 1382, when the synagogues were made into churches and the Jews forced to flee. The church of S. Anna of Trani is still recognizable as a former synagogue, but today's visitor searches in vain for a written trace of its memory or documentation of the violence. With the advent of the Aragonese dynasty in 1442, the Jews in southern Italy enjoyed a privileged interval. Alphonso I (V of Aragon) and others removed jurisdiction over Jews from the bishops' tribunals and instead created a Christian magistrate, the *bajulo*. Alphonso also abolished the obligation to wear the badge. Under Alphonso's son, Don Ferrante (Ferdinand I), Jews enjoyed complete freedom of movement and the rights of full citizenship. According to some estimates, the Jewish population, scattered throughout more than 150 localities, reached 50,000 in the second half of the fifteenth century (Milano 1963). Although many Jews were bankers, there was no dearth of artisans and small businessmen. The Jewish presence was particularly important in the manufacture and sale of silk.

There were also many Jews in Sicily. In 1492, when in the space of several months Ferdinand and Isabella's edict put an end to a thousand-year presence on the island, there were between 35,000 and 50,000 Jews in Sicily, as many as in all the rest of Italy. Medieval Sicilian Jews lived scattered in nearly sixty different localities, with strong concentrations in the main cities; Palermo alone had 5,000. Several features distinguished Sicilian Jewish life from that of the rest of Italian Jewry. For one thing, Sicilian Jewry was marked by an intense and enduring relationship with the Islamic world. In these centuries a considerable number of Jews of North African, Tunisian, or Tripolitan descent still lived in Sicily, where the use of Arabic was widespread, and the Jewish community bore a strong organizational resemblance to other Jewish communities of the Mediterranean (Ashtor 1979). Sicilian Jewry also had a strong link with the Spanish world, accentuated by the rule of the Aragonese dynasty in Sicily. Perhaps the most significant difference in the social and economic organization of Sicilian Jewry was the absence of moneylending, which the crown officially prohibited at the request—of unknown motive and origin—of the communities themselves (Bonfil 1994). Sicilian Jews were therefore merchants, farmers, artisans, fishermen and fishmongers, growers and sellers of wine, and jewelers. This wide range of activities, made possible by the weakness of the Sicilian guilds, would seem to attest to a remarkable level of social integration. Other signs, however, point in the opposite direction. They were outlined by Rabbi Obadiah of Bertinoro in his invaluable account of his pilgrimage to Jerusalem in 1488. He wrote of the poverty of the Sicilian Jews, who were for the most part manual laborers, as well as of the existence of such severe disabilities as the obligation to wear an identifying badge and the requirements that Jews oversee the cleaning of the royal palaces and serve as executioners (Bonfil 1994).

Fourteenth- and fifteenth-century Sicilian Jewish life nevertheless continued under the traditional royal protection. The Jews depended on the king, *servi camerae regiae,* with all the limitations and privileges that this dependence entailed, from exceedingly heavy taxes to a remarkable degree of juridical autonomy. In 1447, the king abolished the office of *dayan kelali,* chief justice of the Jews, which had been filled by a Jew handpicked by the king and was vehemently opposed by the communities, and they became directly dependent on royal justice. Tension and hostility are evident in many episodes during the second half of the fifteenth century, including pogroms and massacres in Noto, Modica, and other parts of Sicily. The expulsion of the Jews was, however, imposed from without by the Spanish monarchy. The viceroy and representatives of the largest cities opposed the expulsion, and on the eve of the Jews' departure, they were still demanding that the decree be revoked in view of the harm the island would suffer. After several postponements, the final date for the expulsion was put at January 12, 1493, the day on which all those who had not accepted conversion—the great majority—left Sicily for good (Ashtor 1983).

In July 1492, the same fate befell the Jews of Sardinia. Jews had been in Sardinia since the thirteenth century, although documents do not provide information on the size of the island's first Jewish settlement. During Aragonese rule in the fourteenth century, the Jewish presence consisted of the two large communities of Cagliari and Alghero, in addition to various small centers scattered around the island. In Alghero, Jews played a particularly important role in commerce with Spain and the Balearic Islands, and enjoyed such special privileges as exemption from wearing the identifying badge. The legal status of Sardinian Jews was very similar to that of their Sicilian coreligionists. Unlike the latter, however, they were moneylenders as well as merchants, and they were also involved in various artisanal activities and mining in the Iglesias region. Although they eventually shared the fate of their Spanish brethren, the situation of the Sardinian Jewish communities does not seem to have deteriorated until 1488, when very restrictive legislation called for separate Jewish residential quarters, strict enforcement of the badge, and considerable limitations on professions. After the edict of expulsion from Spain was extended to Sardinia in 1492, most of the Jews left from the port of Cagliari for North Africa, from whence they subsequently dispersed throughout the Ottoman Empire. The synagogues of Cagliari and Alghero were turned into churches, and only the Jewish tower built in Alghero in 1360 by the Jews of Cagliari remained as a record of their life on the island (Milano 1963).

Most of the Sicilian exiles went instead to the ports of the nearby kingdom of Naples, where the crown had warmly welcomed the Spanish refugees, and where they were immediately granted equal rights with the Jews already residing in the kingdom. A great many Jews found refuge in the kingdom of Naples, and this was certainly one of the factors that contributed to the rise of tensions there. It is also significant that the collective imagination attributed the plague that broke out in November 1492, causing thousands of deaths in the following year, to the Jews arriving from Spain. A French invasion of 1494 brought these tensions to a head. As the French descended on Naples, the masses decided to rid the kingdom of Jews, perhaps in the certainty that the latter would receive neither protection nor help from the French, who had driven the French Jews out a century earlier. Expulsion, looting, and devastation preceded the entrance of the French, and more violence, confiscations, and conversions followed. The return of the Aragonese dynasty did not markedly improve the situation. Despite the attempt by Frederick III of Aragon to return to the previous policy, there were strong pressures from within Neapolitan society to rid the kingdom of Jews. All in all, it was a rather slow, fluctuating process. In 1502, however, Naples became a possession of the Spanish monarchy, making expulsion inevitable. It took place in successive waves in 1510 and 1514 and was finally brought to a conclusion, for the few hundred families still in the kingdom, in 1541.

THE JEWS OF ROME

Jews have lived in Rome continuously since antiquity, making the Roman Jewish community unique in the Diaspora. During the Christian era, there have been no expulsions and nothing has disturbed the succession of generations. Although the community's history is shrouded in darkness until the eleventh century (when the first signs of a Jewish presence begin to appear), we know that it was an uninterrupted presence.

The relationship of the Roman Jews to the surrounding world was anything but ordinary, since they had to deal with the overlapping influences of the civil government and the papacy, the supreme religious authority of the Christian world. It is thus particularly difficult to tell the story of the Roman Jews without taking into account the ideological aspects of the Church's Jewish policy. Although the medieval period witnessed a clear separation of temporal and religious powers, they became increasingly intertwined in the hands of the pontiff after the fourteenth century (Prodi 1987). Religious ideology lay at the root of many aspects of Rome's Jewish policy that might seem purely economic and social, including, for example, its fiscal policy (Stow 1982).

The first medieval description of the Roman Jewish community comes to us from Benjamin of Tudela, a twelfth-century Spanish Jewish merchant who left a priceless chronicle of his voyage through most of the then known world. In Rome, Benjamin found about 200 Jewish families living peacefully, on good terms with the papal court and under no fiscal obligations. After this initial assessment, we possess no data about the size and evolution of the Roman community until more recent centuries. The northward migration of a great many Roman Jews in the fourteenth century must have seriously reduced the size of the community. In the second half of the fifteenth century, incomplete data culled from notarial sources confirm 402 Jewish names—the majority of them masculine—but do not indicate the number of nuclear families to which these correspond (Esposito 1983a and b). This figure predates the influx of refugees from Spain and southern Italy, which changed the composition of Roman Jewry after 1492. We do not know with certainty how many Jews stayed in Rome and how many merely passed through on their way to Islamic countries. New synagogues of both the Spanish and Sicilian rites, family names, and the internal vicissitudes of the community bear witness to the considerable change in communal life and organization brought about by the influx. A 1527 census—the first to describe the Roman population, and hence also the Jews—reported 370 Jewish families, a total of 1,750 individuals.

The Jewish community organization in medieval Rome was of long standing, apparently originating in the eleventh century. References to the *Universitas iudeorum urbis* are quite frequent in documents from the fourteenth and fifteenth centuries, which provide descriptions of the community's organizational structures. These structures were based on a general assembly, ruled by the majority, and an executive power of three *fattori* serving four-month terms. The judicial powers of the community were strictly limited, however, and communal tribunals, composed of voluntary arbiters, were almost exclusively confined to matrimonial matters (Milano 1963).

After having lived in Trastevere until the end of the thirteenth century, Jews began to settle in S. Angelo, where the ghetto would be built in the sixteenth. The community underwent a spontaneous process of concentration similar to those of most other Jewish settlements during this period. Despite the fierce struggles among various factions of the Roman aristocracy that characterized the fourteenth century, Jews continued to enjoy relative stability. Neither Cola di Rienzo's attempt to make the papal state a republic nor the catastrophic appearance of the plague affected relations between the city and the Jewish community or endangered the Jews' safety and legal status. A Senate statute of 1310 defined the Jews as Roman citizens, a ruling reconfirmed in 1402. The 1310 statute also imposed an identifying badge—in this case, a red cloak—and this regulation was renewed by statutes enacted in 1363. Jews living in the Contrada iudeorum (Jewish quarter) were exempted, however, as were foreign Jews during the first ten days of their stay in the city (Milano 1963).

Civil legislation seemed inclined to maintain the status quo and to protect the community. Although they often fluctuated, relations with the papacy, which had reestablished itself in Rome at the beginning of the fifteenth century, appeared similarly inclined. Thus the liberal bulls of 1419 and 1429 with which Pope Martin V renewed the Jews' designation as citizens afforded them free association with Christians and entitled them to a series of other privileges. Martin's successor, Eugene IV, had a more ambiguous policy. Initially, he confirmed the guarantees given to the Jews, but in 1442 he issued a bull that was diametrically opposed to his original position. It subjected Jews to numerous restrictions, from a ban on commerce and lending to a prohibition against studying Talmudic books. The bull, extended to all of Italy, was revoked a few months later, however, following a large donation by the Roman Jews and an agreement between the Curia and the Italian communities to raise the tithe paid by Italian Jews to the excessive sum of 1,130 florins.

During the fourteenth and fifteenth centuries, financial agreements of this sort, together with the payment of exceptional bonuses aimed at modifying dispositions or laws threatening the liberty and existence of Jewish communities, were almost the rule in relations between the Italian states and the Jews. The above agreement seems to indicate that the Roman Jewish community had considerable funds available to it. What professions did Roman Jews pursue, and what was their actual economic significance? Notarial sources of the fifteenth century do not document the existence of Jewish credit. Jewish bankers established relations with the papacy in the fifteenth century only during the pontificate of Martin V, while Christian bankers predominated in the Curia for the entire century. It seems quite probable that pawnshops existed, but neither contracts—not required with secured loans—nor rules for their management are extant (Maire Vigueur 1983; Esposito 1983a). On the other hand, unequivocal documentation of the existence of Jewish bankers in Rome can be found in Daniele da Pisa's *Capitoli,* which reorganized the Jewish community there in 1524, dividing it in three census classes, the first of which consisted of bankers (Milano 1964).

Jewish physicians appear to have been an important and privileged group. Jews very often served as pontifical chief physician. Such was the case with Bonet de Lattes, a Provençal Jew who served Alexander VI, Julius II, and Leo X in this capacity. Jewish physicians enjoyed special treatment and prestige: they were exempted from wearing the badge and permitted to use an honorary title. Among other occupations, fifteenth-century Roman Jews dealt in grain, wine, and cloth, which subsequently became the dominant trade. They also engaged in a wide range of artisanal activities, but did not, at least according to the fragmentary documentation available, grow wine grapes or foodstuffs. Although expressly permitted by law to do so, they did not generally own real estate or land (Esposito 1983a).

Fiscal impositions on the community formed an important element in relations between Roman Jewry and the papacy. As Benjamin of Tudela recounts, twelfth-century Roman Jews were exempted from taxes. By the fourteenth century, however, they were already subjected to considerable financial pressure. The first tax paid by medieval Roman Jews dates back to 1310. At that time they began to pay an annual tribute of ten gold florins to avoid participating in the carnival games of Agone and Testaccio, at which they were subjected to violence and public ridicule. This tax, a kind of ransom, was initially quite modest. It multiplied in the course of the fifteenth century, however, when the Church extended it to all 110 synagogues in the papal states. According to a tradition related by the Roman statutes of 1464, thirty florins were added to the original sum in memory of the thirty coins with which Judas was said to have sold Christ. The total of 1,130 florins (more than 500 scudi) was not a negligible sum, particularly after the disappearance of the other Jewish communities in the papal states at the close of the sixteenth century left only those of Rome and Ancona to pay it (Milano 1963).

The origin of the Church's system of Jewish taxation was thus linked to ideological issues concerning carnival, humiliation of the Jews, and violence and its control. Similarly, in subsequent centuries, the fiscal system would play a repressive and conversionary role, to which, in theory, it should have been completely unrelated. This is another—and not the least—of the anomalies that typified the complex relations between the Jews and the Church of Rome. These relations vacillated between repression and protection, as well as between conversion and stability. Even the high tax levied in the sixteenth century for the maintenance of the house of converts was certainly not merely a financial issue, because it involved Jews directly in the support of the Church's conversionary policy. By the end of the fifteenth century, Roman Jewry was subjected to very heavy financial pressure. This pressure would become even more marked during the ghetto period, in the wake of the Jews' growing impoverishment and the drastic reduction in the number of communities. The *vigesima,* an income tax to help fund a crusade against the Turks, was imposed on Jews in the middle of the fifteenth century during the pontificates of the Spaniard Calixtus III and Pius II (Milano 1963). Although the crusade itself remained largely in the planning stage, various other events served to establish the vigesima in the course of centuries. Opposed, renounced, and then reimposed, it eventually became the main tax on the Jews in the papal states. With the addition of other levies and fines for various infractions, the increasing taxation of Jews assumed a consciously avowed ideological character in the second half of the sixteenth century. Impoverishment and economic oppression might serve to push Jews to convert, making financial pressure an instrument of religious pressure (Stow 1982).

THE ADVENTURE OF DAVID REUBENI

On the threshold of the sixteenth century, conversion had become the central problem in Jewish-Christian relations even in Italy. The converso problem in the Iberian world was of utmost importance, although reverberations in Italy of the events in Spain and Portugal were confused. The messianic fervor accompanying the expulsion was not restricted to Jews, but in fact aroused the interest of a Christian world increasingly permeated by a fervid apocalyptic mysticism. In this context, a Jewish adventurer's journey between Rome and Portugal revived Jewish messianic dreams and gathered unexpected support and interest. In the brief period between his initial appearance and his end at the stake, this adventurer's career seemed symptomatic of the chasm between the Italian Jewish communities and the Jews of the Iberian world, with its heightened tensions.

David Reubeni disembarked in Venice at the close of 1523. He said he came from the Habor desert in Arabia, from a Jewish kingdom of

300,000 souls. He claimed to be the brother of its King Joseph, and his ambassador to the West in search of a political and military alliance against the Ottoman Empire. Although he did not come from an imaginary Jewish kingdom, it can be deduced from the various versions he offered of his voyage and mission, particularly the one in his *Diario*, that David did in fact arrive from Arabia, and that his voyage took him through Nubia, Sudan, and Egypt to Hebron, Jerusalem, and Gaza in the land of Israel, and finally to Venice (Sestieri 1991). In the city on the lagoon, David did not stay in the ghetto, although he admitted he was Jewish and alluded obscurely to his mission (in his past travels he had pretended to be a Muslim). Venetian Jews reacted to him cautiously and diffidently, and he soon left for Rome, arriving there on February 21, 1524. He presented himself to Cardinal Egidio da Viterbo, a learned Hebraist, who introduced him to the papal court.

David stayed in Rome for a year, becoming a member first of Egidio da Viterbo's household and then of that of Daniele da Pisa, one of the most authoritative members of the Roman Jewish community and author of the famous *Capitoli* that reorganized community life. But he was not generally well received by the Roman Jews. In his *Diario*, he refers to tensions and quarrels and recounts that "two evil slanderers went to the Pope and said: Burn this Jewish ambassador who says the Lord sent him, and see if God saves him from the flames" (Sestieri 1991: 161). Nevertheless, David was well regarded at Clement VII's court. According to Daniele da Pisa, the pontiff received him and spoke to him at great length. David stated his requests: "and the result was that this David was sent . . . to make a pact and ask for arms with which to wage war, that is, firearms, *cortetti* and *falconetti* and the like, from the king of Portugal [so that they] could go to war against the Ishmaelite kings to get to the Sanctuary of God" (Sestieri 1991: 200–201).

At the end of his stay in Rome, David obtained letters of introduction to the king of Portugal and the sovereign of Ethiopia. The Portuguese ambassador was reluctant to grant a safe-conduct to a Jew or to allow him to enter a country that a generation ago had forcibly converted all his correligionists. But these problems were resolved, and David left for Portugal, then in the midst of the long negotiations with Rome that eventually led to the introduction of a Spanish-style Inquisition in 1536. In this context, the arrival of such a figure could not but have raised hopes in the increasingly repressed and stifled world of the conversos. The converso world was awash with messianic currents akin to those that had spawned prophetic movements in Castile at the beginning of the century before being violently repressed by the Inquisition (Edwards 1984b). Neither did these currents differ greatly from the millenaristic fears that shook the Christian world, finding expression, for example, in the second half of the century in Sebastianism, the movement nourished by hopes of the resurrection of King Sebastian of Portugal after his death in battle in Morocco in 1578 (Yerushalmi 1991).

Officially, David's mission to Portugal aimed to contract an alliance with King John III against the Turks and to obtain new artillery in exchange. He probably secretly planned to return the masses of Portuguese conversos to Judaism and have them emigrate to the land of Israel once it was retaken from the Turks. His *Diario* alludes openly and repeatedly to this return to Israel, although it is more cautious regarding the problem of the conversos. Despite the fact that David represented himself not as a messiah but as a prince and ambassador, and despite the fact that his project was political and military rather than, strictly speaking, messianic, the Portuguese converso world viewed his arrival as that of a liberator and messiah. In this climate of enthusiasm, a young converso secretary to the royal chancellery, Diogo Pires, was moved by these hopes and caused a sensation by reverting to Judaism and joining David. This incident caused a great scandal in court circles, heightening apprehension about converso faith in David Reubeni and prompting John III to renege on his promise of alliance and expel him from the country.

While Pires, with the new name of Sholomo Molko, escaped to Jerusalem, David left Portugal and spent the following years in difficult voyages. Since his *Diario* ends with his departure from Portugal, we can only approximate the last years of his life. He returned to Italy around 1530, and while in Venice, he encountered Molko, who had become a renowned mystic and scholar in Palestine and Salonika. Molko had arrived in Rome in 1529, surrounding himself with a messianic and prophetic aura. As a converso who had reverted to Judaism, it was obviously very risky for him to sojourn in Rome. Moreover, we know that Clement granted him safe-conduct, expressly forbidding any type of persecution because he had been forcibly baptized (*invitus*) at an early age and had always lived as a Jew, never believing in the Christian faith.

Leaving Italy, Reubeni and Molko went to Regensburg to request an audience with Charles V. We do not know whether they wanted his support for their plan to fight the Turks or were trying—as other Christian sources relate—to convert him to Judaism. We are not even sure that Reubeni joined Molko in Regensburg. The latter's presence is mentioned in the diary of Josel of Rosheim, the head of German Jewry, who not only did not support Reubeni's proposal, but actually left the city so as not to be involved with it. The requested audience did not take place, and Molko, probably along with David, was arrested by the emperor. Molko was burned as a Judaizer in Mantua in 1532. David Reubeni came to the same end in Badajoz in 1538. In the list of the condemned at Badajoz, his name appears like this: "David, who was called 'the Jew of the shoe.' He claimed to be the son of King Solomon and the brother of King Joseph, and to have been born in the Horot Desert. He arrived in the kingdom of Portugal in 1525. He indoctrinated and converted many Christians to the dead law of the Jews. Handed over to the secular arm in the year 1538" (Rodríguez-Moñino 1956).

The early-sixteenth-century Jewish world was evidently fertile soil for adventures of this sort. Similar episodes—such as the appearance of Asher Lemlein, another false messiah, who stirred up Venice and Capodistria in 1502—had prepared the way for outbursts of messianic fervor among Jews and conversos. The Jewish world was not unanimous in its belief in David Reubeni's mission, however, especially in Italy and Germany, where his appearance raised doubts and resistance. On the other hand, he achieved great renown among the Jews in Muslim North Africa and, above all, among Portuguese conversos. In Italy, his supporters included personages of great prominence, such as Daniele da Pisa, the physician Yosef Zarfati, and Bienvenida Abrabanel, a member of a noble family that had settled in Naples after being expelled from Spain. Bienvenida, in fact, sent him a flag, which he carried, along with three others, on his voyages. Regal symbols of a people without a kingdom, these flags struck the imagination of Reubeni's contemporaries. Embroidered in Hebrew, they bore the name of God and the Ten Commandments. The *Mogen David,* the star of David, would only much later become the symbol of the Jewish people (Scholem 1971).

As extreme and paradoxical as they might appear, these events are nevertheless very revealing. First and foremost, they reveal much about the difference between the world of the Italian Jews and that of the Sephardim, particularly the difference between the messianism of the Spanish Jews and conversos and the skepticism of those Venetian and Roman Jews who considered Reubeni a dangerous impostor. Furthermore, they reveal the Church's shift from a policy that attempted to convert the Jews using persuasion to one of inflexibility and harshness. Between Reubeni's initial reception at the papal court and his burning at the hands of Charles V lay much more, in reality, than the story of a false messiah. The safe-conduct granted to Molko by Clement VII seems, in fact, to foreshadow the latter's much more general affirmations in the 1533 bull *Sempiterno regi,* which explicitly designated the conversions of Portuguese Jews in 1497 as forced and removed the conversos' reversion to Judaism from inquisitional jurisdiction (Yerushalmi 1971). This decision did not imply a refutation of the politics of conversion. Rather, it represented an attempt to make a clear-cut distinction between spontaneous and forced conversion, thus safeguarding the very idea of conversion. Pope Paul IV's 1555 decision to persecute the Marranos of Ancona was diametrically opposed to Clement's approach. The burning of Sholomo Molko as an apostate was a prelude to this change.

If the messianic affair of David Reubeni can be interpreted as emblematic, it is because of the complex and confused mixture of religious expectations that typified not only the converso world but also that of the Gentiles, attentive and curious observers of the events of these years. A lively and fertile cultural ferment among scholars formed the common ground of Jewish and Christian messianism. Indeed, it is no accident that the learned Hebraist Cardinal Egidio da Viterbo vouched for the adventurer David Reubeni before the Medici pope. This was, therefore, a specific cultural context that included the kind of mingling of Jewish and Christian cultures that has been considered a specific characteristic of the Renaissance world. The Reubeni/Molko affair seems, in a certain sense, to be the final culmination of that encounter between the Jewish and gentile worlds.

BETWEEN EXTERNAL AND INTERNAL:
THE JEWS IN RENAISSANCE CULTURE

No one can deny that the Renaissance was a moment of great renewal in the history of the Western world. It fused the culture of antiquity harmoniously with a sense of the future and the individualistic pride of the present. Despite attempts at revisionism, this is the image that we still hold of the fifteenth-century Italian world. It differs little from that which Jacob Burckhardt delineated more than a century ago or which led Michelet—more by his heart than his head—to invent the term itself (Febvre 1966). While the period that began with the fifteenth century prompted Christian elites to radically transform their own perceptions and culture, however, this transformation did not bring them to a different consideration of the Jewish minority within their world. Rather, growing intolerance and pressure for cultural and religious uniformity often accompanied the transformation of the medieval world and its passage to the modern era. It is no coincidence that witch burnings studded the European states' push toward modernity in the early modern, rather than the medieval, period. Similarly, nations on the road to centralization gave rise to expulsion and persecution of Jews much more often than did the Church. At least in the field of culture, we should expect—as has often been maintained—that the Renaissance facilitated reciprocal exchange between Christians and Jews (Roth 1959; Shulvass 1973). The proposed image is both flattering and reassuring; it represents the intellectual, humanistic universe of the Renaissance as a world open to the most varied influences, curious about diversity and in love with literature and knowledge to the point of considering its followers members of an ideal society of scholars, regardless of their religious or cultural affiliations. But this is a distorted image. In reality, relations between the two cultures, albeit considerable, were in reality complex and rife with ambiguities. If a koine existed, it was certainly not rooted in closer ties between the Christian and Jewish cultures. Rather, each culture was deeply fascinated by the other's world. This attraction did not challenge the deeply rooted issues of separation and inferiority, but encouraged knowledge of those who were different. It therefore led in some cases to the development of nontraditional points of view, although it did so only as an almost unconscious by-product. Even though this attraction enabled some Jews to yield to the dominant truth, and thus convert, it remained for Christians an ambiguous and dangerous attraction. The scholars and philosophers of Italian humanism thus alternately embraced and repulsed Jewish culture like a passionately desired lover from whom they nevertheless wanted to keep their distance.

With its philosophers, scientists, and men of letters, in addition to its traditional scholars, Italian Jewish culture in these centuries was rich and complex, finding expression in many forms. Some forms emanated strictly from within the Jewish world and its tradition. Others, variously influenced by the Christian universe and its humanistic drive, reflected the intersection of Jewish culture with that of the surrounding world. Rather than attempting to illustrate the overall richness of this universe, I focus here on what issued at the crossroads of the two cultures, avoiding the perhaps unanswerable question of the degree to which they were integrated (and, thus, a judgment on the relationship of the Renaissance with the Jews). Encounters such as that between Christian humanism and the Jewish world in the Platonic Academy of Florence shed light on the complexity of these diverse worlds, which alternately attracted and rejected one another.

In order to approach Hebrew texts, humanists needed, most of all, to master philological, critical, and, especially, linguistic skills. Hence, Christians requested Jews to teach them their language and to guide them through rabbinical and biblical texts. Once in possession of these linguistic tools, however, the humanists were not so much interested in the biblical or rabbinical tradition as in cabalistic thought. In a mid-sixteenth-century responsum defending the legitimacy of teaching Hebrew to non-Jews, Rabbi Elia Menachem Halfan referred to the cabalistic interests of Christians, writing: "In the past twenty years ... many nobles and scholars have attempted to deepen their understanding of this glorious science. And they seem truly exhausted by their effort, because not many of our people are learned in this science, since after the many misfortunes and expulsions there are only a few left. Thus seven scholars grab a Jew by his clothes and say: 'teach us this science'" (Bonfil 1987: 502–3).

But what was this cabalistic tradition, the object of such passionate discovery in the Italian Renaissance world? In Hebrew, *kabbalah* means "received tradition." This term designates the particular form assumed by mysticism in twelfth-century Provence and thirteenth-century Spain. There has been much discussion about the relationship between Cabala and the preceding mystical tradition. The latter found expression at two different moments: from the first to the third century of the common era, and, in different forms, between the seventh and ninth century, in the so-called mysticism of the *Merkabah*. The cabalistic system was strongly linked with a text that was widely diffused in the Middle Ages and ascribable to an uncertain period between the second and sixth century. The Book of Creation, *Sefer Yezirah*, would be at the center of medieval cabalistic comments and reflections. At the origins of the cabalistic movement in twelfth-century Provence, we find a text difficult to date and of uncertain origin and genesis, the *Sefer Bahir*, through which precise gnostic elements penetrate Jewish doctrine, mediated perhaps also by Catharist suggestions. The basic text of Cabala is the Book of Splendor, the *Zohar*, traditionally attributed to the second century, but in reality composed in Spain at the end of the thirteenth century.

Medieval cabalistic thought had an esoteric character. Using mystical interpretation of sacred texts, small groups of intellectuals sought to discover the deep secret of creation, the hidden God. In the wake of the traumatic exile from Spain and the upheaval of European Jewry after 1492, Cabala underwent a profound transformation, becoming at the same time an expanded patrimony and a weapon in everyone's hands. In particular, this transformation was the work of the Lurianic School of Safed, a small town high in the hills of the Galilee. There, an important center of thought developed in the sixteenth century that had among its protagonists Moshe Cordovero and Isaac Luria. Cabala aimed to reconstruct the shattered unity of God through the use of what could be defined as mystical exercises. Both the concept of God's presence and that of the shattering of his unity were reinterpreted as the divine world's equivalent of terrestrial exile, and the recomposition of divine unity became the key to redemption (Scholem 1965). These symbols became exceedingly powerful and played a significant—perhaps decisive—role in Shabbetai Tzevi's great messianic movement in 1666.

The fervor with which the new art of printing was applied in these years to fundamental Hebrew and cabalistic texts testifies materially to the rediscovery of Jewish culture by Christians. Italy was the center of this activity, although these works were for the most part intended for foreign markets beyond the Alps and to the east. Some of the great printers of the early sixteenth century were Jewish, including Gershom Soncino. Others were Christian, such as Soncino's rival Daniel Bomberg, a Flemish printer active in Venice in the first half of the century. After the death of Aldo Manuzio in 1515, Bomberg obtained the exclusive right to print Jewish books in Venice for a period of ten years. In this endeavor, he availed himself of the work of numerous scholars, Jews and converts, particularly that of the convert Felice da Prato. Thus, beginning in 1516, Bomberg undertook several great editorial projects, including the first completely printed editions of the rabbinical Bible, the Babylonian Talmud, and the Jerusalem Talmud. Bomberg's subsequent output fused humanistic and cabalistic interests, and included the cabalistic commentary on the Pentateuch by the great scholar Menahem da Recanati. It was not, however, until the middle of the century—after much controversy—that the basic work of medieval Cabala, the *Zohar*, appeared in two contemporaneous printed editions, in Mantua in 1558 and in Cremona in 1560. By 1553, the humanist Guillaume Postel had completed a Latin translation of the entire *Zohar* (Bonfil 1987).

This world of converts—which revolved around Bomberg's printing shop as it had previously around the Florentine Academy—could not but cause alarm and concern about the risks to Jewish identity entailed in this close cultural collaboration with Christians. Moreover, as Leon Modena would stress in his seventeenth-century anti-cabalistic polemics, learned Christians sought to appropriate Jewish culture, particularly its cabalistic aspects, as a part of their substantially conversionist vision. In its loftiest moments, this project could embrace the utopian belief in an ancient wisdom (*prisca veritas*) common to all philosophers and scholars, whose strongest legacy would remain impressed on the Christian religion. It could, however, also confine itself to furnishing more sophisticated instruments for a widespread policy of attack on and destruction of Jewish thought. Although the conversion of the Jews was essential to his project, Pico della Mirandola clearly belonged to the first of these two camps. Indeed, in addition to such Jewish teachers as Johannan Alemanno, Avraham Farissol, and Elijah Delmedigo, he gathered around him a group of converts who shared in his philosophical ideals and projects. Some of them—such as Flavio Mitridate, who after converting became an erudite humanist—represent the most significant and extreme products of the fascination exercised by Florentine Platonism on some Jewish intellectuals. By adopting a very spiritualized view of Judaism, they arrived at an exotic and substantially heterodox Christianity, in close harmony with the intentions and spirit of Pico's Academy (Ruderman 1981).

Both Avraham Farissol and Elijah Delmedigo had a profound knowledge of the Academy's milieu. Although their message is veiled by concerns of cultural politics, they warn of the cultural syncretism of this world of converts. Nevertheless, Farissol and Delmedigo never relinquished their close relationship with Pico della Mirandola and his world. Perhaps indicative of the prevalence of these diplomatic considerations, their choice was also a further indication of how deeply the hermetic doctrines of a part of the Italian philosophical Renaissance had penetrated Jewish culture, despite fears and obstacles. Farissol and Delmedigo never exceeded the boundaries of orthodox Judaism, however, although they countenanced a close dialogue with Christian culture. This interaction was not without ambivalence and tension for them. It is difficult to determine whether their ambivalence concerned dialogue with Christians and its repercussions or the specific character of a Renaissance culture suffused with elements of ancient paganism. Thus, Jews might, in reality, have been suspicious of the essentially pagan culture that was reemerging, with all its deeply rooted fascination (Ruderman 1981). Taking a different tack, David ben Judah Messer Leon and other exponents of the movement recently designated "Jewish humanism" chose to introduce humanism's new calling into Jewish culture and civic and religious life. They thereby entered into a sort of competition with Christian humanism, but not closer cultural contact with it (Bonfil 1984; Tirosh-Rotschild 1988).

This was not the choice of Avraham Yagel, rabbi, physician, and cabalist, who lived in Mantua between the end of the sixteenth century and the first decades of the seventeenth (Ruderman 1988b). This man's intellectual portrait does not in any way distinguish him from many other naturalists and scholars of his century: he had a lively curiosity about the peculiarities and eccentricities of nature, maintained a keen interest in magic and astrology, and made a close connection between magical thinking and scientific thought. Although his interest in medicine does not single him out from such others as Ambroise Paré, the most important surgeon at the French court in the late sixteenth century, his scientific interests liken him to intellectuals like Cornelio Agrippa di Nettesheim or the Platonist Girolamo Cardano. Yagel's originality lay in his interpretative perspective. He attempted to reconcile Christian and Jewish cultures employing mainly Christian and pagan sources, even though he wrote in Hebrew for a Jewish audience. Yagel constantly referred to a sort of ancient preeminence of Jewish science and knowledge. This was linked, however, to a substantial belief in a *prisca veritas* very similar to Pico's, in which, too, both pagan and Christian wisdom were roads leading to the truth. This affirmation naturally made Yagel "a Jew perched dangerously on a spiritual precipice," at the brink of two worlds (Ruderman 1988b: 60). Intellectuals like Yagel faced the problem of how to reconcile their belief in a *prisca theologia* with their belief that the truth belonged exclusively to Judaism. This is the crux of every syncretistic cultural activity, and the point of greatest divergence in the Jewish cultural world. Already by the early sixteenth century, Isaac Abrabanel, Giuda Abrabanel (better known as Leone Ebreo), and others were supporting the preeminence of Jewish tradition over that of Greece and had criticized the idea of a *prisca theologia*. They rejected out of hand any possibility of arriving at the truth by paths other than those of traditional Judaism (Idel 1986 and 1989).

On the other hand, in order to find acceptance in the Christian world, fascination with Jewish culture had to be inserted into a conversionist scheme. And here, too, there was no dearth of roadblocks, as the history of the Florentine Academy demonstrates. Only polemicists and theologians could freely approach Jewish culture, and even they could do so only with the greatest caution. Such less traditional figures as Cornelius

Agrippa di Nettesheim, attacked in the 1530s as a Judaizer for his cabalistic work *De occulta philosophia,* elicited reactions even in the pre-Counter-Reformation world.

We might also call to mind the controversy involving the learned German humanist and Hebraist Johannes Reuchlin, a colleague of Pico's and Erasmus's, in the opening years of the sixteenth century. Although not a "philo-Semite," Reuchlin opposed the campaign to impound rabbinical books launched by two converts, Johann Joseph Pfefferkorn and Viktor Von Karben. The controversy was the talk of Germany around the second decade of the sixteenth century and led to serious problems for Reuchlin, despite both his ties to the papal court and his adversaries' inexperience. Even Erasmus did not support him unqualifiedly, defending him only after his death. "The enemies and destroyers of our people rose up to suppress the Oral Law. But the Lord performed a miracle within a miracle, and from within the midst of the wise men of the nations a man rose up to bring the Law back to its former recognition," wrote Josel of Rosheim, recounting the episode in a traditional and insular vein (Baron 1952, 13:189). In reality, the disputation between Reuchlin and Pfefferkorn went far beyond the traditional problem of Christianity's relationship with the Talmud and involved the relationship between Christian and Jewish cultures at a level heretofore unknown. By then, however, even Reuchlin's purely intellectual interest began to seem fraught with risks.

These scattered threads bring us back to our initial question: the value and scope of cultural contact between Christians and Jews during the Renaissance. The answers that we have found are full of ambiguity, revealing a very complex picture. Jews and Christians conversed, debated, and created knowledge together. Intense contacts, however, came to a dead end at the insurmountable wall of judgment concerning the ultimate sources of truth or teetered riskily on the border between two worlds, as in the case of Yagel, or at the edges of orthodoxy, as with Cornelio Agrippa di Nettesheim. One of the driving forces along this route was cabalistic thought. In the kaleidoscopic world of Italian humanism, it inspired theologians to new conversionist paths and distorted readings of Hebrew texts. By means of diverse paths, it also brought learned Jews closer to the Christian world. Perhaps it can be said that the fascination that Jewish culture held for the Christian world was merely a fascination with its own mental universe, reflecting back onto Jewish culture after having been transformed by contact with gentile culture, pagan as well as Christian. Thus men like Farissol or Yagel could see their own images reflected in the fascination their culture held for the outside world, and they could extract from this information ways of changing and reelaborating Jewish culture, and, perhaps, find reassurances and hopes for the future of their history. Renaissance culture offers us examples of considerable integration and great narrow-mindedness, of attraction and repulsion, and of different uses of the same cultural tools. Ambivalence, it seems, was the symbol that unified both Christians and Jews.

CHAPTER SIX

The Age of the Ghettos

THE GHETTO: BETWEEN
CONFINEMENT AND PROTECTION

Pope Paul IV's 1555 bull *Cum nimis absurdum* instituted the ghetto of Rome and obligated the Jews to live together in one street, completely separated from the homes of Christians, in all localities of the papal states in which Jews resided. This street was permitted just one outlet to the outside and was to be guarded by a locked gate. In the eventuality that one street was not sufficient, additional streets could be added to the first, provided they were contiguous and closed off from the outside. In addition, the pope decreed that there be only one synagogue in the area intended for the Jews and that no new synagogues be built. Lastly, Jews were not permitted to own property. Whatever they already possessed they had to sell to Christians.

Thus, the Church made a choice in favor of rigid segregation in the middle of the sixteenth century. Ecclesiastical authorities had quite a traditional motivation for this choice, the necessity of safeguarding Jewish inferiority. "Since we have learned," the bull affirmed, "that in Rome and other places under the control of the Church, the impudence of Jews has reached such proportions that they dare not only to live among Christians but to be seen near churches without distinguishing dress, and that they rent houses on the principal streets and in the principal squares, buy and hold property . . . we find ourselves forced to take the following measures" (Milano 1963: 247).

When the bull instituted the ghetto, there already existed another ghetto in Italy, that of Venice. In 1516, the Venetian Republic had decreed "that all the Jews currently living in various neighborhoods of our city . . . must transfer immediately to the courtyard of houses in the *geto* near San Hieronymo, where they will live together" (Ravid 1987c: 248). The decree of the Venetian Senate thus for the first time introduced the term "ghetto" (*geto*) to designate the segregated areas of the Jews, a term whose meaning would eventually expand until it came to be generic for any place of segregation and discrimination. There are many hypotheses for the origin of this word. The most probable from an etymological point of view is that it comes from a place-name. Before it was designated as the dwelling place of the Jews, the area was already called Ghetto, a name probably deriving from the activity of the foundries (*getto,* from *gettare*) that existed there in the fifteenth century (A. Toaff 1973; Ravid 1987c). But there are other hypotheses. One refers back to the term used to define the pier (*gettata*) of the port of Genoa where Jews disembarked during the exodus out of Spain in 1492. There they endured untold outrages, without ever being allowed to enter the city. Certainly the vivid and traumatic memory of this place could have been associated with the ghetto as a place of segregation (Sermoneta 1974). Although it is frequently documented in Venice during the first years of its use, the term "ghetto" did not immediately enter into current usage to designate the area allocated for the enclosure of the Jews. In Christian sources, we frequently find *recinto* (enclosure), *serraglio* (seraglio), or *ridotto degli ebrei* (Jewish enclosure), while the term most used in Jewish documents is *hatser* (enclosure). Provided that we are not dealing with a later interpolation, the first use of the word "ghetto" in a papal document dates to the bull *Dudum a felicis* issued by Pius V in 1562. But it was only at the end of the century that its use became more generalized. The word then also entered the language of Hebrew documents in Rome, where it took the form of *get,* the same spelling as the Hebrew word for bill of divorce. In his *Diario,* written about 1528, David Reubeni found it necessary when talking about his stay in Venice in 1523– 24 to explain the meaning of the word to his readers when referring to the ghetto of Venice: "the Ghetto, the place of the Jews" (Ravid 1987c; Sestieri 1991: 105). By the end of the century, however, it was no longer necessary to explain the term in the Roman ghetto. The association with *get* had been imposed on the original etymology, as if to signify by means of this pun a new perception of the enclosure. By this time, the ghetto seemed a definitive separation from Christian society. The outside world had divorced the Jews (Stow 1992e).

In the course of two centuries, from 1555 until the 1700s, all the Italian states that did not expel the Jews enclosed them in ghettos. This did not merely entail the enclosure of an existing space. Jews from other parts of the city, and often from nearby cities and small villages, had to be gathered together in the area that was to become theirs alone. Ghettoization ended up being a kind of expulsion, although the place in which Jews were forced to live was inside the walls instead of outside them. In this context, the vicissitudes of the papal states were significant. In the first half of the sixteenth century, there were more than a hundred places in the papal states that had a Jewish presence, albeit a reduced one. Immediately after the issuance of *Cum nimis absurdum,* a process of expulsion, concentration, and ghettoization began (Luzzati 1987). Jews originally from other parts of the papal states were concentrated in ghettos established in Bologna, Ancona, Ascoli, Imola, and Recanati. With Pius V's issuance of the bull *Hebraeorum gens* in 1569, only the ghettos of Rome and Ancona remained, while Jews were expelled from some fifty towns in which they still lived. Soon after, in 1593, a bull issued by Clement VIII, *Caeca et obdurata,* ratified only the ghettos in Rome, Ancona, and Avignon. When Ferrara came under the dominion of the Church in 1598, ghettos were planned in Ferrara, Cento, and Lugo. They were built between 1624 and 1639, and housed the Jews of Bologna and Romagna as well. Of particular importance was the Ferrara ghetto, where more than 1,500 Jews lived in the seventeenth century. In Modena and Reggio, notwithstanding the plan that existed from the beginning of the seventeenth century to close off the Jews in one area, ghettos were built only in the second half of the century. After the duchy of Urbino came under the control of the Church, small ghettos were established in Urbino, Pesaro, and Senigallia in 1634. Mantua, where there were more than 2,000 Jews in the first half of the eighteenth century (8 percent of the total population), constructed its ghetto in 1612. The area had six synagogues, three of the Ashkenazic rite and three of the Italian. The grand dukes of Tuscany permitted free settlement of Jews in Pisa and Leghorn (Livorno), but built ghettos in Florence and Siena, as well as in small hamlets such as Monte San Savino and Pitigliano. After becoming a free port in 1658, Genoa permitted a small number of Jews to settle, but made them live in a ghetto. Previously, it had alternated between a policy of allowing temporary and limited residency and one of expulsion. The duchy of Milan never had a ghetto. After flirting with expulsion a number of times, it finally expelled its Jews in 1597. Jews had never been permitted to reside permanently in the city of Milan itself. In Piedmont, ghettos appeared much later on: in Turin in 1679–80, and in about twenty other places inhabited by Jews in 1723. Thus, in Piedmont, the concentration of Jews in a small number of ghettos, prevalent elsewhere, did not come to pass. Ghettos were established in the Venetian Republic in Verona, Padua, Rovigo, and some smaller cities between the end of the sixteenth and the beginning of the seventeenth century. It is important to note that the old network of ghettos left its mark on the territorial distribution of Italian Jews. Eighteen of the twenty-two Jewish communities in existence in the 1970s were situated in localities where ghettos had existed at one time or another (Della Pergola 1974).

The institution of the ghetto in the various regions of Italy, including even the Venetian *terraferma,* was based on the Roman and not the Venetian example. With the creation of the Venetian ghetto, the Serenissima had intended to resolve the rather specific and pressing question of the recent presence of Jewish moneylenders within the city's borders. It had not renounced the principles that had kept Jews far from the city until then. This solution offered a compromise, in which segregation actually allowed for a presence that up to that point had been denied (Ravid 1987c). With the bull *Cum nimis absurdum*—which, after all, was itself a kind of compromise guaranteeing Jewish presence, albeit in a rather deteriorated state—the ghetto distinguished itself as a phenomenon that went far beyond simple segregation (Bonfil 1994). In fact, forced enclosure of the Jews in an area reserved for them, surrounded by walls and gates, was something that had occurred in other places, often earlier than it had in Italy. A ghetto was created in Frankfurt am Main in 1462, and similar quarters characterized many other imperial cities. In Spain, the push to enclose the Jews in quarters reserved for them was quite strong throughout the entire fifteenth century. It became the general rule in 1480, when a royal edict imposed a kind of segregation so similar to ghettoization, even in its ideological motivations, that some scholars have adopted the word "ghetto" in this context as well (Kriegel 1979). What distinguished the ghetto as an Italian phenomenon, however, was not only the word with which it came to be universally designated, but its essential ideology, which went far beyond segregation. With the creation of the ghetto, in fact, the Church reaffirmed once again the necessity of a Jewish presence in its bosom. But more than in the past, the Church felt that this presence had to be consciously and methodically subordinated to the glory of Christian truth. The ghetto ended up being the main tool of the conversionist policy undertaken by the Church of the Counter-Reformation. It signaled the invention of an artificial space in which to enclose the Jews while the Church waited for their conversion, within which it was possible to adopt coercive and punitive methods likely to push them into the arms of the Church. The enclosed ghetto ended up being not very different from a correctional institution, enlarged to contain all the Jews (Stow 1986).

Inasmuch as it was a phenomenon typical of Italy during the Counter-Reformation, however, the Italian ghetto was not characterized only by its ideological foundation. Rather, it was also distinguished by the particular communal structure within which the ideological structure operated by means of constriction and enclosure. This structure was characteristic of late medieval Italian Jewish society and remained fundamentally the same within the new confines signaled by ghettoization. Enclosure in a restricted area and the inability to live outside of its gates altered and modified both reality and individual and group perceptions of that reality. This influenced daily life and social organization. It obliged Jews to build strategies of survival and adjustment, and to create new tools for communication and interaction with the outside world. Enclosure in a ghetto could not help but condition the lives of its inhabitants, could not help but represent a real break in continuity. Nevertheless, a strong permanency and a substantial continuity of communal forms of organization marked life in the ghetto. Continuity and abrupt change were both constituent elements of a compacted and unified reality in which even ambiguity and contradictory pushes and pulls were recomposed and reabsorbed. In a certain sense, and this perhaps is the greatest of its ambiguities, the society of the ghetto was characterized by extreme stability.

The ghetto's barriers closed the segregated Jewish street to the pressures of the outside world. Not that they protected the Jews from the institutionalized pressure of a Church poised and ready for converts, but they isolated them from the diffuse and subtle pressures represented by the ideas, the fascination, and the influences of the outside world. Jews may have experienced the walls of the ghetto as the concrete realization of the invisible walls the Talmud had erected to protect and preserve

Jewish identity. The complementary and opposing forces of protection and discrimination thus both shaped the artificial society of the ghetto. The great nineteenth-century German poet and converted Jew Heinrich Heine depicts the Frankfurt ghetto in his short story *The Rabbi of Bacherach*. It was a ghetto with two gates to block access, which for Jewish holidays were closed from the inside and for Christian ones from the outside. This image perhaps sprang from Heine's desire to live simultaneously both within and outside the Jewish world. He lived in the different context of assimilation, of course, but his image still beautifully renders this profound ambiguity.

Jewish resistance to being enclosed was meager and much weaker than it had been against earlier discrimination, such as the obligation to wear a badge. Jews even saw the ghetto as a form of protection, a defense of their lives and identity against the threats of the outside world. Several communities, Mantua and Verona among them, marked the anniversary of the ghetto's enclosure with celebrations and prayers of thanksgiving (Milano 1963).

THE SPACE OF THE GHETTO

Venice erected the first ghetto, which is also the only one in Italy, or for that matter in Europe, that remains practically intact. Its gates were knocked down during the French occupation after the definitive fall of the Republic in July 1797. "So that there should not appear to be a separation between them (the Jews) and the other citizens of this city," ordered the decree of the provisional municipality, "the gates that, in the past, enclosed the ghetto are to be promptly removed" (Calimani 1987: 114).

The enclosure of what was called the Ghetto nuovo was effected in 1516 by putting gates at the two bridges that connected the island of the ghetto to the other islands. These gates were to be closed during the night and guarded by Christian watchmen, paid for by the Jewish community. The outward-facing windows and doors of the houses in the ghetto were to be bricked over and all other external openings closed up. The decree of the Venetian Republic established that Jews could not be owners of the houses they lived in, a law found in every subsequent decree establishing a ghetto. Existing Christian tenants were evicted, and the owners of the houses were authorized to rent them to Jews and to increase the rent by 30 percent. As we can still see today, the Ghetto nuovo opened onto a vast circular square. Shops and the seats of loan banks

were under the arcades of the houses. There were three synagogues in
the Ghetto nuovo: the Scola Tedesca (1528) and the Scola Canton (1531),
both following the Ashkenazic rite, and the Scola Italiana (1571). As
prescribed by law, the synagogues' exteriors gave no hint as to what
they were.

In 1541, when the conditions of overcrowding induced the Levantine
merchants—that is, Sephardim originally from the Turkish Empire—
to ask for better living conditions in the city, the Republic decided to
create what was called the Ghetto vecchio alongside the Ghetto nuovo
(the descriptions "old" and "new" derived from the previous names
of their respective locations). In reality, this enlargement was to house
only Levantine Jews, who had formerly been compelled to live in the
Ghetto nuovo and were permitted to reside only temporarily in the city
(Ravid 1987c). The Ghetto vecchio had two synagogues following the
Sephardic rite: the Scola Levantina, built immediately after the creation
of the Ghetto vecchio, and the Scola Spagnola, constructed in the second
half of the sixteenth century. By the end of the sixteenth century, the
presence of Levantine and Ponentine Jews—Sephardim originally from
the Iberian peninsula, who had lived there as Christians and who could
now revert to Judaism in Venice—was accepted and institutionalized. A
new enlargement in 1633 created the Ghetto nuovissimo. It rose alongside the first two ghettos in a very small area intended only for dwelling,
not for synagogues or shops.

Rome erected its ghetto with great haste in the months following the
issuance of the bull *Cum nimis absurdum*. In October 1555, three months
after the decree, the surrounding walls were already finished. The financial burden of this project, 300 scudi, fell on the Jewish community. The
gates remained open from dawn until one hour after sunset. The quarter in which the ghetto rose, the district of S. Angelo, had formerly been
inhabited by four-fifths of the Roman Jewish population, according to
the 1527 census. But Christians also lived there, and Jews could own
their own houses, although they rarely did. Pope Paul IV's bull required
the Roman Jews to sell their property in very little time and, consequently, at very low prices. Worth about half a million scudi, according
to some estimates, it appears to have sold at a fifth of its market value
(Milano 1988). The institution of the ghetto had a profound effect on
the organization of public religious life. In the first decades of the sixteenth century, there were nine or ten synagogues in Rome. Early in the
ghetto period, there were already only seven, and then five, huddled together in one building in the Piazza delle Cinque Scole: the Temple Syn-

agogue, the Sicilian Synagogue, the Catalan Synagogue, the New Synagogue, and the Castilian Synagogue. The building that housed the five
synagogues existed until the redevelopment of the ghetto. It was replaced by the present synagogue, dedicated in 1904 and known as "the
Great Synagogue."

More than any other, the Roman ghetto came to represent the quin-
tessential image of segregation and discrimination. In fact, it survived
the age of the ghettos. Its walls and barriers were torn down in 1848.
But its gates, so to speak, were opened once and for all only in 1870,
when the unified Italian monarchy brought an end, even in Rome, to the
temporal reign of the popes. This story of the end of seclusion is striking in that the Jews of Rome burst abruptly and without mediation into
the age of emancipation, making a definitive entrance into secular society in an age that had long before seen the end of ghettos in the rest of
Italy and in Europe.

THE SOCIETY OF THE GHETTO

Overcrowding was the most serious and impelling problem that faced
the inhabitants of the ghetto, at least those in the major ghettos of Rome
and Venice. While the area of the ghetto remained constant, except for
slight adjustments, the population within its walls continued to grow. In
the 60,000 square meters that constituted the total area of the three
ghettos of Venice, the average density per hectare went from 461 in
1581 to 897 in 1642. The high point of more than 1,000 came in 1633,
right before the opening of the Ghetto nuovissimo (Calimani 1987: 237).
There was enormous overcrowding. By 1630, population density in the
ghetto was five times that of the rest of the city. The buildings were very
tall, as we can still see today in certain ghetto buildings, and rooms had
low ceilings to allow for the maximum number of storeys. Pope Sixtus V
enlarged the Roman ghetto in 1589, adding the zone of Via Fiumara and
bringing the total aggregate space to three hectares (surrounded by new
walls). But this was not enough to alleviate overcrowding.

But what caused the growth of the ghetto population? Can we point
to an increase in the birthrate, or should we take into account the migratory fluxes—above all within Italy—that changed the distribution of
Jews in Italy during the ghetto period? The Venetian Jewish population,
according to several estimates, reached approximately 5,000 (3 percent
of the total population of the city) in the course of the seventeenth century. This continual rise seems, more than anything else, to be because

of the influx of Polish Jews escaping the Cossack massacres of 1648–49 (Milano 1963).

Sephardic migration to the states of the Church took place in the years immediately after the expulsion of the Jews from Spain, and thus preceded by several decades the establishment of the ghetto. The 1569 bull *Hebraeorum gens,* which allowed the survival of only the Rome and Ancona ghettos, explicitly proscribed Jews expelled from other areas of the papal states from resettling in these two remaining ghettos. We can hypothesize that some refugees nevertheless did enter Rome, an influx that surely increased after Clement VIII abolished these restrictions in 1593.

The population of the Rome ghetto doubled in the period between the censuses of 1527 and 1592, from 1,772 to 3,500. But the percentage of Jews in the total population of the city remained constant, at slightly more than 3 percent. If one takes into account the hypothesis that there was immigration from other cities, these data do not indicate an increase in the birthrate. The varying demographic situation in the Italian ghettos allows for a comprehensive discussion only in general terms. Various factors have to be taken into account, including the death rate, which seems to have been lower than in the surrounding society, except during the ghetto's initial period and several particularly violent epidemics. There were several reasons for this, including, it has been suggested, the observance of laws of hygiene tied to ritual practices and a lower incidence of alcoholism and venereal disease (Bachi 1962; Livi Bacci 1983). Ghetto life does, however, appear to have affected marriage, which was entered into earlier than in Christian life, in obedience to religious law. In the first century of its existence, the Roman ghetto experienced a decrease in the number of marriages, probably owing to the lack of space for the creation of new nuclear families, but perhaps even more to a general sense of mistrust and discouragement (Stow 1992). Given the impossibility of finding a model of demographic development, it can only be suggested that the initial maintenance or slight increase in the birthrate was followed, in the course of the seventeenth century, by a decline, and that the demographic growth of the larger ghettos was more the result of concentration and movement than of actual increments in the birthrate (Harris 1967).

The lack of space profoundly affected the customs and practices of ghetto inhabitants. They responded to the generalized ban on owning property in a most specific way, one that had major importance in the ghetto's economy. Derived from the adaptation of an old instrument of

Jewish law and already in use decades before the establishment of the ghetto, *hazakah* (possession) furnished Jews with a legal basis for the orderly and stable possession of the house in which they lived. In 1604, this became the *jus gazaga,* a kind of right of tenancy—but not of ownership—which could be sold, mortgaged, divided, and inherited provided the tenant continued to pay an annual rent to the Christian landlord. In the seventeenth-century ghetto, even the smallest portions of the *hazakah,* consisting of one room, or just a space for a bed, were sold or passed on to the next generation. Surviving documents convey images of a people forced to live piled one on top of another in conditions of unbelievable discomfort and reconstruct before our eyes the tall houses and low ceilings that were destroyed during the redevelopment of the Roman ghetto at the beginning of this century. The words of an early-seventeenth-century Jew, a witness at a trial for theft, vividly describe this teeming life in the ghetto's limited space:

> I am Banchiere and I live in the same house with Beniamini, from whom, as I told you, I rent my part of the house, and there are more tenants in that house, that is on the ground floor (bottega) where I am there is another tenant, a certain lady called Camilla Betarbo and Elia her son and my nephew, and Mr. Beniamino is in that house with his mother and two small children and an old woman of about seventy or eighty and a boy called Sciamuelle . . . from Ferrara and there are [*sic*] in that house yet another Jew called Lazzaro Abino to whom Mr. Beniamin gave a bedroom. (Feci 1991: 70)

The social organization of the ghetto did not differ considerably from earlier communal life. Family structure and the network made up of neighbors and relatives remained unchanged. The distribution of trades in the Roman ghetto did not change with respect to the period preceding ghettoization, when it had already been characterized by the clear dominance of the used clothing trade and by the practice of a limited number of artisanal trades. If there really was a transformation of ghetto society, it was mainly the result of its progressive and constant impoverishment, determined in large part by confinement. Jewish society confronted poverty mainly by expanding its use of confraternities devoted to mutual self-help. The origin of such voluntary associations is controversial. Many date them back to the model of Jewish confraternities in Spain from the second half of the thirteenth century onward, and in Germany and southern France in the fourteenth century. Others stress the influence of similar Christian societies, which were already widespread throughout Italy at the beginning of the fourteenth century. The study of Christian confraternities in Venice during the sixteenth and seventeenth centuries, the so-called *scuole grandi* (Pullan 1971), as well as the study of one Christian and one Jewish society in early-sixteenth-century Ferrara, appears to emphasize the structural and functional differences between Christian and Jewish confraternities. However, both belonged to the same social context, a context characterized by growing pauperization, devastating effects of epidemics and wars, and the need for new means of resolving or containing the problem of poverty. The first Hebrew society in Italy was the Gemilut hasadim ("Society of Charity and Death"), founded in Ferrara in 1515 and the model that similar confraternities later followed. In the event of illness, its assistance was limited to indigent members of the community. But unlike Christian societies, it oversaw the burial of all the members of the community, not only the poor (Ruderman 1976).

Confraternities left their greatest mark on Jewish community life between 1600 and 1700, when they formed a veritable network that compensated for the privations caused by progressive impoverishment and eliminated a great many of the internal conflicts within the ghetto. The Gemilut hasadim was the oldest confraternity in Rome as well. Established in the sixteenth century, it benefited from the Church's only concession to the laws forbidding Jews to own real estate. The Gemilut hasadim was, in fact, authorized to acquire lands and houses provided they were destined for cemetery use and, from 1645 on, valued at less than 5,000 scudi. Among the chief confraternities in the Roman ghetto were the Talmud Torah, which taught needy children, the Betulot, a dowry-provider for poor young women, and the Matir Assurim, which settled the debts of incarcerated Jews. There were about forty confraternities, both large and small, committed to assisting a wide segment of the ghetto population in the eighteenth century (Milano 1964).

The Roman ghetto became progressively but appreciably impoverished in the course of the seventeenth century, until it reached the nadir of its degradation and indebtedness in the eighteenth (Rosa 1989). All the data from censuses, tax lists, pontifical government and community records, lists of those in debtor's prison, dowry lists, and so on agree, albeit with perceptible fluctuations. The discussion of percentages is a thorny one, because it is difficult develop criteria for a definition of "poverty." According to some estimates, 40 percent of the inhabitants of the Roman ghetto were poor in the last years of the sixteenth century (A. Toaff 1984), a high figure, but not disproportionately so. We have similar data for the European population in general during these centuries (Mueller 1972). This is not a case of an underclass, but of poor

workers: a stratum of the population within society, even though it included beggars and vagabonds. This is confirmed by evaluations of Jews
incarcerated for debts between the end of the sixteenth century and the
first half of the seventeenth. These evaluations involve people who were
poor but not without property, since they were in a position to contract debts of some magnitude (Stow 1986). The Congregation of the
Holy Office "visited" the ghetto's archive in 1734 with the aim of reor-
ganizing the failing financial situation. It labeled 126 families "capital-
ist" and over 700 "poor people," out of a total population of around
5,000 (Rosa 1989). The average estate of the Jews in the ghetto fell from
250 scudi to 15 scudi between 1555 and 1795, with a precipitous decline (from 150 to 49 scudi) in the two decades after the 1682 closure
of banks (Milano 1964: 169). Significantly, the process of pauperization
did not seem to widen the social rift, especially in Rome. In other words,
while the poor became increasingly so, the wealth of the privileged classes
also diminished. In such a situation, the sum of 8,000 scudi that was administered annually by the confraternities could not substantially have
mitigated the condition of the ghetto poor. Nevertheless, the network of
confraternities represented an important element of economic and social
equilibrium and had a fundamental role in the life of the Roman ghetto.

Above all, the fact that charity was only one of its aims distinguished
a Jewish confraternity from a similar Christian one. Private organizations founded by groups of individual supporters (in some cases even by
women) often gathered together members belonging to the same age
group, creating bonds of solidarity and social cohesion. In addition to
the specific social role of easing tensions within Jewish society, the confraternities had a truly religious function. In the Italian ghettos of the
seventeenth century, devotional practices linked to their activities would
assume a more and more important role, increasingly connected to
significant changes in group and individual religious feelings.

THE GHETTO AND THE OUTSIDE WORLD

The Jewish world was not immediately aware that enclosure in a ghetto
represented an abrupt change. Long accustomed to partial and frequently revoked measures, as well as to threats and vacillation, the Jews
were unable to grasp fully the import of the shift in papal policy. Documents of Jewish notaries that refer to transactions entered into after the
bull *Cum nimis absurdum* imposed the sale of Jewish property provide
the first reference to the ghetto. One such document from 1557 men-

tions only that "the pope had ordered that all Jews must live together" (Stow 1990d).

Jews' perceptions of themselves and their relationship with the outside world in the age of the ghettos were ambivalent and contradictory. On the one hand, a fundamental instability colored ghetto life, owing to the precariousness of existence within the ghetto's walls, marked by over-crowding, conversionary pressure, and growing poverty. On the other hand, Jewish identity was unexpectedly strengthened by the clear-cut delimitation of the community's boundaries. These two contrasting per-ceptions coexisted, representing two different aspects of the very same situation and at the same time expressing the basic paradox of the ghetto.

The Roman ghetto is the most significant example of this paradox also because its direct relationship with the pontifical authorities radicalized several aspects of external pressure—from conversionary drives to fiscal and legal harassment—albeit without cutting the kind of umbilical cord that existed for centuries between the papacy and the Jews of Rome. The ghetto experienced a strong and diffuse sense of precariousness, whose profound influence on Jewish life is only now being evaluated from an internal point of view. Individual and group behavior, including ten-sion and frequent brawls, revealed this uncertainty, especially from the early seventeenth century on, when the community's financial situation became more and more precarious. At the same time, natural disasters, above all such terrible epidemics of plague as that of 1656, struck the overcrowded ghettos (Milano 1964; Harris 1967). At the same time, strengthened Jewish identity was manifested by collective and social be-havior indicating a high degree of ease and self-assuredness. Relations between ghetto Jews and converts can be interpreted in this light, dem-onstrating the persistence of social and family ties, albeit with tensions created by an act as radical and definitive as conversion (Stow 1992c). This behavior, along with such breaks in family bonds as are indicated by attempts to skirt the law preventing new converts from being disin-herited by their Jewish families, reveals neither a particular concern for protecting communal religious identity nor the sense that the commu-nity was truly at serious risk.

Several examples can better illustrate this self-confidence. In 1557–58, following the seizure on the premises of the Scola Ashkenazita of a banned exegetical work, the Inquisition launched a serious attack on everyday Jewish religious life, closing three of the seven synagogues in Rome, the Quattro capi, the Scola Nuova, and the Scola Ashkenazita. The synagogues were reopened after many months, upon payment of

a large fine. At the time of the reopening, a bitter legal dispute broke
out between the Scola Ashkenazita and the Scola Nuova, in which each
side blamed the other for the closing and, hence, the fine. How can this
incident be interpreted other than as an indication of enormous self-
confidence? The community went so far as to allow open dissension on
concrete, everyday matters during a situation that, if nothing else, threatened the very survival of Jewish practices (Stow 1990d).

In this case, the dispute never left the communal tribunals. But things
did not always turn out this way. While civil suits only occasionally
ended up in Christian tribunals, criminal offenses, such as brawls and
thefts, normally did so. In 1736, the governor's tribunal condemned and
hanged two thieves accused of breaking into numerous ghetto shops.
Before the executions, the Christian confraternity that ministered to condemned prisoners tried urgently, but in vain, to persuade the two thieves
to convert. It had been more than one hundred years since a Jew had been
sentenced to death in Rome. The Roman populace, accustomed to attending executions as a form of entertainment, speculated as to whether
the thieves would die as Jews or Christians. Excitement ran high in the
city, and only the deployment of troops on the morning of the executions kept the mood from degenerating. Accustomed to measuring the
mood of the populace, the authorities rejected the confraternity's request to postpone the executions so that greater pressure could be applied on the two Jews. From the point of view of the civil authorities, the
matter had to be resolved quickly. The Jewish community, however, also
had to be aware that such an event put all Jews at risk. Thus, it seems
quite probable that the community itself denounced the two thieves, obviously prompted by the impossibility of turning to other than outside
tribunals (Foà 1987). This denunciation is emblematic of the ambiguity
of the ghetto. Enclosure itself confirmed the relationship with the outside and molded the connection between the Jews and the Christian
world.

When Jews confronted the surrounding culture, the result was even
more ambiguous. In fact, the ghetto's well-defined physical barriers paradoxically facilitated the absorption of this culture (Bonfil 1988a). Cultural life in all the Italian ghettos underwent a lively and rapid transformation. Not only the Venetian ghetto, with its singular culture, but
those of Mantua and Modena as well, were centers of intense publish-
ing activity, open to theater, music, poetry, and literature in addition to
traditional studies. Moreover, a considerable part of this literature
was no longer in Hebrew but in the vernacular, a sign of both a decline

in the knowledge of Hebrew and a deliberate decision to adopt Baroque cultural forms (Bonfil 1988a). Spawned by this openness, interest in Cabala spread. Particularly in the Lurianic version, Cabala's intrinsically Jewish character and its stress on symbolic interpretation permitted the new scientific and rationalistic ideas of the late sixteenth and seventeenth centuries both to be freely reinterpreted and to become part of the traditional Jewish framework. Paradoxically, the more Jews were cut off from the world, the more some of them were able to keep up with its transformations.

This took place even at the devotional level. An outdoor ritual called *tikkun,* whose cabalistic meaning was "intervention by means of *kavvanah* [devotion] in cosmic processes," achieved wide popularity in the seventeenth and eighteenth centuries. With the help of the confraternities, this ritual took place outside the synagogue (Bonfil 1988a: 24). Its most widespread form, the *tikkun hatzot,* consisted of nocturnal prayers of mourning for the destruction of the Temple recited on the eve of some holidays. A vigil of prayer and study, it ushered in nocturnal devotion of direct cabalistic derivation unknown in the preceding centuries. It thus paralleled the analogous preference for nighttime prayers that characterized Christian religiosity in the Baroque age. It was in this period that the practice of a nocturnal vigil on the eve of a child's circumcision spread throughout the Italian ghettos. Characterized on the one hand by festivities and on the other by a dedication to prayer and study, these rites gradually prioritized the former (Horowitz 1989b). Moreover, at the end of the seventeenth and beginning of the following century, confraternity devotions in the Italian ghettos began to take place at night. This change in devotional hours was encouraged by the use of a new drink considered a strong mental stimulant able to produce the lucidity necessary for nighttime studies: coffee (Horowitz 1989a). As with its previous appearance in mystic Islamic sects in the sixteenth-century Ottoman Empire (Saraçgil 1989), coffee's introduction in the Italian ghettos was connected to mystical devotional forms, in this case cabalistic.

Doubtless, the changes in ghetto life introduced by the diffusion of cabalistic culture and new forms of religiosity went very deep and led to a different definition of sacred and profane space. They even prompted a change in the relationship of the individual to tradition, communal organization, and his own capacity for religious and cultural initiative (Bonfil 1988a). The problem of the relationship between these internal changes in the cultural Jewish world and openness to the outside world, however, remained unresolved. Moreover, did these changes lead to transformation? Or, especially in their widest social diffusion, did they serve to reassure the ghetto population and represent an urge to project onto a mythic messianic future their hopes and frustrations? Finally, in the long run, did the ghetto walls rather help interrupt the process of cultural exchange with the outside that had always been, in various forms, an essential component of the dynamic of Jewish life? Notwithstanding the cultural richness of ghetto life, did they create the conditions for a growing cultural marginalization of the Jews? Thus, while the existence of communities permitted the Jews, in the period preceding the ghetto, to "control their own space," after the ghetto, "the space would control the Jews" (Stow 1990d). From the second half of the seventeenth century on, in fact, ghetto cultural life stagnated. With some exceptions (Sermoneta 1989), the Jewish world, which had responded to the enclosure in the ghetto with great creativity, now seemed unable to create instruments that allowed it to adapt itself with the same creativity and cultural autonomy to life outside the ghetto. In Rome, this took place in a particularly distinctive way. It is not by chance that travelers and observers—including Ferdinand Gregorovius in 1853—have handed down to us an image of the Roman ghetto in its last decades characterized not only by poverty and enforced and perpetual backwardness, but also by passivity. Hence, the opening of the ghetto had a violent impact on the Jewish world, and ghetto society confronted the modern world with great difficulty once outside its gates.

CHAPTER SEVEN

The Modern Era

Exodus and Return

The nearly two centuries between the expulsion of the Jews from
Spain in 1492 and the sensational appearance of the false messiah
Shabbetai Tzevi in 1666 constituted a period of change and transformation for the Jews of Europe. The exiles from Spain dispersed around
the Mediterranean toward the Ottoman Empire, while those from Portugal created busy commercial trade routes, giving life to such important
Jewish communities as those of Leghorn and Amsterdam and establishing the first centers of a renewed Jewish presence in England and France.
In the same period, Italy and Germany expelled the Jews or enclosed
them in ghettos. Driven from Germany by violence and war, Jews relo-
cated to the East, in Poland and Lithuania, radically transforming the
geography of their European settlements within the space of a century.
Three distinct areas were thus defined: one characterized by immobility
and insularity, and the other two by mobility. The latter two, however,
were markedly different from one another. One was Sephardic, and its

mobile quality derived from international commerce, cosmopolitanism, and the movement of merchants and capital. The other was Ashkenazic and was characterized by migration and settlement in new lands where Jews were afforded a greater chance of survival both by entering into new occupations and by dispersing in many small villages. (This new pattern replaced the Jews' previous tendency to concentrate in cities and larger settlements.)

But how did Jewish history relate to that of the outside world during this period? How did the events that radically transformed the political, economic, and religious structure of Europe influence Jewish history? To what extent were Jewish change and continuity dependent upon these events? Finally, is it possible—as has been suggested—to attribute the change in Jewish fortunes to the formation and secularization of the modern state, in short, to the predominance in governmental policies of economic and mercantile interests over religious and ideological ones (Israel 1985)?

The transformation of the European Jewish world in the sixteenth and seventeenth centuries was undoubtedly related to changes in the surrounding world, but the complexity of the interaction between the two defies general categorization. Why, for example, were some states inclined to readmit Jews, while both the sovereigns and the people of others continued to entertain the idea of expulsion? Despite transformations in the Christian religious universe, the overlap of politics and religion remained the decisive factor in guiding the relations between Christian states and the Jews. There were also numerous elements of continuity with the past. Many features of imperial Jewish policy, for example, were a legacy of the age-old relationship that had bound Jews to their sovereigns since the Middle Ages. The introduction of Roman law in Germany was a concrete sign of continuity much more than of rupture, offering a starting point and solid juridical justification for the maintenance of a Jewish presence. Other elements seemed decidedly more innovative, including the transformations connected to the dissolution of religious unity in the Christian world, with their political and religious consequences. Innovation also stemmed from economic necessities that emerged over centuries of religious warfare, in which Jews ended up assuming an essential role, supplying liquidity to the warring countries and provisioning the troops. This was a complex age, pervaded by contradictory impulses. The generalized trend of Jewish expansion in Europe was rooted in a complicated intermingling of age-old criteria that had regulated Jewish existence in the past with a new set of emerging values.

THE JEWS IN GERMANY

Whereas growing tensions resulting from Jewish presence led to the radical and definitive outcome of expulsion in many parts of Europe, sporadic violence and a succession of local expulsions and readmissions, not a general and definitive expulsion, characterized the history of the German communities between the fourteenth and sixteenth centuries. The situation stabilized somewhat following the catastrophic Black Death, and the Jewish communities of Augsburg, Ulm, Nuremberg, Mainz, and Worms soon reconstituted themselves in the second half of the fourteenth century after having been destroyed in the wave of pogroms in 1348–49. This lull was followed, in turn, by new violence and repeated expulsions during the fifteenth century, including the massacre and expulsion of the Viennese Jews in 1421 and expulsions from Linz, Cologne, Augsburg, Bavaria, and Moravia in succeeding decades. It was, however, at the end of the fifteenth century and in the first decade of the sixteenth that a campaign for expulsion spread, leading to the eviction of Jews from much of Germany and Switzerland: from Geneva in 1490, from Mecklenburg and Pomerania in 1492, from Halle and Magdeburg in 1493, from Lower Austria, Styria, and Carinthia in 1496, from Württemberg and Salzburg in 1498, and from the free imperial cities of Nuremberg and Ulm in 1499. After serious uprisings in Berlin in 1500, Jews were driven from Brandenburg in 1510, from Colmar, Mulhouse, and Obernai in 1512, and from Regensburg in 1519.

The expulsions thus seemed to spread like an ink blot, although many of these evictions were temporary and the lack of a central power made general implementation difficult. In Cologne and Mainz, the prince-bishop permitted Jews driven from the cities to remain in the countryside or in smaller towns. Shortly after the Jews of Brandenburg were exiled because of a charge of host desecration, its elector proclaimed them innocent and readmitted them to most of the cities in the electorate. Until the Reformation, the campaign for expulsion in the cities seems to have originated for the most part with lower-level clergy and friars. The princes, on the other hand, continued to exercise restraint and tried to maintain traditional policies. Moreover, imperial protection consistently safeguarded Jewish residential rights and personal safety through all the radical changes and permutations of the political scene. This protection was all the more significant for having emerged unscathed from the reunification of Spain and the Empire under Charles V.

The outbreak of the Lutheran Reformation added complexity to the situation. Luther's position on the Jews was one that could have been interpreted initially as a change from traditional Catholic doctrine in favor of the Jews (Ben-Sasson 1971). It was clear from the 1530s on, however, that its roots were to be found in the Pauline tradition expressed in the Letter to the Galatians. In his searing polemics against the Sabbatarians—members of an Anabaptist sect widespread in Moravia that observed the Jewish Sabbath—Luther, in fact, adopted a position very similar to that of the Franciscans in their attacks on Jews. Moreover, like the Franciscans, he called for the Jews' expulsion (Stow 1982; Oberman 1983). Josel of Rosheim, the leader of the German Jews, tried in vain in 1536 to get him to change his mind.

Josel was a key figure in the relations between the German Jewish communities and the Empire. Appointed leader of the German Jews in 1503 by Maximilian of Hapsburg, he retained this preeminent position during the reign of Charles V. His memoirs help us understand what imperial protection really meant in Germany at this time. Threats of expulsion, actual expulsions, and accusations of ritual murder and sacrilege fill the pages of his memoirs, without the slightest sense that these events were exceptional. Before Josel's birth in 1471, three of his uncles had been burned at the stake in Endingen, and his father saved himself only by fleeing. Almost all his family's belongings had been pillaged in 1473. In 1476, in the midst of these years of violence and massacres, his parents had been forced to live for a year hidden in a forest in Alsace. Josel himself had been imprisoned on a charge of ritual murder in 1514, although he had been found innocent and released after several weeks.

As leader of the German Jews, Josel of Rosheim was often forced to intervene to protect Jewish communities from violence and expulsions in the climate of social and political instability created in Germany at the beginning of the Reformation, from 1520 on. During the peasants' uprising in Alsace, he was able to ward off violence by going to the convent of Altdorf to negotiate with the leaders of the insurrection, who threatened to slaughter the Jews. When the elector of Saxony decided, at Luther's urging, to evict the Jews in 1536, Josel tried in vain to have the order stayed. In 1542, however, he succeeded in having the expulsion of the Jews of Prague and Bohemia revoked. Engulfed in the battle between the Reformation and the Counter-Reformation, Jews were caught in a very difficult situation, in which imperial protection naturally represented a guarantee of safety far superior to that offered by the Lutheran states. The policies of the Lutheran princes elicited fear among the Jews and together with their centuries-old tradition of loyalty to the political power—in this case, the emperor—pushed them to side with the Hapsburgs. In 1546, German Jews prayed daily in synagogue for the emperor's victory, even in the free imperial city of Frankfurt, part of the Protestant coalition in the League of Schmalkalden. At the diets of Augsburg in 1530 and Speyer in 1544, Charles V had for the time being reconfirmed Jewish privileges, and at Regensburg in 1546, he had enlarged their scope. Even as the Jews ended up supporting the Hapsburgs, the Lutheran states continued to expel them: from Thuringia in the 1540s, from the duchies of Brunswick, Hannover, and Luneburg in 1553, from Brandenburg in 1573, and from a large part of Silesia in 1582. In 1572, the synagogue of Berlin was sacked. Jews were not, however, driven from the ecclesiastical states that made up about one-fourth of the entire German territory, nor from most of the Hapsburg hereditary possessions, such as Bohemia and Moravia. Hence, the Lutheran states, along with the cities, were in the vanguard of the expulsion process.

Around 1570, the wave of expulsions seemed to have crested. Jews were invited back to some of the areas from which they had been exiled, even settling in such regions as the northern coast, where they had previously maintained a meager presence. The growth of a significant community in the port city of Altona was particularly important. Even the city of Hamburg, which had never accepted Jews in the past, permitted a group of Portuguese to settle there in 1590, although it continued to ban German Jews. In the seventeenth century, the Portuguese community of Hamburg would become the second largest Sephardic community in northern Europe, trailing only that of Amsterdam. In 1582, a general synod of the German Jews sanctioned the reorganization of the German communities. Among other things, it established five main rabbinic courts, one of which was to be in Frankfurt, where Jews had lived in a ghetto since 1462. The Jewish population of the city, maintained until the second half of the sixteenth century at several hundred by a tightly controlled municipal ordinance, reached 3,000 in 1613, 15 percent of the total population. The expansion of activities open to Jews, particularly in the field of commerce, played a principal role in this growth.

What happened to the Bohemian Jews in these years is particularly significant. A hereditary territory of the Hapsburgs, Bohemia had experienced an increase in violence and pogroms during the reign of Ferdinand I, encouraged by the sovereign himself and culminating with the expulsion of the Jews from all the cities of the crown except Prague at the middle of the century. Even in Prague, pressure from the municipal authorities had led in 1557 to a measure of expulsion. Despite its somewhat incomplete implementation, it drastically reduced the size of the community. When Maximilian II ascended the throne in 1570, there were only 413 Jewish families in all of Bohemia, a total of about 2,000 persons. The new sovereign canceled the Bohemian expulsion and granted the Jews of Prague permission to reside in the city indefinitely. His successor, Rudolf II—who also reconstituted the Vienna community during his reign—went even further in 1577, conceding additional privileges and guarantees against expulsion that led to a remarkable economic and demographic growth for the Jews of Bohemia. In Prague alone there were 3,000 Jews in 1600, and in the space of a few decades the community became the second largest in Europe (the largest was that in Rome). This strong demographic spurt was nourished by Rudolph II's liberalization of the professions, which widened the range of commercial opportunities for the Jews of Prague. Additionally, it opened the door to Jewish artisans and craftsmen, especially in goldsmithery, which had previously been a monopoly of the Christian guilds.

Rudolf II's reign during the years when Prague was the seat of the imperial court was a very special time in the life of the Jews of the city. They lived in an area called the Jewish city, a quarter surrounded by walls older, according to legend, than the city itself. Of this ancient Jewish quarter, only five synagogues, the town hall, and the cemetery are still standing. The rest was razed to the ground in the course of urban renewal in 1893, although it survives in the descriptions of poets and storytellers. The cemetery is extraordinary, crammed with tombstones covering innumerable layers of graves. According to legend, they are ancient, but in reality the oldest gravestone, that of the rabbi and poet Avigdor Caro, is only from 1439.

This world of close cultural exchange, over which, however, pogroms and expulsions continued to cast a shadow, was destined to fade quickly. (Not accidentally, stories of pogroms and expulsions reverberate obsessively in popular Czech legends of this period [Ripellino 1994].) In 1620, the battle of the White Mountain would destroy Bohemian culture and the refined court of the Elector Palatine, but not Bohemia's Jews. Mindful of traditional imperial protection of the Jews, Ferdinand II ordered that the Jewish quarter of Prague be spared. It survived intact the destruction inflicted on the city by Hapsburg troops.

The Thirty Years' War does not appear to have seriously interrupted the demographic growth of the German Jewish communities. Not that the general crisis left the Jewish world unscathed. Indeed, war, insecurity, and epidemics did not spare the Jewish quarters, driving Jews to take refuge in walled cities from the plundering troops (Baron [1937] 1969, vol. 14). And many Jews set out for Poland, Holland, and Switzerland, leaving behind a Germany in the throes of the most serious crisis in its history. But the imperial armies and the Swedish and, later, French occupying troops were in many instances ordered to safeguard the existence and security of the Jewish communities. The role of the Jews as wartime suppliers had, in fact, become vital. Without the provisions guaranteed by their commercial networks, the troops would have been left without horses and rations. Had it not been for the contributions of the Jews, the imperial and Swedish troops would have lacked the cash to pay for the supplies necessary to carry on the war. These contributions were more or less imposed on the communities by the parties in battle, who had only protection to offer in exchange. In many German cities and zones, therefore, Jews entered new fields, and their communities consequently grew in number and size (Israel 1985).

A new wave of violence and expulsions, however, struck the German Jewish world in the years between the end of the Thirty Years' War in 1648 and 1670. The cities were again in the vanguard of this movement, while the Hapsburg defeat in the war brought about a crisis in traditional imperial protection of Jews. In this climate, 4,000 Viennese Jews were expelled in 1659. The expulsion was demanded by the city council and the clergy, and the emperor sanctioned it this time as well. It was short-lived, however. By 1673, in fact, the situation had already been resolved almost everywhere, even in Vienna, where the Jewish community was reconstituted at the end of the 1670s, although in a weakened and reduced state compared to its flourishing during the first half of the century.

One might hypothesize that in the long run the rupture in Christian religious unity and the forced acceptance of a plurality of confessions in the Christian world after the religious wars would have made the difficult job of maintaining a Jewish presence in the various states more feasible (Ben-Sasson 1976). But in reality this maintenance of Jewish presence had very little to do with the new concept of tolerance being developed in this period. In fact, the man who was called the father of religious tolerance, Erasmus of Rotterdam, had immediately excluded Jews from this right. And although Luther had fought for a religion free from ecclesiastical intervention, he had invoked repressive measures and expulsions against Jews. In reality, Germany was characterized by adherence to traditional models of behavior, despite war, despite the examples of Spain and Portugal, and despite the Roman Church's new policy. In many ways, the emperor who protected German Jews and the princes who allowed them to reenter their territories were little different from Rudiger of Speyer, who in 1084 invited the Jews to settle in his city to increase its commercial importance. Naturally, seventeenth-century Germany, with its organizational infrastructure of city governments and commercial guilds, was quite different from the Germany of the eleventh century. But this difference implied modifications, rather than radical changes, just as the emergence of the particularly important seventeenth-century Jewish financiers known as court Jews only marginally changed the social status of the Jews in general. For 600 years, the Jewish presence in Germany was characterized primarily by a pattern of alternation of settlement followed by expansion, pogroms, and contraction. The German experience, moreover, was unique because, unlike Italy and Spain during the same period, Germany never attempted to convert the Jews, at least not on a large scale (neither, perhaps, did Luther in the first years of the Reformation). Consequently, Germany never had a converso problem.

THE PORTUGUESE DIASPORA

The German Jews, moreover, were not acquainted with that truly unique phenomenon experienced by the Jews of the Iberian peninsula: an explicitly ethnic Diaspora. This was a Diaspora "of the nation," involving not only open Jews but also all those who, although baptized, were searching for a way back to Judaism and to the open expression of their religious beliefs. Hence, in the first half of the sixteenth century, a constant flow of Spanish Jews migrating to the East traversed the Mediterranean, seeking refuge and protection from Spanish, Sicilian, and Neapolitan expulsions. Formed mainly by open Jews, who had refused baptism and were therefore subject to expulsion, this migratory wave also included conversos driven to test the waters of the East or the safer Italian states by the fears unleashed by the Spanish Inquisition's repressive measures against new Christians (Kamen 1988). The first wave of emigration from Spain and southern Italy was followed, after the mass conversion of the Portuguese Jews, by a second, more expansive and prolonged wave, whose ebb and flow was determined by the alternating concessions of the Portuguese monarchy. First the king would open the borders and allow the exodus of new Christians; then he would close them, making any attempt to leave perilous and clandestine.

This migration overlapped and merged with the world of commerce and the demands of trade, in which the Portuguese soon occupied a position of extreme importance. After 1530, commercial trade routes linking the Ottoman Empire to the West via the Balkans were "directed by and in the hands of Levantine Jewish merchants," as the Venetian Senate wrote in 1541 in instituting the Ghetto vecchio for the Levantines, Portuguese who had already emigrated to the East (Ravid 1987c: 250; Arbel 1988). Their commercial destiny took them all over the Mediterranean before they disembarked in a country where they could revert openly to Judaism. A multitude of strong ties molded the Portuguese into a sort of cosmopolitan class that was able to move easily throughout the Mediterranean and to mediate between different universes (Toaff and Schwarzfuchs 1989). Documents repeatedly recount stories of lives divided by incessant voyages, of separated families, of people with two names, and of frequent passages back and forth between Judaism and Christianity. It is difficult to determine where the religious impulse to reclaim one's Jewish identity ended and the mundane instinct to consolidate both family fortunes and the "nation" began. A Portuguese interrogated by the Venetian Inquisition in 1555 as to whether he valued "his faith or his possessions" responded: "My faith, but after my faith, I want to have my possessions, so that I can live" (Ioly Zorattini 1980–94, 1:260).

Contemporaries of the new Christians from the Iberian peninsula called them "Portuguese," and they then adopted this term to define their geocultural origins. But this label obscured another, more ambiguous, definition of their complex religious identity, that of "Marranos." A derogatory term—in Castilian it means pig, and the Arabic equivalent *mahran* means prohibited—it was already in use in Spain at the end of the fourteenth century to designate converts. Strictly speaking, the word "Marrano" signifies a Spanish or Portuguese Jew who had converted to Christianity but secretly continued to profess Judaism. The name refers, therefore, to an actual historical experience, beginning with the conversions of late-fourteenth- and fifteenth-century Spain. After the expulsion of the Jews, this experience was characterized by well-defined forms of religious behavior based on the dissimulation of a prohibited adherence to Judaism and the simulation of a false membership in Christianity. The Marrano experience has elicited questions and discussions and has given rise to a legitimate "Marrano question" (Netanyahu 1966). Were there really many conversos who continued to practice Judaism, or, to use a term of the Inquisition, "to Judaize"? Was this not, for the most part, exaggeration on the part of an Inquisition intent on seeing a Marrano in every converso? Taking into account that the pressure to assimilate ended up erasing the memory of Judaism in most new Christians, it is impossible to identify all converts with crypto-Judaizing. Yet there is, in fact, much evidence of far-reaching attempts to conceal religious identity in the converso world, not the least of which is the fact that such important Jewish communities as those of Amsterdam and Leghorn issued from the return of hundreds of Portuguese to the public profession of Judaism.

We do not know exactly when the spread of Marranos in the Mediterranean began. Several signs, including the widespread use of the term "Marrano," point to a very early presence. At times, this expression was even used mistakenly as a synonym for the word "Jew"; at other times, it was used appropriately. When the ecclesiastical chronicler Sigismund de' Conti wrote in his *Historia* that the epidemic of syphilis that struck Europe for the first time in 1494 had been brought to Italy by exiled Spanish Marranos, for example, was he really attempting to attribute responsibility for the illness to the Jews driven from Spain (Foa 1990)? Whatever the size of this late-fifteenth-century Marrano Diaspora, it soon intermingled and melded with the broader and more massive movement of 1492 exiles. Only in the first decades of the sixteenth century did the Portuguese join this migratory wave, changing its complexion and making possible the outside world's identification of Marranos with Portuguese conversos.

The principal destination of these migrations was the Ottoman Empire. By 1492, the Turkish sultan had already invited Spanish exiles to settle there, and refugees found a warm welcome and wide-ranging professional and commercial opportunities. To reach the Ottoman Empire meant to find freedom and security again. "Turkey is a land that lacks nothing and where, if you wish, all shall be well with you, . . . Here every man may live in peace under his vine and his fig tree," wrote a German Jew living in Edirne in the first half of the fifteenth century, comparing the situation under Islam to that in Germany (Lewis 1984: 136). Conquered by the Turks in 1430 and developed into one of the chief cities of the Ottoman Empire, the Greek city of Salonika was not yet inhabited by Jews in 1478. Between 1520 and 1530, however, its Jewish population rose to more than 50 percent of the population, and by 1613, to 68 percent. According to census registers of Istanbul, the Jewish population of the capital rose from 1,647 to 8,070 families between 1477 and 1535. The geometric growth of the population within a very limited number of years probably reflected internal migrations as well. Given the use of the *surgun* (a forced transfer of groups within the population), which was employed frequently by the Ottomans to create Jewish settlements in recently conquered Christian cities, these migrations were not always voluntary (Lewis 1984). Even so, the immigration of Spanish and Italian Jews, and of Portuguese Marranos, to the Ottoman Empire was very extensive.

At the end of the sixteenth century, paradoxically, Spain itself became a land of refuge for Portuguese Judaizers, especially between 1580 and 1640, when Portugal was annexed by the Spanish crown. Particularly after the death of Philip II, the duke of Lerma's policies favored Portuguese immigration to Castile by enacting a series of liberalizing concessions and economic incentives to attract Portuguese merchants and financiers. In the space of several decades, the importance of Portuguese Jews in Castilian commerce increased considerably, as did their economic function in the Spanish colonies of the Americas. Spain, naturally, continued to prohibit the presence of Jews and to subject new Christians to the jurisdiction of the Inquisition. But in the first half of the seventeenth century, the Spanish Inquisition was far less concerned with Judaizing than its counterpart in Portugal. With the Spanish Inquisition's renewal of trials and other activity after 1645, this migratory flow ebbed and a new wave of Portuguese Jews flowed from Spain to Holland, England, and Germany.

Italy, where the Inquisition exerted much less pressure than in Spain and Portugal, naturally represented an obligatory stop on the road to the East. Originally fulfilling the need for transitory refuge, stays in Italy could often become prolonged and then permanent. This took place, for example, in Venice. The presence of Spanish Jews there appears to date from as early as the beginning of the fifteenth century. The presence in Venice of "new Christians who keep the rites and customs of Jews" is also documented from the second half of the century on. The tensions provoked by their presence led, however, to a 1497 Senate decree calling for the expulsion from the entire territory of the Republic of "all the Marranos from Spain or from other parts" (Ioly Zorattini 1980–94: 1:27). In the course of the century, this policy was attenuated, and in 1541, as has been noted, the Ghetto vecchio was created. It was constructed, in fact, to house Levantine Jews (those arriving from the Ottoman Empire) who were residing temporarily in Venice. These were ex-

Marranos who had already reverted to the open profession of Judaism in the Levant and who continued to live freely as Jews in Venice, albeit within the ghetto. As subjects of the Ottoman Empire, they enjoyed the sultan's protection and therefore did not hide their Jewish identity. Many Portuguese merchants in Venice lived outside the ghetto, however, pretending to be Christian. They were ambiguous characters who, in some cases, repeatedly crossed the boundary between the world of the ghetto and that of the outside, sometimes wearing the "black beret" of non-Jews and sometimes the distinctive yellow hat worn by Jews. A contemporary called them "worse than Jews because they are neither Christian nor Jew." From 1548 on, the Venetian Inquisition focused its attention on these Portuguese (Ioly Zorattini 1980–94). The Venetian Senate issued a new proclamation for their expulsion in 1550, referring explicitly to the preceding one in 1497. The new proclamation was applied, although it did not substantially change Venetian policy (Pullan 1983).

At the end of the 1570s, the Cyprus war resulted in a particularly difficult time for Levantine merchants. The war created in Venice a climate of extreme distrust of Jews in general, who were perceived as allies of the Turks. This led Venice to issue an expulsion decree for Jews of all nations after the victory of Lepanto in 1571. The Republic rescinded this decree shortly afterward, however, and never put it into effect (Calimani 1987). These events marked a clear-cut turning point in Venetian policy. From 1573 on, Levantine Jews were encouraged to settle in the city, naturally in the ghetto, as were the "Portuguese"—referred to as Ponentine—whose presence was definitively sanctioned in a 1589 decree granting them full liberty to revert to Judaism provided they lived in the ghetto as Jews and wore the yellow hat. Although Jews and Marranos enjoyed relative freedom in Venice, this freedom developed slowly, in a context of expulsion threats and inquisitorial trials. The Inquisition in Venice was, to be sure, greatly tempered and strongly conditioned by its relationship with the Republic. Venetian magistrates sat on the inquisitorial tribunal next to friars sent from Rome (Pullan 1983). Above all, the situation remained basically unstable, at least until the 1589 decree, as the boundaries between de facto tolerance and openly sanctioned rights shifted constantly.

The Venetian experience was radically different from that of the new community of Portuguese origin in Leghorn, who were subjected to neither ghetto nor badge. Different as well was the experience of the Portuguese Jews in the Estense dominion of Ferrara. Ferrara had taken in

Spanish Jews in 1493, and during the first half of the sixteenth century, a large Portuguese community had formed there. In accordance with the privilege granted them by Ercole II Este in 1538, renewed and refined in such successive safe-conducts as Ercole II's in 1555, the Portuguese had to declare at the moment of their arrival in the city whether they were Jewish or Christian. They were subsequently obliged to maintain their chosen religious status. If they declared themselves to be Jews, they were guaranteed the right to live according to the laws of Judaism, and any legal action against them for apostasy was forbidden, even if they had previously lived as Christians. The arrest of Joseph Saralvo, a Portuguese who had reverted to Judaism and secretly performed circumcisions in Ferrara and Venice for thirty years, contributed to the turnabout that led the Este to give in to Roman pressure at the beginning of the 1580s, exactly when Venice was liberalizing its policy regarding the Portuguese. Saralvo was taken to Rome and burned alive in Campo de' Fiori in 1583. The apprehension created by this episode rendered Marrano life in Ferrara more difficult, resulting in an exodus of a large part of the community to Venice.

The migration of Portuguese was determined not only by the need to escape the Inquisition's surveillance but by economic factors as well. Thus, the freedom they enjoyed in Venice did not prevent Venetian and Portuguese Jews from settling in the Dutch city of Haarlem in 1605. Moreover, in the middle of the century, many Jews left Venice for Leghorn. The foundation of the latter community was perhaps the most significant event in the economic life of the Portuguese in seventeenth-century Italy. Cosimo I Medici of Tuscany had already demonstrated a keen understanding of the importance of Sephardic commerce, inviting Portuguese and Levantines to settle in Pisa in 1548 and 1551, with guarantees of religious freedom. The project for the transformation of Leghorn into a commercial hub of trade with the Levant that would supplant Venice got under way after the Turkish defeat at Lepanto. Nevertheless, the difficulties inherent in the theoretical concession of full religious freedom to the Portuguese and Levantines were considerable; in 1571, in fact, the ghettos of Florence and Siena were forming. Only in 1591, after the regulations governing the Portuguese presence had been liberalized in Venice, did Ferdinand I Medici guarantee "Jews, Turks, Moors and others" the right to "live, dwell, and associate in these afore-mentioned cities of ours, Pisa and Livorno," even though they and their families had in the past lived "outside our dominion dressed as Christians or with Christian names." This was the ordinance known as the *livornina,* which was reconfirmed by a second *livornina* in 1593 (Frattarelli Fischer 1987: 17). Jews thus came to make up 20 percent of Leghorn, a city with a population consisting primarily of foreigners and dependent on the traffic of its port, which by 1655 had become the most important in the Mediterranean (R. Toaff 1990).

The privileges with which Tuscany and Venice sanctioned Portuguese Jewish communities and guaranteed them protection from the Inquisition had a precedent in the first half of the sixteenth century. Privileges conceded by Pope Paul III in the early 1540s, and renewed by Pope Julius III in 1553, had invited Levantine and Portuguese merchants to settle in the port of Ancona (Simonsohn 1985; Cooperman 1987). In this case, it was the popes who safeguarded the Portuguese—formally apostates—from the Inquisition and permitted the free practice of Judaism. Economic motivations linked to the need to develop the port of Ancona and to strengthen its role in Adriatic trade must have been central to this policy. But there were other important factors as well, among them, that the severe criticism of the Roman Curia for the forced conversion of Portuguese Jews in 1497 reemerged in Clement VII's 1533 bull, *Sempiterno regi,* and during negotiations with the Portuguese court to establish the Inquisition in Portugal in the 1530s. Thanks to the guarantees conceded by Rome and restated by the municipality, the Portuguese community was able to prosper and, with it, commercial traffic at the port of Ancona. In 1553, the community included a hundred or so families, was organized in its own communal body, the Universitas hebreorum lusitanorum seu portugallensium, had a synagogue in the Hispanic-Portuguese rite, and was strictly separated from the local Jewish community. The latter was of German origin, but it had been enlarged around the 1540s by Neapolitan and Apulian refugees (R. Segre 1985). The advent of Paul IV in 1555, however, led to a clear-cut change of direction. In fact, the new pope ordered the Inquisition's tribunal to investigate the Marranos of Ancona in order to put an end to the scandalous public profession of Judaism by new Christians. After arrests, escapes, and trials, twenty-five Marranos were burned at the stake in 1556. Even Sultan Süleyman the Magnificent himself exerted very strong pressure in an attempt to have the sentences reversed, since several of those arrested were subjects of the Ottoman Empire. But he was unsuccessful, despite economic reprisals and the serious crisis in international relations that followed.

The dramatic episode in Ancona took place in a situation already full of tension between the Portuguese and Italian communities, tension that Paul IV's repressive turnabout had intensified. The sultan ordered a commercial blockade of the port of Ancona in response to the arrests and sentences. The Italian community, which faced heavy economic losses from the blockade, opposed it in every possible way. Italian Jews opposed just as much the effort of the Portuguese in Pesaro, where they had taken refuge from the Inquisition on the invitation of the duke of Urbino, to take advantage of the Ancona blockade to promote the port of Pesaro. This opposition had a purely religious side. Jehoshua Soncino, an Italian rabbi from Salonika, affirmed in a responsum that "these Jews previously practiced the Christian religion in Portugal, and if they wished to put themselves under the protection of God and practice Judaism, they were not to live in Christian lands, despite assurances received. It was common knowledge in fact and evident to anyone who could reason that the future held a severe punishment in store for them, for having abjured their former faith. They have therefore brought evil on themselves and have knowingly approached suicide" (A. Toaff 1974: 275). For Rabbi Soncino, the Marranos of Ancona, like other Portuguese Jews, lived in a sort of marginal state. Although they had reverted to the religion of their fathers, their lives would forever be marked by risk and uncertainty if they did not leave Christian lands forever. The motives of business and trade that drove them to expose themselves to these risks, and even to travel to countries under the control of the Inquisition, were diametrically opposed to their religious motive.

An extraordinary lack of scruples seems to have been the distinctive feature of many of these figures, at least the most important. Let us consider one of the great sixteenth-century families, the Mendeses (Roth 1947 and 1948; Kellenbenz 1987). The two founders of the family fortune, Francisco and Diogo Mendes, were probably descended from the great Spanish dynasty of the Benveniste. At the beginning of the century, they controlled the import of pepper into northern Europe, Francisco from Lisbon and Diogo from Antwerp. After Francisco's death, his widow, Beatrice de Luna, left Portugal and transferred the family business to Antwerp. From Antwerp, the Mendes family also controlled the secret transfer of assets and capital of Portuguese Marranos to the Ottoman Empire. In 1544, the family, by then consisting of Beatrice and her sister Brianda, Diogo's widow, her nephew João Miques, and Francisco's daughter, Reyna, fled the Low Countries, where the Hapsburg court was arranging Reyna's marriage to Charles V's favorite, Francis of Aragon, and settled in Venice. There a letter of safe-conduct allowed them and their retinue to avoid the Inquisition's harassment. Their lives were not, however, carefree, especially after a serious conflict between them prompted Brianda to denounce Beatrice to the Inquisition as a Judaizer. After another transfer to Ferrara, Beatrice arrived in Constantinople in 1553, where she openly reverted to Judaism. In the same year, João Miques, by then Joseph Nasi, married his cousin Reyna. From then on, he would be involved for many years in a whirlwind of political maneuvering. Protected by the Turkish sultan, hated by France, and ambiguously supported by Spain, he was the guiding force behind the blockade of the port of Ancona and took an active role in all the important political and military events of those years. In 1561, he launched a project of Jewish return to Palestine; the Jews were to have settled near Tiberias on land that had been given to him by the sultan. The project failed, as did a subsequent attempt to become the king of Cyprus. In the end, Joseph Nasi received the island of Naxos and its dukedom as a gift from Sultan Selim II.

Just as ambivalent and complex was the life of Righetto Marrano, alias Anrriquez Nuñez, alias Abraham, tried by the Venetian Inquisition as a Judaizer in 1570 and again in 1576 by the Portuguese Inquisition in Lisbon, where he had returned to live. The accused recounted two totally different life stories at his two trials. In Venice, he declared that he had always lived as a Jew and had been born in Ferrara, not Lisbon. If he had admitted that he had been born in Portugal, where there had been no Jews since 1497, he would have been considered a Judaizing Christian. In Lisbon, where the evidence against him was incontestable, he confessed to having been born in Portugal and baptized and to having lived as a Marrano in Antwerp, Tuscany, Ferrara, Venice, and the Levant. Moreover, he asserted that he wanted to return to Christianity. The sentence of life imprisonment was then commuted to a lighter punishment. Thus ended the not in the least exceptional case of a Marrano who passed back and forth between Judaism and Christianity, probably, in the final analysis, not believing in either. In the image used to define another Portuguese tried in the same period by the same Venetian Inquisition, Righetto Marrano was a "ship with two rudders, navigating with one wind with one, and with another wind with the other" (Pullan 1977: 37; Ioly Zorattini 1989).

THE JEWISH COMMUNITY OF AMSTERDAM

The origins of the Jewish community of Amsterdam are closely intertwined both with the war that led to the birth in the late sixteenth century of the Republic of the United Provinces and with Portuguese emigration to the Spanish Low Countries, in particular to Antwerp, the main center of the Portuguese-controlled spice trade and the site of a large Portuguese settlement from the end of the fifteenth century on. Charles V's 1526 general safe-conduct for new Christians arriving from Portugal drew them to Antwerp in large numbers, but trials of Judaizers and attempts to control their religious practices followed. The Portuguese Jews of Antwerp lived so strictly behind a mask of Christianity that when Josel of Rosheim visited Antwerp during those years, he wrote that it was a city without Jews. In 1549, the emperor ordered the expulsion of all Portuguese who had entered Antwerp after 1543, "even if they asserted that they did not leave Portugal due to fear of the Inquisition or wished to demonstrate or prove they were good Christians" (Révah 1963: 124). Opposed by the city authorities, who favored the Portuguese commercial presence, this measure was only sparingly applied and does not seem to have hindered the growth of the Portuguese community. Moreover, in the absence of an inquisitorial tribunal in the Spanish Low Countries, this repressive policy lacked teeth.

The war of independence against Spain, and particularly the blockade of the port of Antwerp in 1595 by the Republic of the United Provinces, caused the collapse of the city's commercial life and the transfer of a sizable number of Portuguese to Amsterdam. It appears that this migration made up at least a part of the original Portuguese community of Amsterdam. Other Marranos arrived straight from Portugal, without encountering any opposition from the Dutch. These refugees were enemies of Spain, persecuted by the same Inquisition that had burned heretics and Calvinists. From the beginning of the revolution, moreover, the States-General of the United Provinces, in an attempt to obtain Jewish financial backing, encouraged the settlement of groups of Ashkenazim in the northeast of the country and in 1577 negotiated with the leaders of the Jewish community at Frankfurt am Main for the transfer of part of the community to Antwerp in exchange for contributions to the Dutch war chest. The ongoing military operations, however, made the project impractical.

The first Jews to settle in Amsterdam were Portuguese, for the most part, followed in growing numbers by Ashkenazim. In 1635, the latter gave birth to their community, and between 1660 and 1673, Polish Jews had their own separate community as well. In the wake of the influx of Ashkenazim, there were about 8,000 Jews in Amsterdam by the beginning of the eighteenth century, 4 percent of the total population (there had been 4,000 in 1650, mostly Portuguese). The Portuguese in Amsterdam at first continued to exercise their traditional role in the spice trade, as they had in Antwerp. But their importance quickly increased thanks to their role as polishers and traders of diamonds arriving from India by way of Portugal. They could devote their energies to this very recently developed trade without encountering resistance from guilds or established interests. In the course of the seventeenth century, the role of Jewish commerce in Holland grew enormously by means of the creation of a virtual commercial triangle with the West Indies for the importation of spices and tobacco.

By the 1670s, poets and historians had already recast the birth of the Amsterdam community in a mythical light. Less than a century after its foundation, they aimed to create the memory of the religious enthusiasm that had led the Portuguese to brave a variety of dangers to reach Amsterdam. But they also intended to create a monument to the founding fathers' difficult reconstruction of religious identity. Born Christian, the founders could not read the Hebrew inscriptions on the door of the Ashkenazic rabbi whom they met in Germany and who would later guide their return to Judaism (Robert Cohen 1987).

The story of the beautiful Maria Nuñes expresses the founders' exaltation in their intense attachment to the faith of their forefathers. Fleeing Portugal, she was captured with her ship by the English, brought to London, and received at Elizabeth's court, where a duke fell in love with her and asked for her hand in marriage. Scorning the enticements of the queen and of love, however, Maria Nuñes asked for and obtained permission to continue her voyage to Holland and return to the faith of her fathers. Several years later, she wed her cousin Manuel Lopes Homem there, "with dancing, music and games" (Robert Cohen 1987: 67). Her marriage was the first to be celebrated in Amsterdam according to Jewish ritual.

Another story recounts that in 1597—1603 in other versions—guards broke into a house where Yom Kippur was being observed, believing they were interrupting a clandestine meeting of Catholics conspiring against the Republic. Only the explanations of Jacob Tirado, one of the Portuguese, finally convinced the authorities that these were not Catholics but Jews. After this episode, even in the absence of public acknowledgment, Jews were able to practice their religion freely and establish the first synagogue in Amsterdam. A mixture of legend and fact, perhaps stories such as the one about the Marranos and their German rabbi guides have more to tell us about the large and varied community of Amsterdam in the second half of the century and about conflicts between

Sephardim and Ashkenazim than about the origins of the community itself. Both Sir Jacob Tirado and Maria Nuñes are, however, historically
documented figures. A ship attempting to escape the Inquisition was actually intercepted by the English in 1597. In addition to five Portuguese
men, there was also a young Portuguese woman in man's clothing on-
board. What the myth leaves out is that several years after her 1612 Jewish wedding in Amsterdam, Maria Nuñes returned to Lisbon with her
husband. They eventually settled in Seville, reverting—at least apparently—to Christianity. Her brother, Manuel Lopez Pereira, had a brilliant career at the court of Philip IV. Other family members remained in
Amsterdam (Israel 1985). The conflicts and difficulties that were created
by the Marrano encounter with Judaism have evidently found neither
space nor, especially, function in myth.

The passage from tacit acceptance of the practice of Judaism to official recognition of public worship—with the concession of synagogues
and cemeteries—was not, however, a foregone conclusion. Indeed, Cal-
vinist reactions—especially in Amsterdam—made this transition difficult. Finally, in 1614, the States-General decided to confront the overall
problem of a Jewish presence in Holland and sought the authoritative
opinion of Hugo Grotius, one of the first great scholars of international
law and considered the founder of the doctrine of natural law. The issue was whether Jews should be allowed to settle in Holland, and, if so,
whether they should enjoy religious freedom, and with what limitations.
Grotius was in favor of maintaining the Jewish presence. In opposition
to the position of many of the city councils and, in fact, to that of Amsterdam, he held that Jews should be given freedom of trade and industry as well. Grotius, however, also proposed such restrictive measures as
a ban on sexual relations between Christians and Jews, the exclusion of
Jews from public office, and a law prohibiting Christian conversion to
Judaism. All these measures were in line with the tradition of justification and limitation of the Jewish presence expressed in Roman law, to
which, among other things, the great jurist made explicit and constant
reference. This was not, therefore, a theorization of principles of religious tolerance or a radical change in the juridical point of view.

Despite these reservations, and despite the prolonged resistance of
many Dutch cities to a Jewish presence, the public practice of Judaism
was authorized in 1615. (Mixed marriages and all polemics against
Christianity were still prohibited.) Even the city of Amsterdam agreed to
allow Jews the free profession of their religion in 1619, which they de
facto already exercised. Legally, the Jews of Amsterdam remained "for-

eigners" until 1657, when the most important merchants were granted citizenship. Amsterdam had by then become the "Jerusalem of Holland," celebrated by writers and poets as a land of liberty for Jews. The great Ashkenazic synagogue was inaugurated in 1671, the Portuguese in 1675. Called the Esnoga, the latter remains one of the largest and most sumptuous buildings in the city. This was the first time European Jews were permitted to build their houses of worship in stone. Until then, laws had imposed strict limitations on the construction and even reconstruction of synagogues, following principles laid down centuries earlier by Theodosius and Justinian in their codes. But here too there was no dearth of protests against these synagogues that rose tall among the houses of Amsterdam. The papal nuncio in Cologne wrote that the Esnoga was a "truly magnificent building of which that vile people are not worthy" (Israel 1985: 220).

The organization of the Portuguese community in Amsterdam had a complex history. In 1618, there were three distinct Portuguese congregations, which united into one large community in 1639. Called Talmud Torah like the Ponentine community in Venice, it was organized on the Venetian model, endowed with broad powers, and guaranteed by the municipal authorities (Israel 1987). This model of one centralized community ended up prevailing over the tendency toward multiplication of community bodies that had previously characterized the Portuguese Jewish world. The new model brought about the union of the existing communities of Hamburg in 1657 and inspired the London Portuguese community to enact constitutional statutes in 1664 explicitly banning the formation of other communities in that city (Bodian 1985). The size of the Amsterdam community and the prominent economic, religious, and cultural role it assumed beginning in the first decades of the seventeenth century easily justified both its incontrovertible political hegemony vis-à-vis the Portuguese of the other Dutch cities and its preeminence in the Portuguese Jewish world.

The Portuguese community of Amsterdam indeed faced difficult problems without precedent in Jewish history. In fact, this community was created entirely by the return to Judaism of Marranos whose families had been baptized for many generations. A people straddling two worlds, they had pretended to be Christian in Portugal or Spain and had imbibed Catholic culture in Spanish schools and universities. Now they had to adjust to a life organized around the rigid observance of Jewish laws. It was not an easy adjustment, and even if they had attempted it with a real desire to eliminate every residue of the Marrano experience, its imprint would have been difficult to erase completely. At first, such outside rabbis as the German Moshe Uri Halevi, the Venetian David Pardo—originally from Salonika—and the Moroccan Jacob Uziel facilitated the return of the Portuguese to Judaism. Many Marranos strongly resisted total compliance with the laws of the community. Some Portuguese lived on the margins of the community, did not pay taxes, and did not participate in communal life. Their link to the Jewish world was exclusively ethnic, and their Jewish identity indeed problematic, an unprecedented phenomenon in the Jewish world (Y. Kaplan 1984). Other members of the community maintained such close ties to their original world that they embarked on voyages to the Low Countries, Spain, and Portugal, where they could not freely practice Judaism and probably had to hide behind a mask of Christianity once more. The community particularly opposed this practice, known as "travels to lands of idolatry." In 1664, it ratified a regulation stipulating that "a circumcised Jew who abandons Judaism and travels to a country belonging to Spain or Portugal, or who practices idolatry in any other place" must, upon returning to the community, be subjected to strict sanctions (Y. Kaplan 1985: 205). Although this phenomenon was necessitated principally by trade and commerce with these countries, it was clearly indicative of the difficulties conversos faced in adapting to the life of the community. The records document cases of individuals who generally returned to Amsterdam after relatively short absences, and who were subjected to communal punishment. But others departed never to return. Between 1644 and 1724, eighty-two members of the Portuguese community were punished for this kind of transgression. Forty-nine of them were not buried in the Portuguese cemetery in Amsterdam, perhaps because they had again departed for "lands of idolatry" or had assimilated into Dutch society (Y. Kaplan 1985).

In such a situation, the community needed tools with which to enforce internal ordinances and regulate its members' observance. The *herem* (excommunication) was such an instrument. Explicitly granted by the civic authorities from the first years of the community's existence, it had a long tradition in the Jewish world. The Portuguese community of Amsterdam strictly reserved its use for the community authorities, the *parnassim*. When, in 1640, Rabbi Menasseh ben Israel claimed that only rabbis had the right to excommunicate, he himself was excommunicated, albeit only for a day, for having disobeyed the community authorities. The herem was essentially a social tool, an interdict that affected community life, social and family ties, and Jewish identity as expressed in ritual and in group bonds. In a situation like the one in Amsterdam, with its fragile religious identity, the use of the herem could just as well lead to the individual's definitive abandonment of the community as to the enforcement of obedience. This explains why the herem was issued frequently but cautiously, and, generally, for brief periods of time. Many different transgressions brought threats of excommunication, including disobedience to the communal authorities and religious heterodoxy—particularly when this was publicly expressed and resulted in the non-observance of the commandments—as well as moral and sexual misbehavior. Of the thirty-six cases of excommunication left on the registers between 1622 and 1683 (these were not all the excommunications issued), only four were definitive (including those of Juan de Prado and Spinoza), and for the most part the others did not exceed six months. In 1683, the town authorities decided to limit the use of the herem. This decision was aimed at circumscribing the administrative and judicial power of the Portuguese community, which had become—according to one of its critics, the Protestant theologian and polemicist Philip van Limborgh—a sort of "republic within a republic."

The problems of adaptation to the practice of Judaism and obedience to communal rules were not the only sources of tension within the Portuguese community. Heterodox circles had actually already begun to form in the first half of the century around Uriel da Costa (or Uriel Acosta), centering after the middle of the century around Daniel de Ribera, Juan de Prado, and Spinoza (with all the ambiguities that the term "heterodoxy" assumes when one uses it to define criticism aimed at a system—i.e., Judaism—free of dogma and sensitive to deviations not from the faith but from the practice of its laws). If Uriel da Costa allowed himself to be subjected to a public abjuration in 1639, of which he has left us a moving but debated description in his autobiography (Acosta 1967; Y. Kaplan 1984), the excommunication of Prado and Spinoza severed all of their ties with the Jewish world and propelled them toward the elaboration of a very radical system of thought based on the rejection of revelation and any personal conception of God. This was soon termed "atheist" by their contemporaries.

Naturally, this heterodox group maintained close contact with the Christian world, especially its heterodox fringe of deists and libertines. They appeared to view religious barriers as destined to fall before the superior demands of philosophy. Orthodox Jewish intellectuals of Amsterdam also maintained a lively cultural exchange with the outside world, however, participating on equal footing in a sort of ideal community of scholars. Their point of view naturally differed from that of the "atheists," being much more attentive to the maintenance of cultural and religious barriers between the two universes. However, despite some limited Jewish measures aimed at avoiding open and explicit controversy between Christians and Jews that could have fallen within the purview of the laws banning anti-Christian polemics, relations were very intense and expressed through public writings, correspondence, and meetings.

Similar though the experiences of Orthodox Jews and Jewish philosophers might have been, their lives took very different turns. Let us compare the journey of Isaac Orobio de Castro, a Portuguese doctor who reverted to Judaism in Amsterdam and a prominent polemicist in defense of rabbinic Orthodoxy, with that of Juan de Prado (Kaplan 1989a). Both their families migrated to Spain from Portugal, taking advantage of the Spanish Inquisition's lesser vigilance. Orobio and Prado met as young men at university in Spain, forced to hide assiduously their crypto-Judaism and new Christian origins. They paid dearly for their double lives: Prado was forced to flee, and Orobio, after having become acquainted with the prisons of Seville, went first to France and finally to Amsterdam, where he returned openly to Judaism. Both came from families that had hidden a deep religious identity and a strong practice of Jewish ritual behind a veil of Christianity. Prado tended toward Deism from his years at Spanish schools, but this did not weaken his attachment to Judaism. Orobio, on the other hand, remained strictly Orthodox throughout his complex journey through life. Both had roots in the Marrano experience, and the profound ambiguities therein led to dire consequences for each.

The heterodoxy of a significant part of seventeenth-century Jewish culture may be considered a product of Marrano dissimulation and passage through different worlds; however, it also resembled the libertine movement and Deist philosophy that emerged contemporaneously in the Christian world. The Jewish world, in fact, was not the only one divided by divergent cultural trends. Christianity too was by then split and in the midst of a severe crisis. Heretical currents swirled across Europe, where the fields of science and philosophy were making rapid progress. It was a Europe poised to exact all possible implications from the critical thinking of the Renaissance and later from the radical criticism of the libertine and Deist currents.

At the end of this process, the figure of Spinoza stands alone. A Jew excommunicated by his people, Christians considered him an "atheist," and his contemporaries viewed him as the very symbol of philosophic impiety and negation of all revelations. Scholars, however, loved and venerated him as a philosopher. For Leibniz, "the Jew of the Hague" presaged "the revolution that was advancing in Europe" (Poliakov 1974b, 2:271). It cannot be denied that Spinoza's roots were deep in the soil of Marrano culture. Born to a Portuguese family who had lived as Catholics in Nantes before reverting to Judaism in Amsterdam, he absorbed the mind-set of that world, perceived its ambivalence, and shared its way of thinking (Yovel 1983 and 1989). By the time Spinoza was born, however, his family had been completely assimilated into the Amsterdam Jewish community. His early education was a traditional Jewish one, and only subsequently, when he frequented the Amsterdam libertine milieu at the school of the ex-Jesuit and freethinker Franciscus van den Enden, did he study Latin and immerse himself in ancient and Christian knowledge and philosophical studies.

Spinoza's journey was therefore different from, if not the opposite of, those of both da Costa and Prado, both of whom went from the Christian world to Judaism (although ideas and behavior usually associated with da Costa and Prado lay at the source of Spinoza's excommunication). His story was nevertheless not unique to the Dutch Jewish world. Spinoza's choice neither to return to the bosom of his community nor to convert to Christianity doubtless represented an element of true innovation in a world in which membership in a church or religious institution was the norm (Yovel 1983). But it was precisely in Amsterdam in the 1680s that some Jews who incurred the sanctions of the community chose to rebel against its authority and to live in the outside world without converting to Christianity. Their choice would compel the Amsterdam Portuguese community to face a situation that the rest of the Jewish world would have to cope with only after emancipation (Y. Kaplan 1984).

THE RETURN OF THE JEWS TO FRANCE

There had been no Jews in the French kingdom since 1394. True, in Provence, the expulsion had taken place much later—on the threshold of the sixteenth century—and Jews continued to live in the region of Avignon (part of the papal states), albeit closed in ghettos (Moulinas 1981). But sixteenth-century France was a kingdom where, in theory, Jews did not have the right to reside. In reality, the first traces of a renewed Jewish presence date back to the end of the fifteenth century, when groups of conversos arriving from the Iberian peninsula settled in

southern and southwestern France even before 1492. Although Jews
were not able to revert openly to Judaism in France, they could live there
as new Christians, far from the surveillance of the Spanish Inquisition.

Not all of the new arrivals were crypto-Judaizers. Fear of the Inquisition and the deterioration of the general climate in Spain vis-à-vis conversos forced even groups or individuals by then resigned to their new
religious identity to consider emigration. This was probably the case with
the Lopez de Villanueva family, ancestors of Michel de Montaigne on
his mother's side, who converted in Spain and found refuge in Toulouse
at the end of the fifteenth century. Most of these conversos, however,
were probably Marranos, as their growing and ever more open practice of Judaism would suffice to prove. In the first decades of the sixteenth century, there was also a heavy influx of Portuguese conversos into
France. The Toulouse Inquisition was alarmed and concerned by the
presence of Marranos. It complained to Rome that the immigrants were
not Christians but Jews, who observed the Sabbath, prayed, and buried
their dead according to Jewish ritual. Despite the apprehension of the
Toulouse Inquisition, and despite sporadic incidents like the one that
took place in 1619 in St. Jean de Luz, when a woman was charged with
host desecration and killed by the crowd, and all the Portuguese were
expelled from the city, it is also true that in sixteenth- and seventeenth-
century France, the presence of groups of converts Judaizing more or
less openly did not create an actual "Marrano problem." Although the
trials of the Toulouse Inquisition in the first decades of the sixteenth
century affected crypto-Judaizers strongly and involved converso Catalan students at the University of Toulouse, they seemed more inspired
by the need to eradicate heresy than by the wish to identify pockets
of Marranism (Mentzer 1982). Thomas Platter, a Protestant medical
student at Montpellier at the end of the sixteenth century, described
Languedoc as a place inhabited by an enormous number of families descended from Jews, who, he maintained, "had arrived from Mauritania
by way of Spain and had settled in the border cities of Montpellier,
Beziers, Narbonne." According to Platter, these converts had "adopted
the customs of all other Christians," but were called "Marranos," in reference, he believed, to the Moors in Mauritania. They were not permitted to hold municipal office and were suspected of preserving Jewish rituals, abstaining from pork, and observing the Sabbath (Philippe 1979).
With its university, Toulouse offered ample opportunities for crypto-
Judaizers. A Portuguese, Baltazar Alvaro, was still able to teach medicine there in the seventeenth century under the name Baltazar Orobio de

Castro before becoming—as Isaac Orobio de Castro—one of the most important members of the Amsterdam Jewish community (Y. Kaplan 1989a).

Interested in developing trade and commerce, the French kings protected the Portuguese from the middle of the sixteenth century on. Henri II granted several families of "Portuguese called new Christians" the right to settle in Bordeaux in 1550, "in order to be employed in our service, to help the kingdom with their assets, manufacturing and trade." At the behest of both the Spanish and Portuguese, Henri III confirmed the privilege in 1574 with a decree that alluded to the controversy stirred up by their presence in the city and forbade anyone "to molest them, maltreat them or force them out of the city and environs of Bordeaux" (Philippe 1979).

The first nucleus of the newly reconstituted French Jewish community did not contain only Spanish and Portuguese conversos. In fact, in the middle of the sixteenth century, a small number of Ashkenazim had already been authorized to settle in Metz, under French control since 1552. The eight original nuclear families had grown to twenty-four by 1595, the year Henri IV reconfirmed their privileges. Guaranteed the opportunity to practice their religion publicly, they organized in an officially recognized community. This was the origin of what was to become one of the premier French Jewish communities (Philippe 1979). During Maria de' Medici's regency, a new edict of expulsion was issued in 1615. Although it mentioned the clandestine presence of Jews in many parts of the kingdom, the edict was directed at Parisian "witches, Jews and sorcerers," and was not applied to the Jews of Metz or to the Marranos of the Bordeaux/Bayonne region (Poliakov 1974b, 1:175–76).

The juxtaposition of Jews and witches was not simply a topos, but rather took its cue from a series of scandals concerning court personages, particularly the queen's favorites, the Italian Concino Concini and his wife, Leonora Galigai. The latter, in particular, was the protagonist of a famous trial in 1617, in which the charge of practicing magic was joined to the false accusation of Judaizing. Maria de' Medici's personal physician, Elia Montalto, was Jewish, however. A Venetian who stipulated the free practice of Judaism as a condition of court service, he was buried in the Jewish cemetery of Amsterdam. The 1615 expulsion edict thus probably came as a reaction to the political climate, growing out of Parisian hatred of the Italian regent. In any event, it remains a mystery, since there were officially no Jews in France in 1615. What is certain is that the parliament of Paris made itself the interpreter of this reaction, asking in 1614 for the expulsion of "Jews, atheists, Anabaptists and others who professed religions not tolerated by royal decrees" (Hertzberg 1990: 12).

The 1615 expulsion decree did not interrupt the process of Jewish resettlement in the cities of the French kingdom. In 1633, there were sixty Portuguese families in Bayonne, eighty in Labastide, forty in Peyrehorade, ten in Dax, forty in Bordeaux, twenty in Rouen, twelve in Paris, and still others in Nantes (Israel 1985). In a 1633 decree, Cardinal Richelieu—whose confidant Alfonso Lopez was "Portuguese"—substantially sanctioned the Portuguese presence in France. Although forced to practice their religion in private, the Portuguese Jews in France had by now reverted almost openly to Judaism, as demonstrated by the fact that Hebrew inscriptions were already appearing on tombstones by 1641. Moreover, they maintained very strong family, matrimonial, and commercial ties with the Portuguese communities in Holland.

The Jewish presence was further strengthened during Richelieu's government and the Thirty Years' War. On the one hand, the Portuguese commercial network—with its close international contacts—proved invaluable in a conflict of such vast scope. On the other, the Jews of Metz played a fundamental role in provisioning the troops and particularly in furnishing horses to the French army. After the French conquest of Alsace in 1638, the same role was played by the Alsatian Jews. Reduced to a few dozen families at the end of the sixteenth century in the wake of local expulsions and a centuries-long decline, they were then in the midst of a rapid expansion. With the annexation of a part of Alsace in 1648, the Alsatian Jews could in theory have been expelled on the basis of the renewed edict of 1615. It was not, however, extended to Alsace and Metz, although expulsion was threatened there as well. Despite strong demographic growth, the condition of Alsatian Jews remained complex and difficult. In 1674, Jews living in upper Alsace, considered a land of perennial French domination, obtained the same rights as Jews in Metz. The Jews in lower Alsace, a land newly governed by France, remained, however, dependent on the local authorities and subjected to discrimination and numerous restrictions. Prevented from owning land and working in most professions, Jews were pushed into the traditional economic outlet of moneylending.

The Portuguese of Bordeaux had to wait until 1723, when the letters patent permitting their residence was renewed, to be openly designated as "Jews, known under the name of Portuguese, otherwise called new Christians" (Philippe 1979). Even Colbert's 1680 decree confirming their privileges had maintained the fiction of membership in the Christian religion. Whereas Colbert's policies had followed those of Richelieu and Henri IV, the second phase of Louis XIV's reign marked a repressive turning point. The expulsion of the Protestants, the war with Holland, and the obsession with religious unity constituted the political and religious premises for a new insularity, in which the specter of new expulsions was present. Eighteenth-century French Jewish history would witness an increasing disparity between the Portuguese of the south and the Ashkenazim of the east. In 1776, the Portuguese obtained the freedom to settle and reside anywhere in the country. At the outbreak of the Revolution, they would be the first to achieve the emancipation that would for some time be denied their coreligionists in Metz and Alsace.

THE REESTABLISHMENT OF THE JEWS IN ENGLAND

The process that led to the reestablishment of the Jews in England in the second half of the seventeenth century was different from the one in France. As in France, there had not been any Jews in England for many centuries. The stereotypes that had fed the climate of expulsion in the thirteenth century, however, were still alive. The image of the Jew thirsting for Christian blood—whether literally or metaphorically by means of usury—which in the Elizabethan period had found expression in Shakespeare's *The Merchant of Venice* and Marlowe's *The Jew of Malta,* reappeared unchanged in the middle of the seventeenth century in the theories of many of those who opposed readmission. This negative mythology, however, was contrasted in the first half of the seventeenth century, and more so in the revolutionary years, with a set of positive myths. Not by chance called "philo-Semitism," these represented a bizarre mixture of millenarian hopes, eagerness for the conversion of the Jews, arguments for tolerance and religious freedom, and intellectual curiosity about Jewish tradition and the Hebrew language (D. S. Katz 1982). There were strong bonds between the intellectual milieu that held these ideas and the Dutch Jewish world, particularly with Rabbi Menasseh ben Israel of Amsterdam, with whom such prominent exponents of English culture as John Dury and Samuel Hartlib traded correspondence and cultural interests. Menasseh ben Israel was born Christian, probably in the Portuguese colony of Madeira. His converso family subsequently migrated to Spain, where it fell into the web of the Inquisition, and went from there to Amsterdam. Coinciding as it did with his strong messianic leanings and interest in Cabala, the world of intellectual philo-Semitism, with its apocalyptic hopes, attracted Menasseh's attention soon after he became prominent in the religious and cultural life of Amsterdam. The attention paid to the Jews by the Christian "philo-Semitic" world was full of ambivalence and contradictory expectations. On the one hand, the philo-Semites recognized the Jews' "election" and their fundamental role in preparation for the advent of the kingdom. Such intellectuals as Isaac de La Peyrère, a French Protestant millenarian and "libertine" who wrote a highly radical work that appeared in 1643 called *Du rappel des Juifs*, developed this point by writing very favorably concerning the Jews. This was a change from the past, when interest in Cabala or Hebrew had never developed into interest in the Jews per se (Popkin 1987). On the other hand, the conversion of the Jews remained the chief objective of all these apocalyptic speculations, even though it often boiled down to conversion to a very "purified" Christianity. In the midst of these conflicting forces, Menasseh ben Israel seems to have assumed the role of spokesman for the Jewish world. In his writings he defined a Judaism that recognized the role of all just people, including non-Jews, in the coming of the messianic world, thereby reassuring the most enlightened Christian circles—the Dutch Arminians and the English sectarians—of the open-mindedness and universalism of the Jews. It was, however, a Judaism also intent on preserving its own religious and cultural identity against any pressure to convert (Mecholulan 1989).

In this context, Menasseh ben Israel developed his project of readmission of the Jews to England. His objective was to annul the 1290 expulsion and have the Jews formally recalled to English soil. He chose, therefore, to push for a recognition of principle, not the gradual extension of the right to worship freely, as in France. (In London, too, there were groups of crypto-Judaizers, "Portuguese," who lived clandestinely. As subjects of Spain and Portugal, they hid behind a mask of Catholicism.) The offensive was launched in 1648–49, with a petition signed by Johanna Cartenright and her son Ebenezer Cartenright, English nationals residing in Amsterdam. They asked "that the cruel and inhuman ban issued against them be revoked, and that under the Christian flag of charity and brotherly love they be allowed to return and permitted to work and live in the land of England, as had taken place in Holland" (D. S. Katz 1982: 177). The petition was sent to the Council of State at the height of the Civil War. Despite the presence of several supporters of religious freedom for Jews, however, the council decided to restrict the concept of religious tolerance to Christians only. A subsequent petition, which narrowly preceded Menasseh ben Israel's arrival in England in 1655, was signed by Manuel Martinez Dormido, a Portuguese who had settled in the Dutch colony in northeastern Brazil and suffered financial ruin as a result of its recapture by the Portuguese. In his petition to Cromwell, Dormido requested that England, Portugal's ally, intercede to help him recover his unlawfully sequestered assets from the Portuguese, and that it readmit the Jews. Dormido lived and did business openly as a Jew in London.

During the struggle between Portugal and Holland in Brazil, and after the fall from office of the duke of Olivares, Philip IV's reforming chief minister, in Spain in 1643 led to a resumption of inquisitorial trials, converso emigration intensified, seeking new outlets in England's New World colonies, particularly in Barbados and throughout the English Caribbean. It is possible that this may have influenced Menasseh ben Israel's project as well. Moreover, although the officers of the Jewish community of Amsterdam did not offer any kind of official support to Menasseh, maintaining a reserve that made sense only in light of their need to safeguard relations with the Dutch Republic, England's rival, this may have been how the Amsterdam community became the spokesman of the Sephardic colonizing drive (Israel 1989). Whatever the dynamic of Menasseh's initiative, it was formulated—as his writings clearly show—from a decidedly messianic perspective, with strong traces of anti-Spanish and anti-inquisitorial politics. The climate created by the Civil War and by Cromwell's dictatorship, which made it feasible in England, was equally religious and political.

The outbreak of war between England and Holland in 1652 delayed the presentation of Menasseh ben Israel's petition requesting the readmission of the Jews. Menasseh arrived in London only in September 1655, carrying a petition for Cromwell, *The Humble Addresses.* It asked that Jews be readmitted to England as citizens and that they be permitted public synagogues and cemeteries, afforded religious tolerance, granted the right to be judged according to their own laws and, lastly, given full trading rights. The first part of his proposal repeated almost word for word many of the mercantilist arguments used twenty years earlier by Simone Luzzatto in his famous *Discorso,* written to persuade the Venetians, who were threatening to expel the Jews, to tolerate their presence because of their economic and commercial usefulness (Ravid 1982a).

The Council of State referred the matter to a commission made up of twenty-eight members, half of them ecclesiastics, the rest merchants and jurists. Inaugurating the sessions on December 4, 1655, of what would go down in history as the Whitehall Conference on the question of Jewish readmission, Cromwell posed the question of whether the Jews should be allowed back into England and, if so, under what conditions. The question immediately proved to be very controversial. Most of the opposition came from the merchants and some of the ecclesiastics. The latter in particular opposed readmission with the most outdated anti-Jewish arsenal. Others, including many ecclesiastics, favored readmission, but also leaned toward a strict limitation on the guarantees of freedom of worship requested by the Jews. Few of the delegates supported readmission unequivocally, despite the fact that the commission had been enlarged after several sessions to admit representatives of the "philo-Semitic" party. Under the latter's influence, the conference seemed for a moment ready to grant all of the Dutch rabbi's petitions. In fact, some of the participants maintained that the Jews had "suffered great abuse, outrages and cruelties" in the course of their history in England, and that it was now the duty of the English to readmit them if they did not want to be struck down by the Lord's wrath (D. S. Katz 1982: 214). With a formulation laden with significance, inasmuch as it would have subsequently opened the way to legalizing a Jewish presence in England, the principal jurists at Whitehall, moreover, expressed the opinion that "there was no law that prohibited the return of Jews to England." But those opposed to readmission prevailed, and the assembly did not express an opinion. Menasseh ben Israel's attempt had failed; England would not become, as the rabbi of Amsterdam had hoped, the center of a new Sephardic emigration.

Menasseh ben Israel's proposal was a principled one. It had formulated the issue of readmission along general lines, leaving no room for compromise or gradual change. It reflected the personal ideas of the Amsterdam rabbi, as well as those of at least a part of the city's Portuguese community and of English apocalyptic and philo-Semitic circles. However, it was much less representative of the policy of the Portuguese of London. There is no doubt that the stir caused by the Whitehall debate helped publicize their Jewishness and permit them to drop a mask that had by then grown superfluous. But the war between Spain and England, which in March 1656 left the assets of Spanish subjects living in England and the English domains liable to confiscation, also helped bring this about. The Marranos of London responded by publicly confessing their Judaism in a petition to the Lord Protector that was signed by the most important members of the group and by Menasseh ben Israel himself. The petition's objective was far more limited than the one expressed a few months earlier in Menasseh's *The Humble Addresses*. It requested a sort of de facto recognition, in short, the maintenance of the status quo. The Jews living in England could henceforth practice their religion without being disturbed and possess synagogues and cemeteries. This situation of de facto tolerance without official sanction lasted until 1664, when Charles II formalized the Jewish presence, despite pressure from the City of London for a new measure of expulsion.

When the statutes of the Jewish community of London were issued in 1664, there were no more than two hundred Jews in the city, all of them Portuguese (Bodian 1985). In the course of the following century, the London community spread, thanks to the growing influx of both German and Portuguese Jews. Until the late eighteenth century, however, no other organized communities arose in England and the role of Jews in the English economy long remained marginal. There was also a high percentage of conversions, especially among Sephardim, who were wealthier and more integrated into general society than their Ashkenazic coreligionists, and who were much more inclined to imitate the customs and lifestyle of upper-class English society (Endelman 1990).

THE JEWS IN EASTERN EUROPE

There were very few Jews in Poland, Lithuania, and the rest of eastern Europe before the sixteenth century: in all, a few tens of thousands, a small minority of the entire European Jewish population. By the twentieth century, the Jews of eastern Europe numbered around seven million, of which three million were in Poland alone. Before the Nazis almost totally annihilated them, the Jews of eastern Europe had become the most substantial part of the Diaspora. Eastern European Jewry had certain features that made it unique, different from the Jews of western Europe. Its settlement patterns were distinctive; its occupations and social conditions were different; and its forms of religious expression were new. Behind these specificities, however, lay fundamental lines of continuity that unite the history of the Polish, Russian, and Lithuanian communities with those of the Jews in the rest of Europe. In particular, these lines of continuity included a shared relationship with tradition, similar forms of communal organization, and a similar relationship with the often hostile world in which the Jews lived.

The slow and prolonged exodus that would lead the Jews, especially the German Jews, to settle in Poland, Lithuania, and, later, Russia, began late in the thirteenth century, when expulsions and massacres caused Jews to move eastward. But this was not the only reason. Some of the first Jews to arrive in Poland belonged to the movement known as Ashkenazic Pietism. They were searching for less crowded spaces in which to practice their particularly rigorous faith. Other Jews followed, attracted both by lands offering ample space on which to settle and other economic opportunities unknown elsewhere. In 1264, Boleslaw of Poland issued a statute—the first of many—that placed the Jews under his direct protection, and under the direct jurisdiction of the kings and the high nobility. This gave them a legal status very similar to that of the Jews in the Empire and the rest of the West. Moneylending was strongly encouraged, and, together with the taxes they paid, made Polish Jews the main source of liquidity for the monarchy and the nobility. It was not, however, until the sixteenth century that the Jews significantly expanded their presence in eastern Europe, first in Poland, Lithuania, and Galicia and, subsequently, in White Russia and the Ukraine. At the beginning of the sixteenth century, the approximately 30,000 Polish Jews were still a very small minority in a population of five million Poles. Less than a century later, in 1575, they numbered more than 100,000, out of a population of seven million. This was a very steep growth, proportionately as well as absolutely. In time, the Jewish population would increase even more, until it had grown to 350,000 at the close of the seventeenth century and 750,000 in 1765 (Israel 1985).

Among the occupations practiced by the Polish Jews, the most typical was the administration of noble lands, a practice known as *arenda* (rent) and widespread from the second half of the sixteenth century on in the territories of eastern Poland. Jews took over estates as tenant farmers or managers who directed the sale of agricultural products for the large Polish landowners, who avoided the direct administration of their landholdings. At least in some cases, Jews thus rented vast estates, even whole cities; they administered the sale of grain and wine, managed distilleries, became involved in the international trade of these products in the Baltic ports, and imported spices and jewels from Holland and Hamburg for consumption by the Polish nobility. Taking advantage of the absence of strong guild organizations and the relative openness of the existing ones, they entered sectors that were prohibited to them in the West, such as artisanship. In the regions of eastern Poland, east of Lublin and Lvov, they had become the chief component of the middle class by the end of the sixteenth century (Israel 1985). The situation was different in western Poland, where strong guilds and an expanding Christian middle class barred Jewish access to both artisanship and commerce and prevented them from settling in those cities, including Warsaw, that enjoyed the juridical right *de non tolerandis iudaeis*. Particularly in the Baltic regions, but also in cities such as Poznan and Kraków, they were subjected to severe restrictions. Although it was not always the case, the settlement of Jews in the East thus followed a pattern unlike that in the West. More rural than urban, eastern European Jews lived in villages and small cities that often ended up having more Jews than Christians.

Into the open spaces of eastern Europe, Jews brought their language, Yiddish—a mixture of German and Hebrew that at the beginning of the sixteenth century began its ascent to a literary form—as well as their model of communal organization. The latter would give life to a sort of institutional pyramid at whose base lay the local communities, the *kehilot,* and at whose apex stood the Council of the Four Lands. With true jurisdictional powers, this council governed the life of the Polish Jews for about two centuries, from the second half of the sixteenth century to the eighteenth century.

Although Jews in the East mostly played the role of middlemen—between the nobles and the peasants and between the city and the country—this does not imply that closer and tighter bonds were created between the Jewish and Christian worlds than existed in the West. Invisible barriers, no less restrictive than the walls of the ghettos, closed off the physical and cultural spaces of Jewish villages; everyday business contact did not imply familiarity or a lowering of social barriers. For its part, the rural Christian world expressed this alienness and diffidence in a pervasive and constant hostility. It viewed the Jew as no less the *longa manus* of the feudal lord than an outsider who spoke a different language, followed incomprehensible customs, and was accused by the Church of having killed Christ. The violent preaching of John of Capistrano had familiarized the fifteenth-century Polish world with the accusations of the most extreme and radical part of the Church. Between the sixteenth and eighteenth centuries, when such charges had almost completely disappeared in western Europe, Poland was the scene of numerous accusations of ritual murder, which often resulted in death sentences and pogroms. Similar accusations would have a very long life in Russia, extending until the first years of the twentieth century.

The most serious incident took place in 1648, when Chmielnicki's Cossacks revolted against the Poles, bringing unprecedented catastrophe to the Ukrainian, Polish, and Lithuanian Jewish communities. The insurrection, which broke out in 1647, provoked a long period of wars known as "the twenty-year flood." Led by Bogdan Chmielnicki, a Cossack chief allied with the Tartars, the insurrection developed in a climate of extreme sociopolitical tension between the Polish monarchy and the Cossacks. Religious tensions between the Cossacks, who belonged to the Orthodox Church, and the Poles, who were Catholic or Uniate (that is, Orthodox recognizing the authority of Rome), contributed significantly to the problem. Moreover, almost the entire Polish nobility was Catholic and owned most of the land in the Ukraine. Religious tensions thus became interwoven with political tensions, and the Cossacks directed their violence against the Catholic clergy as well as the Polish nobility. Jews, however, were the main target of the violence. Ukrainian peasants saw the Jewish tax collectors and tenants of cities and villages as the chief allies of the hated Polish nobility, and those peasants who joined the uprising were particularly relentless against the Jews. Jews fled west and sought refuge in fortified cities, taking an active role in their defense alongside the Polish troops. At the same time, the Cossacks, having crossed the Dnieper, engaged in systematic massacres. They besieged such cities as Lvov, Lublin, and Dubnow, repeatedly defeating the Polish troops and subsequently devastating Galicia, Lithuania, and part of Poland. The Cossacks returned to the territories east of the Dnieper only in August 1648, following a truce with the Polish crown. But the massacres of Jews and the destruction of Jewish cities continued until 1655, albeit with diminished intensity.

Contemporary Jewish sources describe this wave of violence as a great catastrophe; entire communities were destroyed and hundreds of thousands killed. According to recent estimates, the years of the violence left between 40,000 and 50,000 dead (about 20–25 percent of the Jewish population), while about 10,000 Jews left Poland and the neighboring areas to take up permanent refuge in the West (Weinryb 1973). We must include among the refugees those who fled to the West but returned after the violence ended, and those who converted to the Orthodox faith in order to save their lives and were able subsequently to revert freely to Judaism. Polish Jewry was thus struck by a catastrophe of enormous proportions. Nevertheless, the demographic growth of the Jewish world was interrupted for only a brief time, reaching its apogee in the eastern regions of Poland in the second half of the seventeenth century (Israel 1985). The percentage of Jews living in cities there grew, and in many centers Jews became the majority. The process of growth was accompanied, however, by one of pauperization. The social differential widened within the community, and more people engaged in the humblest occupations, such as the ubiquitous ones of itinerant peddler and petty middleman.

Although they must be reevaluated in the light of their socioeconomic significance, the 1648 massacres remained profoundly traumatic in Jewish collective memory, which interpreted them within age-old schemes. As in the massacres in Germany during the Crusades, Jews were attacked for being Jews and could save themselves by converting. Despite the substantially political dynamic behind the Chmielnicki insurrection, Jewish memory viewed it in terms of martyrdom and the "Sanctification of the Name" (J. Katz 1961). The hymn "El Male Rahamim," by Rabbi Sabbatay Horowitz, which religious Jews sang at the moment of their murder in Hitler's death camps, was one of the religious hymns composed to memorialize the Chmielnicki martyrs in synagogue.

The climate engendered by the massacres had severe repercussions for religious life and lay at the root of the messianic hopes that only twenty years later gave rise to the Shabbetai Tzevi phenomenon throughout Poland and the East. These same hopes subsequently gave rise to the Hasidic movement, founded by Yisrael Baal Shem, known as the Baal Shem Tov (the Master of the Good Name), in the second quarter of the eighteenth century in Volhynia and Podolia, the regions at the center of Sabbetian fervor. Hasidism was further nourished by the Lurianic cabalistic tradition born in Safed in the sixteenth century and widespread in most of the eastern Jewish world since the second half of the seventeenth century.

Hasidism transformed religious life and behavior in the Jewish world. This transformation resulted partly from the crisis that struck the Polish and eastern communities in the eighteenth century, weakening their organizational structure and leaving deep internal social rifts. But the Hasidic movement cannot be interpreted in reductive terms as an outgrowth of social hardships and revolution. Rather, it constituted a radical innovation that profoundly changed the entire eastern European Jewish world (J. Katz 1971). An emphasis on individual religious experience lay at the heart of Hasidism, whose essential aim was mystical communion with the divinity. This emphasis on individual experience did not, however, lead Hasidism to devalue traditional religious observance, which it maintained and strengthened as a guide for subjective religious experience. Mystical communion with God made the religious person a "pneumatic," someone inspired by the Holy Spirit, and endowed him with powerful religious authority. In fact, the Hasidic mystic did not live this subjective experience in isolation or in a tight circle of initiates, but within the real life of the community, in continual rapport with the faithful. Despite deep roots in the older cabalistic mystical tradition, Hasidism was actually devoid of original thinking. It ultimately adopted a populist folk mythology that was well suited to Hasidism's deeply innovative relationship with collective life. Hasidism's real innovation was, in fact, its creation of a religious community of believers (Hasidim) and the relationship between this community and all of Jewish society. Another novelty introduced by Hasidism was its accentuation of the charismatic role of the religious leader, the rebbe, and especially of the *tzaddiq* (saint), the intermediary with the divinity, around whom the disciples gathered. The tzaddiq became the principal reference point for popular religion in eighteenth- and nineteenth-century Polish villages (Scholem 1965).

From the second half of the eighteenth century on, Hasidism broke out of its original boundaries and spread among the Jews of Poland, Russia, Bosnia, Hungary, and Romania, reaching its fullest extent in the nineteenth century. This process was bitterly opposed by Jews still bound to rabbinic Judaism. While the movement spread rapidly throughout the Polish Jewish world, it remained a minority in Lithuania. There, Talmudic studies, which had made the country a first-rank Jewish cultural center and had given life to schools of great importance, were still very much alive. The greatest exponent of the rabbinic reaction to the spread of Hasidism in Lithuania was Elijah of Vilna, the so-called Gaon of Vilna, active in the second half of the eighteenth century. He was an expert mathematician as well as a great Talmudist, and he supported a synthesis of the Talmudic tradition and Cabala.

Despite its direct derivation from older traditions of cabalistic mysticism, Hasidic mysticism, as it was elaborated in early-eighteenth-century Poland, renounced the messianism that had characterized mystical Jewish movements for centuries and had been so influential in creating the religious and cultural fabric of Jewish life. This renunciation was the consequence of a sensational episode that generated violent emotions and deep disillusionment in 1666 in the Ottoman Empire, the West, and eastern Poland: the messianic adventure of Shabbetai Tzevi. The Hasidic movement owed a debt to Shabbetai Tzevi's Polish followers for its mysticism, although it also introduced innovations. Indeed, many of the transformations marking the Jewish world in the East and throughout the Diaspora beginning at the close of the seventeenth century can be dated to Shabbetai's adventure.

The extraordinary and paradoxical affair of Shabbetai Tzevi—a Jew from Smyrna, who, in 1666, proclaimed that he was the messiah and profoundly unsettled the entire Jewish world with his preaching, before being imprisoned by the Turks and converting to Islam—has been interpreted as the last episode of medieval Judaism. According to this view, his claim marked the last time that the Jewish universe expressed itself in a utopian form and soon after would be radically transformed. Gershom Scholem has stressed that this episode can likewise be viewed as the emergence of a new way of thinking, an awareness of change (Scholem 1973), and one of the difficult first steps along what Maurice Kriegel has labeled "the paradoxical paths of modern times" (Kriegel 1980a). If one considers that many innovative elements were intrinsic to cabalistic culture—which, although not at the root of Sabbatean thought, certainly nourished it—one is not surprised that an apostate messiah and his prophet, Nathan of Gaza, appeared at the very moment the Jewish world was making the transition to modernity.

CHAPTER EIGHT

Beyond
the Ghetto

THE "IMPROVEMENT" OF THE JEWS

Between the end of the eighteenth and the second half of the nineteenth century, Jews achieved full emancipation throughout western Europe: in England, France, Germany, the Hapsburg Empire,
and Italy. They were thus able to enjoy complete civil and political equality, including the right to serve in legislatures and hold public office. They
could live wherever they desired (not only in ghettos or Jewish quarters),
own property, enter all trades and professions, and attend state schools
and universities. In short, they were completely integrated into the surrounding society.

A lively debate in the course of the eighteenth century had prepared
the way for the painstaking achievement of this objective. Enlightened
European public opinion was shaped not only by concern for the Jews'
fate but above all by the idea that Jewish equality was a necessary con-

dition for the development of civil society. In a world on the road to modernity, in fact, the Jews' existence as a separate group with a distinct legal status represented not so much an injustice unworthy of a civilized society as a roadblock on the way to achieving political homogeneity. Indeed, the constitutional-monarchist deputy Stanislas de Clermont-Tonnerre expressed precisely this concept in his famous speech supporting Jewish equality during the 1789 debate in the Constituent Assembly: "Everything must be denied the Jews as a nation, everything must be granted the Jews as individuals. They must become citizens. Some say that they do not desire it. If that be so, let them say it, and they will be expelled. They cannot be a nation within a nation" (J. Katz 1973: 67).

To be admitted into society, Jews had to renounce their particularism. Enlightenment thinkers considered the Jews' particularism to be a consequence of their backwardness. But in the enlightened view, Jewish degradation had lost its traditional religious connotation, being construed instead as the outcome of centuries of discrimination by which Jews had been excluded from certain occupations and separated from society. "Let us concede," wrote the Prussian Christian Wilhelm Dohm, one of the principal proponents of emancipation,

> that the Jews may be more morally corrupt than other nations; that they are guilty of a proportionately greater number of crimes than the Christians; that their character in general tends more toward usury and fraud in commerce; that their religious prejudice is more antisocial and clannish; but I must add that this supposed greater moral corruption of the Jews is a necessary and natural consequence of the oppressed condition in which they have been living for so many centuries. A calm and impartial consideration will prove the correctness of this assertion. (Dohm 1957)

Thus the supporters of Jewish emancipation at first referred to it as "improvement" or "civil and moral regeneration." In many countries, the battle for emancipation was transformed into a call for the Jews to renounce their distinctive ways and their particularism, in short to "improve" themselves.

HASKALAH

The Jewish world was thus called upon to change. In the past, change had been achieved by transformations within Judaism, many of which emanated from the mystical tradition. This time, change would have to be achieved by adopting entirely new means. A century earlier, the Shabbetai Tzevi episode had spawned important changes in the relationship

between Jews and their religious and cultural tradition. But the enlightened cultural climate rendered obsolete and insufficient the old Jewish
models of internal transformation. Yet decidedly enlightened positions
might reveal unexpected mystical roots. An emblematic case in point is
that of the enigmatic Moses Dobruška. Dobruška was born a Jew in Moravia in a Sabbatean milieu but converted to Catholicism and assumed
the name Thomas von Schönfeld. A crypto-Judaizer and a Mason, he
later became known in Strasbourg and Paris as a Jacobin under the
name Junius Frey. Finally, in 1794, during the Terror, he was charged
with espionage and guillotined along with Danton. The great historian of mysticism Gershom Scholem argued that Dobruška's puzzling
journey exemplifies the Jewish progression toward modernity (Scholem
1981). But suggestive although Dobruška's life might have been, it cannot be considered truly emblematic. Rather, the Jewish encounter with
the outside world and its culture, accompanied by internal reform of
Jewish society, led to modernity.

A product of this interchange between the outside world and Jewish society was the Haskalah, the movement of Jewish enlightenment
that originated in eighteenth-century Germany and subsequently spread
through much of the Jewish world. Clearly influenced by Enlightenment
thought, Haskalah thinkers supported a rationalistic interpretation of
Jewish theology and rejected mysticism and Cabala. They criticized
traditional Talmudic study and maintained that it was necessary to
secularize Jewish culture profoundly by opening it up to philosophic
and scientific thought. The adherents of Haskalah (*maskilim*) accentuated the points of contact between Jewish culture and that of the outside
world. They believed in a universalistic conception of Judaism, which
they saw as a moral beacon of humanity. The ethical principles of Judaism
were valid, in their view, for all nations, not only for the Jews.

Obviously, such a transformation could not leave traditional religious observance unaffected. The maskilim at first did not attack Jewish
law directly. But as the reformers sought to separate halachic laws from
mere customs (*minhagim*), religious practices also came under criticism.
Moses Mendelssohn, the greatest proponent of the Haskalah in Germany during these years, remained religiously observant and spoke out
publicly in defense of the Jewish religion. He refused all invitations to
convert to Christianity in the name of philosophy. But many adherents
of the German Enlightenment perceived a substantial affinity between
an enlightened rational Judaism and a profoundly purified Deistic Christianity. This perception tended to blur religious boundaries rather than

emphasize them. Although he never carried it through, this was the climate in which the philosopher Solomon Maimon attempted in the name of natural religion to convert to Protestantism. Similarly, David Friedlander, a disciple of Mendelssohn's and an outstanding personality of the Berlin Jewish community, proposed unsuccessfully in 1799 that the heads of the most important Jewish families in Berlin convert en masse to a Christianity rationalized and reduced to a form of natural religion.

The boundaries between assimilation and conversion were disappearing in Haskalah Germany. Contacts between Christians and Jews flourished in the famous Berlin salons maintained by outstanding Jewish women of the late eighteenth century. This climate has been described as "an assimilationist utopia in miniature" (Hertz 1987: 49). A number of women shone in this environment. All would eventually convert, including Mendelssohn's daughter Dorothea, who later became the wife of the Romantic philosopher Friedrich von Schlegel, and Rahel Varnhagen, whom Hannah Arendt later transformed into an emblem of frustrated assimilation (Arendt 1974).

Limited to a narrow class of Berlin Jews, conversion represented only the most extreme and radical aspect of a continuing process taking place within the Jewish world. George Mosse has referred to this process as a "secularization of Jewish theology," one that led to the "adaptation of the liturgy and of Jewish thought to the new cultural and political trends of the day" (Mosse 1985b). In Germany, where this process originated and found its most radical expression, Judaism began to resemble a sentimental religion similar to Pietistic Protestantism. Jews came to accentuate religious feeling at the expense of the ritualism and formalism of traditional rites. The traditional liturgy was modified by the introduction of hymns and, above all, by the use of the German language. Reformers waged an all-out struggle to reform behavior during the service. They attempted to transform the synagogue, traditionally filled with the chatter and noise of the faithful, into a place of decorum and edification. As late as the beginning of the twentieth century, the fight in France against synagogue noise was one of Theodor Reinach's ongoing interests. A member of the intellectual avant-garde, a politician, and the founder of the Liberal Jewish Union, Reinach wanted to introduce the organ into French synagogues to distinguish them from "German or Polish synagogues where duties without beauty are performed amidst a deafening brouhaha, in a sometimes indecent confusion" (Birnbaum 1995: 120). The attempt to conform to models of respectability was a ubiquitous theme in Jewish expression between the time of the Enlightenment and the rise of a religious reform movement.

In the course of the nineteenth century, the Haskalah influenced the entire Jewish world. Seeds of doubt and change were planted as far away as the Russian and Polish yeshivot, and Jews divided themselves into two camps: the traditionalists and the maskilim. In some cases maskilic thought melded either with the rationalist tradition within traditional Judaism or with the fruits of Jewish Renaissance thought in Italy, which had entered central and eastern European Jewish culture primarily through the work of the Maharal of Prague in the late sixteenth century. This was how the Haskalah entered Russia at the end of the eighteenth century. But even where the Haskalah found nourishment in Jewish cultural traditions or internal criticism of tradition, an external influence—Enlightenment thought—always remained fundamental (Etkes 1987).

THE PATHS OF EMANCIPATION

The emancipation of the Jews was only one stage in the more general transformation of the European states as they moved toward modernity after the French Revolution and the first Industrial Revolution. Emancipation was thus a secondary product of secularization. Secularization produced a different relationship between Jews and Christians, eliminating—or at least reshaping—the ideological and religious motivations for balancing the Jews' legal presence with their inferiority and subordination. During an earlier stage in the secularization of the modern state, a similar imbalance in the late medieval period had brought about not the integration of the Jews into society, but rather their expulsion from most of the West. Their readmission in the seventeenth century was only de facto at first and only later came on the basis of partial concessions and increased tolerance. It had not originally implied complete integration into the surrounding society, that is, political emancipation. Rather, readmission of the Jews merely signified their naturalization, the establishment of a legal basis for their ongoing residence. The dichotomy between emancipation and mere naturalization was possible in a society traditionally divided into social hierarchies and groups with separate statutes. In such a society, naturalization did not imply equal rights or the elimination of privileges, and relations between the state and the Church permitted discrimination among citizens based on their religion (J. Katz 1973). It is not by chance that at the end of the seventeenth century and the beginning of the eighteenth, such theoreticians of the separation of Church and state as John Locke and John Toland were the first to advocate linking the naturalization of Jews with their attainment of equal rights. In the age of enlightened secularization, the question of emancipation became unavoidable.

The Catholic Church remained fiercely opposed to all such views, taking a hard line based on religious principles; the Catholic clergy everywhere defended the subordination of the Jews. Nor, for that matter, did the Protestant leadership, in its varied manifestations, take up arms to advance Jewish equality.

As recent historiography stresses, the paths that led to Jewish emancipation were just as varied and numerous as the roads that led to modernity in the various countries of the West (Birnbaum and Katznelson 1995). In many cases, social integration preceded political emancipation, and reform was a gradual process for most European states. A belief in gradual reform still characterized enlightened opinion in France on the eve of the Revolution. Dohm, who was linked to Mendelssohn's Berlin group, believed that this was the way to achieve reform in Germany. The Hapsburg emperor Joseph II's Edict of Tolerance, issued in 1781 and received enthusiastically by the Jews, belongs to the category of gradual gains. It granted citizenship to the Austrian, Bohemian, and Hungarian Jews, even as it maintained discriminations and inequalities.

Only revolutionary France, where emancipation was based on the idea of equality for all, accomplished a rapid and complete emancipation of the Jews. The first decree of the Constituent Assembly, issued in January 1790, emancipated the Sephardim in southwestern France, while the second, adopted in September 1791 after prolonged resistance, emancipated all other French Jews, that is, the Ashkenazim living in Alsace, Lorraine, and Metz. Thus, the juridical paradox of the Jewish presence fell under the egalitarian ax of the French Revolution, which no longer permitted favoritism or privileges and made all men citizens with equal rights and equal duties.

The French Revolution was preceded by the American Revolution, which was largely informed by the theories of none other than John Locke. Locke's ideas were brought into even sharper focus by Roger Williams of Rhode Island and perfected in debates launched by various Protestant sects fighting to disestablish Congregationalism in New England. In the Declaration of Independence, the Founding Fathers politically emancipated the adherents of all religions, including the approximately 2,000 Jews living in the American territories at that time.

In the course of the revolutionary and Napoleonic wars, the French armies imposed Jewish equality in many parts of Europe: in Belgium, Holland, the Italian states, and many of the German states. Even Prussia, after its defeat by Napoleon, granted the Jews almost complete emancipation in 1812, the sole limitation being their disqualification for government posts. After the fall of the Napoleonic empire, emancipation remained a definitive right under the Bourbon Restoration in France, but Austria, Prussia, and the German states reintroduced many limitations. In reality, this return to the past was connected to a slowdown in the general pace of modernization. The 1848 German revolution granted the Jews full equality according to the French model. In fact, the Frankfurt parliament passed a law guaranteeing the fundamental rights of the German people and forbidding the limitation of political or civil rights on the basis of religion. The defeat of the revolution and the subsequent climate of reaction rendered this law inoperative. In Germany and Austria, the future of emancipation was thus linked to the liberalization of the state, as it was contemporaneously in Risorgimento Italy.

The Austro-Hungarian Empire emancipated its Jews in 1867. Prussia and most of the German states followed suit in 1869, on the eve of the unification of the Reich. Emancipation was preceded, however, by a general process of economic transformation, which radically changed the face of German Jewry. The eighteenth-century German Jewish community was still impoverished and socially disparate, scattered throughout the countryside or in small towns. By the mid nineteenth century, this picture had undergone a radical change: Jews were highly urbanized and making rapid economic strides. Social inequalities within the community were quickly disappearing, and even the lowest classes were being transformed into a respectable and relatively homogeneous "middle class." The embourgeoisement of German Jewry also influenced its mentality and behavior, its family structure, and its education. "The Jews exhibited the characteristics of being bourgeois to so disproportionately high a degree that their transformation preceded by at least a generation that of the general German populace" (Sorkin 1987: 110). The economic and social transformation of the German Jewish world thus preceded the attainment of full emancipation and appears to have resulted from the more general process of social and economic modernization within Germany. Even so, contemporary Jews perceived this transformation to be a product of the rights that emancipation, although not yet complete, had granted them. According to some interpretations, it is precisely the gradualness of German emancipation that accounts for the German Jews' deep internalization of this process and therefore for their active participation in their own acculturation. Nevertheless, the history of German Jewry is far from representing the irremediable conflict between the maintenance of identity and its loss. Rather, German Jewry during emancipation continued to create a highly specific subculture that, although identified with Judaism, was permeated by emancipatory and universalist values critical of tradition (Sorkin 1992).

Although France continued to recognize the Revolution's 1789 vote of emancipation, the social and political integration of the French Jews was not rapid. The strong push for assimilation during the Napoleonic period created high levels of tension between the Jewish world and the authoritarian Napoleonic officials. Afterward, Jews remained substantially marginal to French society and political life until around 1870. There was practically no significant Jewish participation in the great development of French industry, and very few unconverted Jews held important public posts before 1848.

Only after 1870, during the Third Republic, did Jewish integration into French society and political life reach its apex. The French experience was characterized by Jewish entry into the highest offices of the state. "The strong French State," writes Pierre Birnbaum, "was the only one in modern history, indeed in all history, to open its various Grand Corps to Jewish statesmen. Paradoxically, at the same time that France was undergoing so many major social and ideological crises, Jews became prefects or underprefects, state councilors, presidents of courts of appeal, judges in the most important court, first president of the Supreme Court of Appeal, or even generals without being obliged to convert, as they were in Germany or Austria-Hungary" (Birnbaum 1995: 117). Despite their high degree of integration under the Third Republic, French Jews did not, as has been suggested, abandon Jewish identity. Indeed, the French Jewish world was revitalized at that time by its remarkable geographic mobility and by the continual influx of Jews from the East. Between the Revolution and 1861, the Jewish population grew from 40,000 to 80,000. In the nineteenth century, a veritable demographic revolution moved the center of Jewish life from Alsace to the capital: the Rabbinical Academy transferred to Paris from Metz in 1859; 15,000 Jews left Alsace and Lorraine for Paris after France lost the provinces in 1870; after the Russian pogroms of the 1880s, 80,000 Russian Jews migrated to Paris. By the 1880s, 45,000 Jews lived in or near Paris.

The influx of Jews from the East brought about a resurgence of Jewish particularism and a reaffirmation of ethnic identity. At the end of the nineteenth century, Russian Jews established their own quarter in Paris in the Marais. There they founded community and welfare organizations, forming an "ethnic island" (Birnbaum 1995) similar to the one later created by North African Jewish immigrants to France.

The road to full emancipation for the Jews of England was also very specific. In Germany and France, the surrounding society specifically requested that the Jews enter the modern world, and the Jews responded with such ideological and religious movements as the Haskalah. In England, by contrast, the process of modernization was spontaneous, failing to give rise to any particular ideological and theoretical trends. "Parliament did not expect Jews to reform any of their beliefs or practices as a prerequisite to full political equality; in fact, Parliament had little interest in what Jews thought or prayed or how they acted in their shops and synagogues" (Endelman 1987a: 242). Consequently, the English Jews felt only a superficial need to alter their beliefs or practices. Indeed, the Haskalah had only a minor impact on England, and Reform Judaism was scarcely a factor. English Jews of the highest social levels, both "highly civilized" Sephardim and the most "backward" Ashkenazim, had by the mid eighteenth century adopted a life-style similar to that of non-Jews: they had cut their beards, and they frequented cafes and theaters. It took only a little longer for Jews from even the lowest social levels to become acculturated. Thus, widespread social integration came quickly, inasmuch as the surrounding society put up little resistance to the acceptance of Jews.

In the political realm, all English-born Jews enjoyed the right of citizenship, as they had since the reestablishment of Jews in England in the second half of the seventeenth century. They did not possess full civil and political equality, but this meant only that they could not be elected to public office or attend Oxford and Cambridge, limitations that affected very few people and for many years elicited no reaction in the Jewish community. In 1829, however, the elimination of similar clauses regarding Catholics and nonconformists brought the problem to a head for Jews as well. Full political and civil rights were formally and totally granted in 1871. The greatest controversy revolved around whether a Jew could be elected to the House of Commons, a point that Commons conceded in 1833 and the House of Lords in 1858. In short, social emancipation preceded political emancipation by roughly fifty years.

EMANCIPATION IN ITALY

The Jewish experience of emancipation in Italy has been singular and clearly differs from the history of other Jewish communities in the Western world. The most significant aspect of the Italian process was undoubtedly the lack of a consolidated and sustained movement of either Haskalah or Reform. The reasons for this uniqueness, both in the nineteenth century and before, are, however, still open to historical debate. On one hand, to what degree did the physical experience of the ghetto, for example, influence the Jews' entrance into the modern world? Or, on the other hand, to what extent can the uniqueness of the Italian emancipation model be traced to the fact that Jewish emancipation accompanied rather than followed the emancipation of civil society? (This was also to some degree the case in Germany, but contrary to what happened in France.) Finally, can the absence of a true Haskalah be attributed to a lack of cultural and religious development, or, rather, to the fact that Italian Judaism had been more progressive and modern ever since the Renaissance and therefore did not need to undergo a process of internal transformation such as occurred in Germany?

The emancipation of Italian Jewry was undoubtedly a nineteenth-century phenomenon, without roots in the Enlightenment. It developed alongside the movement for Italian unification. Liberty was first bestowed on the Jews by the French armies and later introduced in the Jacobin republics and the kingdom of Italy. But with the end of the Napoleonic era, age-old discriminations were reintroduced in Italy. Modena, the kingdom of Sardinia, and the papal states once again confined Jews in ghettos. Only regions controlled by Austria or, like Tuscany, under Austrian influence realized reform projects in the spirit of the Enlightenment. In this situation, it was inevitable that the fate of Jewish emancipation would follow that of the unification process. The constitutional movement and the later revolutionary movement of 1848 brought equality once more to all citizens, including Jews. After the defeat of the 1848 revolutions, emancipation was again abrogated in Modena, Tuscany, and Rome. Only in Piedmont did Victor Emmanuel II leave intact the 1848 edict granting equality to the Jews of his kingdom.

The vicissitudes through which the Roman Jews lived are particularly significant. The gates of the Roman ghetto were torn down for the first time in 1799 and again in 1848. But the Jews did not leave the ghetto once and for all until September 20, 1870. The ghetto of Rome was thus the last to open, and the Roman Jews, the most ancient community in the western Diaspora and the largest in Italy, were the last to attain freedom. And they did so the moment they stepped outside the ghetto's gates, finally obtaining parity with other citizens a few days after the fall of papal temporal power. By that time the oppressive and humiliating aspects of segregation were already so strongly perceived that traditional resistance to the opening of the ghetto could no longer exist.

As steeped in poverty and immobility as the Roman Jews were, they fully understood that their fate was linked to the creation of an Italian state. Not that they actively supported unification. Indeed, only a very few elite Jews in papal Rome were considered Jacobins, that is, revolutionaries—if they can truly be called that. It seems that Italian Jewry's strong support for the Risorgimento, recently stressed again as one of the specificities of the emancipation process in Italy (D. V. Segre 1995), came more from the Piedmontese or Lombard community than the Roman ghetto.

Successive events in the Roman community quickly brought to light the difficulties inherent in an unplanned and hasty exit from the ghetto. The community's transformation into a voluntary association was one of the reasons for the severe crisis into which it fell immediately after emancipation. Many Jews chose not to belong to the community, living apart from it. The first impulse of many Jews seems to have been to accelerate their integration into the surrounding society, making it difficult to achieve internal cohesion. Meanwhile, the community faced a series of urgent material problems, including the reformation of the old Jewish occupational structure and persistent poverty among the population. With the demolition of the old ghetto, the community also needed to redefine Jewish space, relocating the former ghetto inhabitants to other areas and reconstructing new communal institutions, including a new synagogue.

Although the contributions—mainly economic but also political and cultural—of Jews who came to the capital from other communities after 1870 eased the transformation of Roman Jewry, the process was neither linear nor painless. As a recent interpretation stresses, the crux of the problem was the clash between support of Italian nationalism and adherence to Judaism (Caviglia 1996). This tension was never resolved. Periods of Jewish identification alternated with periods of Italian national identification. If this interpretation is not merely part of a larger picture, but encapsulates the essential direction of contemporary Italian Jewish history, important inferences can be made. Support for Zionism, in this view, constitutes not only a revival of interest in Jewish issues after a period of assimilation, but also an internal redefinition of Judaism, a kind of substitute for a reform movement. Modern Italian Jewry, with its greater emphasis on moving from the ghetto than on changes within Judaism itself, thus underwent a belated internal reform. But unlike earlier movements for reform in other Jewish communities, which were based on universalistic Enlightenment values and sought to rationalize Jewish ritual, Italian Jewry predicated its own transformation on the reconstruction of a Jewish national identity (Zionism). Italian Judaism, accordingly, experienced emancipation without Haskalah. In other countries, particularly Russia, the path to modernity was diametrically opposite; there was neither emancipation nor assimilation (Lederhendler 1992).

JEWISH RESPONSES TO MODERNITY

Jewish responses to emancipation were manifold and varied. From the outset, there were deep concerns about the risks to tradition posed by the new relationship between the Jews and the outside world. The term "assimilation" is still used to define—and to lament—the loss of Jewish identity that resulted from political emancipation, social integration, and the attractions of the larger society. In reality, an analysis of Jewish emancipation reveals that a stark dichotomy between assimilation and retention of identity characterizes only a fraction of the Jewish encounter with the outside world. For the most part, such a dichotomy describes the fears of traditionalists rather than the realities of cultural and religious transformation. As has been seen, this reality was generally much more complex and is less clearly understandable in terms of assimilation versus identity than is usually assumed. This was true even in France and Germany, countries commonly described as champions of assimilation. Most recent studies question the very use of the term "assimilation," replacing it with "acculturation," which describes the process of reshaping identity rather than that of losing it (Sorkin 1992).

This is not to say that there were no pressures on Jews to renounce their specificity and assimilate. Indeed, one of the tensest moments occurred in France in 1806, during the first years of the Napoleonic regime. The Jewish community was officially requested to speak its mind on the fundamental issues of its relationship with civil society, and on the possibility of reconciling Jewish law with the civil laws of the state. In substance, Jews were being called upon to formally identify themselves with the new homeland and accept its precepts. The questions submitted to the Jews' representatives—at first an assembly of notable rabbis and laymen, later a more authoritative one with the high-sounding name of Grand Sanhedrin (from the supreme tribunal of ancient Israel)—concerned Jewish matrimonial law and its relationship to civil marriage laws, the possibility of mixed marriages, and loyalty to the French state. As expected, the issue of mixed marriage, which Napoleon viewed as a very efficient means of integration, aroused the greatest discussion. Marriage between Jews and Christians was a recent innovation, permitted only since the separation of Church and state and the introduction of civil marriage. Both the Catholic Church and the Jewish world had forbidden mixed marriages through the centuries, and both now denied the religious validity of such unions. Some of the assembly's representatives proposed that it deny recognition to mixed marriages, but the prevailing opinion was more flexible, reaffirming their civil value and renouncing religious sanctions against those contracting them. In general, the delegates' responses to the questions point to a highly integrated Jewish community, which identified wholeheartedly with the French state that had granted citizenship to its members.

One of the Sanhedrin's decisions was to replace the traditional governing bodies of the communities with local consistories subordinate to a central consistory, a reform that with various changes has remained in effect until today. Even more than the push to assimilate, the disintegration of the old community organizations, under pressure from without by the state and from within by the erosion of its authority, fragmented Jewish identity. Then, in the process of transformation, Jewish identity lost most of its traditional communal expression, allowing for a greater degree of individual initiative. An important part of this process was the universal adoption of family names, which was decreed by Napoleon and instituted in the rest of Europe during the nineteenth century. The use of family names accentuated the vast changes then occurring in age-old communal structures and also inserted the Jews into the wider structures of the outside world. Jewish mentalities and perceptions changed, and the emphasis on collective identity shifted to that of the individual. The community ceded its hitherto central role to the organs of the state, which now governed over each Jewish *citizen*.

In the course of the nineteenth century, the Jewish encounter with the outside world and with change touched the very core of religious doctrine and practice. Profoundly influenced by the Berlin Haskalah movement, the first attempt at reform took place in Hamburg in 1818, when a group of Hamburg Jews founded a temple—as modern parlance had by then renamed the synagogue—with a modified service and prayers mainly in German. The Reform movement spread throughout Germany in the 1830s, the work of a new generation of rabbis educated in German universities. Among them was Abraham Geiger, considered the father of the Reform movement. Geiger advocated a Reform Judaism whose fundamental assumption was the typically maskilic reduction of Judaism's essence to a universal ethical principle. The reformers sought to identify nonessential precepts and laws so that these could be abolished or modified to fit with modern rationalistic sensibilities. Reform concentrated on the religious service, advocating the use of the vernacular in prayers. In 1845, the movement, whose leaders met at periodic rabbinical conferences, split as a result of Zacharias Frankel's more conservative positions. Reform lost its momentum in the years after 1848, when the involvement of many Reform rabbis in the German revolution alienated German authorities. The latter banned the Reform movement, and many of its rabbis emigrated to America, where an Americanized brand of Reform eventually gained wide acceptance. In the 1870s, the movement regained its strength in Germany, generally taking positions more moderate than those of the preceding decades.

The encounter with the modern world produced another development: the birth of a new and modern type of Jewish learning. Founded in Germany in the first half of the nineteenth century, the Wissenschaft des Judentums movement pioneered a critical study of the Jewish past, particularly in the fields of philosophy and history. Among its founders were Abraham Geiger, Leopold Zunz, and Heinrich Graetz. Despite their intention—in Zunz's words—to present Judaism with a worthy funeral, the Wissenschaft scholars opened the way to a Jewish cultural renaissance in Europe. By inserting Jewish culture into the larger field of European culture, from both a philosophical and an ideological perspective, they furnished the Jewish world with the modern cognitive tools necessary to interpret its past and historical memory.

Meanwhile, the traditionalists also reorganized, with the intent of combating Reform and change. They adopted the label "Orthodox"—or "neo-Orthodox"—a concept without precedent in Jewish history. The Orthodox reaffirmed the integral value of observance of the laws of Halakhah. Nevertheless, they were not simply a continuation of the medieval rabbinic tradition, but another product of the new context in which the Jewish world found itself. Like the Reform movement, the Orthodox movement was a response to modernity. The founder of neo-Orthodoxy was the Frankfurt rabbi Samson Raphael Hirsch, who considered Jewish emancipation and integration to be positive developments and shared with the Haskalah the idea of a Jewish universalistic ideal. He identified this ideal not with an ethical principle, however, but with observance of Torah. Although it reaffirmed continuity, neo-Orthodoxy thus also represented an innovation in the Jewish world. By contrast, radical separation from the outside world, self-exclusion, and absolute rejection of modernity were the exclusive territory of the ultra-Orthodox movement, which flourished primarily in Hungary and eastern Europe— that is, where Jews were still living apart and unemancipated.

FROM RUSSIA TO AMERICA

The Jews of eastern Europe experienced strong and continual demographic growth from the eighteenth century on. In the nineteenth century, the majority of the Jews in Europe lived in Russia, Poland, Lithuania, and Hungary. Russia had a particularly large number of Jews. The partition of Poland in the second half of the eighteenth century had placed over two million Polish Jews under the dominion of the czar, and Russian expansion into Belorussia and Bessarabia had added more. While emancipation in the West was coming to a head at the end of the Napoleonic period, the Russian Jews were still far from attaining it. The capitals of Moscow and St. Petersburg were off-limits to Jews, and Jewish residence in such cities as Kiev and Warsaw was strictly limited. As a result, only 10 to 15 percent of the Jewish population resided in important urban areas in the course of the nineteenth century. In 1835, Czar Nicholas I (1825–55) formed the Pale of Settlement. In the Pale— a swath of territory extending from the Baltic Sea to the Black Sea, including Lithuania, Belorussia, and the Ukraine—Jews lived in conditions of extreme poverty and oppression. They were subject to particularly harsh conscription laws, under which youths were drafted to serve terms of twenty-five years. Jewish boys as young as twelve years old were torn from their families and made into soldiers. While Jewish communal organizations were severely restricted or destroyed, the Russian Orthodox clergy were given much leeway for conversionary and anti-Semitic activities, and lower-class hatred of the Jews was allowed to run rampant. Yet despite stagnation and repression, and despite the lack of any prospect of emancipation, the social and cultural trends that had profoundly transformed the Jewish world in the West also touched the shtetl. Since the first decades of the nineteenth century, maskilic influence had grown within the eastern European communities. Rather than fostering religious reform, however, they concentrated their efforts in the field of education. Against the wishes of Orthodox Jewish groups, the followers of the Haskalah sought to add scientific and secular studies to the traditional curriculum. Despite their small numbers, the maskilim were able to steer Jewish public opinion through their newspapers. As their influence grew, they assumed a position of leadership that the traditionalists could seldom challenge (Lederhendler 1994).

Along with a general trend toward modernization, the reign of Alexander II witnessed a perceptible improvement in the living conditions of Jews in Russia. The new czar reduced military service to five years, permitted greater freedom of movement, and partially opened the universities to Jews. It seemed as if the door to gradual emancipation had been opened. But Alexander's 1881 assassination by a group of socialist revolutionaries again led to a deterioration of the Jewish condition. Very soon a series of anti-Jewish pogroms broke out, many of them triggered by accusations of ritual murder or desecration. A number of factors motivated the attacks on Jewish communities: theological anti-Jewish hatred, which was particularly widespread in the Russian Orthodox Church; pan-Slavic hostility toward modernity and the West, of which the Jews became symbols; and, finally, the specifically political motive of czarist hostility toward the Jews, who were viewed as revolutionaries. The terrible Kishinev pogrom was particularly traumatic. Jews made up almost half of the Bessarabian city's population of 100,000, and an anti-Semitic mob unleashed its fury against them there on Easter Sunday 1903. Acting with the complicity of the authorities and the blessing of the Orthodox Christian clergy, the mob massacred more than forty Jews, including women and children, and destroyed the Jewish quarter. The Kishinev pogrom resonated throughout the West. It also helped widen the great divide that violence and repression had already opened between the Russian Jews and the czarist regime since 1881.

As traditional communal structures weakened, growing impoverishment in the last decades of the nineteenth century had resulted in a sizable Jewish proletariat. Socialist and revolutionary ideas spread throughout the increasingly secularized Jewish world, creating a wider gulf between generations than had the Haskalah a generation earlier. Young people from traditional pious families rid themselves of their religious baggage and became political. They participated in illegal revolutionary movements, filling the ranks of such workers' parties as the Jewish Bund, founded in 1897, and supporting the nascent Zionist movement. It was a radical change that was at once social, economic, and cultural. Without this change it would be difficult to explain the mass migration of millions of Jews from Russia westward, to Europe and especially America. Public discussions among Russian Jews laid the groundwork for the decision to leave Russian soil forever and emigrate to a new world. This decision was rightly perceived as a renunciation of the fight for emancipation and a different life in Russia. But the situation was desperate, and for the first time there was someplace to go, someplace Jews would be taken in. As a delegate from Kiev to the Jewish conference on emigration in St. Petersburg in 1882 said: "Either we get civil rights or we emigrate. Our dignity is being trampled on, our wives and daughters are being dishonored, we are looted and pillaged; either we get human rights or else let us go wherever our eyes may lead us" (Howe 1976: 25).

In the thirty-three years between 1881 and the outbreak of World War I, two million Russian Jews, a third of the entire eastern European Jewish population, emigrated to America. A new life was beginning for those who embarked on emigrant ships, despite their fears, doubts, and difficulties. In America, the emigrants found Jews with full civil and political rights, the equals of other American citizens. When they disembarked on American soil at the great immigration center Ellis Island, the Russian Jews encountered immigration inspectors who often Americanized their names on the spot, doctors who examined them and detained the ill, and Jewish agency personnel who aided newcomers. Later they found housing in the overcrowded tenements on the Lower East Side of Manhattan, where Jewish families lived next-door to Italian and Irish immigrants and with them found equal opportunities in an expanding society. During the period of mass immigration before World War I, the United States never seriously curbed the influx of European immigrants, despite attempts to enact more restrictive immigration laws.

THE NEW ANTI-SEMITISM

The revolution emancipated Russian Jewry. But then Russian Jews, whether traditionalist or revolutionary, had to contend with anti-Semitic attacks under various communist regimes. Although the Russian and eastern European variety was particularly dramatic, all of twentieth-century Europe shared a modern form of anti-Semitism. Its roots date back to the very origins of the emancipation movement. Obviously, Jewish traditionalists were not the only adversaries to Jewish emancipation.

Ever since eighteenth-century European cultural and political circles had begun to debate the question, many intellectuals had opposed integrating Jews into society and granting them civil and political rights. Only some of these adversaries of Jewish emancipation drew from the tradition of Christian anti-Judaism. Even many of the French *philosophes* opposed Jewish emancipation. Only Montesquieu openly advocated tolerance of the Jews, reasoning from his skeptical and relativistic background. But personalities of the caliber of Diderot, Holbach, and Voltaire opposed toleration, going so far as to deny that Jewish backwardness resulted from the Jews' segregation from the rest of society. Rather they regarded negative character traits as essential to Jewish nature. Some scholars have assumed that the *philosophes* used Judaism to mask their principal targets, the Church and Christianity (Gay 1959). Other interpreters, however, have seen in Voltaire's thinking the foundation of a new, modern, secularized anti-Semitism. They point to his exaltation of paganism over the Judeo-Christian tradition, as well as his use of Greek and Roman classics to demonstrate the unbending hostility of the Jews toward Western civilization (Hertzberg 1990: 313). Regardless of what motivated the anti-Jewish polemics of Enlightenment thinkers, it is certain that opposition to emancipation during the revolutionary age did not come solely from the clerical camp. Even such exponents of the Jacobin left as the Alsatian representative Jean-François Rewbell bitterly opposed the emancipation of the Ashkenazic Jews, as did such prominent figures as Desmoulins and Marat. Voltairean anti-Semitism thus coalesced with various elements: with a populism attentive to the moods of the masses, with the Jacobin struggle against religious cults, which led during the Terror to persecution of observant Jews and Christians alike, and with mistrust of Jews as foreigners who were likely to betray the homeland and the revolution.

By the mid nineteenth century, Jewish emancipation was a fait accompli in most of western Europe and had become inevitable even where opposition to it was strong. Despite the resistance of those who reaffirmed their allegiance to tradition, a corresponding transformation had profoundly touched the Jewish world. The modernization of Judaism should have led to a progressive disappearance of anti-Semitism, which was a vestige of the dark days of discrimination and religious hatred. As we know, this is not what happened; in modern times, anti-Semitism adopted a new character in keeping with changed conditions. Modernizing its arsenal, it displayed an unparalleled ability to wield power until, with Hitler, it destroyed almost the entire European Jewish population.

The new anti-Semitism consisted of many different components, the most obvious of which was racism. A product of the new cultural climate, nineteenth-century anti-Semitism arose from the idea that humanity was divided into distinct biologically determined races, and that the "Aryan race" was superior to other races. Unknown to both Christian and secular Enlightenment universalists, the so-called Aryan myth took shape and established itself in nineteenth-century Germany. Rooted in the discovery of the existence of a homogeneous Indo-European linguistic area, and culturally abetted by the rise of positivist philosophy, this myth was a pure and simple invention. It posited the existence of a pure Indo-European, or Aryan, race made up of Germanic and Nordic peoples and superior to other races, particularly the Jews (Poliakov 1974a). Even before racial doctrines became fully established, however, the cultural climate of post-Restoration Europe had changed. The universalist and rationalist doctrines that had sustained the call for emancipation had given way to romantic exaltation of Christian spirituality. Particularly in Germany, the resulting cultural void allowed mistrust of Jews to resurface, later to be interwoven with racial theories.

Even as traditional and conservative an institution as the Catholic Church modernized its anti-Jewish arsenal after the middle of the nineteenth century. The famous Mortara case of 1858 exemplifies the Church's new isolation. In the final years of its dominion in Bologna, the Church of Pius IX kidnapped a Bolognese Jewish child in order to convert him. It did so in a climate of remarkable isolation, steadfastly defying the condemnation of the entire Western world, including its own political protector, Second Empire France. The new Catholic anti-Semitism gave new credence to age-old stereotypes that in the past had been accepted solely by fringe elements of the Christian world. At the end of the century, Catholic newspapers close to the Curia, including the Jesuit organ, *La civiltà cattolica*, fully supported recent ritual murder accusations against Jews in Russia, Czechoslovakia, and Hungary. Popes and theologians had rejected such charges in no uncertain terms during the "dark" Middle Ages. Now, for the first time in the long history of the Church, its highest levels lent credence to them. The nature of the Jewish enemy had changed; for the Church of the second half of the nineteenth century, the Jews were heirs to the French Revolution and the Enlightenment, representatives of a detested modernity against which the Church had fought hard and long.

It is difficult to fully understand why these age-old myths reappeared in the nineteenth-century Church. Certainly, the Church was disoriented by the loss of its temporal power, which for centuries had constituted its very essence. Deprived of the responsibilities of political power, the Church fell under the influence of an extremist fringe. Catholic policy toward the Jews thus displayed greater rigidity and closed-mindedness than ever before.

The last two decades of the century saw the rise of what has been called "political anti-Semitism," especially in France, Germany, and Austria. Political anti-Semitism associated the Jews with the bourgeois and utilitarian values typical of a materialistic society. After having been attacked as the symbol of backwardness, the Jew thus came to symbolize modernity, a modernity rejected and condemned for its materialism and soullessness (Mosse 1985b). This identification of the Jews with bourgeois modernity was more central to the intellectual foundations of German political anti-Semitism than was biological racism. German nationalism contributed its rejection of liberalism, encouraging the growth of violent and aggressive political movements, and laying the groundwork for Nazi anti-Semitism (Pulzer 1988).

In France, the anti-Semitic movement gained ground at the beginning of the 1880s, when liberal supporters of the Third Republic clashed with reactionary anti-democratic forces. Books like Edouard Drumont's violent and wildly popular *La France juive,* widely circulated newspapers, and organizations all spread stories about a Jewish plot against France and called for an end to Jewish equality. Although these ideological currents belonged to the nationalist Right, anti-Semitism also spread through contemporary leftist circles. By the end of the century, the Left had become revolutionary and voluntarist, disavowing the founding myth of the French Revolution. Taking its lead from Marx's *On the Jewish Question,* the Left attacked capitalism, clearly identifying it with Jews.

These forces coalesced with a nascent virulent nationalism, reactionary Catholicism's resurgent anti-Semitism, and racial myths (Sternhell 1994) to form the backdrop of the Dreyfus Affair, the high point of French anti-Semitism, during which crowds in the squares shouted, "Death to the Jews." But the Dreyfus case also helped marshal a solid secular and republican bloc that vanquished the nationalist and anti-Semitic right for many decades. In fact, republicans, democrats, liberals, socialists, and the entire left and center wings of the Third Republic lined up behind Alfred Dreyfus, the captain unjustly found guilty in 1894 of spying for Germany and deported to Devil's Island. Siding against Dreyfus were the clergy, the army, monarchists, and nationalists, all inciting hatred of the Jews. The case quickly developed into a clash of republican institutions. The two sides had very different concepts of power, one authoritarian and reactionary, the other liberal and democratic. They also had differing ideas about the place of public opinion and the role of intellectuals.

The Dreyfus Affair was a watershed in the political life of the Third Republic, and among its consequences was the separation of Church and state in France. The case ended with a victory for the Dreyfusards. Dreyfus was pardoned and freed, and, in 1906, France formally rehabilitated him. The case, however, also represents a watershed in the history of the French Jewish community's relationship with society at large, as well as of its perception of itself and the surrounding world. The Consistory, the organ created by Napoleon to govern the French Jews, took a cautious approach. Claiming only a religious function, it refused to fight for Dreyfus or to confront the country's rampant anti-Semitism (Albert 1992). According to some historians, greater concern with the fate of Jewish integration than with anti-Semitism led much of French Jewish society to exhibit the same caution. In the heat of the discussion, one of Dreyfus's most ardent defenders, the French socialist Bernard-Lazare, condemned his fellow Jews for their timidity.

Leon Blum, the future premier of France, was one of the first Dreyfusards. Noting that Dreyfus himself was a respectable bourgeois, disciplined and faithful in his service to the state, Blum wrote, "Dreyfus himself, had he not been Dreyfus, would probably not have been a Dreyfusard." The Dreyfus case thus brought to light the existence of an insoluble problem, the persistence of anti-Semitism in a highly integrated society.

What price were Jews willing to pay for their integration? What was the relationship between assimilation and integration on the one hand and anti-Semitism on the other (Marrus 1971)? Theodore Herzl, a Hungarian Jew who had been Paris correspondent for a Viennese newspaper during the Dreyfus Affair, offered a radical answer to these questions. According to Herzl, emancipation had failed and anti-Semitism remained a constant factor in society. The only way for Jews to save themselves, according to Herzl, was to leave the Diaspora and create a state of their own. The publication of Herzl's book *The Jewish State* in 1896 and the first Zionist Congress in Basel two years later politicized Zionism.

Examining the climate of anti-Semitism that gave rise to the Dreyfus Affair, some recent historians have argued that France rather than Germany was the true birthplace of the Nazis' anti-Semitic ideology. They note that a violently anti-Semitic right-wing culture survived the political victories of the Left to infuse much of France's great literature. Moreover, they argue, this persistent anti-Semitism later informed French collaborationism during World War II (Sternhell 1994).

In France during the Dreyfus Affair, in 1897 or 1898, French and Russian anti-Semites—financed by the Okrana, the czarist secret service—were forging a weapon against the Jews that would have great historical significance, the infamous *Protocols of the Elders of Zion*. This book purported to present the accidentally discovered minutes of a mysterious world council of Jewish elders plotting to conquer the world for the great Jewish financiers and capitalists. The book hinged on two basic premises that had great significance for the future. The first, obviously religious in its origins, was that the Jews planned to overthrow Christian civilization. The second, the existence of a plot, was intended primarily to mobilize the masses. At first the *Protocols* were distributed only in Russia, in the wake of the Kishinev pogrom. Although the *Times* of London proved in 1921 that the book was a fabrication, it subsequently became a best-seller and was translated into many languages; it was Hitler's favorite book. It is still published today, especially in Arab countries and by neo-Nazi groups in western Europe.

The rapid spread of anti-Semitism in both emancipated Western societies and eastern European societies where Jews remained unemancipated poses the question of whether there exists an unvarying anti-Semitism. Are we dealing with a substantially homologous phenomenon? What is the relationship between anti-Semitism and integration? Can the new anti-Semitism be interpreted as a reaction to integration, a refusal by a part of society to accept the Jewish minority (Arendt 1951)? And what elicited this negativity toward the Jew, his "difference" or his invisibility? For decades, Jews in the Western world had renounced all signs of diversity, including their clothing and their beards. They were indistinguishable from others. But this did not lead to an abandonment of the view that Jews were physically alien. Rather, influenced by positivistic and racial theories, emancipated society seemed continually to add new characteristics to the Jewish stereotype. Anti-Semitic cartoons now identified the Jew, not by his caftan and beard, but by his supposedly essential physical characteristics, the "Jewish" foot and, especially, the long and hooked "Jewish" nose (Gilman 1991). Integration thus seemed to pose new problems. Despite years of movement toward Jewish integration, assimilation, and equality, the sense that Jews were essentially different from others seemed to restate itself in mythic, threatening terms.

Afterword

In Modern Times

This book closes at the end of the nineteenth century. During this period the Jews throughout western Europe consolidated their emancipation, secured full political and civil rights, and mounted the various rungs of non-Jewish society. The Jews of eastern Europe did not obtain political and social emancipation, however, despite their attempts at modernization, and they thus fixed their sights on emigration to western Europe or to America. Meanwhile, a new anti-Semitism appeared in the West. "Modern," aggressive, and organized like a political party, it quickly appropriated age-old anti-Jewish images, to which it added new racial theories. This is a general picture of the Jewish condition in Europe at century's end, as it might have appeared to a contemporary of Dreyfus and Herzl, as it likely appeared to most Jews of the time. An epoch was closing; another, potentially more promising, one was opening.

I shall go no further. I shall not recount the two cardinal facts of twentieth-century Jewish history, Zionism and the Holocaust, which have made it profoundly different from the long Jewish Middle Ages and even from the more recent period of emancipation and modernization. I shall, however, attempt to examine some aspects of continuity and disruption in Jewish life during this century. The breaks with tradition have been decisive and clear-cut. But there is also an inevitable continuity bridging the past, subtending facts and mentalities, which permits one to trace the many anticipations and connections of every phenomenon.

The growth of a new American center in the Diaspora, the Holocaust, and the birth of the state of Israel were the twentieth century's most radical breaks in the continuum of the Jewish past. The Nazi extermination of six million Jews resulted in the almost total disappearance of the eastern European Jewish world and a great diminution of the western European one. Not only did it take place on a larger scale than previous anti-Semitic phenomena; it was qualitatively different, totally without precedent in the long history of anti-Semitism. No previous massacre, expulsion, or pogrom was informed by the same ideological context, had the same significance, and arrived at the same outcome.

Likewise, although with positive implications, the rise of political Zionism and the birth of the state of Israel were completely new phenomena. Zionism radically changed both the self-image of European Jews and their relationship with the surrounding milieu. It created a crisis in traditional Jewish identity, revolutionized the categories of political affiliation, and placed the concept of Jewish peoplehood on new foundations. The birth of Israel in 1948 transformed the Jews from a dispersed minority into a state, with all its attendant characteristics: political bodies, representation, a national culture. The relationship between a Diaspora that refuses to disappear and a state that often proposes itself as the legitimate political body of all Jews, including those scattered among the nations of the world, remains complex and problematic. But all this is radically new and represents a clear break with Diaspora history. Indeed, many of the builders of Israeli culture wanted to cut all ties to the Diaspora past, refusing even to recognize its value as a creative force (Yerushalmi 1982b).

To be sure, there is real continuity. Zionism, for example, has a long history that dates back to before the nineteenth century. Its roots are to be found in the myths and fantastic projects of return that were interwoven with messianism, and in the hope for return constantly repeated in daily prayer. But the antecedents of Zionism are also to be found in the Jews' concrete relationship with the land of Israel: beginning in the Renaissance, young men went there to study in Jerusalem, Hebron, and later Safed, and for centuries aged Jews migrated to Israel to find their final resting place. But there is a world of difference between these acts and political Zionism. The latter calls for a return to the ancestral land, not for its own sake, but as a way of giving the Jews a homeland, a state, indeed, a modern national identity. A world of difference exists as well between those earlier acts of allegiance to Israel and both Herzl's formula and the ways in which the various waves of immigrants began to implement it. Moreover, political Zionism was launched by changes in the Jewish world. It took root in the encounter with modernity, in the appearance of new forms of identity, often antithetical to religion, and in widespread transition from strict ritual observance to secular commitments.

Historians have at times striven to emphasize continuity in order to bridge the gap between the known and the unknown. Not a few historians have thus interpreted the Holocaust as the dramatic confirmation of the failure of emancipation. Questioning the sincerity of the liberal position vis-à-vis the Jews, they have searched the deficiencies and ambiguities of the liberal states for the source of anti-Semitism's spread in the twentieth century. The theory that ascribes the extermination of the Jewish people to the failure of emancipation or, in its more sophisticated versions, to the deficiencies and ambiguities of emancipation, has particular valences. On the one hand, this theory arises from the idea that anti-Semitism is a constant in society from which the Jew cannot escape, even through total assimilation. Indeed, the attempt to destroy the Jewish people in its entirety took place at the moment of greatest integration, an integration interpreted too often as a renunciation of identity. On the other hand, this theory is an interpretation born of hindsight, of the awareness that the Holocaust was, after all, the terminus of the road to emancipation. Despite their differences, assimilated and religious Jews died together in Auschwitz's gas chambers.

This, then, was the course of Jewish history. But was it really an inevitable course? Was the destruction of so great a part of the Jewish people really the price of the Jewish world's entry into modernity, its insertion into the surrounding society, with which Jews had centuries-old ties and in which they had in some cases lived from time immemorial? Whatever today's interpreters think, the rise of politically organized anti-Semitic groups capable of mobilizing public opinion was, however disquieting, a marginal phenomenon to the Jews at the end of the last century. When Jews analyzed anti-Semitism between the turn of the century and World War I, they were led, not to predict the slaughter of the Jewish people, but to deplore the persistence of age-old prejudices, bound to disappear as civilization progressed. Whatever current historians looking for continuity with twentieth-century anti-Semitism read into the statements of that period's politicians, writers, and liberal thinkers, contemporaries—at least in the West—had faith in the future.

Did the nineteenth-century Jewish world give in to cowardice, incomprehension, and renunciation of identity in favor of the enticements of assimilation? This is how Bernard Lazare and others judged the behav-

ior of French Jewry vis-à-vis the Dreyfus Affair. Hannah Arendt reiter-
ated this judgment in her attempt to shed light on the conflict between
assimilation and identity (Arendt 1951). Gershom Scholem offered a
similar opinion about the dialogue between Germans and Jews, a one-
way dialogue, to his way of thinking, that was advanced only by the
Jews. Of the same fabric was his scathing criticism in 1944 of Wissenschaft scholars for their proposal to give "a decent burial to Judaism"
(Scholem 1976).

Arendt and Scholem offered radical critiques of assimilation in an effort to reclaim Jewish identity. Unlike Arendt, Scholem was a Zionist,
but both viewed Jewish identity in opposition to the entire process of
Jewish emancipation in the West. And the awareness of the almost total
destruction of the Jewish people informed both critiques.

These are problems that have echoed far and wide in Jewish thought
during the past few decades, and not only in historiography. And yet,
despite the variety of views it incorporates, the interpretation that sees
the entire course of Jewish history—or at least the transition to modernity—as a prelude to the Holocaust is a distorted one. Casting a shadow
on the past, this interpretation calls into question the role of Jewish protagonists, transforming them into passive victims. It tends to annul creativity, innovation, and choice, and thus all of the important moments
of pre- and postemancipation Jewish history. But can we deny this interpretation some measure of legitimacy? Can we ignore hindsight or the
questions it must raise in our minds, deeply marking our profession as
historians and interpreters? The historian's work is rendered even more
difficult by the complex and indissoluble intermingling of historiography and memory, of historiographic rigor and defense of identity. Historians must always confront complexity. But the weight of the events
and their resistance to objective interpretation pose special problems to
the Jewish historian. Perhaps, too, the weight of today's knowledge on
the recounting of past history must be accepted and recognized. History
is primarily the way in which the historian imposes sense and order on
the past. As a consequence, writing post-Auschwitz Jewish history
means posing today's questions to the Jewish past.

The role that the Holocaust plays in modern Jewish historiography is
merely another aspect of the more general role it has assumed in the
transformation and remodeling of Jewish identity. In truth, the Holocaust experience became basic to Jewish identity only belatedly. In neither America nor Europe did its influence become apparent immediately
following the war. The first postwar years represent a parenthesis, a

need, as it were, to put the trauma on hold. But from the early 1960s, after the Eichmann trial and the appearance of such famous memoirs as *The Diary of Anne Frank,* Holocaust memory became a central element of discussions of the Jewish people and its destiny. Even more so, it became the driving force of a reaffirmation of Jewish identity, an identity, however, quite unlike that of tradition. The memory of recent persecution now filled the void left by the loss of religious identity.

The fragmentation and redefinition of Jewish identity—or, rather, of Jewish identities—is in reality the most significant development to confront today's Jewish world. This is the moment of no return, when the Jewish world came face-to-face with modernity—if we accept Zygmunt Bauman's definition of modernity as "emancipation of individual life from collective destiny" (Bauman 1988: 45). Who is Jewish, and how can one define a Jew? There are manifold answers to these questions. They all, however, focus on individual attachment to something variously defined as a community, a tradition, a people, a culture, and a perception of one's self. This transformation of Jewish identity is doubtless a twentieth-century phenomenon. All the same, it is strongly rooted in a history rife with conflicts and ruptures, in that very same past that the traditionalists would have us accept as immutable. By means of this fragmentation, this multiplication of identities, Jews entered the modern world. For better or worse, this is a reality with which current Jewish historians must deal.

These thoughts derive, first and foremost, from the need to map out a specific area for Jewish modernity and to assess whether the recent past displays continuity or discontinuity with the period immediately preceding it, that is, with the era of transition to modernity. But these thoughts also relate, albeit in a different way, to the rest of Jewish history, particularly the premodern period. They determine which questions today's historian will direct to the long "Middle Ages" of Jewish history, which ended only at the dawn of emancipation.

All of which brings me to my final observation. The most interesting recent historiography has dealt with what David Biale fittingly calls the "new past" (Biale 1996), that is, a past continually revisited and stripped of its clichés. To highlight this new history has been the aim of my book. First, it is a history of creativity, of a continual effort to take action not only in the Jewish but also in the surrounding world. This history thus portrays the Jews of the Diaspora as active protagonists and clears the field of the infinite varieties of "lachrymose history" that have demonstrated an incredible vitality, despite authoritative attempts to bury them. In this new past, not even the myth of an eternal anti-Semitism can so easily take root.

Second, this history offers us an image of transformation and intrinsic change. The communities change, the ways of adapting to the outside are transformed, new cultural models develop and are continually redefined, and the Halakhah itself is constantly evolving. Although the most traditionalist interpretation would have us believe so, it is not the case that premodern Jewry lived in a static world, which in turn was superseded by a Jewish world that continually changes and renews itself, or that is assimilated and has lost its way. Jewish history, like that of the rest of the world, has always been accompanied by continuity and disruption, although the periods of transformation and continuity in the two worlds have not always coincided.

And this brings us to another basic point of Jewish history; its connection to the surrounding milieu, to the surrounding culture, whether dominated by the Catholic Church, Protestantism, or nation-states. Based methodologically on socioanthropological rather than historical assumptions, the image ought to be one of rapport between societies and cultures. It should not be informed by legends with happy or sad endings, by fairy tales about symbiosis and cohabitation or, conversely, of persecution and impervious alienation. It has in fact become an unchallenged point of historical knowledge that there was an ongoing rapport between the two worlds, that the reciprocal influences and cultural exchanges were articulated in innumerable forms.

Emancipation, the transition to modernity, was the source of Jewish nineteenth-century historiography. Later, as a reaction to "assimilationist" Wissenschaft historiography, historians found new sources in Jewish nationalism and in Zionism. What is expressed by today's new historiography? What image of Jewish history is traced by recent historians who draw upon the tools of the social sciences and of non-Jewish historiography and assume the destructive task of wiping the slate clean of clichés, consoling myths, and apologias? These are questions that the historian can at present only ask.

Bibliography

Acosta, Uriel [Uriel da Costa (ca. 1585–1640)]. 1922. *Die Schriften des Uriel da Costa*. Edited by Carl Gebhardt. Curis Societatis Spinozanae. Amsterdam: M. Hertzberger.

———. 1967. *Uriel Acosta: A Specimen of Human Life*. New York: Bargman.

Adelman, Howard. 1988a. "Leon Modena: The Autobiography and the Man." In *The Autobiography of a Seventeenth-Century Venetian Rabbi: Leon Modena's "Life of Judah,"* edited by Mark R. Cohen, 19–49. Princeton: Princeton University Press.

———. 1988b. "Rabbi Leon Modena and the Christian Kabbalists." In *Renaissance Rereadings: Intertext and Context,* edited by Maryanne Cline Horowitz, Anne J. Cruz, and Wendy A. Furman, 271–86. Urbana: University of Illinois Press.

———. 1991. "Rabbis and Reality: Public Activities of Jewish Women in Italy during the Renaissance and Catholic Restoration." *Jewish History* 5.1: 27–40.

———. 1993. "The Educational and Literary Activities of Jewish Women in Italy during the Renaissance and the Catholic Restoration." In *Shlomo Simonsohn Jubilee Volume: Studies in the History of the Jews in the Middle Ages and Renaissance Period,* edited by Daniel Carpi et al., 9–23. Tel Aviv: Tel Aviv University, Faculty of Humanities, Chaim Rosenberg School of Jewish Studies.

———. 1995. "Servants and Sexuality: Seduction, Surrogacy, and Rape: Some Observations concerning Class, Gender and Race in Early Modern Italian Jewish Families." In *Gender and Judaism: The Transformation of Tradition,* edited by Tamar M. Rudavsky, 81–97. New York: New York University Press.

Adler, Elkan Nathan, ed. 1987. *Jewish Travellers in the Middle Ages: Nineteen Firsthand Accounts.* New York: Dover.

Albert, Phyllis Cohen. 1977. *The Modernization of French Jewry: Consistory and Community in the Nineteenth Century.* Hanover, N.H.: Brandeis University Press, distributed by University Press of New England.

———. 1992. "Israelite and Jew: How Did Nineteenth-Century French Jews Understand Assimilation?" In *Assimilation and Community: The Jews in Nineteenth-Century Europe,* edited by Jonathan Frankel and Steven Zipperstein, 88–109. New York: Cambridge University Press.

Allegra, Luciano. 1990. "L'ospizio dei catecumeni di Torino." *Bolletino storico-bibliographico subalpino* 88: 513–73.

———. 1993. "A Model of Jewish Devolution: Turin in the Eighteenth Century." *Jewish History* 7.2: 29–58.

———. 1996. *Identità in bilico: Il ghetto ebraico di Torino nel Settecento.* Turin.

Almog, Shmuel, ed. 1988. *Antisemitism through the Ages.* Translated by Nathan H. Reisner. New York: Pergamon Press for the Vidal Sassoon International Center for the Study of Antisemitism, Hebrew University of Jerusalem.

Anchel, Robert. 1946. *Les Juifs de France.* Paris: J. B. Janin.

Antoniazzi Villa, Anna. 1986. *Un processo contro gli Ebrei nella Milano del 1488.* Bologna: Cappelli.

Arbel, Benjamin. 1989. "Venice and the Jewish Merchants of Istanbul in the Sixteenth Century." In *The Mediterranean and the Jews: Banking, Finance and International Trade (XVI–XVIII Centuries),* edited by Ariel Toaff and Simon Schwarzfuchs, 39–56. Ramat-Gan, Israel: Bar-Ilan University Press.

———. 1995. *Trading Nations: Jews and Venetians in the Early-Modern Eastern Mediterranean.* Leiden: E. J. Brill.

Arendt, Hannah. 1951. *The Origins of Totalitarianism.* New York: Harcourt Brace Jovanovich.

———. [1957] 1974. *Rahel Varnhagen: The Life of a Jewish Woman.* New York: Harcourt Brace Jovanovich.

———. 1978. *The Jew as Pariah: Jewish Identity and Politics in the Modern Age.* New York: Grove Press.

Ashtor, Eliyahu. 1975. "New Data for the History of Levantine Jewries in the Fifteenth Century." *Bulletin of the Institute of Jewish Studies* 3: 67–102.

———. 1979. "Palermitan Jewry in the Fifteenth Century." *Hebrew Union College Annual* 50: 219–51.

———. 1983a. "La Fin du judaïsme sicilien." *Revue des Etudes juives* 142: 323–47.

———. 1983b. *The Jews and the Mediterranean Economy, Tenth–Fifteenth Centuries.* London: Variorum Reprints.

Assis, Yom Tov. 1988. "Sexual Behaviour in Mediaeval Hispano-Jewish Society." In *Jewish History: Essays in Honour of Chimen Abramsky,* edited by Ada Rapaport-Albert and Steven J. Zipperstein, 25–59. London: P. Halban.

Avisar, Samuel. 1980. *Tremila anni di letteratura ebraica.* Vol. 1. Rome.

Bachi, Roberto. 1938. "La demografia dell'Ebraismo italiano prima dell'Emancipazione." *La rassegna mensile di Israel* 12.7–9: 256–320.

———. 1962. "The Demographic Development of Italian Jewry from the Seventeenth Century." *Jewish Journal of Sociology* 4: 172–91.

Bachi, Roberto, and Sergio Della Pergola. 1984. "Gli Ebrei italiani nel quadro della demografia della diaspora." *Quaderni storici* 19: 155–91.

Baer, Fritz (Yizhak). 1929–36. *Die Juden im Christlichen Spanien: Urkunden und Regesten.* Berlin: vol. 1, Akademie Verlag; vol. 2, Schocken Verlag.

———. [1945] 1961–66. *A History of the Jews in Christian Spain.* 2 vols. Philadelphia: Jewish Publication Society of America.

———. 1989. "The Origins of Jewish Communal Organisation in the Middle Ages." In *Studies in Jewish History*, edited by Joseph Dan, 59–82. Binah, vol. 1. New York: Praeger.

Barnai, Jacob. 1992. "La diaspora sefardita nell'impero ottomano (dal quindicesimo al diciottesimo secolo)." In *Oltre il 1492*, edited by Anna Foa, Myriam Silvera, and Kenneth Stow, *La rassegna mensile di Israel* 58.1–2: 203–40.

Baron, Salo Wittmayer. 1942. *The Jewish Community.* 3 vols. Philadelphia: Jewish Publication Society of America.

———. [1937] 1952–83. *A Social and Religious History of the Jews.* 2d ed., rev. and enl. 18 vols. New York: Columbia University Press; Philadelphia: Jewish Publication Society of America.

Barzilay, Isaac E. 1960. "The Italian and Berlin Haskalah: Parallels and Differences." *Proceedings of the American Academy for Jewish Research* 29: 17–54.

Baskin, Judith R. 1991a. *Jewish Women in Historical Perspective.* Detroit: Wayne State University Press.

———, ed. 1991b. "Some Parallels in the Education of Medieval Jewish and Christian Women." *Jewish History* 5.1: 41–51.

———. 1994. *Women of the Word: Jewish Women and Jewish Writing.* Detroit: Wayne State University Press.

Basnage, Jacques, sieur de Beauval [1653–1723]. [1710] 1716. *Histoire des Juifs depuis Jesus Christ jusqu'à présent: Pour servir de continuation à l'Histoire de Joseph.* 9 vols. in 15. The Hague: H. Scheurleer.

Bataillon, Marcel. 1956. "Les Nouveaux Chrétiens de Ségovie en 1510." *Bulletin hispanique* 58: 207–31.

Bauman, Zygmunt. 1988. "Exit Visa and Entry Tickets: Paradoxes of Jewish Assimilation." *Telos* 77: 45–77.

Beinart, Haim. 1971. "The Converso Community in Sixteenth- and Seventeenth-Century Spain." In *The Sephardi Heritage: Essays on the History and Cultural Contribution of the Jews of Spain and Portugal*, edited by Richard D. Barnett, 1: 457–78. New York: Ktav.

———. 1980. *Trujillo: A Jewish Community in Extremadura on the Eve of the Expulsion from Spain.* Jerusalem: Magnes Press, Hebrew University.

———. 1981. *Conversos on Trial: The Inquisition in Ciudad Real.* Translated by Yael Guiladi. Jerusalem: Magnes Press, Hebrew University.

———. 1985. "La Inquisicion española y la expulsion de los judios de Andalucia." In World Congress of Jewish Studies 1985, 103–23.

Bennassar, Bartolomé, et al. 1979. L'Inquisition espagnole: XVe–XIXe siècle. Paris: Hachette.

Ben-Sasson, Haim Hillel. 1966. "Jewish-Christian Disputation in the Setting of Humanism and Reformation in the German Empire." Harvard Theological Review 59: 369–90.

———. 1971. "The Reformation in Contemporary Jewish Eyes." Proceedings of the Israel Academy of Sciences and Humanities 4: 239–326.

———. [1969] 1976. A History of the Jewish People. Cambridge, Mass.: Harvard University Press.

———. 1989. "The Generation of the Spanish Exiles Considers Its Fate." In Studies in Jewish History, edited by Joseph Dan, 83–98. Binah, vol. 1. New York: Praeger.

Berger, David, ed. 1986a. History and Hate: The Dimensions of Anti-Semitism. Philadelphia: Jewish Publication Society of America.

———. 1986b. "Mission to the Jews and Jewish-Christian Contacts in the Polemical Literature of the High Middle Ages." American Historical Review 91: 576–91.

Berliner, Abraham. 1893. Geschichte der Juden in Rom von der ältesten Zeit bis zur Gegenwart (2050 Jahre). Frankfurt a./M.: J. Kauffmann.

Bernardi Saffiotti, Simonetta. 1983. "Gli Ebrei e le Marche nei secoli XIV e XV: Bilancio di studi, prospettive di ricerca." In Aspetti e problemi della presenza ebraica nell'Italia centro-settentrionale (secoli XIV e XV), edited by Sofia Boesch Gajano, 227–72. Rome: Istituto di scienze storiche dell'Università di Roma.

———. 1990. "Presenze ebraiche nelle Marche: Un caso nella valle del Fiastra." In La valle del Fiastra tra antichità e Medioevo, 505–44. Macerata.

Bernardino da Siena [Saint, 1380–1444]. 1958. Le prediche volgari, edited by Ciro Cannarozzi. Pistoia: Alberto Pacinotti, 1934–40. Florence.

Berti, Silvia. 1996. "A World Apart? Gershom Scholem and Contemporary Readings of Seventeenth-Century Jewish-Christian Relations." Jewish Studies Quarterly 3.1: 212–24.

Bethencourt, Francisco. 1995. L'Inquisition à l'époque moderne: Espagne, Portugal, Italie, XVe–XIXe siècle. Paris: Fayard.

Biale, David. 1979. Gershom Scholem: Kabbalah and Counter-History. Cambridge, Mass.: Harvard University Press.

———. 1986. Power and Powerlessness in Jewish History. New York: Schocken Books.

———. 1992. Eros and the Jews: From Biblical Israel to Contemporary America. New York: Basic Books.

———. 1994. "Confessions of an Historian of Jewish Culture." Jewish Social Studies 1.1: 40–51.

———. 1996. "Between Polemics and Apologetics: Jewish Studies in the Age of Multiculturalism." Jewish Studies Quarterly 3: 174–84.

Biondi, Albano. 1994. "Gli Ebrei e l'Inquisizione negli Stati estensi." In L'Inqui-

sizione e gli Ebrei in Italia, edited by Michele Luzzati, 265–85. Rome: Laterza.

Biraben, Jean-Noël. 1975–76. *Les Hommes et la peste en France et dans les pays européens et méditerranéens.* 2 vols. Paris: Mouton.

Birnbaum, Pierre. 1995. "Between Social and Political Assimilation: Remarks on the History of Jews in France." In *Paths of Emancipation: Jews, States and Citizenship,* edited by id. and Ira Katznelson, 94–127. Princeton: Princeton University Press.

Birnbaum, Pierre, and Ira Katznelson. 1995. "Emancipation and the Liberal Offer." In *Paths of Emancipation: Jews, States and Citizenship,* edited by id., 3–36. Princeton: Princeton University Press.

Blumenkranz, Bernhard. 1960. *Juifs et chrétiens dans le monde occidental, 430–1096.* Paris: Mouton.

———. 1963. *Les Auteurs chrétiens latins du Moyen Age sur les juifs et le judaïsme.* Paris: Mouton.

———. 1966. *Le Juif médiéval au miroir de l'art chrétien.* Paris: Etudes augustiniennes.

Bodian, Miriam. 1985. "The Escamot of the Spanish-Portuguese Jewish Community of London, 1664." *Michael* 9: 9–26.

———. 1987. "The 'Portuguese' Dowry Societies in Venice and Amsterdam." *Italia* 6: 30–61.

———. 1989. "Amsterdam, Venice and the Marrano Diaspora in the Seventeenth Century." In *Dutch Jewish History: Proceedings of the Fourth Symposium on the History of the Jews in the Netherlands, 7–10 December–Tel Aviv–Jerusalem, 1986,* edited by Jozeph Michman, 2: 47–65. Giv'at Ram: Institute for Research on Dutch Jewry; Jerusalem: Hebrew University of Jerusalem.

———. 1994. "Men of the Nation: The Shaping of Converso Identity in Early Modern Europe." *Past & Present* 143: 48–76.

Boesch, Gajano Sofia. 1979. "Per una storia degli Ebrei in Occidente tra Antichità e Medioevo: La testimonianza di Gregorio Magno." *Quaderni medievali* 8: 12–43.

———. 1983. "Il comune di Siena e il prestito ebraico nei secoli XIV e XV: Fonti e problemi." In *Aspetti e problemi della presenza ebraica nell'Italia centrosettentrionale (secoli XIV e XV),* edited by id., 175–225. Rome: Istituto di scienze storiche dell'Università di Roma.

Boiteux, Martine. 1977. "Carnaval annexé: Essai de lecture d'une fête romaine." *Annales ESC* 32.2: 356–80.

Bonazzoli, Viviana. 1979. "Gli Ebrei del regno di Napoli all'epoca della loro espulsione. I parte: Il periodo aragonese (1456–1499)." *Archivio storico italiano* 127: 495–559.

———. 1981. "Gli Ebrei del regno di Napoli all'epoca della loro espulsione. II parte: Il periodo spagnolo (1501–1541)." *Archivio storico italiano* 129: 179–287.

———. 1990. *Il prestito ebraico nelle economie cittadine delle Marche fra '200 e '400.* Ancona.

Bonfil, Roberto. 1983. "Some Reflections on the Place of Azariah de Rossi's
  Meor'eynayim in the Cultural Milieu of Italian Renaissance Jewry." In
  Jewish Thought in the Sixteenth Century, edited by Bernard Dov Cooper-
  man, 23–48. Cambridge, Mass.: Harvard University Center for Jewish
  Studies.

———. 1984. "The Historian's Perception of the Jews in the Italian Renaissance: Towards a Reappraisal." *Revue des Etudes juives* 143: 59–82.

———. 1987. "Cultura e mistica a Venezia nel Cinquecento." In *Gli Ebrei e
  Venezia,* edited by Gaetano Cozzi, 469–506.

———. 1988a. "Change in the Cultural Patterns of a Jewish Society in Crisis:
  Italian Jewry at the Close of the Sixteenth Century." *Jewish History* 3.2:
  11–30.

———. 1988b. "How Golden Was the Age of the Renaissance in Jewish His-
  toriography?" In *Essays in Jewish Historiography: In memoria Arnaldo
  Dante Momigliano,* edited by Ada Rapoport-Albert, 78–102. Middletown,
  Conn.: Wesleyan University Press.

———. [1979] 1990. *Rabbis and Jewish Communities in Renaissance Italy.*
  Translated by Jonathan Chipman. Oxford: Published for the Littman Library
  by Oxford University Press.

———. 1992. "Preaching as Mediation between Elite and Popular Cultures:
  The Case of Judah del Bene." In *Preachers of the Italian Ghetto,* edited by
  David B. Ruderman, 67–88. Berkeley and Los Angeles: University of Cali-
  fornia Press.

———. [1991] 1994. *Jewish Life in Renaissance Italy.* Translated by Anthony
  Oldcorn. Berkeley and Los Angeles: University of California Press.

———. 1996a. "Lo spazio culturale degli Ebrei d'Italia fra Rinascimento ed età
  barocca." In *Gli Ebrei in Italia,* vol. 1: *Dall'Alto Medioevo all'età dei ghetti,*
  edited by Corrado Vivanti, 413–73. Turin.

———. 1996b. *Tra due mondi: Cultura ebraica e cultura cristiana nel Medioevo.* Naples: Liguori.

Bori, Pier Cesare. 1983. *Il vitello d'oro: Le radici della controversia antigiu-
  daica.* Turin: Boringhieri.

Borromeo, Agostino. 1994. "Inquisizione e *conversos* nella Sardegna spagnola."
  In *L'Inquisizione e gli Ebrei in Italia,* edited by Michele Luzzati, 197–216.
  Rome: Laterza.

Boureau, Alain. 1986. "L'Inceste de Judas: Essai sur la genèse de la haine anti-
  semite au XIIᵉ siècle." *L'Amour de la Haine: Nouvelle Revue de Psych-
  analyse* 33: 25–41.

Bowsky, William M., ed. 1971. *The Black Death: A Turning Point in History?*
  New York: Holt, Rinehart & Winston.

Braude, Benjamin. 1994. "Les Contes persanes de Menasseh ben Israel:
  Polémique, apologétique et dissimulation à Amsterdam au XVII siècle." *Annales ESC* 49.5: 1107–38.

Braudel, Fernand. 1972. *The Mediterranean and the Mediterranean World in
  the Age of Philip II.* Translated from French by Siân Reynolds. New York:
  Harper & Row.

Brault-Noble, Catherine, and Marc, Marie-José. 1980. "L'unificazione religiosa e sociale: La repressione delle minoranze." In *Storia dell'Inquisizione spagnola*, edited by Bartolomé Bennassar. Milan: Davis.

Breuer, Mordechai. 1988. "The 'Black Death' and Antisemitism." In Almog 1988, 139–51.

Browe, Peter. 1942. *Die Judenmission im Mittelalter und die Päpste*. Miscellanea historiae pontificiae, 6. Rome: SALER, rappresentanza della Case editrice Herder. Reprint, Rome: Università Gregoriana, 1973.

Caciorgna, Maria Teresa. 1983. "Presenza ebraica nel Lazio meridionale: Il caso di Sermoneta." In *Aspetti e problemi della presenza ebraica nell'Italia centrosettentrionale (secoli XIV e XV)*, edited by Sofia Boesch Gajano, 127–73. Rome: Istituto di scienze storiche dell'Università di Roma.

Calimani, Riccardo. [1985] 1987. *The Ghetto of Venice*. Translated by Katherine Silberblatt Wolfthal. New York: M. Evans.

Cantera Montenegro, Enrique. 1979. "Judios de Torrelaguna: Retorno de algunos expulsados entre 1493 y 1495." *Sefarad* 39: 333–46.

Caro Baroja, Julio. [1961] 1986. *Los Judios en la España moderna y contemporanea*. 3 vols. Madrid.

Carpentier, Elizabeth. 1971. "The Plague as a Recurrent Phenomenon." In *The Black Death: A Turning Point in History?* edited by William M. Bowsky, 35–37. New York: Holt, Rinehart & Winston.

Carrete Parrondo, Carlos. 1978. "Fraternisation between Jews and Christians in Spain before 1492." *American Sephardi* 9: 15–21.

Cassuto, Umberto. [1918] 1965. *Gli Ebrei a Firenze nell'età del Rinascimento*. Florence: L. S. Olschki.

Castro, Américo. 1961. *De la edad conflictiva*. Madrid: Taurus.

———. [1954] 1966. *La realidad historica de España*. Mexico City: Editorial Porrúa.

———. 1971. *The Spaniards: An Introduction to Their History*. Translated by Willard F. King and Selma Margaretten. Berkeley and Los Angeles: University of California Press. Reprinted 1985.

Caviglia, Stefano. 1996. *L'identità salvata: Gli Ebrei di Roma tra fede e nazione, 1870–1938*. Rome: Laterza.

Chazan, Robert. 1973. *Medieval Jewry in Northern France: A Political and Social History*. Baltimore: Johns Hopkins University Press.

———. 1980. *Church, State, and Jew in the Middle Ages*. New York: Behrman House.

———. 1987. *European Jewry and the First Crusade*. Berkeley and Los Angeles: University of California Press.

———. 1989. *Daggers of Faith: Thirteenth-Century Christian Missionizing and Jewish Response*. Berkeley and Los Angeles: University of California Press.

———. 1992. *Barcelona and Beyond: The Disputation of 1263 and Its Aftermath*. Berkeley and Los Angeles: University of California Press.

Cipolla, Carlo M. 1976. *Before the Industrial Revolution: European Society and Economy, 100–1700*. New York: Norton.

Cohen, Esther. 1989. "Symbols of Culpability and the Universal Language of Justice: The Ritual of Public Executions in Late Medieval Europe." *History of European Ideas* 11: 407–17.

———. 1993. *The Crossroads of Justice: Law and Culture in Late Medieval France.* Leiden: E. J. Brill.

Cohen, Esther, with Elliott Horowitz. 1990. "In Search of the Sacred: Jews, Christians and Rituals of Marriage in the Later Middle Ages." In *Journal of Medieval and Renaissance Studies* 20.2: 225–49.

Cohen, Gerson D. 1960–61. "The Story of the Four Captives." *Proceedings of the American Academy for Jewish Research* 29: 55–131.

———. 1967a. "Esau as Symbol in Early Medieval Thought." In *Jewish Medieval and Renaissance Studies,* edited by Alexander Altmann, 19–48. Cambridge, Mass.: Harvard University Press.

———. 1967b. "Messianic Postures of Ashkenazim and Sephardim (Prior to Sabbethai Zevi)." In *Studies of the Leo Baeck Institute,* edited by Max Kreutzberger. New York: F. Ungar.

Cohen, Jeremy. 1982. *The Friars and the Jews: The Evolution of Medieval Anti-Judaism.* Ithaca, N.Y.: Cornell University Press.

———. 1983. "The Jews as the Killers of Christ in the Latin *traditio,* from Augustine to the Friars." *Traditio* 39: 1–27.

———. 1986. "Scholarship and Intolerance in the Medieval Academy: The Study and Evaluation of Judaism in European Christendom." *American Historical Review* 91: 592–613.

———. 1987. "The Mentality of the Medieval Jewish Apostate: Peter Alfonsi, Hermann of Cologne, and Pablo Christiani." In *Jewish Apostasy in the Modern World,* edited by Todd Endelman, 20–47. New York: Holmes & Meier.

———. 1989a. *Be Fertile and Increase, Fill the Earth and Master It: The Ancient and Medieval Career of a Biblical Text.* Ithaca, N.Y.: Cornell University Press.

———. 1989b. "Recent Historiography on the Medieval Church and the Decline of European Jewry." In *Popes, Teachers, and Canon Law in the Middle Ages,* edited by J. R. Sweeney and Stanley Chodorow, 251–62. Ithaca, N.Y.: Cornell University Press.

———, ed. 1991. *Essential Papers on Judaism and Christianity in Conflict: From Late Antiquity to the Reformation.* New York: New York University Press.

———. 1996. "The Muslim Connection: On the Changing Role of the Jew in High Medieval Theology." In *From Witness to Witchcraft: Jews and Judaism in Medieval Christian Thought,* edited by Jeremy Cohen, 141–62. Wiesbaden: Harrassowitz.

Cohen, Mark R. 1972. "Leone da Modena's Riti: A Seventeenth-Century Plea for Social Toleration of Jews." *Jewish Social Studies* 37: 287–319.

———. 1980. *Jewish Self-Government in Medieval Egypt: The Origins of the Office of Head of the Jews.* Princeton: Princeton University Press.

———. 1994. *Under Crescent and Cross: The Jews in the Middle Ages.* Princeton: Princeton University Press.

Cohen, Mark R., with Theodore K. Rabb. 1988. "The Significance of Leon Modena's Autobiography for Early Modern Jewish and General European History." In *The Autobiography of a Seventeenth-Century Venetian Rabbi:*

Leon Modena's "Life of Judah," edited by Mark R. Cohen, 3–18. Princeton: Princeton University Press.

Cohen, Richard I. 1991. "Conversion in Nineteenth-Century France: Unusual or Common Practice?" *Jewish History* 5.2: 47–56.

Cohen, Robert. 1987. "Memoria para os siglos futuros: Myth and Memory on the Beginning of the Amsterdam Sephardi Community." *Jewish History* 2.1: 67–72.

———. 1992. "Dal commercio alla colonizzazione: Livorno ed Amsterdam nella prima metà del XVII secolo." In *Oltre il 1492,* edited by Anna Foa, Myriam Silvera, and Kenneth Stow, *La rassegna mensile di Israel* 58.1–2: 137–45.

Cohen, Shaye J. D. 1985. "The Origins of the Matrilinear Principle in Rabbinic Law." *AJS Review* 1: 19–53.

Cohen, Thomas V. 1988. "The Case of the Mysterious Coil of Rope: Street Life and Jewish Persona in Rome in the Middle of the Sixteenth Century." *Sixteenth Century Journal* 19: 209–21.

Cohn, Norman. [1957] 1961. *The Pursuit of the Millennium: Revolutionary Messianism in Medieval and Reformation Europe and Its Bearing on Modern Totalitarian Movements.* New York: Harper.

———. 1969. *Warrant for Genocide: The Myth of the Jewish World-Conspiracy and the Protocols of the Elders of Zion.* New York: Harper & Row. 3d ed. Chico, Calif.: Scholars Press, 1981.

Colafemmina, Cesare. 1980. "Insediamenti e condizioni degli Ebrei nell'Italia meridionale e insulare." In *Gli Ebrei nell'Alto Medioevo,* 197–229.

———. 1991. *Ebrei e cristiani novelli in Puglia: Le comunità minori.* Bari.

———. 1996. *Per la storia degli Ebrei in Calabria: Saggi e documenti.* Soveria Mannelli: Rubbettino.

Colorni, Vittore. 1935. "Prestito ebraico e comunità ebraiche nell'Italia centrale e settentrionale." *Rivista di Storia del diritto italiano* 8.3: 1–55.

———. 1945. *Legge ebraica e leggi locali.* Milan: A. Giuffrè.

———. 1956. *Gli Ebrei nel diritto comune fino alla prima emancipazione.* Milan: A. Giuffrè.

———. 1969. "Ebrei in Ferrara nei secoli XIII e XIV." In *Miscellanea di studi in memoria di Dario Disegni,* 69–106. Istituto di studi ebraici, Scuolo rabbinica S. H. Marguilies-Disegni pubblicazioni, 2. Turin.

———. 1980. "Gli Ebrei nei territori italiani a nord di Roma dal 568 agli inizi dal secolo XIII." In *Gli Ebrei nell'Alto Medioevo,* 241–309.

Concina, Ennio. 1991. "Parva Jerusalem." In *La città degli Ebrei. Il ghetto di Venezia: Architettura e urbanistica,* edited by id., Ugo Camerino, and Donatella Calabi, 11–155. Venice: Albrizzi Editore.

Contreras, Jaime. 1982. *El Santo Oficio de la Inquisición en Galicia, 1560–1700: Poder, sociedad y cultura.* Madrid: Akal.

Cooperman, Bernard. 1987. "Venetian Policy towards Levantine Jews and Its Broader Italian Context." In *Gli Ebrei e Venezia,* edited by Gaetano Cozzi, 65–84.

Coulet, Noël. 1978. "Juif intouchable et interdits alimentaires." In *Exclus et systèmes d'exclusion dans la littérature médiévale. Sénéfiance* 5: 207–21.

———. 1979. "De l'integration à l'exclusion: La Place des juifs dans les céré-
monies d'entrée solennelle au Moyen Age." *Annales ESC* 34.4: 672–83.

Cracco Ruggini, Lelia. 1980. "Pagani, Ebrei e Cristiani: Odio sociologico e odio
teologico nel mondo antico." In *Gli Ebrei nell'Alto Medioevo*, 15–101.

Dahan, Gilbert, ed. 1985. *Les Juifs au regard de l'histoire: Mélanges en l'honneur de Bernard Blumenkranz.* Paris: Picard.

———. 1988. "L'Eglise et les Juifs au Moyen-Age (XIIᵉ–XIVᵉ siècles)." In *Ebrei
e cristiani nell'Italia medievale e moderna: Conversioni, scambi, contrasti*,
edited by Michele Luzzati, Michele Olivari, and Alessandra Veronese, 19–
43. Rome: Carucci.

———. 1990. *Les intellectuels chrétiens et les Juifs au Moyen Age.* Paris: Editions du Cerf.

Dan, Joseph. 1987. *Gershom Scholem and the Mystical Dimension of Jewish
History.* New York: New York University Press.

Davis, Natalie Zemon. 1975a. "The Reasons for Bad Government." In id., *Society and Culture in Early Modern France: Eight Essays.* Stanford: Stanford
University Press.

———. 1975b. "The Rites of Violence." In id., *Society and Culture in Early
Modern France: Eight Essays*, 152–87. Stanford: Stanford University Press.

———. 1987. "Fame and Secrecy: Leon Modena's Life as an Early Modern Au-
tobiography." In *The Autobiography of a Seventeenth-Century Venetian
Rabbi: Leon Modena's "Life of Judah,"* translated and edited by Mark R.
Cohen, 50–71. Princeton: Princeton University Press.

———. 1995. *Women on the Margins: Three Seventeenth-Century Lives.* Cambridge, Mass.: Harvard University Press.

Dedieu, Jean-Pierre. 1980. "I quattro tempi dell'Inquisizione." In *Storia dell'Inquisizione spagnola*, edited by Bartolomé Bennassar. Milan: Davis.

Della Pergola, Sergio. 1974. "The Geography of Italian Jews: Countrywide Patterns." In *Studi sull'ebraismo italiano in memoria di Cecil Roth*, edited by
Elio Toaff, 93–128. Rome: Barulli.

———. 1983. *La trasformazione demografica della diaspora ebraica.* Turin:
Loescher.

Della Pergola, Sergio, and Roberto Bachi. 1984. "Gli Ebrei italiani nel quadro
della demografia della diaspora." *Quaderni storici* 19: 155–91.

Despres, Denise. 1996. "Mary of the Eucharist: Cultic Anti-Judaism in Some
Fourteenth-Century English Devotional Manuscripts." In *From Witness
to Witchcraft: Jews and Judaism in Medieval Christian Thought*, edited by
Jeremy Cohen, 375–401. Wiesbaden: Harrassowitz.

Di Segni, Riccardo. 1981. *Le unghie d'Adamo: Studi di antropologia ebraica.*
Naples: Guida.

———. 1985. *Il Vangelo del Ghetto.* Rome: Newton Compton editori.

———. [1976] 1986. *Guida alle regole alimentari ebraiche.* Rome: Carucci.

———. 1988. "Il folklore delle comunità ebraiche italiane." In *La cultura folk-
lorica*, edited by Franco Cardini, 309–37. Busto Arsizio: Bramante Editrice.

———. 1989. "Il padre assente: La trasmissione matrilineare dell'appartenenza
all'ebraismo." *Quaderni storici* 24: 143–204.

———. 1990a. "Colei che non ha mai visto il sangue: Alla ricerca delle radici ebraiche dell'idea della concezione verginale di Maria." *Quaderni storici* 25: 757–90.

———. 1990b. "Spazi sacri e spazi maledetti nella Roma ebraica." In *Luoghi sacri e spazi della santità*, edited by Sofia Boesch Gajano and Lucetta Scaraffia, 113–20. Turin: Rosenberg & Sellier.

Dohm, Christian Wilhelm von. [1781–83] 1957. *Concerning the Amelioration of the Civil Status of the Jews*. Translated by Helen Lederer. Cincinnati: Hebrew Union College–Jewish Institute of Religion. Originally published as *Über die bürgerliche Verbesserung der Juden* (2 vols.; Berlin: F. Nicolai). Note also French edition, *De la reforme politique des Juifs*, edited by Dominique Bourel (Paris, 1984).

Domínguez Ortiz, Antonio. 1988. *Los Judeoconversos en España y America*. Madrid: ISTMO.

———. 1992. *Los Judeoconversos en la España moderna*. Madrid: Editorial MAPFRE.

Douglas, Mary. 1966. *Purity and Danger: An Analysis of Pollution and Taboo*. London: Routledge & Kegan Paul.

———. 1972. "Deciphering a Meal." *Daedalus* 101: 61–82.

Drumont, Edouard Adolphe. 1886. *La France juive devant l'opinion*. Paris: Marpon & Flammarion.

Dubin, Lois. 1987. "Trieste and Berlin: The Italian Role in the Cultural Politics of the Haskalah." In *Toward Modernity: The European Jewish Model*, edited by Jacob Katz, 189–224. New Brunswick, N.J.: Transaction.

———. 1991. "The Ending of the Ghetto of Trieste in the Late Eighteenth Century." In *Il mondo ebraico: Gli Ebrei tra Italia nord-orientale e l'Impero asburgico dal Medioevo all'età moderna*, edited by Pier Cesare Ioly Zorattini and Giacomo Todeschini, 287–310. Pordenone: Studio tesi.

———. 1994. "Les Liaisons dangereuses: Mariage juif et état moderne à Trieste au XVIII siècle." *Annales ESC* 49.5: 1139–70.

Edwards, John. 1984a. "Elijah and the Inquisition: Messianic Prophecy among Conversos in Spain, C. 1500." *Nottingham Medieval Studies* 28: 79–94.

———. 1984b. "Jewish Testimony to the Spanish Inquisition: Teruel 1484–7." *Revue des Etudes juives* 143: 333–50.

———. 1988a. "Religious Faith and Doubt in Late Medieval Spain: Soria circa 1450–1500." *Past and Present* 120: 3–25.

———. 1988b. *The Jews in Christian Europe, 1400–1700*. London: Routledge.

———. 1992. "Religiosità maschile e femminile presso i nuovi cristiani spagnoli tra il 1450 e il 1550." In *Oltre il 1492*, edited by Anna Foa, Myriam Silvera, and Kenneth Stow, *La rassegna mensile di Israel* 58.1–2: 13–21.

Eisen, Arnold. 1994. "Rethinking Jewish Modernity." *Jewish Social Studies* 1.1: 1–21.

Endelman, Todd M. 1979. *The Jews of Georgian England (1714–1830). Tradition and Change in a Liberal Society*. Philadelphia: Jewish Publication Society of America.

———. 1987a. "The Englishness of Jewish Modernity in England." In *Toward Modernity: The European Jewish Model*, edited by Jacob Katz, 225–46. New Brunswick, N.J.: Transaction Books.

————, ed. 1987b. *Jewish Apostasy in the Modern World*. New York: Holmes & Meier.

————. 1990. *Radical Assimilation in English Jewish History, 1656–1945*. Bloomington: Indiana University Press.

————. 1991. "Anti-Semitism and Apostasy in Nineteenth-Century France: A Response to Jonathan Helfand." *Jewish History* 5.2: 57–64.

————. 1992. "German Jews in Victorian England: A Study in Drift and Defection." In *Assimilation and Community: The Jews in Nineteenth-Century Europe,* edited by Jonathan Frankel and Steven Zipperstein, 57–87. New York: Cambridge University Press.

Esposito, Anna. 1983a. "Gli Ebrei a Roma nella seconda metà del '400, attraverso i protocolli del Notaio Giovanni Amati." In *Aspetti e problemi della presenza ebraica nell'Italia centro-settentrionale (secoli XIV e XV),* edited by Sofia Boesch Gajano and Michele Luzzati, 29–125. Rome: Istituto di scienze storiche dell'Università di Roma.

————. 1983b. "Gli Ebrei a Roma tra Quattro e Cinquecento." In *Quaderni storici,* edited by Sofia Boesch Gajano and Michele Luzzati, 18: 815–45.

————. 1988. "Notai, medici, convertiti: Figure di intermediari nella società romana del tardo Quattrocento." In *Ebrei e cristiani nell'Italia medievale e moderna: Conversioni, scambi, contrasti,* edited by Michele Luzzati, Michele Olivari, and Alessandra Veronese, 113–21. Rome: Carcucci.

————. 1990. "Le comunità ebraiche di Roma prima del Sacco (1527): Problemi di identificazione." *Henoch* 12: 165–89.

————. 1995. *Un'altra Roma: Minoranze nazionali e comunità ebraiche tra Medioevo e Rinascimento*. Rome: Il Calamo.

Esposito, Anna, and Diego Quaglioni. 1990. *Processi contro gli Ebrei di Trento (1475–1478)*. Padua: CEDAM.

Etkes, Emanuel. 1987. "Immanent Factors and External Influences in the Development of the Haskalah Movement in Russia." In *Toward Modernity: The European Jewish Model,* edited by Jacob Katz, 13–32. New Brunswick, N.J.: Transaction Books.

Fabre-Vassas, Claudine. 1997. *The Singular Beast: Jews, Christians and the Pig*. Translated by Carol Volk. New York: Columbia University Press.

Febvre, Lucien. [1950] 1966. "Come Jules Michelet inventò il Rinascimento." In *Studi su Riforma e Rinascimento e altri scritti su problemi di metodo e di geografia storica,* translated by Corrado Vivanti. Turin: G. Einaudi. See also Lucien Febvre, *Michelet et la Renaissance* (Paris: Flammarion, 1992).

Feci, Simona. 1991. "In Roma ci era buona giustizia: I processi del Tribunale Criminale del Governatore contro Ebrei (1619–29)." Tesi di laurea dell' Università La Sapienza di Roma.

————. 1993. "The Death of a Miller: A Trial *contra Hebreos* in Baroque Rome." *Jewish History* 7.2: 9–28.

Finkelstein, Louis. 1924. *Jewish Self-Government in the Middle Ages*. New York: Jewish Theological Seminary of America.

Foa, Anna. 1988. "Il gioco del proselitismo: Politica delle conversioni e controllo della violenza nella Roma del Cinquecento." In *Ebrei e cristiani nell'Italia medievale e moderna: conversioni, scambi, contrasti,* edited by Michele Luzzati, Michele Olivari, and Alessandra Veronese, 155–69. Rome: Carucci.

———. 1990. "The New and the Old: The Spread of Syphilis, 1494–1530." In *Sex and Gender in Historical Perspective,* edited by Edgar Muir and Guido Ruggiero, 26–45. Baltimore: Johns Hopkins University Press.

———. 1992. *Ebrei in Europa: Dalla peste nera all'emancipazione XIV–XVIII secolo.* Storia e società. Rome: Laterza.

———. 1994. "L'immagine dell'ebreo tra magia e superstizione (XVII–XVIII secolo)." In *La questione ebraica dall'Illuminismo all'Impero (1700–1815),* edited by Paolo Alatri and Silvia Grassi, 3–13. Naples: Edizioni scientifiche italiane.

———. 1996. "The Witch and the Jew: Two Alikes That Were Not the Same." In *From Witness to Witchcraft: Jews and Judaism in Medieval Christian Thought,* edited by Jeremy Cohen, 361–74. Wiesbaden: Harrassowitz.

Foà, Simona, ed. 1987. *La giustizia degl'Ebrei.* Rome: Carucci.

Francastel, Pierre. 1952. "Un Mystère parisien illustré par Uccello: Le Miracle de l'hostie d'Urbino." *Revue archéologique* 39: 180–91.

Frankel, Jonathan. 1981. *Prophecy and Politics: Socialism, Nationalism and the Russian Jews, 1862–1917.* Cambridge: Cambridge University Press.

———. 1992. "Assimilation and the Jews in Nineteenth-Century Europe: Toward a New Historiography?" In *Assimilation and Community: The Jews in Nineteenth-Century Europe,* edited by Jonathan Frankel and Steven Zipperstein, 1–37. New York: Cambridge University Press.

Frattarelli Fischer, Lucia. 1983. "Proprietà e insediamenti ebraici a Livorno dalla fine del Cinquecento alla seconda metà del Settecento." In *Ebrei in Italia,* edited by Sofia Boesch Gajano and Michele Luzzati, *Quaderni storici* 18: 879–96.

———, ed. 1987. *Le "livornine" del 1591 e del 1593.* Leghorn.

Funkenstein, Amos. 1993. *Perceptions of Jewish History.* Berkeley and Los Angeles: University of California Press.

———. 1995. "The Dialectics of Assimilation." *Jewish Social Studies* 1.2: 1–14.

Gager, John. 1983. *The Origins of Antisemitism.* Oxford: Oxford University Press.

Gampel, Benjamin R. 1989. *The Last Jews on Iberian Soil: Navarrese Jewry 1479–1498.* Berkeley and Los Angeles: University of California Press.

García Càrcel, Ricard. 1976. *Orígenes de la inquisición española: El tribunal de Valencia, 1478–1530.* Barcelona: Ediciones Península.

Garin, Eugenio. 1996. "L'umanesimo italiano e la cultura ebraica." In *Gli Ebrei in Italia,* vol. 1: *Dall'Alto Medioevo all'età dei ghetti,* edited by Corrado Vivanti, 361–83. Turin.

Gay, Peter. 1959. *Voltaire's Politics: The Poet as Realist.* Princeton: Princeton University Press. 2d ed., Yale University Press, 1988.

———. 1966. *The Enlightenment: An Interpretation.* Vol. 1: *The Rise of Modern Paganism.* New York: Knopf. Norton reprint, 1977.

———. 1978. *Freud, Jews and Other Germans: Masters and Victims in Modernist Culture.* New York: Oxford University Press.

Gilchrist, John. 1969. *The Church and Economic Activity in the Middle Ages.* London: Macmillan; New York: St. Martin's Press.

———. 1988. "The Perception of Jews in the Canon Law in the Period of the First Two Crusades." *Jewish History* 3.1: 9–24.

Gilman, Sander L. 1991. *The Jew's Body.* New York: Routledge.

———. 1994. "The Visibility of the Jew in the Diaspora: Body Imagery and Its Cultural Context." In *Judaism in the Modern World,* edited by Alan Berger, 87–121. New York: New York University Press.

———. 1996. *Smart Jews: The Construction of the Image of Jewish Superior Intelligence.* Lincoln: University of Nebraska Press.

Ginzburg, Carlo. [1989] 1991. *Ecstasies: Deciphering the Witches' Sabbath.* New York: Pantheon Books.

———. 1992. "Just One Witness." In *Probing the Limits of Representation: Nazism and the "Final Solution,"* edited by Saul Friedlander, 82–96. Cambridge, Mass.: Harvard University Press.

———. 1995. "Representations of German Jewry: Images, Prejudices, Ideas— A Comment." In *In and Out of the Ghetto: Jewish-Gentile Relations in Late Medieval and Early Modern Germany,* edited by R. Po-chia Hsia and Hartmut Lehmann, 209–12. Cambridge, Mass.

Gli Ebrei e Venezia: Secoli XIV–XVIII: Atti del convegno internazionale organizzato dall'Istituto di storia della società e dello Stato veneziano della Fondazione Giorgio Cini, Venezia, Isola di San Giorgio Maggiore, 5–10 giugno 1983. 1987. Edited by Gaetano Cozzi. Milan: Edizioni Comunità.

Gli Ebrei nell'Alto Medioevo: 30 marzo–5 aprile 1978. 1980. Centro italiano di studi sull'Alto Medioevo. Spoleto: Presso la sede del Centro.

Glückel of Hameln [1646–1724]. [1932] 1977. *The Memoirs of Glückel of Hameln.* Translated with notes by Marvin Lowenthal; new introd. by Robert S. Rosen. New York: Schocken Books.

Goitein, Shlomo D. [1955] 1964. *Jews and Arabs: Their Contacts through the Ages.* New York: Schocken Books.

———. 1967–93. *A Mediterranean Society: The Jewish Communities of the Arab World as Portrayed in the Documents of the Cairo Geniza.* 6 vols. Berkeley and Los Angeles: University of California Press.

Grabois, Aryeh. 1975. "The Hebraica Veritas and Jewish Christian Intellectual Relations in the Twelfth Century." *Speculum* 59: 613–34.

Graetz, Heinrich Hirsch. [1853–70] 1946. *A History of the Jews.* 6 vols. Philadelphia: Jewish Publication Society of America.

Grayzel, Solomon. 1958. "The Confessions of a Medieval Convert." *Historia Judaica* 17: 89–120.

———. [1933] 1966. *The Church and the Jews in the Thirteenth Century: A Study of Their Relations during the Years 1198–1254, Based on the Papal Letters and Conciliar Decrees of the Period.* Vol. 1. New York: Hermon Press.

———. 1989. *The Church and the Jews in the Thirteenth Century,* vol. 2: 1254–1314, edited by Kenneth R. Stow. New York: Jewish Theological Seminary of America; Detroit: Wayne State University Press.

Grégoire, Henri. [1789] 1988. *Essai sur la régénération physique, morale et politique des Juifs.* Paris: Stock.

Gregorovius, Ferdinand. 1966. *The Ghetto and the Jews of Rome.* New York: Schocken Books.

Grossman, Avraham. 1988. "The Historical Background to the Ordinances on Family Affairs Attributed to Rabbenu Gershom Me'or ha-Golah ('The Light of the Exile')." In *Jewish History: Essays in Honour of Chimen Abramsky,* edited by Ada Rapaport-Albert and Steven J. Zipperstein, 3–23. London: P. Halban.

———. 1991. "Medieval Rabbinic Views on Wife-Beating, 800–1300." *Jewish History* 5.1: 53–62.

Guerchberg, Seraphine. 1948. "La Controverse sur les prétendus semeurs de la 'Peste Noire' d'aprés les traites de peste de l'époque." *Revue des Etudes juives* 118: 3–40.

Gutwirth, Eleazar. 1984. "The Jews in Fifteenth-Century Castilian Chronicles." *Jewish Quarterly Review* 74: 379–96.

———. 1985. "Elementos etnicos e historicos en las relaciones judeo-conversas en Segovia." In World Congress of Jewish Studies 1985, 83–102.

———. 1988. "The Expulsion from Spain and Jewish Historiography." In *Jewish History: Essays in Honour of Chimen Abramsky,* edited by Ada Rapaport-Albert and Steven J. Zipperstein, 141–61. London: P. Halban.

———. 1989a. "Abraham Seneor: Social Tensions and the Court-Jew." *Michael* 11: 169–229.

———. 1989b. "Duran on Ahitophel: The Practice of Jewish History in Late Medieval Spain." *Jewish History* 4.1: 59–74.

———. 1993. "Conversions to Christianity amongst Fifteenth-Century Spanish Jews: An Alternative Explanation." In *Shlomo Simonsohn Jubilee Volume: Studies in the History of the Jews in the Middle Ages and Renaissance Period,* edited by Daniel Carpi et al., 97–121. Tel Aviv: Tel Aviv University, Faculty of Humanities, Chaim Rosenberg School of Jewish Studies.

Hacohen, Joseph, and the Anonymous Corrector. 1971. *The Vale of Tears* (Emek Habacha), translated and edited by Harry S. May. The Netherlands: Martinus Nijoff.

Haliczer, Stephen. 1973. "The Castilian Urban Patriciate and the Jewish Expulsions of 1480–92." *American Historical Review* 78: 35–62.

Harris, Alan Charles. 1967. *La demografia del ghetto in Italia (1516–1797 circa).* Rome.

Heine, Heinrich [1797–1856]. 1947. *Heinrich Heine: The Rabbi of Bacherach. A Fragment,* edited by Erich Loewenthal. New York: Schocken Books.

Helfand, Jonathan I. 1988. "Passport and Piety: Apostasy in Nineteenth-Century France." *Jewish History* 3.2: 59–83.

———. 1991. "Assessing Apostasy: Facts and Theories." *Jewish History* 5.2: 65–71.

Hertz, Deborah. 1987. "Seductive Conversion in Berlin, 1770–1809." In *Jewish Apostasy in the Modern World,* edited by Todd M. Endelman, 48–82. New York: Holmes & Meier.

———. 1988. *Jewish High Society in Old Regime Berlin*. New Haven: Yale University Press.

Hertzberg, Arthur. [1968] 1990. *The French Enlightenment and the Jews: The Origins of Modern Anti-Semitism*. New York: Columbia University Press.

Herzl, Theodor. [1896] 1988. *The Jewish State*. New York: Dover Publications.

Herzog, Dagmar. 1996. *Intimacy and Exclusion: Religious Politics in Pre-Revolutionary Baden*. Princeton: Princeton University Press.

Heyd, Michael. 1989. "Menasseh ben Israel as a Meeting Point of Jewish and European History: Some Summary Comments." In *Menasseh ben Israel and His World,* edited by Yosef Kaplan, Henry Méchoulan, and Richard Popkin, 262–67. Leiden: E. J. Brill.

Hill, Christopher. 1972. *The World Turned Upside Down: Radical Ideas during the English Revolution*. London: Temple Smith.

Hook, David. 1989. "Some Problems in Andres Bernaldez's Account of the Spanish Jews." *Michael* 11: 231–55.

Horowitz, Elliott. 1985. "A Jewish Youth Confraternity in Seventeenth-Century Italy." *Italia* 5: 36–97.

———. 1986. "The Way We Were: Jewish Life in the Middle Ages." *Jewish History* 1.1: 75–90.

———. 1987. "Jewish Confraternal Piety in the Veneto in the Sixteenth and Seventeenth Centuries." In *Gli Ebrei e Venezia,* edited by Gaetano Cozzi, 301–13.

———. 1989a. "Coffee, Coffeehouses and the Nocturnal Rituals of Early Modern Jewry." *AJS Review* 14: 17–46.

———. 1989b. "The Eve of the Circumcision: A Chapter in the History of Jewish Nightlife." *Journal of Social History* 23: 45–69.

———. 1992. "Speaking of the Dead: The Emergence of the Eulogy among Italian Jewry of the Sixteenth Century." In *Preachers of the Italian Ghetto,* edited by David B. Ruderman, 129–62. Berkeley and Los Angeles: University of California Press.

———. 1994. "Visages du judaïsme: De la barbe en monde juif et de l'élaboration de ses significations." *Annales ESC* 49.5: 1065–90.

Horowitz, Elliott, and Esther Cohen. 1990. "In Search of the Sacred: Jews, Christians and Rituals of Marriage in the Later Middle Ages." *Journal of Medieval and Renaissance Studies* 20.2: 225–49.

Howe, Irving. 1976. *World of Our Fathers*. New York: Harcourt Brace Jovanovich.

Hsia, R. Po-chia. 1988. *The Myth of Ritual Murder: Jews and Magic in Reformation Germany*. New Haven: Yale University Press.

———. 1992. *Trent 1475: Stories of a Ritual Murder Trial*. New Haven: Yale University Press in cooperation with Yeshiva University Library.

———. 1995. "The Usurious Jew: Economic Structure and Religious Representations in an Anti-Semitic Discourse." In *In and Out of the Ghetto: Jewish-Gentile Relations in Late Medieval and Early Modern Germany,* edited by R. Po-chia Hsia and Hartmut Lehmann, 161–76. Cambridge, Mass.

———. 1996. "Witchcraft, Magic and the Jews in Late Medieval and Early Modern Germany." In *From Witness to Witchcraft: Jews and Judaism in Me-*

dieval Christian Thought, edited by Jeremy Cohen, 361–74. Wiesbaden: Harrassowitz.

Hughes, Diane Owen. 1986. "Distinguishing Signs: Ear-Rings, Jews and Franciscan Rhetoric in the Italian Renaissance." *Past and Present* 112: 3–59.

Hyman, Paula E. 1995. *Gender and Assimilation in Modern Jewish History: The Roles and Representation of Women.* Seattle: University of Washington Press.

Idel, Moshe. 1983. "The Magical and Neoplatonic Interpretations of the Kabbalah in the Renaissance." In *Jewish Thought in the Sixteeenth Century,* edited by Bernard Dov Cooperman, 186–242. Cambridge, Mass.

———. 1986. "Major Currents in Italian Kabbalah between 1550–1660." In *Italia judaica* 1986, 2: 243–62.

———. 1987. "Differing Conceptions of Kabbalah in the Early Seventeenth Century." In *Jewish Thought in the Seventeenth Century,* edited by Isadore Twersky and Bernard Septimus, 137–200. Cambridge, Mass.

———. 1988. *Kabbalah: New Perspectives.* New Haven: Yale University Press.

———. 1989. "Kabbalah, Platonism and Prisca Theologia: The Case of R. Menasseh ben Israel." In *Menasseh ben Israel and His World,* edited by Yosef Kaplan, Henry Méchoulan and Richard Popkin, 207–19. Leiden: E. J. Brill.

———. 1992. "Judah Moscato: A Late Renaissance Jewish Preacher." In *Preachers of the Italian Ghetto,* edited by David B. Ruderman, 41–66. Berkeley and Los Angeles: University of California Press.

———. 1995. *Hasidim: Between Ecstasy and Magic.* Albany: State University of New York Press.

Infessura, Stefano. 1890. *Diario della città di Roma di Stefano Infessura scribasenato.* Nuova edizione a cura di Oreste Tommasini. Rome: Forzani. Fonti per la storia d'Italia pubblicate dall'Istituto storico italiano. Scrittori, secolo XV, no. 5.

Ioly Zorattini, Pier Cesare, ed. 1980–94. *Processi del S. Uffizio di Venezia contro Ebrei e giudaizzant.* 12 vols. Florence: L. S. Olschki.

———. 1988. "Battesimi invitis parentibus nella Repubblica di Venezia durante l'età moderna: I casi padovani." In *Ebrei e cristiani nell'Italia medievale e moderna: conversioni, scambi, contrasti,* edited by Michele Luzzati, Michele Olivari, and Alessandra Veronese, 171–82. Rome: Carucci.

———. 1989. "Anrriquez Nunez alias Abraham alias Righetto: A Marrano Caught between the S. Uffizio of Venice and the Inquisition of Lisbon." In *The Mediterranean and the Jews: Banking, Finance and International Trade (XVI–XVIII Centuries),* edited by Ariel Toaff and Simon Schwarzfuchs, 291–307. Ramat-Gan, Israel: Bar-Ilan University Press.

Isaac, Jules. 1948. *Jésus et Israël.* Paris: A. Michel. Translated by Sally Gran and edited by Claire Huchet Bishop under the title *Jesus and Israel* (New York: Holt, Rinehart & Winston, 1971).

———. 1956. *Genèse de l'antisémitisme: Essai historique.* Paris: Calmann-Lévy.

Israel, Jonathan. 1985. *European Jewry in the Age of Mercantilism, 1550–1750.* Oxford: Clarendon Press; New York: Oxford University Press.

———. 1987. "The Jews of Venice and Their Links with Holland and with Dutch Jewry (1600–1710)." In *Gli Ebrei a Venezia,* edited by Gaetano Cozzi, 95–116.

———. 1989. "Menasseh ben Israel and the Dutch Sephardic Colonisation Movement of the Mid-Seventeenth Century (1645–1657)." In *Menasseh ben Israel and His World,* edited by Yosef Kaplan, Henry Méchoulan, and Richard Popkin, 139–63. Leiden: E. J. Brill.

Italia judaica: Atti del I convegno internazionale, Bari, 18–22 maggio 1981. 1983. Rome: Ministero per i beni culturali e ambientali.

Italia judaica: Gli Ebrei in Italia dalla segregazione alla prima emancipazione: Atti del III convegno internazionale, Tel Aviv, 15–20 giugno 1986. 1989. Rome: Ministero per i beni culturali e ambientali.

Italia judaica: Gli Ebrei in Italia tra Rinascimento ed età barocca: Atti del II convegno internazionale, Genova, 10–15 giugno 1984. 1986. Rome: Ufficio centrale per i beni archivistici, Divisione studi e pubblicazioni.

Jacoby, David. 1987. "Venice and Venetian Jews in the Eastern Mediterranean." In *Gli Ebrei e Venezia,* edited by Gaetano Cozzi, 29–58.

Jordan, William Chester. 1976. "Problems of the Meat Market of Béziers 1240–1247: A Question of Anti-Semitism." *Revue des Etudes juives* 135: 31–49.

———. 1978. "Jews on Top: Women and the Availability of Consumption Loans in Northern France in the Mid-Thirteenth Century." *Journal of Jewish Studies* 29: 39–56.

———. 1986. "Christian Excommunication of the Jews in the Middle Ages: A Restatement of the Issues." *Jewish History* 1.1: 31–38.

———. 1989. *The French Monarchy and the Jews: From Philip Augustus to the Last Capetians.* Philadelphia: University of Pennsylvania Press.

———. 1996. "Princely Identity and the Jews in Medieval France." In *From Witness to Witchcraft: Jews and Judaism in Medieval Christian Thought,* edited by Jeremy Cohen, 257–73. Wiesbaden: Harrassowitz.

Kamen, Henry. 1965. *The Spanish Inquisition.* London: White Lion. See also id., *The Spanish Inquisition: A Historical Revision* (New Haven: Yale University Press, 1998).

———. 1985. *Inquisition and Society in Spain in the Sixteenth and Seventeenth Centuries.* Bloomington: Indiana University Press.

———. 1988. "The Mediterranean and the Expulsion of Spanish Jews in 1492." *Past and Present* 119: 30–55.

Kaplan, Marion. 1992. "Gender and Jewish History in Imperial Germany." In *Assimilation and Community: The Jews in Nineteenth-Century Europe,* edited by Jonathan Frankel and Steven Zipperstein, 199–224. New York: Cambridge University Press.

Kaplan, Yosef. 1984. "The Social Functions of the Herem in the Portuguese Community of Amsterdam in the Seventeenth Century." In *Dutch Jewish History: Proceedings of the Symposium on the History of the Jews in the Netherlands, November 28–December 3, 1982, Tel Aviv–Jerusalem,* ed. Jozeph Michman and Tirtsah Levie, 1: 111–55. Jerusalem: Tel Aviv University.

———. 1985. "The Travels of Portuguese Jews from Amsterdam to the 'Lands of Idolatry' (1644–1724)." In World Congress of Jewish Studies 1985, 197–223.

———. [1980] 1988. "Jews and Judaism in the Political and Social Thought of Spain in the Sixteenth and Seventeenth Centuries." In Almog 1988, 153–60.

———. [1982] 1989a. *From Christianity to Judaism: The Story of Isaac Orobio de Castro.* Oxford: Oxford University Press for the Littman Library.

———. 1989b. "Political Concepts in the World of the Portuguese Jews of Amsterdam during the Seventeenth Century: The Problem of Exclusion and the Boundaries of Self-Identity." In *Menasseh ben Israel and His World,* edited by Yosef Kaplan, Henry Méchoulan, and Richard Popkin, 45–62. Leiden: E. J. Brill.

———. 1989c. "The Portuguese Community in the Seventeenth-Century Amsterdam and the Ashkenazi World." In *Dutch Jewish History: Proceedings of the Fourth Symposium on the History of the Jews in the Netherlands, 7–10 December—Tel Aviv–Jerusalem, 1986,* vol. 2, edited by Jozeph Michman, 23–45. Giv'at Ram: Institute for Research on Dutch Jewry; Jerusalem: Hebrew University of Jerusalem.

———. 1990. "Karaites in Early Eighteenth-Century Amsterdam." In *Sceptics, Millenarians and Jews,* edited by David Katz and Jonathan Israel, 196–236. Leiden: E. J. Brill.

———. 1992. "Devianza e punizione nella diaspora sefardita occidentale del XVII secolo: I portoghesi ad Amsterdam." In *Oltre il 1492,* edited by Anna Foa, Myriam Silvera, and Kenneth Stow, *La rassegna mensile di Israel* 58.1–2: 163–202.

Katz, David S. 1982. *Philo-Semitism and the Readmission of the Jews to England, 1603–1655.* Oxford: Clarendon Press; New York: Oxford University Press.

———. 1994. *The Jews in the History of England, 1485–1850.* Oxford: Clarendon Press; New York: Oxford University Press.

Katz, Jacob. 1961. *Exclusiveness and Tolerance: Studies in Jewish-Gentile Relations in Medieval and Modern Times.* London: Oxford University Press.

———. 1970. *Jews and Freemasons in Europe, 1723–1939.* Cambridge, Mass.: Harvard University Press.

———. [1958] 1971. *Tradition and Crisis: Jewish Society at the End of the Middle Ages.* New York: Schocken Books.

———. 1972. *Emancipation and Assimilation: Studies in Modern Jewish History.* Farnborough: Gregg.

———. 1973. *Out of the Ghetto: The Social Background of Jewish Emancipation, 1770–1870.* Cambridge, Mass.: Harvard University Press.

———, ed. 1975. *The Role of Religion in Modern Jewish History: Proceedings of Regional Conferences of the Association for Jewish Studies, held at the University of Pennsylvania and the University of Toronto in March–April 1974.* Cambridge, Mass.: The Association.

———. 1983. "Post-Zoharic Relations between Halakhah and Kabbalah." In *Jewish Thought in the Sixteenth Century,* edited by Bernard Dov Cooper-

man, 283–307. Cambridge, Mass.: Harvard University Center for Jewish
Studies.

————, ed. 1987. *Toward Modernity: The European Jewish Model.* New Brunswick, N.J.: Transaction Books.

————. 1989. *The "shabbes goy": A Study in Halakhic Flexibility.* Philadelphia: Jewish Publication Society of America.

————. 1995. *With My Own Eyes: The Autobiography of an Historian.* Translated by Ann Brenner and Zipora Brody. Hanover, N.H.: University Press of New England for Brandeis University Press.

————. 1997. "Da'at Torah—The Unqualified Authority Claimed for Halakhists." *Jewish History* 11.1: 41–50.

Kedar, Benjamin Z. 1984. *Crusade and Mission: European Approaches toward the Muslims.* Princeton: Princeton University Press.

Kellenbenz, Hermann. 1987. "I Mendes, i Rodriguez d'Europa e i Ximenes nei loro rapporti commerciali con Venezia." In *Gli Ebrei a Venezia,* edited by Gaetano Cozzi, 143–61.

Kieval, Hillel. 1992. "The Social Vision of Bohemian Jews: Intellectuals and Community in the 1840s." In *Assimilation and Community: The Jews in Nineteenth-Century Europe,* edited by Jonathan Frankel and Steven Zipperstein, 246–83. New York: Cambridge University Press.

————. 1994a. "Antisemitisme ou savoir social? Sur la gènese du proces moderne pour meurtre rituel." *Annales ESC* 49.5: 1091–1105.

————. 1994b. "Representation and Knowledge in Medieval and Modern Accounts of Jewish Ritual Murder." *Jewish Social Studies* 1.1: 52–72.

————. 1996. "Death and the Nation: Ritual Murder as Political Discourse in the Czech Lands." *Jewish History* 10.1: 75–92.

Kisch, Guido. 1943. "The Jewish Execution in Mediaeval Germany." *Historia Judaica* 5: 103–32.

————. 1944. "The Jew's Function in the Medieval Evolution of Economic Life." *Historia Judaica* 6: 1–12.

————. 1949. *The Jews in Medieval Germany: A Study of Their Legal and Social Status.* Chicago: University of Chicago Press.

————. 1957. "The Yellow Badge in History." *Historia Judaica* 19: 89–146.

Kohn, Roger. 1988. *Les Juifs de la France du Nord dans la seconde moitié du XIVᵉ siècle.* Louvain: E. Peeters.

Kriegel, Maurice. 1976. "Un Trait de psychologie sociale dans les pays méditerranéens du Bas Moyen Age: Le Juif comme intouchable." *Annales ESC* 31.2: 326–30.

————. 1978a. "Mobilisation politique et modernisation organique: Les Expulsions de Juifs au Bas Moyen Age." *Archives de Sciences Sociales des Religions* 46: 5–20.

————. 1978b. "Prémarranisme et Inquisition dans la Provence des XIIIᵉ et XIVᵉ siècles." *Provence historique* 29: 313–23.

————. 1978c. "La Prise d'une décision: L'Expulsion des Juifs d'Espagne en 1492." *Revue historique* 260: 49–90.

————. 1979. *Les Juifs à la fin du Moyen Age dans l'Europe méditerranéenne.* Paris: Hachette.

———. 1980a. "La Juridiction inquisitoriale sur les Juifs à l'époque de Philippe l'Hardi et Philippe le Bel." In Yardeni 1980, 70–77.

———. 1980b. "Sabbatai Zevi ou les chemins paradoxaux de la modernité." *Le Débat* 3: 133–141.

———. 1985. "Gershom Scholem: Ecriture historique et renaissance nationale au XXe siècle." *Le Débat* 33: 126–39.

———. 1992. "La definitiva soppressione del pluralismo religioso nella Spagna dei re cattolici: Limiti e efficacia dell'approccio intenzionalista." In *Oltre il 1492*, edited by Anna Foa, Myriam Silvera, and Kenneth Stow, *La rassegna mensile di Israel* 58.1–2: 1–12.

———. 1997. "Le Messianisme confessionalise: L'Orthodoxie juive au défi de l'Emancipation." In *Figures du Messie*, edited by Claude Cohen-Boulakia and Shmuel Trigano, 45–62. Paris.

Ladero Quesada, Miguel-Angel. 1975. "Le Nombre des Juifs dans la Castille du XVeme siècle." In *Papers in Jewish Demography*, 2: 45–52.

Langmuir, Gavin I. 1960. "*Judaei Nostri* and the Beginning of Capetian Legislation." *Traditio* 16: 203–39.

———. 1963. "The Jews and the Archives of Angevin England: Reflections on Medieval Anti-Semitism." *Traditio* 19: 183–244.

———. 1972. "The Knight's Tale of Young Hugh of Lincoln." *Speculum* 47: 459–82.

———. 1977. "L'Absence d'accusation de meurtre rituel à l'ouest du Rhône." In *Juifs et Judaïsme de Languedoc: XIIIe siècle–début XIVe siècle*, edited by Bernhard Blumenkranz and Marie-Humbert Vicaire, 235–49. Toulouse.

———. 1980a. "From Ambrose of Milan to Emicho of Leiningen: The Transformation of Hostility against Jews in Northern Christendom." In *Gli Ebrei nell'Alto Medioevo*, 313–68.

———. 1980b. "*Tanquam Servi*: The Change in Jewish Status in French Law about 1200." In Yardeni 1980, 24–54.

———. 1984. "Thomas of Monmouth: Detector of Ritual Murder." *Speculum* 59: 822–47.

———. 1985. "Historiographic Crucifixion." In *Les Juifs au regard de l'histoire: Mélanges en l'honneur de Bernhard Blumenkranz*, edited by Gilbert Dahan, 109–27. Paris: Picard.

———. 1987. "Toward a Definition of Antisemitism." In *The Persisting Question: Sociological and Social Contexts of Modern Antisemitism*, edited by Helen Fein, 86–127. New York: De Gruyter.

———. 1990a. *History, Religion, and Antisemitism*. Berkeley and Los Angeles: University of California Press.

———. 1990b. *Toward a Definition of Antisemitism*. Berkeley and Los Angeles: University of California Press.

Laras, Giuseppe. 1979. "Le Grand Sanhédrin de 1807 et ses conséquences en Italie: Organisation des concistoires et réactions des communautés." In *Le Grand Sanhédrin de Napoléon*, edited by Bernhard Blumenkranz and Albert Soboul, 101–17. Collection franco-judaïca, 8. Toulouse: Privat.

Lasker, Daniel J. 1980. "Averroistic Trends in Jewish-Christian Polemics in the Late Middle Ages." *Speculum* 55: 294–304.

Lassner, Jacob. 1990. "The Origins of Muslim Attitudes towards the Jews and Judaism." *Judaism* 39: 494–507.

Lea, Henry Charles. [1905–7] 1966. *A History of the Inquisition of Spain.* 4 vols. New York: American Scholar Publications.

———. [1890] 1967. "El Santo Niño de La Guardia." In *Chapters from the Religious History of Spain connected with the Inquisition,* 437–79. New York: Burt Franklin.

Lederhendler, Eli. 1989. *The Road to Modern Jewish Politics: Political Tradition and Political Reconstruction in the Jewish Community of Tzarist Russia.* New York: Oxford University Press.

———. 1992. "Modernity without Emancipation or Assimilation? The Case of Russian Jewry." In *Assimilation and Community: The Jews in Nineteenth-Century Europe,* edited by Jonathan Frankel and Steven Zipperstein, 324–43. New York: Cambridge University Press.

———. 1994. *Jewish Responses to Modernity: New Voices in America and Eastern Europe.* New York: New York University Press.

Le Goff, Jacques. 1977. *Pour un autre Moyen Age: Temps, travail et culture en Occident: 18 essais.* Paris: Gallimard. Translated by Arthur Goldhammer as *Time, Work and Culture in the Middle Ages* (Chicago: University of Chicago Press, 1980).

Leroy, Beatrice. 1985. "La Vie économique des Juifs de Navarre au XIVe siècle." In World Congress of Jewish Studies 1985, 39–61.

Lesley, Artur. 1982. "Hebrew Humanism in Italy: The Case of Biography." *Prooftexts* 2: 163–77.

Lewis, Bernard. 1984. *The Jews of Islam.* Princeton: Princeton University Press.

Liberles, Robert. 1985. *Religious Conflict in Social Context: The Resurgence of Orthodox Judaism in Frankfurt am Main, 1838–1877.* Westport, Conn.: Greenwood Press.

Livi Bacci, Massimo. 1983. "Ebrei, aristocratici e cittadini: Precursori del declino della fecondità." In *Ebrei in Italia,* edited by Sofia Boesch Gajano and Michele Luzzati, *Quaderni storici* 18: 913–39.

Lopez de Meneses, Amada. 1959. "Una consequencia de la peste negra en Cataluña: El pogrom de 1348." *Sefarad* 19: 92–131; 321–64.

Lotter, Friedrich. 1988. "Die Judenverfolgung des 'Koenig Rintfleisch' in Franken um 1298." *Zeitschrift für historisches Forschung* 4: 385–422.

———. 1989. "The Scope and Effectiveness of Imperial Jewry Law in the High Middle Ages." *Jewish History* 4.1: 31–59.

Lourie, Elena. 1986. "A Plot Which Failed? The Case of a Corpse Found in the Jewish Call of Barcelona (1301)." *Mediterranean Historical Review* 1: 187–220.

———. 1990. *Crusade and Colonisation: Muslims, Christians, and Jews in Medieval Aragon.* Aldershot, Hants: Variorum; Brookfield, Vt.: Gower.

Luzzati, Michele. 1983. "Ebrei, Chiesa locale, 'principe' e popolo: Due episodi di distruzione di immagini sacre alla fine del Quattrocento." In *Ebrei in Italia,* edited by Sofia Boesch Gajano and Michele Luzzati, *Quaderni storici* 18: 847–77.

———. 1985. *La casa dell'Ebreo: Saggi sugli Ebrei a Pisa e in Toscana nel Medioevo e nel Rinascimento.* Pisa: Nistri-Lischi.

———. 1987. *Il ghetto ebraico: Storia di un popolo rinchiuso.* Florence.

———. 1989. "Le ricerche prosopografiche sulle famiglie ebraiche italiane (secoli XIV–XVI)." In Muzzarelli and Todeschini 1989, 58–63.

———. 1992. "Fuggire dalla Spagna per convertirsi in Italia: Ebrei sefarditi a Lucca alla fine del Quattrocento." In *E andammo dove il vento ci spinse: La cacciata degli Ebrei dalla Spagna,* edited by Guido Nathan Zazzu, 103–14. Genoa: Marietti.

Luzzatto, Aldo. 1988. *Biblioteca italo-ebraica: Bibliografia per la storia degli Ebrei in Italia, 1974–1985.* Milan.

MacKay, Angus. 1972. "Popular Movements and Pogroms in Fifteenth-Century Castile." *Past and Present* 55: 33–67.

Maimonides, Moses [1135–1204]. 1983. "Epître sur la persécution." Translated from the Hebrew by Jean de Hulster. In *Epitres,* 9–43. Lagrasse: Verdier. See also *Crisis and Leadership: Epistles of Maimonides,* translated and annotated by Abraham Halkin; commentary by David Hartman (Philadelphia: Jewish Publication Society of America, 1985).

Maire Vigueur, Jean-Claude. 1983. "Les Juifs à Rome dans la seconde moitié du XIV siècle: Informations tirées d'un fond notarie." In *Aspetti e problemi della presenza ebraica nell'Italia centro-settentrionale (secoli XIV e XV),* edited by Sofia Boesch Gajano, 19–28. Rome: Istituto di scienze storiche dell'Università di Roma.

Malino, Frances. 1978. *The Sephardic Jews of Bordeaux: Assimilation and Emancipation in Revolutionary and Napoleonic France.* Tuscaloosa: University of Alabama Press.

———. 1982. "Attitudes toward Jewish Communal Autonomy in Prerevolutionary France." In *Essays in Modern Jewish History: A Tribute to Ben Halpern,* edited by Frances Malino and Phyllis Cohen Albert, 95–117. Rutherford, N.J.: Fairleigh Dickinson University Press; London: Associated University Presses.

Manzini, Vincenzo. 1925. *L'omicidio rituale e i sacrifici umani con particolare riguardo alle accuse contro gli Ebrei.* Turin.

Marcus, Ivan G. 1981. *Piety and Society: The Jewish Pietists of Medieval Germany.* Leiden: E. J. Brill.

———. 1986. "Hierarchies, Religious Boundaries and Jewish Spirituality in Medieval Germany." *Jewish History* 1.2: 7–26.

———. 1996. *Rituals of Childhood: Jewish Acculturation in Medieval Europe.* New Haven: Yale University Press.

Marcus, Jacob R. [1938] 1983. *The Jew in the Medieval World: A Source Book, 315–1791.* New York: Atheneum.

Marín Padilla, Encarnación. 1981–82. "Relacion judeoconversa durante la secunda mitad del siglo XV en Aragon: Nacimientos, hadas, circuncisiones." *Sefarad* 41: 273–300; 42: 59–77.

———. 1983. "Relacion judeoconversa durante la secunda mitad del siglo XV en Aragon: Enfermedades y muertes." *Sefarad* 43: 251–344.

Marrus, Michael. 1971. *The Politics of Assimilation: A Study of the French Jewish Community at the Time of the Dreyfus Affair.* Oxford: Clarendon Press.

Martínez Marina, Francisco. 1799. "Antigüedades hispano-hebreas, convencidas de supuestas y fabulosas: Discurso histórico-crítico sobre la primera venida de los judíos a España." *Memorias de la Real Academia de la Historia* 3: 317–468.

Méchoulan, Henry. 1979a. "Abraham Pereyra, juge des Marranes et censeur de ses coreligionnaires à Amsterdam au temps de Spinoza." *Revue des Etudes juives* 138: 391–400.

———. 1979b. *Le Sang de l'autre, ou, L'honneur de Dieu: Indiens, Juifs, Morisques dans l'Espagne du Siècle d'or.* Paris: Fayard.

———. 1989. "Menasseh ben Israel and the World of the Non-Jew." In *Menasseh ben Israel and His World,* edited by Yosef Kaplan, Henry Méchoulan, and Richard Popkin, 83–97. Leiden: E. J. Brill.

———. 1990a. *Amsterdam au temps de Spinoza: Argent et liberté.* Paris: Presses universitaires de France.

———. 1990b. "Au dossier du Sabbataisme: Une Relation italienne du XVIIe siècle." In *Sceptics, Millenarians and Jews,* edited by David Katz and Jonathan Israel, 185–95. Leiden: E. J. Brill.

———, ed. 1992. *Les Juifs d'Espagne: Histoire d'une diaspora (1492–1992).* Paris: Liana Levi.

Meijer, Jacob. 1955. "Hugo Grotius' Remonstrantiae." *Jewish Social Studies* 17: 91–104.

Meiss, Willard. 1951. *Painting in Florence and Siena after the Black Death.* Princeton: Princeton University Press.

Melamed, Abraham. 1986. "The Perception of Jewish History in Italian Jewish Thought of the Sixteenth and Seventeenth Centuries. A Re-Examination." In *Italia judaica* 1986, 2: 139–70.

Melammed, Levine Renee. 1986. "The Ultimate Challenge: Safeguarding the Crypto-Judaic Heritage." *Proceedings of the American Academy for Jewish Research* 53: 91–109.

Menache, Sophia. 1987. "The King, the Church, and the Jews: Some Considerations on the Expulsions from England and France." *Journal of Medieval History* 13: 223–36.

———, ed. 1996. *Communication in the Jewish Diaspora: The Pre-Modern World.* Leiden: E. J. Brill.

Menasseh ben Israel [1604–57]. [1650] 1987. *The Hope of Israel.* Edited by Henry Méchoulan and Gerard Nahon. English translation by Moses Wall, 1652. New York: Published for the Littman Library by Oxford University Press.

Meneghin, Vittorino. 1974. *Bernardino da Feltre e i monti di pietà.* Vicenza: L.I.E.F.

Mentzer, Raymond A. 1982. "Marranos of Southern France in the Early Sixteenth Century." *Jewish Quarterly Review* 72: 303–11.

Metzger, Thérèse, and Mendel Metzger. 1982. *Jewish Life in the Middle Ages: Illuminated Hebrew Manuscripts of the Thirteenth to the Sixteenth Centuries.* New York: Alpine Fine Arts Collection.

Meyerson, Mark D. 1991. *The Muslims of Valencia in the Age of Fernando and Isabel: Between Coexistence and Crusade.* Berkeley and Los Angeles: University of California Press.

———. 1992. "Aragonese and Catalan Jewish Converts at the Time of the Expulsion." In Walfish 1992–93, vol. 2 [= *Jewish History* 6.1–2]: 131–49.

Michman, Jozeph. 1979. "Les Juifs des Pays-Bas et le Grand Sanhédrin." In *Le Grand Sanhédrin de Napoléon,* edited by Bernard Blumenkranz and Albert Soboul, 86–100. Collection franco-judaïca, 8. Toulouse: Privat.

Migne, J.-P. *Patrologiae cursus completus, sive biblioteca universalis, integra, uniformis, commoda, oeconomica, omnium SS. Patrum, doctorum scriptorumque ecclesiasticorum . . . : Series latina . . .* 221 vols. Paris: Migne, 1844–91. Cited as Migne, *PL.*

Milano, Attilio. 1935–36. "I *Capitoli* di Daniele da Pisa e la comunità di Roma." *La rassegna mensile di Israel* 10: 324–38; 409–26.

———. 1963. *Storia degli Ebrei in Italia.* Turin: Giulio Einaudi.

———. 1964. *Il Ghetto di Roma: Illustrazioni storiche.* Rome: Staderini.

———. 1970. "Battesimi di Ebrei a Roma dal Cinquecento all'Ottocento." In *Scritti in memoria di Enzo Sereni: Saggi sull'ebraismo romano,* edited by Daniel Carpi, Attilio Milano, and Umberto Nahon, 133–67. Jerusalem: Fondazione Sally Mayer.

Modena, Leon. [1678] 1979. *Historia de' riti hebraici.* Bologna: Forni.

———. 1988. *The Autobiography of a Seventeenth-Century Venetian Rabbi: Leon Modena's "Life of Judah,"* edited by Mark R. Cohen. Princeton: Princeton University Press.

Momigliano, Arnaldo. 1994. *Essays on Ancient and Modern Judaism,* edited by Silvia Berti. Chicago: University of Chicago Press.

Montaigne, Michel de [sixteenth century]. 1906. *Journal de voyage,* Paris: Hachette.

Moore, Robert Ian. 1987. *The Formation of a Persecuting Society: Power and Deviance in Western Europe, 950–1250.* New York: B. Blackwell.

Morisi Guerra, Anna. 1987. "Incontri ebraico-cristiani: Il salterio poliglotto di Santi Pagnini." In *Itinerari ebraico-cristiani: Società, cultura, mito,* edited by Marina Caffiero, Anna Foa, and Anna Morisi Guerra, 9–37. Fasano: Schena.

———. 1988. "Cultura ebraica ed esegesi biblica cristiana tra Umanesimo e Riforma." In *Ebrei e cristiani nell'Italia medievale e moderna: Conversioni, scambi, contrasti,* edited by Michele Luzzati, Michele Olivari, and Alessandra Veronese, 209–23. Rome: Carucci.

Moses ben Nahman [Nahmanides] [thirteenth century]. 1982. "Account of the Barcelona Disputation." In *Judaism on Trial: Jewish-Christian Disputations in the Middle Ages,* edited and translated by Hyam Maccoby, 102–46. London: Associated University Presses; Rutherford, N.J.: Fairleigh Dickinson University Press.

Mosse, George L. 1970. *Germans and Jews: The Right, the Left, and the Search for a "Third Force" in Pre-Nazi Germany.* New York: H. Fertig.

———. 1980. "The Secularisation of Jewish Theology." In id., *Masses and Man: Nationalist and Fascist Perceptions of Reality,* 249–62. New York: H. Fertig.

————. 1985a. *German Jews beyond Judaism*. Bloomington: Indiana University Press; Cincinnati: Hebrew Union College Press.

————. 1985b. "Jewish Emancipation: Between *Bildung* and Respectability." In *The Jewish Response to German Culture: From the Enlightenment to the Second World War*, edited by Jehuda Reinharz and Walter Schatzberg, 1–16. Hanover, N.H.: Published for Clark University by University Press of New England.

Moulinas, René. 1981. *Les Juifs du pape en France: Les Communautés d'Avignon et du Comtat Venaissin aux 17e et 18e siècles*. Paris: Privat.

Mueller, Reinhold C. 1972. "Charitable Institutions, the Jewish Community, and Venetian Society. A Discussion of the Recent Volume by Brian Pullan." *Studi veneziani* 14: 37–81.

————. 1975. "Les Préteurs juifs de Venise au Moyen Age." *Annales ESC* 30.6: 1277–1302.

Muzzarelli, Maria Giuseppina. 1983. *Ebrei e città d'Italia in età di transizione: Il caso di Cesena dal XIV al XVI secolo*. Bologna: CLUEB.

————. 1989. "Storia degli Ebrei e storia locale." In Muzzarelli and Todeschini 1989, 72–80.

————, ed. 1996a. *Banchi ebraici a Bologna nel XV secolo*. Bologna: Il Mulino.

————. 1996b. *Verso l'epilogo di una convivenza: Gli Ebrei a Bologna nel XVI secolo*. Florence: Giuntina.

Muzzarelli, Maria Giuseppina, and Giacomo Todeschini, eds. 1989. *La storia degli Ebrei nell'Italia medievale: Tra filologia e metodologia*. Istituto per i beni artistici, culturali, naturali della Regione Emilia-Romagna, documenti, 29. Bologna: Grafiche Zanini.

Nahon, Gerard. 1977. "Les Marranes espagnoles et portugais et les communautés juives issues du marranisme dans l'historiographie récente (1960–1975)." *Revue des Etudes juives* 136: 297–367.

Neher, André. 1986. *Jewish Thought and the Scientific Revolution of the Sixteenth Century: David Gans (1541–1613) and His Times*. Translated from the French by David Maisel. New York: Published for the Littman Library by Oxford University Press.

Nelson, Benjamin. 1949. *The Idea of Usury, from Tribal Brotherhood to Universal Otherhood*. Princeton: Princeton University Press.

Netanyahu, Benzion. 1966. *The Marranos of Spain, from the Late XIVth to the Early XVIth Century, According to Contemporary Hebrew Sources*. New York: American Academy for Jewish Research. 3rd ed., updated and expanded, Ithaca, N.Y.: Cornell University Press, 1999.

————. [1953] 1968. *Don Isaac Abravanel, Statesman and Philosopher*. Philadelphia: Jewish Publication Society of America.

————. 1995. *The Origins of the Inquisition in Fifteenth-Century Spain*. New York: Random House.

Nirenberg, David. 1996. *Communities of Violence: Persecution of Minorities in the Middle Ages*. Princeton: Princeton University Press.

Noonan, John. 1957. *The Scholastic Analysis of Usury*. Cambridge, Mass.: Harvard University Press.

Oberman, Heiko A. 1983. "Three Sixteenth-Century Attitudes to Judaism:

Reuchlin, Erasmus and Luther." In *Jewish Thought in the Sixteeenth Century*, edited by Bernard Dov Cooperman, 326–64. Cambridge Mass.: Harvard University Center for Jewish Studies.

———. 1984. *The Roots of Anti-Semitism in the Age of Renaissance and Reformation*. Philadelphia: Fortress Press.

———. 1988. "Gli ostinati giudei: Mutamenti nelle strategie nell'Europa tardomedioevale (1300–1600)." In *Ebrei e cristiani nell'Italia medievale e moderna: Conversioni, scambi, contrasti*, edited by Michele Luzzati, Michele Olivari, and Alessandra Veronese, 123–40. Rome: Carucci.

Olivari, Michele. 1986. "Note sui rapporti tra Ebrei e cattolici nel Cinquecento." *Quaderni storici* 21: 951–70.

———. 1988. "Ebraisti spagnoli e Inquisizione. Echi di una vicenda giudiziaria e culturale." In *Ebrei e cristiani nell'Italia medievale e moderna: Conversioni, scambi, contrasti*, edited by Michele Luzzati, Michele Olivari, and Alessandra Veronese, 225–30. Rome: Carucci.

———. 1994. "Inquisizione spagnola ed ebraismo." In *L'Inquisizione e gli Ebrei in Italia*, edited by Michele Luzzati, 35–46. Rome: Laterza.

Orfali, Moises. 1996. "Jews and Conversos in Fifteeenth-Century Spain: Christian Apologia and Polemic." In *From Witness to Witchcraft: Jews and Judaism in Medieval Christian Thought*, edited by Jeremy Cohen, 337–60. Wiesbaden: Harrassowitz.

Pales-Gobilliard, A. 1977. "L'Inquisition et les Juifs: Le Cas de Jacques Fournier." In *Juifs et judaisme de Languedoc: XIIIe siècle–début XIVe siècle*, edited by Marie-Humbert Vicaire and Bernhard Blumenkranz, 97–114. Toulouse.

Papers in Jewish Demography, 1973: Proceedings of the Demographic Sessions Held at the Sixth World Congress of Jewish Studies, Jerusalem, August 1973, edited by U. O. Schmelz, P. Glikson, and S. Della Pergola. 1977. Jerusalem: Institute of Contemporary Jewry, Hebrew University of Jerusalem.

Parente, Fausto. 1983. "Il confronto ideologico tra l'ebraismo e la Chiesa in Italia." In *Italia judaica* 1983, 1: 303–81.

———. 1996. "La Chiesa e il Talmud." In *Gli Ebrei in Italia*, vol. 1: *Dall'Alto Medioevo all'età dei ghetti*, edited by Corrado Vivanti, 523–643. Turin.

Parkes, James. 1934. *The Conflict of the Church and the Synagogue: A Study in the Origins of Antisemitism*. London: Soncino Press.

———. 1938. *The Jew in the Medieval Community: A Study of His Political and Economic Situation*. London: Soncino Press.

Patlagean, Evelyne. 1989. "La Dispute avec les Juifs de Nicolas d'Otrante (vers 1220) et la question du Messie." In Muzzarelli and Todeschini 1989, 19–27.

Pavoncello, Nello. 1978. *I toponimi del vecchio ghetto di Roma*. Rome: Carucci.

———. 1987. "L'educazione ebraica a Roma nel periodo del Ghetto (1555–1870)." *I problemi della pedagogia* 3: 231–258.

Perani, Mauro. 1985. "Appunti per la storia degli Ebrei in Sardegna durante la dominazione aragonese." *Italia* 5: 104–44.

———. 1994. "Confisca e censura di libri ebraici a Modena fra Cinque e Seicento." In *L'Inquisizione e gli Ebrei in Italia*, edited by Michele Luzzati, 287–320. Bari: Laterza.

————. 1996. "Vestigia della cultura ebraica a Bologna tra Medioevo e Rinascimento nella testimonianza dei manoscritti." *Italia* 12: 89–139.

Philippe, Béatrice. 1979. *Etre juif dans la société française, du Moyen Age à nos
jours.* Paris: Montalba.

Pini, Antonio Ivan. 1983. "Famiglie, insediamenti e banchi ebraici a Bologna e
nel bolognese nella seconda metà del Trecento." In *Ebrei in Italia,* edited by
Sofia Boesch Gajano and Michele Luzzati. *Quaderni storici* 18: 783–814.

Poliakov, Léon. 1974a. *The Aryan Myth: A History of Racist and Nationalist
Ideas in Europe.* Translated by Edmund Howard. New York: Basic Books.

————. 1974b. *The History of Anti-Semitism.* Translated by Richard Howard.
4 vols. London: Routledge & Kegan Paul.

————. [1965] 1977. *Jewish Bankers and the Holy See: From the Thirteenth to
the Seventeenth Century.* Translated by Miriam Kochan. Boston: Routledge
& Kegan Paul.

Popkin, Richard H. 1987. *Isaac La Peyrère (1596–1676): His Life, Work and
Influence.* Leiden: E. J. Brill.

————. 1989. "The Rise and Fall of the Jewish Indian Theory." In *Menasseh
ben Israel and His World,* edited by Yosef Kaplan, Henry Méchoulan, and
Richard Popkin, 63–82. Leiden: E. J. Brill.

Porges, Nathan. 1923–24. "Elie Capsali et sa Chronique de Venise." *Revue des
Etudes juives* 77: 20–40; 78: 15–34.

Prodi, Paolo. [1982] 1987. *The Papal Prince: One Body and Two Souls: The Papal Monarchy in Early Modern Europe.* Cambridge: Cambridge University
Press.

Prosperi, Adriano. 1989. "La Chiesa e gli Ebrei nell'Italia del '500." In
Ebraismo e antiebraismo: Immagine e pregiudizio, edited by Cesare Lu-
porini, 171–83. Florence: Giuntina.

————. 1994. "L'Inquisizione romana e gli Ebrei." In *L'Inquisizione e gli Ebrei
in Italia,* edited by Michele Luzzati, 67–120. Rome: Laterza.

————. 1996. "Incontri rituali: Il papa e gli Ebrei." In *Gli Ebrei in Italia,* vol. 1:
Dall'Alto Medioevo all'età dei ghetti, edited by Corrado Vivanti, 497–520.
Turin.

Pullan, Brian S. 1971. *Rich and Poor in Renaissance Venice: The Social Institutions of a Catholic State.* Cambridge, Mass.: Harvard University Press.

————. 1977. "A Ship with Two Rudders: 'Righetto Marrano' and the Inquisition in Venice." *Historical Journal* 20: 25–58.

————. 1983. *The Jews of Europe and the Inquisition of Venice, 1550–1670.*
Totowa: N.J.: Barnes & Noble.

————. 1994. "L'Inquisizione e gli Ebrei a Venezia." In *L'Inquisizione e gli
Ebrei in Italia,* edited by Michele Luzzati, 251–64. Rome: Laterza.

Pulzer, Peter G. J. [1964] 1988. *The Rise of Political Anti-Semitism in Germany
and Austria.* Cambridge, Mass.: Harvard University Press.

Quaglioni, Diego. 1983. "Inter Iudeos et Christianos commertia sunt permissa:
'Questione ebraica' e usura in Baldo degli Ubaldi (c. 1327–1400)." In *Aspetti e problemi della presenza ebraica nell'Italia centro-settentrionale,* edited by Sofia Boesch Gajano, 273–305. Rome: Istituto di scienze storiche
dell'Università di Roma.

———, ed. 1987. *Battista de' Giudici, Apologia Iudaeorum —Invectiva contra Platinam: Propaganda antiebraica e polemiche di Curia durante il pontificato di Sisto IV (1471–84)*. Rome: Gestisa.

———. 1988. "I giuristi medievali e gli Ebrei: Due consultationes di G. F. Pavini (1478)." In *Ebrei e cristiani nell'Italia medievale e moderna: Conversioni, scambi, contrasti*, edited by Michele Luzzati, Michele Olivari, and Alessandra Veronese, 63–73. Rome: Carucci.

———. 1989. "Storia della presenza ebraica e dimensione giuridica." In Muzzarelli and Todeschini 1989, 64–71.

Raphaël, Freddy, and Robert Weyl. 1977. *Juifs en Alsace: Culture, société, histoire*. Collection franco-judaïca, 5. Toulouse: Privat.

Ravid, Benjamin. 1976. "The First Charter of the Jewish Merchants of Venice, 1589." *AJS Review* 1: 187–222.

———. 1977. "The Jewish Mercantile Settlement of Twelfth and Thirteenth Century Venice: Reality or Conjecture?" *AJS Review* 2: 201–25.

———. 1978. *Economics and Toleration in Seventeenth-Century Venice: The Background and Context of the "Discorso" of Simone Luzzatto*. Jerusalem: American Academy for Jewish Research.

———. 1982a. "'How Profitable the Nation of the Jewes are': The Humble Addresses of Menasseh ben Israel and the Discorso of Simone Luzzatto." In *Mystics, Philosophers, and Politicians: Essays in Jewish Intellectual History in Honor of Alexander Altmann*, edited by Jehuda Reinharz and Daniel Swetschinski with the collaboration of Kalman P. Bland, 159–80. Durham, N.C.: Duke University Press.

———. 1982b. "The Socioeconomic Background of the Expulsion and Readmission of the Venetian Jews: 1571–1573." In *Essays in Modern Jewish History: A Tribute to Ben Halpern*, edited by Frances Malino and Phyllis Cohen Albert, 27–55. Rutherford, N.J.: Fairleigh Dickinson University Press; London: Associated University Presses.

———. 1982–83. "*Contra Judaeos* in Seventeenth-Century Italy: Two Responses to the Discorso of Simone Luzzatto by Melchiore Palontrotti and Giulio Morosini." *AJS Review* 7–8: 301–51.

———. 1987a. "The Legal Status of the Jews in Venice to 1509." *Proceedings of the American Academy for Jewish Research* 54: 169–202.

———. 1987b. "Moneylending in Seventeenth-Century Jewish Vernacular Apologetica." In *Jewish Thought in the Seventeenth Century*, edited by Isadore Twersky and Bernard Septimus, 257–83. Cambridge, Mass.: Harvard University Center for Jewish Studies; distributed by Harvard University Press.

———. 1987c. "The Religious, Economic, and Social Background and Context of the Establishment of the Ghetti of Venice." In *Gli Ebrei e Venezia*, edited by Gaetano Cozzi, 211–59.

———. 1992. "From Yellow to Red: On the Distinguishing Head-Covering of the Jews of Venice." In Walfish 1992–93, vol. 2 [= *Jewish History* 6.1–2]: 179–210.

———. 1993. "New Light on the Ghetti of Venice." In *Shlomo Simonsohn Jubilee Volume: Studies in the History of the Jews in the Middle Ages and*

Renaissance Period, edited by Daniel Carpi et al., 149–74. Tel Aviv: Tel Aviv University, Faculty of Humanities, Chaim Rosenberg School of Jewish Studies.

Reeves, Marjorie. 1969. *The Influence of Prophecy in the Later Middle Ages: Study in Joachimism.* Oxford: Clarendon Press. Reprint, Notre Dame, Ind.: University of Notre Dame Press, 1993.

Révah, Israel S. 1958. "David Reubeni executé en Espagne en 1538." *Revue des Etudes juives* 117: 128–135.

———. 1959. *Spinoza et le Dr. Juan de Prado.* Paris: Mouton.

———. 1959–60. "Les Marranes." *Revue des Etudes juives* 118: 29–77.

———. 1963. "Pour l'histoire des marranes à Anvers: Recensements de la nation portugaise de 1571 à 1666." *Revue des Etudes Juives* 122: 123–47.

———. 1968. "L'Hérésie marrane dans l'Europe catholique du 15ᵉ au 18ᵉ siècle." In *Hérésies et sociétés dans l'Europe pré-industrielle, 11ᵉ–18ᵉ siècles,* ed. Jacques Le Goff, 327–39. Paris: Mouton.

———. 1971. "Les Marranes portugais et l'Inquisition au XVIᵉ siècle." In *The Sephardi Heritage: Essays on the Historical and Cultural Contribution of the Jews of Spain and Portugal,* edited by Richard D. Barnett, 1: 479–526. London: Vallentine, Mitchell.

Riley-Smith, Jonathan. 1984. "The First Crusade and the Persecution of the Jews." *Studies in Church History* 21: 51–72.

———. 1986. *The First Crusade and the Idea of Crusading.* Philadelphia: University of Pennsylvania Press.

Ripellino, Angelo Maria. [1973] 1994. *Magic Prague.* Translated by David Newton Marinelli. Edited by Michael Heim. Berkeley and Los Angeles: University of California Press.

Rivkin, Ellis. 1957–58. "The Utilisation of Non-Jewish Sources for the Reconstruction of Jewish History." *Jewish Quarterly Review* 48: 183–203.

Rodríguez-Moñino, Antonio. 1956. "Les Judaisants à Badajoz de 1493 à 1599." *Revue des Etudes juives* 115: 73–86.

Romeo, Giovanni. 1994. "La suggestione dell'ebraismo fra i napoletani del tardo Cinquecento." In *L'Inquisizione e gli Ebrei in Italia,* edited by Michele Luzzati, 179–95. Rome: Laterza.

Rosa, Mario. 1989. "Tra tolleranza e repressione: Roma e gli Ebrei nel Settecento." In *Italia judaica* 1989, 3: 81–98.

Rossi, Rosa. 1983. *Teresa d'Avila: Biografia di una scrittrice.* Rome.

Roth, Cecil. 1933. "The Feast of Purim and the Origins of the Blood Accusation." *Speculum* 8: 520–526.

———. 1941a. *A History of the Jews in England.* Oxford: Clarendon Press.

———. 1941b. *A History of the Marranos.* Philadelphia: Jewish Publication Society of America.

———. [1934] 1945. *A Life of Menasseh ben Israel, Rabbi, Printer, and Diplomat.* Philadelphia: Jewish Publication Society of America.

———. 1946. *The History of the Jews of Italy.* Philadelphia: Jewish Publication Society of America.

———. 1947. *The House of Nasi: Doña Gracia.* Philadelphia: Jewish Publication Society of America.

———. 1948. *The House of Nasi: The Duke of Naxos.* Philadelphia: Jewish Publication Society of America.

———. 1957. "Le Martyre de David Reubeni." *Revue des Etudes juives* 116: 93–95.

———. 1959. *The Jews in the Renaissance.* Philadelphia: Jewish Publication Society of America.

Rowland, Robert. 1994. "L'Inquisizione portoghese e gli Ebrei." In *L'Inquisizione e gli Ebrei in Italia,* edited by Michele Luzzati, 47–66. Rome: Laterza.

Rubin, Miri. 1995. "Imagining the Jew: The Late Medieval Eucharistic Discourse." In *In and Out of the Ghetto: Jewish-Gentile Relations in Late Medieval and Early Modern Germany,* edited by R. Po-chia Hsia and Hartmut Lehmann, 177–208. Cambridge, Mass.

Ruderman, David B. 1976. "The Founding of a Gemilut Hasadim Society in Ferrara in 1515." *AJS Review* 1: 233–58.

———. 1979. "A Jewish Apologetic Treatise from Sixteeenth-Century Bologna." *Hebrew Union College Annual* 50: 253–75.

———. 1981. *The World of a Renaissance Jew: The Life and Thought of Abraham ben Mordecai Farissol.* Cincinnati: Hebrew Union College Press.

———. 1988a. "The Italian Renaissance and Jewish Thought." In *Renaissance Humanism: Foundations and Forms,* edited by Albert Rabil, Jr., 1: 382–433. Philadelphia: University of Pennsylvania Press.

———. 1988b. *Kabbalah, Magic, and Science: The Cultural Universe of a Sixteenth-Century Jewish Physician.* Cambridge, Mass.: Harvard University Press.

———, ed. and trans. 1990. *"A Valley of Vision": The Heavenly Journey of Abraham ben Hananiah Yagel.* Philadelphia: University of Pennsylvania Press.

———. 1992a. "Contemporary Science and Jewish Law in the Eyes of Isaac Lampronte de Ferrara, and Some of His Contemporaries." In Walfish 1992–93, vol. 2 [= *Jewish History* 6.1–2]: 211–24.

———. 1992b. "Jewish Preaching and the Language of Science: The Sermons of Azariah Figo." In *Preachers of the Italian Ghetto,* edited by David B. Ruderman, 89–104. Berkeley and Los Angeles: University of California Press.

———. 1993. "The Language of Science as the Language of Faith: An Aspect of Italian Jewish Thought in the Seventeenth and Eighteenth Centuries." In *Shlomo Simonsohn Jubilee Volume: Studies in the History of the Jews in the Middle Ages and Renaissance Period,* edited by Daniel Carpi et al., 177–89. Tel Aviv: Tel Aviv University, Faculty of Humanities, Chaim Rosenberg School of Jewish Studies.

———. 1995. *Jewish Thought and Scientific Discovery in Early Modern Europe.* New Haven: Yale University Press.

Rudt de Collenberg, Wipertus H. 1986–88. "Le Baptême des Juifs à Rome de 1614 à 1798 selon les registres de la 'Casa dei Catecumeni.'" *Archivium Historiae Pontificiae* 24: 91–231; 25: 105–261; 26: 119–294.

Ruether, Rosemary. 1974. *Faith and Fratricide: The Theological Roots of Antisemitism.* New York: Seabury Press.

Sánchez-Albornoz, Claudio. 1956. *España, un enigma histórico.* 2 vols. Buenos Aires: Editorial Sudamericana. Translated by Colette Joly Dees and David

Sven Reher under the title *Spain: A Historical Enigma,* 2 vols. (Madrid: Fundación Universitaria Española, 1975).

Saperstein, Marc. 1986. "The Conflict over the Rashba's Herem on Philosophical Study: A Political Perspective." *Jewish History* 1.2: 27–38.

———. 1989. *Jewish Preaching 1200–1800: An Anthology.* New Haven: Yale University Press.

———. 1992a. "Christians and Christianity in the Sermons of Jacob Anatoli." In Walfish 1992–93, vol. 2 [= *Jewish History* 6.1–2]: 225–42.

———, ed. 1992b. *Essential Papers on Messianic Movements and Personalities in Jewish History.* New York: New York University Press.

———. 1992c. "Italian Jewish Preaching: An Overview." In *Preachers of the Italian Ghetto,* edited by David B. Ruderman, 22–40. Berkeley and Los Angeles: University of California Press.

Saraçgil, Aise. 1989. "Introduzione, uso e divieto del caffè nell'Impero ottomano." Diss., Università La Sapienza di Roma.

Sartre, Jean-Paul. 1946. *Réflexions sur la question juive.* Paris: P. Morihien. Translated by George J. Becker as *Anti-Semite and Jew* (1948; New York: Schocken Books, 1965).

Satta, Fiamma. 1987. "Predicatori agli Ebrei, catecumeni e neofiti a Roma nella prima metà del Seicento." In *Itinerari ebraico-cristiani: Società, cultura, mito,* edited by Marina Caffiero, Anna Foa, and Anna Morisi Guerra, 11–127. Fasano: Schena.

Scaraffia, Lucetta. 1993. *Rinnegati: Per una storia dell'identità occidentale.* Rome: Laterza.

Schaeffer, Peter. 1989. "The Ideal of Piety of the Ashkenazi Hasidim." *Jewish History* 4.2: 9–23.

Schoeps, Hans-Joachim. 1952. *Philosemitismus im Barock: Religions-und geistesgeschichtliche Untersuchungen.* Tubingen: J. C. B. Mohr.

———. 1956–57. "Philosemitism in the Baroque Period." *Jewish Quarterly Review* 47: 139–44.

Scholem, Gershom G. [1938] 1946. *Major Trends in Jewish Mysticism.* New York: Schocken Books.

———. 1965. *On the Kabbalah and Its Symbolism.* Translated by Ralph Manheim. New York: Schocken Books.

———. 1971. *The Messianic Idea in Judaism and Other Essays on Jewish Spirituality.* New York: Schocken Books.

———. [1957] 1973. *Sabbatai Sevi, the Mystical Messiah, 1626–1676.* Translated by R. J. Zwi Werblowsky. Princeton: Princeton University Press.

———. 1974. *Kabbalah.* New York: Quadrangle/New York Times.

———. 1976a. *On Jews and Judaism in Crisis: Selected Essays.* Edited by Werner J. Dannhauser. New York: Schocken Books.

———. 1976b. "Reflections on the Science of Judaism" (in Hebrew). In *Devarim bego,* edited by Anita Shapira, 385–406. Tel Aviv.

———. 1981. *Du frankisme au jacobinisme: La Vie de Moses Dobruška alias Franz Thomas von Schönfeld alias Junius Frey.* Paris: Gallimard, Seuil.

Schwarzfuchs, Simon. 1967. "The Expulsion of the Jews from France (1306)." *Jewish Quarterly Review* 75: 482–89.

———. 1986. *Kahal: La Communauté juive de l'Europe médiévale*. Paris: Maisonneuve & Larose.

———. 1993. *A Concise History of the Rabbinate*. Cambridge, Mass.: Blackwell.

Secret, François. 1964. *Les Kabbalistes chrétiens de la Renaissance*. Paris: Dunod.

———. 1971. "Juifs et Marranes au miroir de trois médecins de la Renaissance." *Revue des Etudes juives* 130: 183–90.

Segre, Dan V. 1995. "The Emancipation of Jews in Italy." In *Paths of Emancipation: Jews, States and Citizenship*, edited by Pierre Birnbaum and Ira Katznelson, 207–37. Princeton: Princeton University Press.

Segre, Renata. 1978. "Bernardino da Feltre, i Monti di Pietà e i banchi ebraici." *Rivista storica italiana* 90: 818–33.

———. 1985. "Nuovi documenti sui marrani d'Ancona (1555–1559)." *Michael* 9: 130–233.

———, ed. 1986–90. *The Jews in Piedmont*. 3 vols. Jerusalem: Israel Academy of Sciences and Humanities.

———. 1987. "Banchi ebraici e Monti di Pietà." In *Gli Ebrei e Venezia*, edited by Gaetano Cozzi, 565–70.

———. 1989. "Flussi e correnti migratorie nel mondo ebraico: Fonti e storiografia." In Muzzarelli and Todeschini 1989, 81–90.

Sereni, Enzo. [1935] 1970. "L'assedio del ghetto di Roma, 1793, nelle memorie di un contemporaneo." In *Scritti in memoria di Enzo Sereni: Saggi sull' ebraismo romano*, edited by Daniel Carpi, Attilio Milano, and Umberto Nahon, 168–98. Jerusalem: Fondazione Sally Mayer.

Sermoneta, Josef B. 1974. "Sull'origine della parola ghetto." In *Studi sull' ebraismo italiano in memoria di Cecil Roth*, edited by Elio Toaff, 185–201. Rome: Barulli.

———. 1986. "Aspetti del pensiero moderno nell'ebraismo italiano tra Rinascimento e età barocca." In *Italia judaica* 1986, 2: 17–35.

———. 1988. "L'incontro culturale tra Ebrei e cristiani nel Medioevo e nel Rinascimento." In *Ebrei e cristiani nell'Italia medievale e moderna: Conversioni, scambi, contrasti*, edited by Michele Luzzati, Michele Olivari, and Alessandra Veronese, 183–207. Rome: Carucci.

———, ed. 1989. *Ratto della Signora Anna del Monte trattenuta a' catecumini tredici giorni dalli 6 fino alli 19 maggio anno 1749*. Rome: Carucci.

———. 1993. "Il mestiere del neofito nella Roma del Settecento." In *Shlomo Simonsohn Jubilee Volume: Studies in the History of the Jews in the Middle Ages and Renaissance Period*, edited by Daniel Carpi et al., 213–43. Tel Aviv: Tel Aviv University, Faculty of Humanities, Chaim Rosenberg School of Jewish Studies.

Sestieri, Lea, ed. 1991. *David Reubeni: Un ebreo d'Arabia in missione segreta nell'Europa del Cinquecento*. Genoa: Marietti.

Shachar, Isaiah. 1974. *The Judensau: A Medieval Anti-Jewish Motif and Its History*. London: Warburg Institute.

Shahar, Shulamit. 1980. "The Relationship between Kabbalism and Catharism in the South of France." In Yardeni 1980, 55–62.

Sharot, Stephen. 1976. *Judaism: A Sociology*. Newton Abbott, Devon: David & Charles; New York: Holmes & Meier.

———. 1980. "Jewish Millenarianism: A Comparison of Medieval Communities." *Comparative Studies in Society and History* 22: 394–415.

Shatzmiller, Joseph. 1973a. "L'Inquisition et les Juifs de Provence au XIIIᵉ siècle." *Provence historique* 23: 327–38.

———. 1973b. "Rationalisme et orthodoxie religieuse chez les Juifs provençaux au commencement du XIVᵉ siècle." *Provence historique* 22: 261–86.

———. 1973c. *Recherches sur la communauté juive de Manosque au Moyen Age (1241–1329)*. Paris: Mouton.

———. 1974. "Les Juifs de Provence pendant la Peste Noire." *Revue des Etudes juives* 133: 457–80.

———. 1977a. "Contacts et échanges entre savants juifs et chrétiens à Montpellier vers 1300." In *Juifs et judaïsme de Languedoc: XIIIᵉ siècle–début XIV siècle*, edited by Marie-Humbert Vicaire and Bernhard Blumenkranz, 337–44. Toulouse: Privat.

———. 1977b. "*Tumultus et rumor in sinagoga*: An Aspect of Social Life of Provençal Jews in the Middle Ages." *AJS Review* 2: 227–55.

———. 1980. "L'Excommunication, la communauté juive et les autorités temporelles au Moyen Age." In Yardeni 1980, 63–69.

———. 1985. "Politics and the Myth of Origins: The Case of the Medieval Jews." In *Les Juifs au regard de l'histoire: Mélanges en l'honneur de Bernhard Blumenkranz*, edited by Gilbert Dahan, 49–61. Paris: Picard.

———. 1987. "La Famille juive au Moyen Age." *Provence historique* 37: 489–600.

———. 1988. "Rabbi Isaac Ha-Cohen of Manosque and His Son Rabbi Peretz: The Rabbinate and Its Professionalisation in the Fourteenth Century." In *Jewish History: Essays in Honour of Chimen Abramsky*, edited by Ada Rapaport-Albert and Steven J. Zipperstein, 61–83. London: P. Halban.

———. 1990. *Shylock Reconsidered: Jews, Moneylending, and Medieval Society*. Berkeley and Los Angeles: University of California Press.

———. 1994. *Jews, Medicine, and Medieval Society*. Berkeley and Los Angeles: University of California Press.

Shulvass, Moses A. 1964. *Between the Rhine and the Bosporus: Studies and Essays in European Jewish History*. Chicago: College of Jewish Studies Press.

———. [1955] 1973. *The Jews in the World of the Renaissance*. Leiden: E. J. Brill.

Sicroff, Albert A. 1960. *Les Controverses des statuts de "pureté de sang" en Espagne du XVᵉ au XVIIᵉ siècle*. Paris: Didier.

Siegmund, Stephanie. 1996. "La vita nei ghetti." In *Gli Ebrei in Italia*, vol. 1: *Dall'Alto Medioevo all'età dei ghetti*, edited by Corrado Vivanti, 846–92. Turin.

Simon, Marcel. [1948] 1986. *Verus Israel: A Study of the Relations between Christians and Jews in the Roman Empire (135–425)*. Translated from the French by H. McKeating. New York: Published for the Littman Library by Oxford University Press.

Simonsohn, Shlomo. [1962–64] 1977. *History of the Jews in the Duchy of Mantua.* 2 vols. Jerusalem: Kiryath Sepher.

———, ed. 1982–86. *The Jews in the Duchy of Milan.* 4 vols. Jerusalem: Israel Academy of Sciences and Humanities.

———. 1985. "Marranos in Ancona under Papal Protection." *Michael* 9: 234–67.

———. 1988–91. *The Apostolic See and the Jews.* 8 vols. Toronto: Pontifical Institute of Mediaeval Studies.

———. 1989. "Some Well Known Jewish Converts in the Renaissance." *Revue des Etudes juives* 148: 17–52.

Smith, Jonathan Z. 1987. *To Take Place: Toward Theory in Ritual.* Chicago Studies in the History of Judaism. Chicago: University of Chicago Press.

Soloveitchik, Haym. 1972. "Pawnbroking: A Study in Ribbit and of the Halakhah in Exile." *Proceedings of the American Academy of Jewish Research* 38–39: 203–68.

———. 1987. "Religious Law and Change: The Medieval Ashkenazic Example." *AJS Review* 12: 205–23.

Sonne, Isaiah. 1947. "On Baer and His Philosophy of Jewish History." *Jewish Social Studies* 9: 61–80.

Sorkin, David. 1987. *The Transformation of German Jewry, 1780–1840.* New York: Oxford University Press.

———. 1992. "The Impact of Emancipation on German Jewry: A Reconsideration." In *Assimilation and Community: The Jews in Nineteenth-Century Europe,* edited by Jonathan Frankel and Steven Zipperstein, 177–98. New York: Cambridge University Press.

———. 1996. *Moses Mendelssohn and the Religious Enlightenment.* Berkeley and Los Angeles: University of California Press.

Stacey, Robert. 1985. "Royal Taxation and the Social Structure of the Medieval Anglo-Jewry: The Tallages of 1239–1242." *Hebrew Union College Annual* 56: 175–249.

———. 1988. "1240–1260: A Watershed in Anglo-Jewish Relations?" *Historical Research* 61: 135–50.

———. 1990. "The Expulsion of 1290: Economics, Sociology, Politics." Unpublished paper. Ithaca, N.Y.

———. 1992a. "The Conversion of Jews to Christianity in Thirteenth-Century England." *Speculum* 67.2: 263–83.

———. 1992b. "Thirteenth-Century Anglo-Jewry and the Problem of the Expulsion." In *The Expulsion of the Jews from England in 1290 and Its Aftermath,* edited by Yosef Kaplan and David Katz. Jerusalem.

Stampfer, Shaul. 1988. "Remarriage among Jews and Christians in Nineteenth-Century Eastern Europe." *Jewish History* 3.2: 85–114.

Starr, Joshua. 1946. "The Mass Conversion of Jews in Southern Italy, 1290–1293." *Speculum* 21: 203–11.

Sternhell, Zeev. [1983] 1986. *Neither Right nor Left: Fascist Ideology in France.* Translated by David Maisel. Berkeley and Los Angeles: University of California Press.

Sternhell, Zeev, Mario Sznajder, and Maia Asheri. [1978] 1994. *The Birth of Fascist Ideology: From Cultural Rebellion to Political Revolution*. Translated by David Maisel. Princeton: Princeton University Press.

Stone, Lawrence. 1975. "The Rise of the Nuclear Family in Early Modern England." In *The Family in History: Lectures Given in Memory of Stephen Allen Kaplan under the Auspices of the Department of History at the University of Pennsylvania*, edited by Charles E. Rosenberg. Philadelphia: University of Pennsylvania Press.

Stow, Kenneth R. 1972. "The Burning of the Talmud in 1553, in the Light of Sixteenth-Century Catholic Attitudes toward the Talmud." *Bibliothèque d'Humanisme et Renaissance* 34: 435–59.

———. 1974. "Agobard of Lyons and the Medieval Concept of the Jew." *Conservative Judaism* 29: 58–65.

———. 1977. *Catholic Thought and Papal Jewry Policy, 1555–1593*. New York: Jewish Theological Seminary of America.

———. 1981. "Papal and Royal Attitudes toward Jewish Lending in the Thirteenth Century." *AJS Review* 6: 161–84.

———. 1982. *Taxation, Community, and State: The Jews and the Fiscal Foundations of the Early Modern Papal State*. Stuttgart: Hiersemann.

———. 1984. *The "1007 Anonymous" and Papal Sovereignty: Jewish Perceptions of the Papacy and Papal Policy in the High Middle Ages*. Cincinnati: Hebrew Union College / Jewish Institute of Religion.

———. 1986. "Delitto e Castigo nello Stato della Chiesa: Gli Ebrei nelle carceri Romane dal 1572 al 1659." In *Italia judaica* 1986, 2: 173–92.

———. 1987. "The Jewish Family in the Rhineland: Form and Function." *American Historical Review* 92: 1085–1110.

———. 1988a. "Expulsion Italian Style: The Case of Lucio Ferraris." *Jewish History* 3.1: 55–64.

———. 1988b. "Hatred of the Jews or Love of the Church: Papal Policy toward the Jews in the Middle Ages." In Almog 1988, 71–89.

———. 1988c. "Life and Society in the Roman Community in the Sixteenth Century" (in Hebrew). *Pa'amim* 37: 55–66.

———. 1989. "La storiografia del ghetto romano: Problemi metodologici." In Muzzarelli and Todeschini 1989, 43–57.

———. 1992a. *Alienated Minority: The Jews of Medieval Latin Europe*. Cambridge, Mass.: Harvard University Press.

———. 1992b. "The Consciousness of Closure: Roman Jewry and Its 'Ghet.'" In *Essential Papers on Jewish Culture in Renaissance and Baroque Italy*, edited by David B. Ruderman, 386–400. New York: New York University Press.

———. 1992c. "The Papacy and the Jews, Catholic Reformation and Beyond." In Walfish 1992–93, vol. 2 [= *Jewish History* 6.1–2]: 257–80.

———. 1992d. "Prossimità o distanza: Etnicità, sefarditi e assenza di conflitti etnici nella Roma del sedicesimo secolo." In *Oltre il 1492*, edited by Anna Foa, Myriam Silvera, and Kenneth Stow, *La rassegna mensile di Israel* 58.1–2: 61–74.

———. 1992e. "Sanctity and the Construction of Space: The Roman Ghetto as

Sacred Space." In *Jewish Assimilation, Acculturation, and Accommodation: Past Traditions, Current Issues. and Future Prospects,* edited by Menachem Mor. Lanham, Md.: University Press of America; Omaha: Center for the Study of Religion and Society, Creighton University.

———. 1993. "A Tale of Uncertainties: Converts in the Roman Ghetto." In *Shlomo Simonsohn Jubilee Volume: Studies in the History of the Jews in the Middle Ages and Renaissance Period,* edited by Daniel Carpi et al., 257–81. Tel Aviv: Tel Aviv University, Faculty of Humanities, Chaim Rosenberg School of Jewish Studies.

———. 1994. "Ebrei e Inquisitori: 1250–1350." In *L'Inquisizione e gli Ebrei in Italia,* edited by Michele Luzzati, 3–18. Rome: Laterza.

———, ed. 1995–97. *The Jews in Rome.* 2 vols. Leiden: E. J. Brill.

———. 1996. "The Avignonese Papacy, or After the Expulsions." In *From Witness to Witchcraft: Jews and Judaism in Medieval Christian Thought,* edited by Jeremy Cohen, 275–97. Wiesbaden: Harrassowitz.

Strack, Hermann I. [1900] 1971. *The Jew and Human Sacrifice: Human Blood and Jewish Ritual, an Historical and Sociological Inquiry.* New York: B. Blom.

Suárez Fernández, Luis. 1964. *Documentos acerca de la expulsión de los judíos.* Valladolid: Biblioteca "Reyes Católicos."

———. [1980] 1983. *Les Juifs espagnols au Moyen Age.* Translated from the Spanish by Rachel Israël-Amsaleg. Paris: Gallimard.

Tirosh-Rotschild, Hava. 1988. "In Defense of Jewish Humanism." *Jewish History* 3.2: 31–57.

———. 1991. *Between Worlds: The Life and Thought of Rabbi David ben Judah Messer Leon.* Albany: State University of New York Press.

Toaff, Ariel. 1970. "Lotte e fazioni tra gli Ebrei di Roma nel Cinquecento." *Studi romani* 27: 25–32.

———. 1973. "Getto-Ghetto." *American Sephardi* 6: 70–77.

———. 1974. "Nuova luce sui Marrani di Ancona (1556)." In *Studi sull' ebraismo italiano in memoria di Cecil Roth,* edited by Elio Toaff, 261–80. Rome: Barulli.

———. 1975. *Gli Ebrei a Perugia.* Perugia: Deputazione di storia patria per l'Umbria.

———. 1979a. *The Jews in Medieval Assisi (1305–1487): A Social and Economic History of a Small Jewish Community in Italy.* Florence: L. S. Olschki.

———. 1979b. "Lotte e fazioni tra gli Ebrei di Roma nel Cinquecento." *Studi romani* 27: 25–32.

———. 1983. "Gli Ebrei romani e il commercio del denaro nei comuni dell' Italia centrale alla fine del Duecento." In *Italia judaica* 1983, 1: 183–96.

———. 1984. *The Roman Ghetto in the Sixteenth Century: Ethnic Conflicts and Socioeconomic Problems.* In Hebrew. Ramat-Gan, Israel.

———. 1986. "Il commercio del denaro e le comunità ebraiche 'di confine' tra Cinquecento e Seicento." In *Italia judaica* 1986, 2: 99–117.

———. 1989a. "The Jewish Communities of Catalonia, Aragon and Castile in Sixteenth-Century Rome." In *The Mediterranean and the Jews: Banking, Finance and International Trade (XVI–XVIII Centuries),* edited by Ariel Toaff and Simon Schwarzfuchs, 249–70. Ramat-Gan, Israel: Bar-Ilan University Press.

———. 1989b. "La storia degli Ebrei in Italia nel tardo Medioevo: Un problema di fonti?" In Muzzarelli and Todeschini 1989, 36–42.

———. 1989c. *Il vino e la carne: Una comunità ebraica nel Medioevo.* Bologna: Il Mulino.

———. 1992. "Ebrei spagnoli e marrani nell'Italia ebraica del Cinquecento: Una presenza contestata." In *Oltre il 1492,* edited by Anna Foa, Myriam Silvera, and Kenneth Stow, *La rassegna mensile di Israel* 58.1–2: 47–59.

———, ed. 1993. *The Jews in Umbria.* 3 vols. Leiden: E. J. Brill.

———. 1996a. *Mostri giudei.* Bologna: Il Mulino.

———. 1996b. "La vita materiale." In *Gli Ebrei in Italia,* vol. 1: *Dall'Alto Medioevo all'età dei ghetti,* edited by Corrado Vivanti, 239–63. Turin.

Toaff, Ariel, and Simon Schwarzfuchs, eds. 1989. *The Mediterranean and the Jews: Banking, Finance and International Trade (XVI–XVIII Centuries).* Ramat-Gan, Israel: Bar-Ilan University Press.

Toaff, Renzo. 1990. *La nazione ebrea a Livorno e a Pisa (1591–1700).* Florence: L. S. Olschki.

Todeschini, Giacomo. 1989a. "Gli Ebrei medievali come minoranza attiva nella storiografia italiana degli ultimi trent'anni." In Muzzarelli and Todeschini 1989, 28–35.

———. 1989b. *La ricchezza degli Ebrei: Merci e denaro nella riflessione ebraica e nella definizione cristiana dell'usura alla fine del Medioevo.* Spoleto: Centro italiano di studi sull'Alto Medioevo.

———. 1990. "Familles juives et chrétiennes en Italie à la fin du Moyen Age: deux modèles de développement économique." *Annales ESC* 45.4: 787–818.

———. 1996. "Usura ebraica e identità economica cristiana: La discussione medievale." In *Gli Ebrei in Italia,* vol. 1: *Dall'Alto Medioevo all'età dei ghetti,* edited by Corrado Vivanti, 291–318. Turin.

Touati, Charles. 1968. "La Controverse de 1303–1306 autour des études philosophiques et scientifiques." *Revue des Etudes juives* 127: 21–37.

———. 1977. "Les Deux Conflits autour de Maimonide et des études philosophiques." In *Juifs et judaïsme de Languedoc: XIIIᵉ siècle–début XIVᵉ siècle,* edited by Marie-Humbert Vicaire and Bernhard Blumenkranz, 173–84. Toulouse.

———. 1979. "Le Grand Sanhédrin de 1807 et le droit rabbinique." In *Le Grand Sanhédrin de Napoléon,* edited by Bernard Blumenkranz and Albert Soboul, 27–48. Collection franco-judaïca, 8. Toulouse: Privat.

Trachtenberg, Joshua. 1939. *Jewish Magic and Superstition: A Study in Folk Religion.* New York: Behrman's Jewish Book House.

———. 1943. *The Devil and the Jews: The Medieval Conception of the Jew and Its Relation to Modern Antisemitism.* New Haven: Yale University Press.

Trasselli, Carmelo. 1954. "Sull'espulsione degli Ebrei dalla Sicilia." *Annali della Facoltà di Economia e Commercio dell'Università di Palermo* 8: 131–50.

Trevor-Roper, Hugh R. 1967. *Religion, the Reformation and Social Change.* London: Macmillan.

Vauchez, André. 1984. "Antisemitismo e canonizzazione popolare: San Werner o Vernier (+1287) bambino martire e patrono dei vignaioli." In *Culto dei santi, istituzioni e classi sociali in età preindustriale,* edited by Sofia Boesch Gajano and Lucia Sebastiani, 490–508. Rome: L. U. Japadre.

Vogelstein, Hermann, and Paul Rieger. 1895–96. *Geschichte der Juden in Rom.* 2 vols. Berlin: Mayer & Müller.

Walfish, Barry, ed. 1992–93. *The Frank Talmage Memorial Volume.* 2 vols. Haifa: Haifa University Press; Hanover, N.H.: University Press of New England in association with Brandeis University Press.

Weinberg, Joanna. 1985. "Azaria de' Rossi and Septuagint Traditions." *Italia* 5: 7–35.

———. 1988. "The Quest for Philo in Sixteenth-Century Jewish Historiography." In *Jewish History: Essays in Honour of Chimen Abramsky,* edited by Ada Rapaport-Albert and Steven J. Zipperstein, 163–87. London: P. Halban.

———. 1992. "Preaching in the Venetian Ghetto: The Sermons of Leon Modena." In *Preachers of the Italian Ghetto,* edited by David B. Ruderman, 105–28. Berkeley and Los Angeles: University of California Press.

Weinryb, Bernard D. 1950. *Texts and Studies in the Communal History of Polish Jewry.* New York: Jewish Publication Society of America.

———. 1973. *The Jews of Poland: A Social and Economic History of the Jewish Community in Poland from 1100 to 1800.* Philadelphia: Jewish Publication Society of America.

———. 1974. "Reappraisals in Jewish History." In *Salo Wittmayer Baron Jubilee Volume on the Occasion of His Eightieth Birthday,* edited by Saul Lieberman and Arthur Hyman, 938–74. Jerusalem: American Academy for Jewish Research.

Weissler, Chava. 1987. "The Religion of Traditional Ashkenazic Women: Some Methodological Issues." *AJS Review* 12: 73–94.

———. 1991. "Woman as High Priest: A Kabbalistic Prayer in Yiddish for Lighting Sabbath Candles." *Jewish History* 5.1: 9–26.

Wickersheimer, Ernest. 1927. *Les Accusations d'empoisonnement portées dans la première moitié du 14 siècle contre les lépreux et les Juifs, leurs relations avec les épidémies de peste.* Antwerp.

Wolff, Philippe. 1971. "The 1391 Pogrom in Spain: Social Crisis or Not?" *Past and Present* 50: 4–18.

World Congress of Jewish Studies. 1985. *Jews and Conversos: Studies in Society and the Inquisition: Proceedings of the Eighth World Congress of Jewish Studies held at the Hebrew University of Jerusalem, August 16–21, 1981.* Edited by Yosef Kaplan. Jerusalem: World Union of Jewish Studies; Magnes Press. In Spanish.

Yardeni, Myriam, ed. 1980. *Les Juifs dans l'histoire de France: Premier colloque international de Haïfa.* Leiden: E. J. Brill.

Yates, Frances A. 1972. *The Rosicrucian Enlightenment.* London: Routledge & Kegan Paul. Reprint, Boulder, Colo.: Shambhala, 1978.

Yerushalmi, Yosef Hayim. 1970. "The Inquisition and the Jews of France in the Time of Bernard Gui." *Harvard Theological Review* 63: 317–76.

————. 1971. *From Spanish Court to Italian Ghetto: Isaac Cardoso: A Study in Seventeenth-Century Marranism and Jewish Apologetics.* New York: Columbia University Press.

————. 1972. Prolegomenon to Alexandre Herculano, *History of the Origin and Establishment of the Inquisition in Portugal.* New York: Ktav.

————. 1974. "Professing Jews in Post-Expulsion Spain and Portugal." In *Salo Wittmayer Baron Jubilee Volume on the Occasion of His Eightieth Birthday,* edited by Saul Lieberman and Arthur Hyman, 1023–58. Jerusalem: American Academy for Jewish Research.

————. 1976. *The Lisbon Massacre of 1506 and the Royal Image in the Shebet Yehudah.* Cincinnati: Hebrew Union College–Jewish Institute of Religion.

————. 1982a. *Assimilation and Racial Anti-Semitism: The Iberian and the German Models.* New York: Leo Baeck Institute.

————. 1982b. *Zakhor: Jewish History and Jewish Memory.* Seattle: University of Washington Press.

————. 1991. *Freud's Moses: Judaism Terminable and Interminable.* New Haven: Yale University Press.

Yovel, Yirmiahu. 1983. "Marrano Patterns in Spinoza." *La Rassegna mensile di Israel* 49: 543–64.

————. 1989. *Spinoza and Other Heretics.* Princeton: Princeton University Press.

Yuval, Yisrael. 1993. "Vengeance and Damnation, Blood and Defamation: From Jewish Martyrdom to Blood Libel Accusations" (in Hebrew). *Zion* 58.1: 33–90.

Ziegler, Philip. 1969. *The Black Death.* New York: John Day.

Zimmels, Hirsch Jakob. [1958] 1976. *Ashkenazim and Sephardim: Their Relations, Differences, and Problems as Reflected in the Rabbinical Responsa.* London: Oxford University Press.

Zipperstein, Steven. 1985. *The Jews of Odessa: A Cultural History, 1794–1881.* Stanford: Stanford University Press.

————. 1992. "Ahad Ha'am and the Politics of Assimilation." In *Assimilation and Community: The Jews in Nineteenth-Century Europe,* edited by Jonathan Frankel and Steven Zipperstein, 344–65. New York: Cambridge University Press.

Illustration Credits

Chapter 1. Erna Michael Haggadah, fol. 40, Germany, 7
c. 1400. Collection Israel Museum, Jerusalem.
Photograph courtesy of Israel Museum.

Chapter 2. *Left:* Church, Cathedral of Strasbourg, c. 1230. 23
Right: Synagogue, Cathedral of Strasbourg,
c. 1230. Photographs courtesy of Manuela
Fugenzi.

Chapter 3. Rothschild Misc. 24, fol. 78v, northern Italy, 49
c. 1450–1480. Collection Israel Museum, Jerusalem. Photograph courtesy of Israel Museum.

Chapter 4. Ms. OR 2884, fol. 17v, Spain, c. 1350. Courtesy 74
of The British Library.

Chapter 5. Rothschild Misc. 24, fol. 121v, northern Italy, 108
c. 1450–1480. Collection Israel Museum, Jerusa-
lem. Photograph courtesy of Israel Museum.

Chapter 6. Giuseppe Vasi, Piazza Giudea fuori dal Ghetto, 138
1752. Rome. Photograph courtesy of Valerio
Ricciardi.

Chapter 7. Bernard Picart, Jewish marriage, 1722. Private 154
collection. Photograph courtesy of Manuela
Fugenzi.

Chapter 8. Photograph of young and old Jews in a park on 192
New York's Lower East Side, c. 1910. Photograph
courtesy of Brown Brothers.

Index

Abrabanel, Bienvenida, 129
Abrabanel, Giuda (Leone Ebreo), 135
Abrabanel, Isaac, 79, 135
Abraham Ibn Daud, 74–75
Abraham Ibn Hasdai, 30
Acculturation, use of term, 203. *See also* Assimilation of Jews
Acosta, Uriel (Uriel da Costa), 175
Adret, Solomon Ibn, 63, 69, 82
Agimet (Jewish silk merchant), 14
Agnadello, battle of (1509), 116
Agone carnival games, 46, 125
Agrippa di Nettesheim, Cornelius, 135–36
Ahasuerus (legendary Jew), 50
Alemanno, Johannan, 134
Alexander II (czar), 207
Alexander VI (pope), 66, 125
Alghero (Sardinia), 121, 122
Almohades, 78, 90
Alphonso I (king of Sicily), 120
Alphonso V (king of Aragon), 94
Alphonso X (king of Castile), 83
Alsatian Jews, 180
Altona (Germany), 158
Alvaro, Baltazar (Baltazar Orobio de Castro), 178–79
Amedeo VI (count of Aosta), 14
American Jews, 197, 205, 208
American Revolution, 197
Amsterdam (Holland), 154, 163; Ashkenazim community of, 68, 170; first synagogue in, 171; population statistics of, 170; public worship in, 172–73
Amsterdam Portuguese community: commercial trades of, 171; community model of, 173; excommunication as tool of, 174–75; heterodox groups of, 175–77; identity problems of, 173–74; mythical recollections of, 171–72; origins of, 169–70; and philo-Semitism, 181–82, 183; public worship by, 172–73
Anatoli, Jacob, 93
Ancona (Italy), 125, 130, 140, 146, 167–68
Andalusia (Spain), 78, 86
Andrea de Monte, 45
Angevin monarchy, 119
Anti-Judaism, defined, 17
Anti-Semitic stereotype: Christian identity's ties to, 24–26, 27–28; contamination formula of, 17, 21–22, 24–25; of Host profanation, 17–18; of moneylending, 39–40; of ritual murder, 18–21; transformation of, 16–17
Anti-Semitism: assimilation and, 212, 213, 217; in France, 211–13; of modern Catholic Church, 210–11; of Nazis, 212–13, 216; racial component of, 16–17, 106–7, 210, 213; of Russian Orthodox clergy, 206, 207; Voltairean, 209
Antwerp (Holland), 170

Apparatus (papal bull), 29
Apulia (Italy), 1, 119
Arabic language, 77
Aragonese Dominicans, 32, 33; conversionist sermons of, 45, 86–87
Aragonese Jewish community: exiled Jews from, 101; forced sermons to, 87; in inquisitorial trials, 98; judicial autonomy of, 81–83; migration from France to, 83–84; in pogrom of 1391, 85; population of, 75, 94; reconstruction of, 94–95; trades/occupations of, 80
Arbues, Pedro de, 97–98, 102
Archisynagogus (communal leader), 64
Arenda (rent) practice, 186
Arendt, Hannah, 195, 218
Aretine bankers, 117
Armleder massacres (1336), 8
Artisan trades, 80, 118, 186–87
Aryan myth, 210
Ashkenazic Pietism, 186
Ashkenazim: Amsterdam community of, 68, 170; communal organization of, 59–60, 62; emancipation of, 197, 200; French communities of, 179, 181; Italian loan banks of, 109–11; London community of, 185; martyrdom of, 89, 91; massacres of, in 1348, 14–16; on moneylending to non-Jews, 37–38; origins of, 2, 9; Venice community of, 67–68; *yeshivah* life of, 56
Assimilation of Jews: and anti-Semitism, 212, 213, 217; in France, 203–4; in Germany, 198–99; Haskalah's impact on, 194–96; and Jewish identity, 203–4, 217–18. *See also* Emancipation of Jews
Assisi (Italy), 61, 118
Atheist movement, 175, 176–77
Augsburg (Germany), 156; 1530 diet of, 158
Augustine, Saint, 24, 25
Averroism, 90–91
Avignon (France), 40, 109, 177
Avila (Spain), 76

Baal Shem Tov (Yisrael Baal Shem), 189
Badge, identification: abolition of, in Italy, 120; creation of, 34; exemptions from wearing, 121, 125; in Muslim Spain, 77; for Roman Jews, 124; for Venetian Jews, 115, 165
Baer, Yizhak, 50
Bajulo (Christian magistrate), 120
Balearic Islands, 80

Banks. *See* Moneylenders, Christian; Moneylenders, Jewish
Barcelona (Spain): contamination anxiety in, 86; disputation of 1263 in, 88–89; ritual murder charges in, 19–20
Baron, Salo Wittmayer, 9, 51
Baruch (a Judaizer), 96
Bauman, Zygmunt, 219
Bavaria, 156
Bayle, Pierre, 50
Bayonne (France), 180
Belorussia, 206
Benedict XIII (anti-pope), 88–89, 94
Benjamin of Tudela, 123
Benveniste, Abraham, 63–64, 95
Berlin (Germany), 156, 158, 195
Bernaldez, André, 101
Bernardino da Feltre, 20, 118
Bernardino da Siena, 117
Bernard-Lazare, 212, 217–18
Bernard of Clairvaux, Saint, 37
Bessarabia, 206, 207
Betulot confraternity (Rome), 148
Biale, David, 219
Biblical texts. *See* Hebrew texts
Birnbaum, Pierre, 199
Black Death. *See* Plague
Blois (France), 19
Blum, Leon, 212
Boarding schools, 44. *See also* Houses of converts
Bohemian Jews, 158–59
Boleslaw (ruler of Poland), 186
Bologna (Italy): expulsion of Jews from, 117; ghettos of, 140; house of converts in, 44; loan banking in, 111, 116–17
Bomberg, Daniel, 133
Bonet de Lattes, 62, 125
Bordeaux Portuguese, 179, 180–81
Brandenburg region, 156, 158
Brazil, 183
Brunswick (Germany), 158
Brussels (Belgium), 15
Das Buch der Natur (Konrad of Megenberg), 14
Burckhardt, Jacob, 130

Cabalistic system: and ghettoization, 152; and Hasidism, 189–90; Haskalah on, 194; humanist interest in, 132–34, 136; impact of, on traditional Judaism, 91; and philo-Semitism, 181–82; transformation of, after 1492, 132–33
Caeca et obdurata (papal bull), 117, 140
Cagliari (Sardinia), 27, 121–22
Callistus II (pope), 27, 28
Callistus III (pope), 126

Campsores guild, 116
Canon law: meal prohibitions of, 53; on moneylending, 35, 36–37; Roman juridical elements of, 26–27; servitude concept of, 27–28
Capitoli (Daniele da Pisa), 67, 125, 127
Capsali, Elijah, 56
Cardano, Girolamo, 135
Carinthia, 156
Caro, Avigdor, 159
Cartenright, Ebenezer, 182
Cartenright, Johanna, 182
Casale (Italy), 62
Castilian Jewish community: centralization of, 63–64; court Jews of, 79, 82–83; exiled Jews from, 101; Ferrer's sermons to, 88; Inquisition of, 97; judicial autonomy of, 81, 82; Marranos' migration to, 164; in pogrom of 1391, 85, 86, 101; population of, 75; reconstruction of, 94, 95; trades/occupations of, 80
Castilian Synagogue (Rome), 145
Catalan Synagogue (Rome), 145
Catalonia (Aragon), 13, 63, 84, 86
Catholic Church. *See* Church
Cento (Italy), 140
Charles II (king of England), 185
Charles V (emperor), 106, 156, 158
Chioggia, war of (1378–81), 114
Chmielnicki, Bogdan, 187–88
Christiani, Pablo, 32, 88
Christianity: anti-Judaism identity of, 24–26, 27–28; heterodox movements in, 175–76; Jewry's perception of, 57–58, 92–93; nocturnal devotions of, 152; Portuguese Jews' mediation with, 162–63, 165, 171–72, 173–74, 176; Renaissance encounters with, 130–37
Christians: cabalistic interests of, 132–34, 136–37; contamination anxiety of, 16–22; education of, 57; ghettos' relations with, 143, 151–53; and Jewish dietary laws, 53, 58, 111–12; Jews distinguished from, 34; Jews' subordination to, 9–10, 24–26, 27–28, 77, 138–39; marriage of Jews to, 26, 70, 96, 172, 204; moneylending to, 35–39, 80–81, 111–12, 118–19; perception of time by, 51–52
Christian slaves, banned ownership of, 26, 27, 38
Chrysostom, Saint John, 25
Church: anti-Judaism theme of, 24–26, 27–28; contamination symbolism of, 16–22; conversionist project of, 41–

43; in Eastern Europe, 187; on emancipation of Jews, 197; on flagellation, 15; ghettoization policy of, 41, 47–48, 138–39, 141–42, 149–50; jurisdiction of, over Judaism, 26–29; modern anti-Semitism of, 210–11; on moneylending, 35–37, 110, 118; Plague theory of, 13–14; pure blood measures of, 106; on ritual murder charges, 19, 20–21; Talmud policy of, 31–32, 33; taxation policy of, 125–26. *See also* Papacy
Circumcision rites, 152
Citizenship. *See* Juridical status
La civiltà cattolica (Jesuit newspaper), 210
Clement IV (pope), 30
Clement VI (pope), 13–14
Clement VII (pope), 127, 128, 129–30, 167
Clement VIII (pope), 140, 146
Clermont-Tonnerre, Stanislas de, 193
Coffee, 152
Colbert, Jean-Baptiste, 180–81
Colmar, 156
Cologne (Germany), 15, 156
Commercial trades, 162, 166, 167, 170, 171, 179
Communitas Hebreorum, 61
Community, the: assimilation's impact on, 204; centralization of, 63–65; ethnicity element of, 66–69; ghettoization's impact on, 142–43, 150–53; governing bodies of, 61; Italian model of, 59–60; juridical foundation of, 60; jurisdictional autonomy of, 62–63, 81–83; loan banking networks of, 109–11; rabbis' role in, 61–62; reconstruction of, in Spain, 94–96; terms for, in Italy, 61
Concini, Concino, 179
Condotta (moneylending charters), 52, 61; on moneylending, 34, 110; on ritual slaughter, 111–12
Confraternities: homogenization role of, 65, 66; model for, 148; nocturnal devotions of, 152; origin of, 147–48; religious function of, 149
Conjugal duty *(onah)*, 69
Consistories, 204, 212
Constantine, 26
Contamination: dietary fears of, 53, 83, 111–12; formulation of concept, 16–17, 21–22; from Host profanation, 17–18; Paul on, 24–25; Plague's ties to, 16–17, 21, 86; from ritual murder, 18–21

Contarini, Gasparo, 43
Conti, Sigismund de', 163
Contra Apionem (Josephus), 20
Conversion: assimilation's replacement
of, 195; eschatological basis of, 42–
43; ethnicity's repression of, 68–69;
incentives for, 87; Maimonidean
justification of, 92–93; martyrdom
versus, 89–90, 91; Mortara case of,
210; mysticism and, 91; rationalism
and, 90–91; spontaneous versus
forced, 27, 130; statistics on, 46–
47; theatrical element of, 46
Conversion campaigns, 3–4; of Benedict XIII, 88–89; compulsory sermons
of, 45–46, 86–87, 88; of Counter-
Reformation, 41–43; of Dominicans,
8, 86–87; as failure, 47–48, 97, 98; of
Ferrer, 88–89; ghetto as tool of, 41, 48,
142; of humanist intellectuals, 133–34;
in Italy, 5, 119–20; in Portugal, 103–
4; in Spain, 5, 8, 84–89, 93; of Visigoth kings, 76–77. See also Ghettos
Converts: confiscated assets of, 87; designated as Jews, 76, 77, 93, 95–96, 104;
forced sermons by, 87; and ghetto
Jews, 150; houses of, 44–45, 126; inquisitorial jurisdiction over, 29–30,
97–98, 130; pogrom against, in Lis-
bon, 104; pure blood statutes against,
106; reentry into Judaism by, 68–69,
95–96, 161–63; ritual murder charges
against, 98–99. See also Portuguese
Jews
Córdoba (Spain), 75
Cordovero, Moshe, 133
Cosimo I Medici, 166
Cossack massacres, 146, 187–88, 189
Costa, Uriel da (Uriel Acosta), 175
Council of Paris (1213), 37
Council of the Four Lands (Poland), 64,
187
Counter-Reformation, 41–43, 142
Court Jews, 79, 82–83, 161
Coutinho, Fernand de, 103
Crescas, Hasdai, 94–95
Criminal offenses, 81, 151
Cromwell, Oliver, 183, 184
Crusades, 2, 16–17; of the Little Shep-
herds, 13, 84, 101
Crypto-Jews. See Converts
Cum nimis absurdum (papal bull), 138,
140, 141, 144, 149

Daniele da Pisa, 67, 125, 127, 129
Danton, Georges-Jacques, 194
Dax (France), 180

Dayan kelali (communal leader), 64, 65,
121
Decretals (Gregory IX), 29
Deist movement, 175, 176; Haskalah's
ties to, 194–95
De Iudaeis et aliis infidelibus (de Susan-
nis), 36, 43
De la Sala, Pons, 85
Delmedigo, Elijah, 134
De Luna Mendes, Beatrice, 168–69
De Luna Mendes, Brianda, 168–69
De occulta philosophia (Agrippa di
Nettesheim), 135–36
Desmoulins, Camille, 209
De Susannis, Marquardus, 36
Diamond trade, 171
Diario (Reubeni), 127, 128
The Diary of Anne Frank, 219
Diderot, Denis, 209
Dietary laws, 52–53, 58, 111–12
Directorium Inquisitorum (Eymerich), 82
Discorso (Luzzatto), 183
Divorce, 70
Dobruška, Moses, 194
Dohm, Christian Wilhelm, 193, 197
Dominicans, 8, 29, 32, 33, 45, 86–87
Donin, Nicholas, 31
Dormido, Manuel Martinez, 183
Dreyfus Affair, 211–13, 218
Drumont, Edouard, 211
Dubnow (Poland), 188
Dudum a felicis (papal bull), 140
Dulcia (wife of Eleazar ben Judah of
Worms), 56–57
Du rappel des Juifs (La Peyrère), 182
Dury, John, 181

Earrings, as identifier, 34
Eastern Europe: Christian-Jewish rela-
tions in, 187; Hasidic movement in,
189–91; maskilic influence in, 206–7;
population statistics in, 8–9, 185; rea-
sons for migrations to, 185–86; wo-
men's role in, 72. See also Polish
Jews; Russian Jews
Edict of Tolerance (1781, Joseph II), 197
Education, 55–57
Egidio da Viterbo, 127, 130
Eichmann, Adolf, 219
Eleazar ben Judah of Worms, 56
Elijah of Vilna, 190
Elizabeth I (queen of England), 171
"El Male Rahamim" (Horowitz), 189
Emancipation of Jews: in America, 197;
in England, 200; Enlightenment view
of, 192–93; in France, 197, 199–200;
in Germany, 198–99; in Holland, 198;

in Italy, 201–3; lack of, in Russia, 206–8; opposition to, 197, 209; secularization's ties to, 196–97. *See also* Assimilation of Jews

Emech Habacha (Hacohen), 102

Emilia (Italy), 110

Encyclopaedia Judaica, 9

England: emancipation of Jews in, 200; expulsion of Jews from, 2, 8, 9, 11–12; Jewish population of, 12; juridical status in, 11, 12, 39; readmission of Jews to, 182–85; ritual murder charges in, 18–19

Enlightenment, 192–96

Episcopus judaeorum (communal leader), 64

Erasmus, 136, 160

Ercole II Este, 166

Esnoga Synagogue (Amsterdam), 173

Espina, Alonzo de, 98–99

Etsi Iudaeos (papal bull), 27

Eugene IV, 124

Eulenburg region, 21

Excommunication *(herem),* 62, 174–75

Exiled Jews: destinations of, 101–3, 122, 163–64, 170; first record of, 74; Israel's relationship with, 58–59; modern relocation of, 154–55

Expulsions of Jews: from Antwerp, 170; from Bologna, 117; canceled in Prague, 158–59; conversion policy against, 47; from England, 2, 8, 9, 11–12; from France, 2, 8, 9, 11, 12, 40, 83–84, 179–80; from Germany, 9, 154, 156, 157–58; from Milan, 141; from Naples, 9, 108, 122; from Navarre, 102; during Reformation, 157–59, 160; for ritual murder charges, 20–21; from Rome, 40; from Sardinia, 121–22; from Sicily, 121, 122; from Spain, 2, 11, 20, 23, 100–102, 122, 154, 161; from Umbria, 118; from Venice, 115; from Vienna, 160. *See also* Exiled Jews

Eymerich, Nicolas, 82

Family names, universal adoption of, 204

Family structure, 69–73

Farissol, Avraham, 134

Farnese, Cardinal Alessandro, 43

Ferdinand I (Don Ferrante), 120

Ferdinand I (emperor), 158

Ferdinand I Medici, 166

Ferdinand II (emperor), 159

Ferdinand II (king of Aragon), 79, 81, 89, 97; expulsion edict of, 100

Ferrara (Italy), 44, 110, 117, 140, 148, 165–66

Ferrer, Saint Vincent, 88, 89

First Letter to the Corinthians (Paul), 25

Flagellation movements, 15

Florence (Italy), 111, 140

Fortalitium fidei (Espina), 98, 99

Fournier, Jacques, 96

Fourth Lateran Council (1215), 34–35

France: Ashkenazim communities of, 179, 181; assimilationist policies in, 203–4; confiscation of Talmud in, 31–32; Dreyfus Affair in, 211–13; emancipation of Jews in, 197, 199–200; expulsion of Jews from, 2, 8, 9, 11, 12, 40, 83–84, 179–80; Jewish populations of, 8, 180, 199; pogrom of 1321 in, 21; polygamy in, 69; Portuguese communities of, 178–79, 180–81

La France juive (Drumont), 211

Franciscans, 106, 157; inquisitorial authority of, 29; on meat sales, 111–12; on moneylending, 36; *monte di pietà* of, 112–14, 118; papacy's position on, 40

Franconia region, 21

Frank, Jacob, 194

Frankel, Zacharias, 205

Frankfurt (Germany), 15, 141, 143, 158

Frederick Barbarossa, 10

Frederick II (emperor), 10, 19

Frederick III (king of Aragon), 122

French Revolution, 197

Friedlander, David, 195

Fulda (Germany), 19

Galigai, Leonora, 179

Geiger, Abraham, 205

Gemilut hasadim (Jewish confraternity), 148

Geneva (Switzerland), 156

Genoa (Italy), 114, 141

Gentiles. *See* Christians

Germany: Aryan myth of, 210; Ashkenazic origins in, 9; bourgeois Jewry of, 198, 211; emancipation of Jews in, 198–99; expulsion of Jews from, 9, 154, 156, 157–58; family life in, 71; flagellation movement in, 15; Haskalah movement in, 194–95; imperial protection policies of, 156, 157–58, 159; martyrdom in, 71, 89, 91; pogroms in, 8, 12–13, 15–16, 156; polygamy in, 69; Reform movement in, 204–5; Roman law in, 155; during Thirty Years' War, 159–60; *Wissenschaft* movement in, 205

Gershom ben Judah (Rabbenu), 69, 70
Ghetto nuovissimo (Venice), 144, 145
Ghetto nuovo (Venice), 67, 143–44
Ghettos: cabalistic culture of, 152;
    Church's motivation for, 41, 47–48,
    138–39, 141–42; conditions in, 145–
    46, 148–49, 153; and conflicted iden-
    tity, 51, 142–43, 150–52; confraterni-
    ties of, 147–48, 149; criminal offenses
    in, 151; death rate in, 146; in Italy, 4,
    140–42, 201; origin of term, 139–40;
    Paul IV's creation of, 25–26, 138, 144,
    149–50; publishing activities of, 151–
    52; of Rome, 47–48, 138–39, 144–
    45, 148–49, 201–2; tenancy rights of,
    147; of Venice, 67–68, 143–44, 162,
    164–65
Ghetto vecchio (Venice), 67, 144, 162,
    164–65
Giacomo della Marca, 34
Gioacchino da Fiore, 43
Giordano da Rivalto, 119
Giudici, Battista de' (bishop of
    Ventimiglia), 41
Giustiniani, Paolo, 43
Gloucester (England), 19
Glückel of Hameln, 71–72
Graetz, Heinrich, 50, 205
Granada (Spain), 75, 76, 78
Grand Sanhedrin (France), 204
Great Revolt (66–70 C.E.), 1
Great Synagogue (Rome), 145
Gregory the Great (pope), 26–27
Gregory IX (pope), 29, 31
Grotius, Hugo, 172
Gubbio (Italy), 118
Gui, Bernard, 96

Haarlem (Holland), 166
Hacohen, Joseph, 102
Halakhah, defined, 51
Halevi, Jehudah, 58
Halevi, Moshe Uri, 174
Halfan, Elija Menachem, 132
Halle (Germany), 156
Ha-Lorki, Josue (Jerónimo di Santa Fe),
    88, 90
Hamburg (Germany), 158, 173, 204–5
Ha-Meiri, Menahem, 92–93
Hannover (Germany), 158
Hartlib, Samuel, 181
Hasidic movement, 5, 189–91
Haskalah (maskilim) movement, 200,
    201; assimilation role of, 195; in East-
    ern Europe, 196, 206–7; Enlighten-
    ment views of, 194–95; and Reform
    Judaism, 204–5

Hazakah (possession) rights, 147
Hebraeorum gens (papal bull), 140, 146
Hebrew language, 77, 151–52
Hebrew texts: humanist interest in, 42,
    131–32; mystical interpretation of, 91;
    papacy's confiscation of, 31–32; print-
    ing of, 133; rationalistic readings of,
    90–91; required study of, 55–57
Heine, Heinrich, 143
Henri II (king of France), 179
Henri III (king of France), 179
Henri IV (king of France), 179
Henry III (king of England), 12, 19
Henry IV (emperor), 10
Herem (excommunication), 62, 174–75
Heresy and Judaizers, 29–30
Herzl, Theodore, 212, 216
Hirsch, Samson Raphael, 205–6
Historia (Conti), 163
History of Jewish Rites (Modena), 38
Hitler, Adolf, 209, 213
Holbach, Paul-Henri, 209
Holland, 172–73, 183, 198. See also
    Amsterdam
Holocaust, 216, 217, 218–19
Holy Shower of Stones (Sassaiola Santa),
    46
Horowitz, Rabbi Sabbatay, 189
Host profanation, 16, 17–18, 39
Houses of converts, 44–45, 126
Huesca Inquisition, 96
Humanists: cabalistic interests of, 132–
    34, 136; Jewry's encounter with, 42,
    131, 134–37
The Humble Addresses (Menasseh ben
    Israel), 183, 185
Hungary, 8–9

Ibn Adret, Solomon, 63, 69, 82
Ibn Daud, Abraham, 74–75
Ibn Ezra, Moshe, 77–78
Ibn Hasdai, Abraham, 30
Ibn Hasdai, Judah, 30
Ibn Verga, Solomon, 66, 97
Ignatius of Loyola, Saint, 44, 106
Imola (Italy), 140
Imperial protection policies: in Germany,
    156, 157–58, 159; in Spain, 78–79,
    86; during Thirty Years' War, 159–
    60
Index of Prohibited Books, 33
Informers (malsinos), 82
Innocent III (pope), 27
Innocent IV (pope), 19, 29, 32
Inquisition: of Judaizers, 29–30, 52; of
    Maimonides' writings, 30–31; in
    Spain, 97–99, 161, 164; of Talmud,

31–33; in Toulouse, 178; trials of, 97–
98; in Venice, 165
Interest rates: of Jewish moneylenders,
110, 114–15; of *monte di pietà*, 113;
for non-Jews, 37–38
Isabella I (queen of Castile), 79, 81, 97,
100, 120
Islam. *See* Muslims
Israel: exiled relationship with, 58–59;
Reubeni's mission of return to, 128–
30; state of, 216
Istanbul (Ottoman Empire), 163–64
Italian Jews: badge of, 34; communal
rabbi of, 62; community model of, 59–
60, 63; emancipation of, 201–3; forced
conversion of, 5; fourteenth-century
migrations of, 108–9; ghettoization
of, 4, 139–42; moneylending by, 36,
109–11, 114–16, 117–19; origins of,
1–2; populations of, 8, 116, 117, 120;
Renaissance culture of, 131; taxes on,
119, 124. *See also* Ghettos; Roman
Jews
Italy: Jewish expansion in, 108–9;
Sephardim's migrations to, 161, 164–
65; unification movement in, 201, 202

Jacob ben Meir, Tam (Rabbenu Tam),
38, 57–58, 70
Jacobins, 209
James I (king of Aragon), 32, 83
Jehiel ben Josef, 31
Jerónimo di Santa Fe (Josue Ha-Lorki),
88, 90
Jesuits, 106
Jewish Bund (Russian Jewish party), 207
Jewish history: of exile, 58–59; as organic whole, 50–51; role of Holocaust
in, 218–19; tension of separateness in,
51–55; transformations/continuity in,
154–55, 215–17, 219–20
Jewish identity: assimilation's impact on,
203, 204, 217–18; concrete elements
of, 51; ghettoization's impact on, 51,
142–43, 150–52; historiography's interpretation of, 50–51; Holocaust element of, 218–19; humanist encounter
with, 42, 131–37; of Portuguese Jews,
162–63, 171–72, 173–75; religious
criteria of, 24–26, 27–28; Sartre on,
49; separateness of, 51–55; transmission of, 55–56, 69–71; Zionist
redefinition of, 202–3, 216
The Jewish State (Herzl), 212
The Jew of Malta (Marlowe), 181
Jews: anti-Semitic stereotype of, 16–22;
badge for, 34, 77, 88, 115, 124, 165;

communal organizations of, 59–62;
conversionary sermons to, 45–46, 86–
87, 88; conversion of, 41–43; converts designated as, 76, 77, 93, 95–96,
104; emancipation of, 192–93, 196–
97, 201–3; England's readmission of,
182–85; family structure of, 69–73;
flagellation movements against, 15; inquisitorial jurisdiction over, 29–31;
juridical status of, 9–11, 59, 77, 155;
marriage of Christians to, 26, 70, 96,
172, 204; modernity tied to, 210, 211;
papal jurisdiction over, 28–29; Plague
accusations against, 14–16; as racially
defined, 106–7, 210, 213; subordinate
position of, 9–10, 24–26, 27–28,
138–39; as wartime suppliers, 160,
180; witches tied to, 179–80. *See also*
Jewish history; Jewish identity
Joan I (queen of Naples), 119
John of Capistrano, Saint, 40
John I (king of Castile), 84
John III (king of Portugal), 105, 128
John XXII (pope), 32, 40
Josel of Rosheim, 128–29, 136, 157, 170
Joseph II (emperor), 197
Josephus, Flavius, 20
Judah Ibn Hasdai, 30
Judaism: Christian identity's ties to, 24–
26, 27–28; converts' reentry into, 4,
68–69, 95–96, 161–63; and Hasidism, 190; Haskalah movement in,
194–95; inquisitorial jurisdiction over,
29–31; of Menasseh ben Israel, 182;
and mysticism, 91; Orthodox movement in, 205–6; papal jurisdiction
over, 28–29; of Portuguese heterodox
groups, 175–77; Portuguese Jews' mediation with, 162–63, 165, 171–72,
173–74; practice of, in Holland, 172–
73; and rationalism, 90–91; Reform
movement in, 195–96, 200, 201, 204–
5; sacredness in, 53–54; *Wissenschaft*
study of, 205
Judaizers. *See* Converts
Judicial autonomy of Sephardim, 81–83
Julius II (pope), 125
Julius III (pope), 33, 167
Juridical status: based on servitude, 10–
11; of converts, 95; deterioration of,
11–13; in the Enlightenment, 192–93;
in Holland, 172–73; in Italy, 120, 121,
124; and jurisdictional issues, 59; and
land ownership, 39; in Muslim Spain,
77; under Roman law, 9–10, 26, 155
Jus gazaga (right of tenancy), 147
Justinian Code, 10, 26, 173

Kabbalah (received tradition), 132. *See also* Cabalistic system
Kehilla kedoshah (sacred community), 54
Kiddush ha-shem (sanctification of the Name), 16–17
Kiev (Russia), 206
Kishinev pogrom (1903), 207, 213
Konrad of Megenberg, 14
Kraków (Poland), 187
Kriegel, Maurice, 191
Al Kuzari (Halevi), 58

Labastide (France), 180
Ladislas (king of Naples), 119
La Guardia case, 98–99
Lainez (a Jesuit), 106
Landesrabbiner of the Empire (communal leader), 64
Languedoc (France), 9, 79, 83, 178
La Peyrère, Isaac de, 182
League of Cambrai, 116
League of Schmalkalden, 158
Leghorn (Italy), 140, 154, 163, 165, 166–67
Leibniz, Gottfried Wilhelm, 177
Lemlein, Asher, 129
Leone Ebreo (Giuda Abrabanel), 135
Leo X (pope), 125
Lepanto, battle of (1571), 165, 166
Lepers, 21
Letter to the Galatians (Paul), 17, 25, 41, 157
Letter to the Romans (Paul), 24, 25
Levantine Jews, 67, 68, 144, 164–65, 166, 167
Libellus ad Leonem Decem (Querini and Giustiniani), 43
Liberal Jewish Union (France), 195
Libertine movement, 175, 176
Limpieza de sangre (pure blood), 105–7
Linz (Germany), 156
Lisbon (Portugal), 104
Literacy, 57
Lithuania, 154, 190
Livornina ordinances, 166–67
Livorno. *See* Leghorn
Loan banks. *See* Moneylenders, Christian; Moneylenders, Jewish
Locke, John, 197
London Portuguese community, 173, 182, 184–85
Lopes Homem, Manuel, 171
Lopez, Alfonso, 180
Lopez de Villanueva family, 178
Lopez Pereira, Manuel, 172
Louis IX (king of France), 31, 32
Louis XIV (king of France), 181

Lower Austria, 156
Lublin (Poland), 186, 188
Lucena (Spain), 75
Lucrum cessans (moneylending exception), 36
Lugo (Italy), 140
Luna, Pedro de (Benedict XIII), 88–89, 94
Luneburg (Germany), 158
Luria, Isaac, 133
Lurianic School (Safed), 133
Lutheranism, 41, 157
Luzzatto, Simone, 183
Lvov (Poland), 186, 188

Magdeburg (Germany), 156
Magister judaeorum (communal leader), 64
Maimon, Solomon, 195
Maimonides, 30–31, 92
Mainz (Germany), 15, 156
Majorca (Spain), 80
Malsinos (slanderers), 82
Mantua (Italy), 61, 110, 117, 119; excommunication function in, 62; ghettos of, 140, 143, 151
Manuel (king of Portugal), 102
Manuzio, Aldo, 133
Marat, Jean-Paul, 209
Marcellus II (pope), 43
Marches, the (Italy), 110
Marrano, Righetto, 169
Marrano, use of term, 162–63. *See also* Portuguese Jews
Marriage: arranged, 71–72; of Christians with Jews, 26, 70, 96, 172, 204; of converts, 95; and divorce, 70; in ghettos, 146; and polygamy, 69; of Sephardim and Italian Jews, 67; sexuality in, 69; women's status in, 70
Marseilles (France), 13
Martinez, Ferran (archdeacon of Ecije), 84, 88
Martini, Raimon, 33
Martin V (pope), 40, 94, 124
Martyrdom *(Qiddush ha-Shem)*, 89–90, 91, 92
Marx, Karl, 211
Maskilim. See Haskalah movement
Massacres. *See* Pogroms
Matir Assurim confraternity (Rome), 148
Maximilian II (emperor), 157, 159
Mecklenburg (Germany), 156
Medici, Maria de' (queen of France), 179
Menahem da Recanati, 133
Menasseh Ben Israel, 174, 181–84
Mendelssohn, Dorothea, 195

Mendelssohn, Moses, 194
Mendes family, 168–69
Mendicant orders: participation of, in
pogroms, 85; on Talmud, 31, 32, 33.
See also Dominicans; Franciscans
The Merchant of Venice (Shakespeare),
39, 181
Merkabah, 132
Messer Leon, David ben Judah of
Worms, 134–35
Messianism: Hasidic rejection of, 190–
91; of imperial Spain, 106–7; and
mysticism, 91; Reubeni's mission of,
126–30
Mestre (Italy), 114, 115, 116
Metz (France), 179, 180
Michelet, Jules, 130
Midrashim, 33
Milan (Italy), 110, 141
Mintz, Judah, 56, 62, 112
Miques, João (Joseph Nasi), 168, 169
Mitridate, Flavio, 134
Modena (Italy), 44, 140, 151, 201
Modena, Leon, 38, 133–34
Modena, Solomon, 29
Modernity: anti-Semitism of, 208–13;
assimilationist pressures of, 203–4,
217–18; Church's reaction to, 210–11;
Haskalah movement of, 194–96, 206–
7; Jewish transformation/continuity of,
154–55, 215–17, 219–20; Orthodox
movement of, 205–6; Reform move-
ment of, 195, 204–5; Zionist response
to, 216–17
Mogen David (star of David), 129
Molko, Sholomo (Diogo Pires), 128–30
Moneylenders, Christian, 37, 112–14,
116–17
Moneylenders, Jewish: absence of, in
Sicily, 120; anti-Semitic stereotype of,
17–18, 39–40; in Bologna, 116–17;
in Christian Spain, 80–81; Church's
position on, 35–37, 110, 118; communal requirements for, 61; condotte
contracts with, 34, 54, 61, 110, 111–
12; England's restrictions on, 12;
Franciscans' attack on, 112–14; interest charged by, 37–38, 110, 114–15;
Italy's acceptance of, 110–11, 118–
19; land alienation of, 38–39, 80; location of, in ghettos, 143–44; in Poland, 186; in Rome, 124–25; in Siena,
117; in Umbria, 117–18; in Venice,
114–16
Monferrato (Italy), 110
Montaigne, Michel de, 45, 178
Montalto, Elia, 179

Monte di pietà, 112–14, 117, 118. See
also Moneylenders, Christian
Monte San Savino (Italy), 141
Montesquieu, Baron de, 209
Moravia, 156, 158
Moriscos (Muslim converts), 44, 106
Morone, Giovanni, 43
Mortara case (1858), 210
Moscow (Russia), 206
Moses ben Maimon (Maimonides), 30–
31, 92
Moses ben Nahman (Nahmanides), 32–
33, 88–89
Moshe Ibn Ezra, 77–78
Mosse, George, 195
Mozarabs (Spanish Christians), 77, 78
Mulhouse, 156
Muslim converts (Moriscos), 44, 106
Muslims, 5, 78; dietary restrictions of,
52; forced conversions by, 92; and
Sephardim, 77; and Sicilian Jews,
120
Mysticism. See Cabalistic system

Nagid (chief), 64
Nahmanides, 32–33, 88–89
Nantes (France), 180
Naples (Italy), 9, 108, 122
Napoleon, 198, 203–4
Nasi, Joseph (João Miques), 168, 169
Nathan of Gaza, 191
Naturalization, emancipation versus,
196–97
Navarre, 84, 101–2
Nazis, 212–13, 216
Nebuchadnezzar, 75
Neo-Orthodox Judaism, 205–6
New Synagogue (Rome), 145
Nicholas I (czar), 206
Nicholas V (pope), 40
Norwich (England), 18
Nuñes, Maria, 171, 172
Nuremberg (Germany), 156

Obadiah of Bertinoro, Rabbi, 120–21
Obernai, 156
Okrana (czarist secret service), 213
Olivares, duke of, 183
Omar, pact of, 77
On the Jewish Question (Marx), 211
Oratory of Divine Love, 43
Orobio de Castro, Baltazar (Baltazar Al-
varo), 178–79
Orobio de Castro, Isaac, 176, 179
Orthodox Judaism, 205–6
Ottoman Empire, 126, 127, 128; Jewish
migrations to, 163–64

Pablo de Santa Maria (Solomon Halevi), 90
Padua (Italy), 62, 110, 141
Pale of Settlement, 206
Palermo (Sicily), 27, 120
Palestine, 58–59
Pamplona (Spain), 102
Papacy: conversion policy of, 27, 28; on Franciscan preaching, 40; ghettoization policy of, 138–39, 141–42, 149–50; Jewish physicians of, 125; jurisdiction of, over Judaism, 28–29; Roman Jewry's relation with, 122–23, 124, 125–26; Talmud policy of, 31–32, 33; transferred seat of, 109
Pardo, David, 174
Paré, Ambroise, 135
Paris (France), 179–80, 199, 200
Parnassim (Jewish community authorities), 174–75
Passau (Bavaria), 18
Paul, Saint, 17, 24–25, 41, 157
Paul III (pope), 167
Paul IV (pope), 130, 167; and ritual murder, 43; Roman ghettos of, 25–26, 138–39, 144
Pentateuch, 55
Perugia (Italy), 61, 117
Pesaro (Italy), 140, 168
Pethahiah of Regensburg, Rabbi, 56
Peyrehorade (France), 180
Pfefferkorn, Johann Joseph, 136
Philip II (king of Spain), 164
Philip IV (king of Spain), 183
Philip V (king of France), 21
Philo-Semitism, 181–82
Physicians, Jewish, 125
Piazza delle Cinque Scole (Rome ghetto), 144–45
Pico della Mirandola, Giovanni, 134, 135
Piedmont (Italy), 9, 110, 141, 201
Pietistic Protestantism, 195
Pilpul ha-Yeshivah (academic disputation), 56
Pires, Diogo (Sholomo Molko), 128–30
Pisa (Italy), 13, 140, 166
Pitigliano (Italy), 141
Pius II (pope), 115, 126
Pius V (pope), 140
Pius IX (pope), 210
Plague: Church's position on, 13–14; and contamination anxiety, 21, 122; demographic/cultural impact of, 1–2, 7–8; pogroms during, 13–16
Platina, Bartolomeo, 41

Platter, Thomas, 178
Pogroms: contamination fears and, 16–17, 21, 86; during the Crusades, 2, 16–17; flagellants' role in, 15; in France, 21; in Germany, 8, 12–13, 15–16, 156; of Holocaust, 216, 217, 218–19; in Lisbon, against converts, 104; during the Plague, 13–16; in Poland, 187–89; in Russia, 207; in Spain, 83–85, 93
Pole, Reginald, 43
Polish Jews, 5; community organization of, 61, 64; Cossack revolt against, 187–88; Hasidism of, 189–91; pogroms against, 187–89; population of, 8–9, 185, 186; trade/occupations of, 186–87
Polygamy, 69
Pomerania, 156
Ponentines, 67, 68, 144, 165
Pons de la Sala, 85
Pontoise (France), 19
Poor, the: banks for, 113, 116; confraternities for, 147–48; of Polish communities, 188–89; of Roman ghetto, 148–49
Population statistics: in Amsterdam, 170; in Bessarabia, 207; in Bohemia, 159; in Bologna, 116; in England, 12; in France, 8, 180, 199; in Hamburg, 158; in Hungary, 9; in Istanbul, 163–64; in Italy, 116, 117, 120, 123, 145–46; in Paris, 199; in Poland, 9, 185, 186; in Portugal, 8; in Prague, 159; in Rome, 123, 146; in Salonika, 163; in Sicily, 120; in Spain, 8, 75–76, 101; in Umbria, 117; in Venice, 145–46
Pork prohibitions, 52
Portugal: in Brazil conflict, 183; conversion policy of, 3, 103–4; Jewish population of, 8; Reubeni's mission to, 127–28; Spanish Inquisition in, 105; travel prohibited to, 174
Portuguese Jews (Marranos): Ancona community of, 130, 167–68; Antwerp community of, 170; commercial trades of, 162, 166, 167, 170, 171, 179; community model of, 173; complex religious identity of, 162–63, 165, 168, 169, 170, 171–72, 173–75, 176; ethnicity legacy of, 67–69, 161–62; in Ferrara, 165–66; forced conversion of, 3, 103–4; French communities of, 177–79, 180–81; Leghorn settlement of, 166–67; London community of, 173, 182, 184–85; messianism of,

127–28; migratory destinations of, 154, 162, 163–65; in Venice, 165; women's role for, 71. *See also* Amsterdam Portuguese community
Postel, Guillaume, 133
Poznan (Poland), 187
Practica Inquisitionis (Gui), 96
Prado, Juan de, 175, 176
Prague, 158–59
Prato, Felice da, 133
Presbyter judaeorum (communal leader), 64
Printing/publishing, 133, 151–52
Prisca veritas (ancient wisdom), 134, 135
Property ownership restrictions, 38–39, 80; exemption from, 148; in ghettos, 138, 143, 144, 146–47
Protocols of the Elders of Zion, 213
Provence (France), 2, 9, 13, 63, 83, 90, 177
Prussia, 198
Pugio fidei (Martini), 33
Pure blood statutes, 105–7

Qiddush ha-Shem (martyrdom), 89–90, 91, 92
Quattro capi (synagogue), 150
Querini, Pietro, 43

Rabbenu Gershom (ben Judah), 69, 70
The Rabbi of Bacherach (Heine), 143
Rabbis, 54–55, 61–64
Rab de la corte of Castile (communal leader), 64
Racism, 16–17, 106–7, 210, 213
Raymond de Peñafort, 32, 33, 86
Readmission rites of converts, 96
Rebbe (religious leader), 190
Recanati (Italy), 140
Reformation, 157–61
Reform Judaism, 195–96, 201, 204–6
Regensburg, 156
Reggio (Italy), 44, 140
Reinach, Theodor, 195
Renaissance, 131–37
Republic of the United Provinces, 169, 170
Reubeni, David: "ghetto" reference of, 139–40; messianic mission of, 126–30; supporters of, 129
Reuchlin, Johannes, 136
Rewbell, Jean-François, 209
Ribera, Daniel de, 175
Richelieu, Cardinal, 180
Rienzo, Cola di, 124

Rindfleisch massacres (1298), 8, 13
Ritual murder accusations: in Apulia, 119; of cannibalism, 19–20; Church's use of, 20–21, 210; against converts, 98–99; of crucifixion, 18–19; against Josel of Rosheim, 157; in Poland, 187; in Rome, 43; in Simon of Trent episode, 40–41; usury's ties to, 39
Ritual slaughter *(shehitah)*, 52–53, 111–12
Robert (king of Naples), 40, 119
Romagna (Italy), 140
Roman Inquisition, 97
Roman Jews: communal rabbis of, 62; community organization of, 61, 123; conversion of, 44–47; edict on expulsion of, 40; emancipation of, 201–3; ethnic diversity of, 66–67, 123; ghettoization of, 47–48, 138–39, 144–45, 148–49, 201–2; juridical status of, 124; migrations of, from Rome, 109; nationalism-Judaism tension of, 202–3; papacy's relation with, 122–23, 124, 125–26; population of, 123, 146; professions of, 124–25; Reubeni's reception by, 127, 129; ritual murder case of, 43; taxes on, 124, 125–26
Roman Law: in Germany, 155; Grotius's use of, 172; Jews' juridical status under, 9–10, 26, 155
Rome: conversion policy of, 45–47; ghetto policy of, 47–48; papacy's transfer from, 109; Reubeni's mission to, 126–27; ritual murder case in, 43. *See also* Roman Jews
Rosh golah (exilarch), 64
Rouen (France), 180
Rovigo (Italy), 141
Rudiger of Speyer, 161
Rudolf II (emperor), 159
Russian Jews, 200, 206–7, 208
Russian Orthodox Church, 206, 207

Sabbatarians, 157
St. Jean de Luz (France), 178
St. Petersburg (Russia), 206
Salonika (Ottoman Empire), 163
Salzburg (Austria), 156
S. Anna of Trani (church), 119–20
Santo niño de La Guardia case, 98–99
Saralvo, Joseph, 166
Sardinia, 9, 121–22, 201
Sartre, Jean-Paul, 49
Savoy, 9, 13, 14
Schlegel, Friedrich von, 195
Scholem, Gershom, 191, 194, 218

Scola Ashkenazita (synagogue), 150–51
Scola Canton (synagogue), 144
Scola Italiana (synagogue), 144
Scola Levantina (synagogue), 144
Scola Nuova (synagogue), 150–51
Scola Spagnola (synagogue), 144
Scola Tedesca (synagogue), 144
Scuole grandi (Christian confraternities),
  148
Sebastian (king of Portugal), 128
Sebastianism movement, 128
Secularization, 155; emancipation's ties
  to, 196–97; of Jewish liturgy, 195
Sefer Bahir, 132
Sefer Yezirah (Book of Creation), 132
Selim II (sultan of Turkey), 169
Semikhah (rabbinic ordination), 54
Sempiterno regi (papal bull), 130, 167
Seneor, Abraham, 79, 101
Senigallia (Italy), 140
Separateness: of dietary laws, 52–53; of
  rabbinic figure, 54–55; of Sabbath
  celebration, 52; of sacredness concept,
  53–54
Separation of church and state, 196–97,
  204, 212
Sepharad (biblical land), 74
Sephardim: bilingual culture of, 77–78;
  conversion of, 5, 8, 76–77, 86–87,
  93, 94; as court Jews, 79, 82–83;
  emancipation of, 197, 200; expulsion
  of, from Spain, 2, 11, 20, 23, 100–
  102, 122, 154, 161; Hamburg community of, 158; judicial autonomy of,
  81–83; London community of, 185;
  martyrdom of, 89–90; messianism of,
  91, 129; monarchical dependency of,
  78–79, 86; Muslim treatment of, 77;
  origins of, 74–75; population of, in
  Spain, 8, 75–76, 101; reconstructed
  Spanish communities of, 94–96;
  trades/occupations of, 79–81, 154–
  55; Venice community of, 67–68,
  144
Sermons, conversionary, 45–46, 86–87,
  88
Servi camerae (concept), 28–29
Servitude: canon law on, 27–28; and juridical status, 10–11
Severus (bishop of Majorca), 75
Seville (Spain), 84, 94
Sexual relations, 69, 115, 172
Shabbetai Tzevi, 5, 133, 154, 189, 190–
  91, 193
Sicilian Jews, 1, 9, 64, 65, 120–21, 122
Sicilian Synagogue (Rome), 145

Sicut Iudaeis (papal bull), 27, 28
Siena (Italy), 117, 140
Las siete partidas (Alphonso X), 83
Silesia, 158
Simon of Trent, 40–41
Sisebuto (king of Visigoths), 76
Sixtus IV (pope), 97
Sixtus V (pope), 145
Slanderers (malsinos), 82
Slaughter rituals (shehitah), 52–53, 111–
  12
Society of Charity and Death (Jewish
  confraternity), 148
Solomon Halevi (Pablo de Santa Maria),
  90
Solomon Ibn Verga, 66, 97
Soncino, Gershom, 133
Soncino, Jehoshua, 168
Sovereigns. See Imperial protection
  policies
Spain: Arab conquest of, 77; biblical
  identification of, 74; contamination
  anxiety in, 83, 86; conversion campaigns in, 5, 8, 76–77, 86–87, 93, 94;
  court Jews of, 79, 82–83; expulsion of
  Jews from, 2, 11, 20, 23, 100–102,
  122, 154, 161; Ferrer's preaching in,
  88, 89; imperial protection policy of,
  78–79, 86; Inquisition in, 97–99,
  161, 164; Jewish communities of, 65,
  77–78; Marranos' migration to, 164;
  martyrdom in, 89–90; moneylending in, 80–81; origin of Jews in, 74–
  75; pogrom of 1391 in, 83–85, 93;
  polygamy in, 69; population of Jews in,
  8, 75–76, 101; pure blood statutes of,
  105–7; reconstructed Jewish communities of, 94–96; travel prohibited to,
  174
Spanish Inquisition, 102, 161, 164; creation of, 97; trials/executions of, 97–
  99
Spello (Italy), 118
Speyer, diet of (1544), 158
Spice trade, 170, 171
Spinoza, 175, 176–77
Stalin, Joseph, 208
States-General of the United Provinces,
  170, 172
Stefano di Bourbon, 35
Strasbourg, 15
Study of Hebrew texts, 55–57
Styria (Austria), 156
Süleyman the Magnificent (sultan of
  Ottoman Empire), 167–68
Sumptuary laws, 66

Surgun (forced transfer of populations), 164
Switzerland, 15, 156
Synagogues: in Amsterdam, 171, 173; Church policy on, 25, 26–27; converted into churches, 119–20, 122; instructional role of, 55; mixed membership of, 67; Reform of, 195, 205; in Rome, 138, 144–45, 150–51; in Venice, 144; women's galleries in, 71
Syphilis, 21, 163

Talmud: Bomberg's printing of, 133; burning of, in 1322, 40; on Christianity as idolatrous, 57–58, 92–93; Church policy on, 31–32, 33; and Hasidism, 190; Haskalah's view of, 194; on identity of converts, 95; *midrashim* of, 33; on moneylending to non-Jews, 37; Nahmanides on, 32–33; required study of, 55–56; Tortosa disputation of, 88–89; in western Jewish world, 77
Talmud Torah community (Amsterdam), 173
Talmud Torah confraternity (Rome), 148
Taqqanot (decrees and ordinances), 60
Tarragona (Spain), 75
Taxes: on converts, 104; intercommunal payment of, 64; on Italian Jews, 119, 124; land as payment for, 12; for protection, 79; on Roman Jews, 125–26
Temple Synagogue (Rome), 144–45
Teruel (Spain), 84
Testaccio carnival games, 46, 125
Theodosian Code, 10, 26, 27, 173
Thirty Years' War, 159–60, 180
Thuringia (German state), 158
Tikkun hatzot (an outdoor ritual), 152
Times (London), 213
Tirado, Jacob, 171, 172
Toland, John, 197
Toledo (Spain), 75, 78, 88, 94
Torah study, 38, 55, 60
Torquemada, Tomàs de, 97
Tortosa disputation, 88–89, 90
Toulon (France), 13
Toulouse Inquisition, 178
Trani (Italy), 119–20
Trastámara Revolution, 83
Treatise on the Sanctification of the Name (Maimonides), 92
Trent (Italy), 40–41, 111
Treviso (Italy), 114

Tudela (Spain), 76, 102
Turbato corde (papal bull), 29–30
Turin (Italy), 44, 141
Turks, 126, 127, 128
Tuscany (Italy), 110, 201
Tzaddiq (saint), 190

Uccello, Paolo, 17, 39
Ulm (Germany), 156
Ultra-Orthodox Judaism, 206
Umbria (Italy), 46, 110, 117–18
Universitas Hebreorum, 61
Universitas iudeorum urbis, 123
University of Paris, 31
University of Toulouse, 178–79
Urbino (Italy), 140
U.S. Declaration of Independence, 197
Usury. *See* Moneylenders, Christian; Moneylenders, Jewish
Uziel, Jacob, 174

Valencia (Spain), 84–85
Valladolid ordinances, 64, 82, 88, 89, 94
Valreas, 19
Van den Enden, Franciscus, 177
Varnhagen, Rahel, 195
Vaud, 21
Venetian Chronicle (Capsali), 56
Venetian Inquisition, 165
Venice (Italy): excommunication in, 62; ghettos of, 67–68, 139, 141, 143–44, 145–46, 151; house of converts in, 44; Jewish banking in, 114–16; Marranos' migrations to, 164–65; Plague in, 13; Reubeni in, 126–27
Verona (Italy), 62, 110, 141, 143
Vicenza (Italy), 110
Vico, Giambattista, 50
Victor Emmanuel II (king of Italy), 201
Viennese Jews, 160
Vigesima (income tax), 126. *See also* Taxes
Vineam sorec (papal bull), 87
Vineyards, 38–39
Visigoth kings, 27, 76–77
Voltaire, 209
Von Karben, Viktor, 136

Warsaw (Poland), 187, 206
Whitehall Conference, 184
White Mountain, battle of (1620), 159
William of Norwich, 18
Williams, Roger, 197
William the Conqueror, 12
Wine prohibitions, 53, 58

Wissenschaft des Judentums movement, 205, 218
Women: in Eastern Europe, 72; education of, 56–57; religious role of, 70–71; ritual slaughter by, 112
Worms (Germany), 156
Württemberg (Germany), 156

Yagel, Avraham, 135
Yeshivah (higher education), 55–56

Yiddish language, 187
Yisrael Baal Shem, 189

Zamora, synod of, 83
Zaragoza (Spain), 75, 95
Zarfati, Yosef, 129
Zionist movement, 202–3, 208, 212, 216–17
Zohar (Book of Splendor), 132, 133
Zunz, Leopold, 205

Text:	10/13 Sabon
Display:	Sabon
Composition:	G&S Typesetters, Inc.
Printing and binding:	Thomson-Shore, Inc.